Necessity and Philosophy in Plato's *Republic*

Necessity and Philosophy in Plato's *Republic*

Russell Winslow

LEXINGTON BOOKS
Lanham • Boulder • New York • London

Published by Lexington Books
An imprint of The Rowman & Littlefield Publishing Group, Inc.
4501 Forbes Boulevard, Suite 200, Lanham, Maryland 20706
www.rowman.com

86-90 Paul Street, London EC2A 4NE

Copyright © 2024 by The Rowman & Littlefield Publishing Group, Inc.

All rights reserved. No part of this book may be reproduced in any form or by any electronic or mechanical means, including information storage and retrieval systems, without written permission from the publisher, except by a reviewer who may quote passages in a review.

British Library Cataloguing in Publication Information Available

Library of Congress Cataloging-in-Publication Data

Names: Winslow, Russell (Russell E.), author.
Title: Necessity and philosophy in Plato's Republic / Russell Winslow.
Description: Lanham : Lexington Books, [2024] | Includes bibliographical references.
Identifiers: LCCN 2024019867 (print) | LCCN 2024019868 (ebook) | ISBN 9781666958577 (cloth) | ISBN 9781666958584 (epub)
Subjects: LCSH: Plato. Republic. | Necessity (Philosophy)
Classification: LCC JC71.P6 W49 2024 (print) | LCC JC71.P6 (ebook) | DDC 123/.7—dc23/eng/20240626
LC record available at https://lccn.loc.gov/2024019867
LC ebook record available at https://lccn.loc.gov/2024019868

∞™ The paper used in this publication meets the minimum requirements of American National Standard for Information Sciences—Permanence of Paper for Printed Library Materials, ANSI/NISO Z39.48-1992.

For David, my partner of 31 years

Contents

Acknowledgments	ix
Introduction	xi
Chapter 1: Philosophical Nature: Natural Necessity	1
Chapter 2: The Necessity of the Greatest Study: The Good	35
Chapter 3: The Child of the Good: On Light and Desire	51
Chapter 4: Necessity in the Intelligible Region of the Divided Line	69
Chapter 5: Necessity in the Cave	79
Chapter 6: Necessity and the Highest Studies	107
Chapter 7: Necessity and the Song [*nomos*] Itself (Dialectic)	147
Chapter 8: On Bastards and Orphans	175
Chapter 9: Necessity and Democracy	197
Chapter 10: The Spindle of Necessity	213
Bibliography	237
Index	243

Acknowledgments

The principal idea for this book germinated within the productive soils and hospitable environments provided by the classes and reading groups that I have led over the last few years. The participants in these settings—Ben Acree, Brittany Hagar, Bob Loomis, Justin Spain, Ed Stroupe and Vidya Ravilochan—made the conversations remarkably rich and exciting. I wish to thank them. In addition, several friends and colleagues helped me to formulate many of the ideas found within this book. Charles Bambach, Claudia Baracchi, David Carl, John Cornell, Veronique Dupont-Roc, Ian Moore, Raoni Padui, Zhen Liang, Arcelia Rodriguez, Gregory Schneider, Kit Slover, Caleb Thompson and Michael Weinman have all offered care and encouragement. Llyd Wells, in particular, lent a patient ear and a helping hand for editing what finally emerged here. The support of my deans at St. John's College, Walter Sterling and Sarah Davis, has occasioned the writing of this book. In addition, I would like to express my gratitude to my reviewers for taking the time to read the work carefully and to offer considered criticisms. Finally, I am thankful for the enthusiasm expressed for the project by Jana Hodges-Kluck and all at Lexington Press.

The translations of Plato in this work are mine, unless otherwise indicated.

Introduction

"Interpretation of Plato is not a reproduction but a creation."

(Tigerstedt 1977, 100, emphasis added).

Necessity and the good differ *necessarily*. In book VI of the *Republic*, Socrates defends the practice of philosophy from Adeimantus' slander against it. Given that everywhere in cities philosophy has the reputation of being at best "useless" and at worst "malicious" (487 d), Adeimantus had resisted handing the keys to the citadel of the "beautiful city" to the philosopher (487 e). In the course of his defense, Socrates claims, among other things, that this reputation of philosophy in cities grows out of the perception of the practice of the private educators (the sophists). Such men educate in nothing other than the opinions of the many (*oi* polloi), he says (493 a). Consequently, neither the private wage earners nor their students are able to see or to show "how much necessity and the good differ by nature" (493 c). Thus, such men are "strange [*atopos*]" educators (493 c). Without being in possession of this distinction, their teachings (misconceived as philosophy) bring the discipline into bad repute.

There are many reasons to raise doubts about the success of Socrates' attempts to answer the polemic of Adeimantus. One of them might be that neither the interlocutors nor the readers are, in fact, ever able to make this distinction from the arguments found in the text. Socrates makes it clear that he does not know what the good is by nature (505 a). Moreover, he does not have the time to offer his opinions about it (506 e). Even if Socrates knew the being of the good, the interlocutors are not prepared to receive a dialectical account of it (533 a). Therefore, if knowledge of the good is necessary to know "how much necessity and the good differ by nature" (493 c), then perhaps the defense of philosophy remains doubtful or outside of the range of the discussants' abilities.

Despite this absence (or perhaps because of it), many works have been written analyzing the nature of the good in the *Republic*. Indeed, perhaps all works on the *Republic* could be said to be about the nature of the good in one way or another. But what about the other side of the opposition in this claim? What about *necessity*? Does the text provide an account of the nature of necessity? As readers, if we are to distinguish between the good and necessity, do we have a sense of how the concept of necessity operates in the ontology of the *Republic*, such that we are prepared to give an account of it in Socratic or Platonic terms?

The term translated as necessity, *anagkē* (or one of its grammatical variants—verb *anagkazō* and adjective *anagkaios*), appears hundreds of times in the text—about as often as "the good." Yet, there exists very little commentary on it.[1] By the time we encounter the term in this formal way in book VI, the discussants have used one of the forms of "necessity" already more than a hundred times. It is true that the word most often occurs as a banal response in the flow of the conversation. For instance, when Socrates concludes an argument about the misological consequences resulting from exposing inappropriate humans to the practice of dialectic, he says that such a human "becomes a lawless man from a lawful one." Glaucon then replies, "necessarily [*anagkē*]" (539 a). However, in addition to these more emphatic forms of affirmation, the term is employed in a technical sense too—as shows our original example in which Socrates argues that a mark of philosophy is its ability to distinguish "the good" from "necessity." Moreover, it appears in the dialogue in an image or mythological form as well: the great deity and her "spindle of necessity" in the concluding *apologos* of Er (616 c). That is to say, throughout the *Republic*, we find necessity in all the forms of speech presented there: stylistic, argumentative, metaphorical and mythological.[2]

As such, the characters in the *Republic* (as well as its readers) are in very much the same position regarding the concept of "necessity" as those of the *Theaetetus* regarding the concept of "knowledge." In that text, Plato has Socrates say: "but really, Theaetetus, we've been infected for a long time with impure talk. For tens of thousands of times we've said "we recognize' and 'we don't recognize,' and 'we know' and 'we don't know,' as though we understand one another in some way while still being ignorant of knowledge" (Plato 2004, 196 d-e). Thus, just as the interlocutors in the *Theaetetus* employ the concept of "knowledge" without knowing what they mean, the characters in the *Republic* speak of "necessity" without an explicit account of it. Yet, if the happiness of *kallipolis* relies on the practice of philosophy, and if philosophy is distinguished from sophistry in part or in whole by its capacity to separate the good from necessity, then understanding what we (and the text) mean when we say "necessity" is urgent, perhaps as urgent as knowing what we mean by "the good." For, we have been tossing around this crucial concept without knowing what we mean.

This book offers a reading of Plato's *Republic* through the lens of necessity. From ancient to modern times, the history of western philosophy grapples with the meaning of necessity. As will become clear over the course of the monograph, Plato presents an image of necessity in the drama of the *Republic* that encompasses a much broader expression of nature than modernist accounts. One way of conceiving of necessity is reflected in classical Newtonian mechanics. In this setting, necessity becomes expressed in universal laws that govern all the movements of nature: "No variation of things arises from blind metaphysical necessity, which must be the same always and everywhere" (Newton 1999, 942). In the ancient world too, Aristotle offers an interpretation of necessity upon which the former conception may rely for its persuasive force.[3] He devotes a chapter in *Metaphysics delta* to isolating the many ways in which *anagkē* becomes said. There, Aristotle argues that all the senses of necessity he articulates are derived from the fourth one: "we say that that which cannot be otherwise is necessarily so" (Aristotle 1924, 1015 a 20–1015 b 9). Despite their radically different cosmologies, in both the ancient and the modernist interpretation, necessity is said to govern over that which cannot be otherwise.[4]

In these two accounts, one can observe a similar organization in *natural* necessity and in what might be called *logical* necessity. What governs the motions of the planets? A law of force that necessarily rules over the predictable path of the planet around the sun. What governs the movement of the syllogism? A law of force that necessarily rules over the predictable path from premise to conclusion. However, as I will suggest, for Plato, the relation between logical necessity [a *technē*] and natural necessity [*physis*] remains a question. Therefore, on my reading, not only does the concept of necessity in Plato express movements in the cosmos that reach farther than these traditional examples, but also the dialogues frequently force one to raise doubts about the happy coincidence between the kind of necessity (logical) that is supposed to govern human thinking and that which rules nature.

By way of an introduction, I will summarize a few of the features of necessity that appear in the dialogues and in this book's analysis, features which demonstrate Plato's novel conception. First, in a way that differs dramatically from traditional concepts of it, Plato's *Timaeus* gives voice to a "necessity" conceived as a "wandering cause" [*to tēs planōmenēs eidos aitias*] (Plato 2001, 48 a).[5] As we know from book VI of the *Republic*, the things in the world which "wander" are the things in becoming. Becoming and wandering are, thus, synonyms. Moreover, the philosopher according to Socrates in book VI hates *what wanders* and loves *what is always* (485 b). Consequently, what wanders is perhaps superficially opposed there to *what is always*, or *being*, *or what cannot be otherwise*. But "wandering" means more than becoming or movement. The verb "to wander" in both the *Republic* and the *Timaeus* translates "*planaō*." The English word "planet" comes from this Greek term because the planets are those entities in the sky that appear to move in irregular and unorderly ways. While the constellations move in a manner that is consistent and perfectly rational, the planets do not. Sometimes they move backwards, sometimes forwards, and sometimes they stop moving in relation to the constellations. One might even say that there is something *arbitrary* to their retrograde movements. If one conceives of necessity as a "wandering" cause, then such a causality might suggest the existence of movements outside of those legally governed in a way that "cannot be otherwise" (Aristotle 1924, 1015 a 20–1015 b 9) or "always the same" (Newton 1999, 942). With this formulation, Plato has his characters present us with a necessity that is surprising and perplexing, insofar as it is potentially capable of randomness and unpredictable irrationality.

In the context of the *Timaeus*, the quality of irrationality is a constitutive element within the concept of necessity. Halfway through his presentation of the birth of the cosmos, Timaeus realizes that he has left out an account of necessity. He must begin again, as it were, "from the beginning" (Plato 2001, 48 b).[6] Similarly to the condition of the discussants regarding the concept of "knowledge" in the *Theaetetus* above, Timaeus had been using the concept of necessity all along without offering an account of it. Prior to the birth of the cosmos, necessity was already there; indeed, the demiurge relies upon it to perform his creations. Thus, Timaeus must begin his mythological origin story again with an account of necessity. As we learn, prior to the demiurge's "construction" of the cosmos, it was irrational: "these different kinds [the elements] held a different place . . . before the all was arrayed . . . Before that time, all these things were in a condition that was without ratio and measure [*alogōs kai ametrōs*]" (Plato 2001, 53a). Thus, in its condition without interference by the demiurge, necessity is *without reason* and *without measure*. In the era prior to the demiurge's compositions, necessity ruled in such a way that no meaningful distinctions could be made between elements. However, the demiurge persuaded[7] her to "lead *most* of what comes to be toward what is best" (Plato 2001, 48 a, emphasis added). That is to say, the demiurge persuades necessity to allow becoming in the manner of "forms and number" (Plato 2001, 53 b). Fire, water, air and earth take the form of geometrical structure. Thus, the demiurge persuades necessity to allow him to organize becoming into something of a rational form. Still, the qualification that the demiurge leads only "most" of what comes to be towards what is best, rather than "all," signals that there remains an irrationality in the cosmological order. As we will see, necessity as a "wandering cause" continues to haunt even these geometrical compositions. In the *Republic*, this irrationality shows itself often. For instance, it appears in the new studies of book VII—all of which are mathematical, save the ultimate study (dialectic). I will show that at the heart of each of these mathematical disciplines lies a destabilizing irrationality—the calling card of the "wandering cause." Moreover, this disruptive "wandering cause" appears not only in the region of formal mathematics, but in living systems too: the muses elaborate the *necessary* mortal dissolution of even perfectly ordered entities like *Kallipolis* (546 a).

Similarly, necessity as a "wandering cause" also gives rise to those movements that "happen to be" [*tugxanō*]—another way of speaking of unpredictable chance.[8] Not only does necessity govern the movements of those entities for which a law may be found, a law by which they can be shown to move in a way that is predictable and, thus, cannot be otherwise, but also necessity governs those movements that just "happen" to be [*tugxanō*]. Throughout the *Republic*, there are movements Socrates describes with this term, movements that occur in a system without a clear origin, movements that appear to disrupt it and that reflect an instability in the system. For example, unless a noble nature "happens" to be planted in a favorable environment, or unless a god "happens" to intervene, she will become malicious or useless (492 a). The "natural" course of things would have ushered the noble soul toward tyranny; however, the wandering cause may intervene to save her, opening up the otherwise closed system to which she belongs: neither city nor man will become perfect "before some necessity [*anagkē*] from chance embraces [*peribalē*] those few philosophers who are not malicious [*poneros*]" (499 b).

Another manifestation of the "wandering cause" in the discourse of the *Republic* is *erōs*. While it is conspicuously absent from the *birth* of Timaeus' technological description of the production of the cosmos, *erōs* remains intimately connected to necessity in the *Republic*. Like necessity, *erōs*' reach is wider than reason's. For instance, it is precisely *erōs* which inserts irrationality into the calculation that initiates the dissolution of *Kallipolis*. The muses announce that the constraints that rational calculation attempts to place upon *erōs* will fail in the city, engendering its decline (546 a—b). Erotic love inevitably slips out of reason's control. As such, *erōs*, qua necessity, governs not only the mortal compulsion toward sexual generation and growth, it also remains inseparable from the drive toward mortal death.

Moreover, erotic necessity is distinguished in the *Republic* from the logical necessity that governs reason. While describing the common activities between male and female guardians, Socrates says that "commingled together in [nude] gymnastics and other ways, they'll be led by an innate *necessity* to sexual intercourse with one another. Do I not speak of necessities?" To which, Glaucon replies, "not *geometrical*, but *erotic* necessities" (458 d, emphasis added). Here, the pervasive force of *erōs* is explicitly connected to necessity's movements. Moreover, a question is raised about the need to distinguish between geometrical and erotic necessities. On my reading, geometrical necessity refers to the force that logical necessity exerts on systematic thinking, like that within the propositions of geometry. As we will see, erotic necessity subtends and remains prior to logical necessity. Folding logical necessity into itself, erotic necessity marshals *logos* into the service of its own—sometimes irrational and wandering—ends.

If all of these movements and irregular rotations belong in an unavoidable sense to necessity, it means that all systems are subject to wandering for Plato. While certainly bodies are subject to the "wandering cause" and to what "happens to be" [*tugxano*], it may be that soul cycles too—discursive and intellectual systems as well as the syllogisms and propositions that constitute them—are subject *to wandering* when viewed from the point of view of Platonic necessity. A common thread in all three features introduced above is that *anagkē* not only bestows regularity, but inserts instability and irrationality into systems, both those composed by nature and those composed or discovered by humans. Systems like individual plants, political constitutions and even perhaps achievements in the disciplines of science wander. When the muses speak to us through Socrates "in the manner of *tragedy* [*tragikōs*], as if we were children" (545 e, emphasis added), they convey that the city, like all mortal beings, must die. All entities that come to be have their rotations and life cycles; when they reach this temporal determination, they begin to fail. As alluded to before, the perfection of *Kallipolis* and the unimpeachable wisdom of its guardians will not save it. "Even though they are wise, those you have raised as rulers of the city will nonetheless not happen upon [*tugxanō*] the [right] prosperous birth and barrenness for your kind with calculation and sensation" (546 a—b). They will breed when they should not. That is to say, erotic necessity will slip through the rulers' calculating fingers and engender the city's mortal end. One would expect such a description for the biological entities subject to necessity's wandering. However, the "tragic" speech of the Muses suggests that there exists wandering in the intellectual systems too. Such wandering, on my reading, betrays a tragic finitude inherent in the Platonic ontological organization of the human (and its *logos*) in the world. Necessity folds all human endeavors into itself and serves as a limit for human achievement. In other words, the wandering, irrational, and erotic features of necessity reinscribe the human within finitude at the very moment that human reason expects to transcend and escape its limitations. As we will observe in our analysis of the *apologos* of Er, this finitude is felt as tragedy;[9] and the wakeful encounter with this finitude produces the art forms of tragedy, comedy and philosophy.

I employ the language of tragedy throughout this book in an ancient sense. That is to say, I do not mean to suggest that philosophy and human existence is "tragic" in the modern sense of a singular devastation. Rather, I mean an ontological condition that resembles that Greek term frequently found in tragedies: *deinos*. What makes philosophy and human existence tragic is the fact that it is both wonderful and terrible at the same time. The human is both blessed and cursed with *logos*. As an ancient example, consider the quality most associated with Odysseus: his wiliness. Odysseus' wiliness remains the outstanding quality that makes him capable of great works and heroic deeds. In a way a bit like Socratic irony, it is Odysseus' wiliness that makes him the man of many masks. He can make himself appear to his interlocutors in any way he chooses; he possesses the gift of exceptional *logos*, such that he can rearrange his appearance as if he were a human chameleon. However, this heroic quality equally prevents him from doing what he claims he wants the most: it keeps him from returning home. While it may be a blessing to be in possession of a nature that enables the indefinite capacity to shift masks, it may also be a curse. Is there an actual nature under the mask at all? If he can find it and bring it forward, will it be recognized at home? Odysseus' wiliness is *deinos*: it is both wonderful and terrible at the same time. In the present monograph, I develop a reading of the *Republic's* philosophical nature and its *logos* in this tragic light.[10] It may be that tragedy, comedy and philosophy are mirrors that reflect the human being in its wandering in accordance with necessity.

I will conclude this introduction by providing a brief precis about how this book will contend with the dialogue form of Plato. One consequence of offering an interpretation of necessity in the *Republic* is that it allows one to develop another way of understanding the relation between the dramatic elements of the dialogue and its arguments. For decades now, there have been a plethora of books written on the importance of including the dramatic elements of the dialogues when formulating interpretations of Plato's thought.[11] In this book, I take this necessity for granted. When one considers the operation of necessity in the *Republic*, it becomes clear that, from a certain point of view, the dramatic elements in fact *are* the features of necessity that subtend the coming to be of the dialogue *and* its arguments. That is to say, the argument belongs to the ecosystem provided in the text. The system of necessity that subtends the *Republic*, its ecosystem, occasions the argument and provides the motive force by which it comes into being. The novel occurrence of the festival of Bendis, the location and features of Piraeus, the characters and natures of the foreigners and the citizens present for the discussion, the political atmosphere of its setting, and much more. All of these features (which will be discussed in detail in the course of the monograph) weave together the powers and motive forces of the ecosystem of the *Republic*. They constitute the soil out of which this particular argument grows. By way of comparison, one might argue that the ecological setting of Plato's *Republic* is to its argument as Simondon's system of individuation is to its individual (Simondon 2020). The near infinity of processes and energies that compose a field of individuation occasions the individual. However, the field of individuation is not exhausted by the individual, neither its form nor content; quite the contrary, the individual is merely one production made possible by the composition of the system of individuation (Simondon 2020, 32). Similarly, the field of necessary conditions that constitute the dramatic setting of the *Republic* occasion the individual argument. But the individual argument does not exhaust the conditions of necessity present in the dramatic setting. As such, each dialogue has its conditions of necessity—its dramatic setting and its arbitrary movements—that occasion the identity of its arguments. One of the tasks of the present monograph will be to offer an interpretation of the *Republic* by means of these *wandering* necessary conditions.

NOTES

1. One exception to the absence of commentary is Rachel Barney's (2008) "Eros and Necessity in the Ascent from the Cave." As will become clear, especially in Chapter 5, her conclusions regarding the meaning and role of the concept of necessity in the *Republic* differ from mine.

2. In this book, I adopt Mariana McCoy's understanding of the role of images in the dialogues when she writes, "in the *Republic*, there is no image-free way of speaking about philosophical objects. That is, there is no philosophical language that can wholly free us from the limits of images. In this way, Plato's understanding of what counts as philosophical language challenges many contemporary understandings of philosophical language as precise and non-imagistic . . . For Plato, a central task of philosophy is to help us to understand ourselves as image-makers who need the imagination to access reality and yet must be cautious of not too easily accepting our images uncritically" (McCoy 2020, 7). On my reading, staging the drama of the dependence of human discourse on images helps to illuminate one of the ways that *necessity* shapes human life in Plato. Because images "both disclose and distort reality" (McCoy 2020, 7), there is something finite, even tragic, about the human relation to knowledge.

3. It should be noted that the corpus of Aristotle offers more nuance on the meaning of necessity. In the *Physics*, for instance, Aristotle offers an understanding of necessity [*anagkē*] as an accidental [*sumbebkos*] and arbitrarily spontaneous [*automaton*] cause. While considering the formation of sharp teeth, he contrasts *telos* and *anagkē* as causes of generation, suggesting that sharp teeth are not generated by accident or by chance spontaneity (qua necessity), but rather "for the sake of" cutting food (Aristotle 1998, 198 b 24–33).

4. I recognize the immense difference between the ontologies of Newton and Aristotle. Here, I simply wish to point out how Plato's conception of necessity is original and must be distinguished from both of them, even Aristotle's. As we will see shortly, Plato's texts articulate a conception of necessity that includes what "wanders," the "wandering cause." This differs a lot from Aristotle's "what cannot be otherwise."

5. As will become clear in chapter seven, I do not think of the dialogues as expressing a unified argument. The *Timaeus* and the *Republic* ought to be read as self-contained works. Each dialogue has a different primary speaker, and neither of these is Plato. Moreover, I do not read the dialogues in the developmental tradition either. That said, I think that it is perfectly legitimate to draw together conceptual phenomena that are frequently repeated in the dialogues with the caveat that the ecosystem of any given dialogue may necessitate a different interpretation. Just as we may compare "love" in the *Phaedrus* and the *Symposium* (even though "love" is not the same in each dialogue), we may compare necessity as "wandering cause" in the *Timaeus* with the necessity of "what wanders" in the *Republic*. I make this comparison in the book while espousing a commitment neither to the tradition that reads the dialogues as a *unified whole* nor to the tradition that reads the dialogues as *developmental*.

6. See John Sallis' *Chorology* (1999) for a careful study of these new beginnings in the *Timaeus*.

7. In addition to its description as a "wandering" causality, the notion that necessity could be "persuaded" to change its course is obviously also perplexing and has generated literature. In fact, much of the literature on necessity in Plato (despite its prevalence throughout the dialogues) is on the *Timaeus*. A trend among these writings is to reduce the complexity and, thus, the perplexity of necessity as "wandering cause" and something capable of "being persuaded." For instance, Andrew Mason's goal is to show that, even though Timaeus' necessity is different from ours, "the difference is not as great as it might first appear" (Mason 2006, 283). In older literature, Cornford challenges Taylor's and Archer-Hind's attempts to explain away the difficulty by making the demiurge omnipotent. He helpfully recognizes the tragic character of this necessity to some degree (Cornford (1937 159–177). However, as Vlastos points out (Vlastos 1941, 296), he still equates this notion of necessity in Plato with that of chance in Aristotle's *Physics*. I agree with Vlastos when he writes that this "does not explain the element of disorder" (Vlastos 1941, 296). In fact, this "chance" in Aristotle only appears to be something by chance to the human being. From the point of view of natural necessity, chance is still something that "cannot be otherwise." It seems to me that many reductive interpretations are compelled by a desire to ensure that Plato is articulating a coherent system. For me, by having his characters use these formulations, Plato is rather raising questions about the human rational comprehension of nature through systematic *technai*.

8. In his reading of the *Apology*, Shane Ewegen suggests a connection between *tuchē* and *anagkē* when he argues that "Socrates's way will proceed 'by chance,' by *tuchē*, using only those words that happen to occur to him . . . this passage indicates the extent to which Socrates, rather than making or constructing a speech of *his own*, will instead *make way for* a *logos* that comes about not by means of his own will but

rather by means of *tuchē*: chance, accident, or even <u>necessity</u>" (Ewegen 2020, 11, underline added).

9. With David Roochnik, I disagree with Martha Nussbaum's claim that the Platonic dialogue is an "anti-tragic theater" or that Plato's is "a pure crystalline theater of the intellect" (Nussbaum 1986,133). What follows in this monograph will seek to elaborate the role of necessity in the *Republic*'s tragic articulation of human finitude. As such, it has much in common with Roochnik's *The Tragedy of Reason* insofar as it affirms the existence in the Platonic dialogues of a "a conception of *logos* that is compatible with the . . . insights of tragedy" (Roochnik 1990, xi).

10. To suggest that, for Plato, philosophy has a tragic character is not the same as to say that Plato is a skeptic. The articulation of a tragic human finitude is already a positive accomplishment. For analyses of the traditional schools of platonic interpretation, especially the systematic and the skeptical varieties, see Gonzales 1995, Annas 1994, Tiegerstedt 1977. Further, David Roochnik asserts that "it is skepticism, and not Platonism, that is truly, even systematically, 'antitragic'" (Roochnik 1990, 204).

11. See, for instance, Tanner 2017, McCoy 2008, Baracchi 2002, Gordon 1999, Gonzales 1998, Hyland 1995, Roochnik 1990, Griswold 1988, Saxonhouse 1978, Klein 1977, Strauss 1964.

Chapter 1
Philosophical Nature: Natural Necessity

In this chapter we consider the contrast between the philosophical nature and natural necessity in book VI. Beginning our analysis in the middle of the text, we offer an interpretation of Socrates' reformulation of the definition of the philosophic nature as a human being erotically compelled toward "what is." There, Socrates argues that philosophic natures not only love "what is," but hate "what wanders"—a characteristic we have seen associated with necessity. Thus, ostensibly, the text produces an argument in which philosophy and necessity are in opposition to one another. However, by developing a reading of the dramatic details of this portion of the text in relation to others, we are able to articulate reasons why the radical separation of the philosophical nature and necessity may be called into question. Necessity, in the shape of *erōs* (erotic love), wandering movement, and *tugxano* (chance happenings) will be shown to condition the emergence of the philosophical nature in a way that renders a radical separation between philosophy and necessity problematic. In addition to working through Socrates' positive formulation of the characteristics necessary for the philosophical nature, our analysis will take us through Adeimantus' famous interruption of the argument. He charges into the discussion in order to insist, with skepticism, that Socrates offer an explanation; for, despite the *ideal* qualities Socrates presents, in *reality*, philosophical natures appear everywhere either at best *useless* and at worst *malicious* in cities. Moreover, we develop a reading of a classically tragic element in the philosophical nature, insofar as its heroic characteristics depend upon the necessary conditions of growth into which it arbitrarily finds itself planted in its youth. By means of these analyses, we perforate the rigid wall between philosophy and necessity.

At the beginning of book VI, Plato has Socrates assert that the philosophers and those who are not philosophers have "somehow" appeared from out of a long and painful discourse (484 a). A few sentences later, the reader observes that the fruit of this labor shows itself in the following way: philosophers "are capable of laying hold of what is always the same" (484 b), while "those who are not capable [of doing this] . . . wander (*planaō*) in what is many and various" (484 b). Here, at the middle point of the dialogue, we arrive at a certain new development in the drama that presents what is called the philosophic nature; it is another appearance of the odyssey of a principal narrative thread in the dialogue that began much earlier. Moreover, Socrates says that it would have been better if this were the only question that had to be treated (484 a), leaving the reader to wonder if the "philosophic nature" has been the subject of inquiry all along.

The earliest *explicit* reference of the philosopher's nature in the *Republic* came through an image of the canine variety. In book II, in an effort to come to terms with a description of the necessary nature of a successful guardian—a nature whose "impossible" (375 d) composition appears to violate one characteristic of the principle of noncontradiction (it must be both gentle and cruel at the same time)—Socrates arrives at an example that lies on the periphery of (but still present within) human society: the dog. Insofar as the guardians will possess a nature that is at once cruel to enemies and gentle with their own, their philosophical nature is like the nature of dogs; for, a dog barks and exhibits anger at a person he does not know, "even if he never had suffered anything bad" (376 a) from the person, while the dog greets a person he knows warmly, even if the person previously abused the dog (376 a). The guardians will be philosophical if the lawgivers can cultivate in them a hostility toward what is alien and a gentleness toward what is one's own. Indeed, the guardian in the model of the philosopher dog is "a lover of learning [*philomathēs*], defining what is its own and what is foreign by intelligence [*sunesis*] and ignorance" (376 b). Obviously, this image of the philosophical nature in Socrates' speech, unquestioned by Glaucon, does not square with the actual activity frequently observed in our protagonist. In overly simplified terms, Socrates' love of learning involves hostility toward what is his own and an eager flirtatiousness toward that which he does not know.

Nevertheless, despite this opposition of the theory presented by the argument with the practice of Socrates, there are ways that this canine in the *Republic* is shown to share certain characteristics with the philosophic nature. Both the dog and the philosopher are liminal figures. Even though dogs are not humans, they nevertheless occupy an important space within human society insofar as they have one foot, as it were, in the human family and at least one outside of it. The liminal position of the philosopher in between the city (what is one's own) and the foreign (what is strange or alien) appears throughout the dialogues, including in the very setting of the *Republic*; for, the Piraeus in which philosophy occurs is both inside and outside of Athens. It strikes me that these liminal images occurring within what must finally be admitted are often unconvincing and unacceptable arguments are, nevertheless, reliable ways that the images both in and peripheral to the arguments convey something of the meaning that the *drama* of the *Republic* presents to the reader. My interpretation of the philosophic nature in the dialogue makes use of the complexity subtending the text's development of these liminal images. Already in the early image of the philosopher dog, we have reference to the philosophic nature as something existing both within and without society.

In book VI, Socrates reformulates the duality of the philosophic nature in terms of a new love and a new hostility. The philosophic nature's blanket "love of learning" is revised to become an *erotic* love of learning that *which is always*: "regarding philosophic natures, it is agreed that they always erotically desire [*erōsin*] the learning which reveals to them something of each being that is always and is not wandering [*planaō*] between generation and decay" (485 a—b). Moreover, just like erotic men (and perhaps those that genuinely love anything), these natures love the whole of the things they love. Philosophic natures are erotically compelled toward learning *that which is*, and not just some of it, but all of it. Here we have some further qualification of what learning that *which is always* means. That *which is always* does not become, does not change, does not pass away; it does not *appear like* something at one moment and then *appear like* something else at another moment. That which possesses this sort of being, therefore, must be as it is always. According to this line of argument, that which does not possess this *what-is-ness* must not have any proper metaphysical standing. Nothing can be "learned" of that which shifts and turns, of that which wanders [*planaō*]. Socrates suggests that the only thing that can be learned of that which wanders is its inability to hold itself still—and for him, at this point in the argument, wandering reveals the measure of its falsity. The measure of the truth lies in the metaphysical status of being always. The measure of the false lies in the metaphysical status of becoming. Moreover, the philosophical nature is completely unwilling to admit anything other than *what is* into the field of things one should want to learn. Thus, the philosophic nature *hates* the false and *loves* [*stergō*] the truth, insofar as s/he hates wandering (becoming) and loves being.[1] Indeed, in reaction to Glaucon's answer to the question of the truth of this claim, that it "is likely [*eikos*]," Socrates responds that it is not only likely, but "there is every necessity [*pasa anagkē*] that the person with this nature . . . will yearn exceedingly for all truth" (485 d). It appears, then, that the contradictory characteristics of the philosophic nature from book II— that it has a "love for one's own" and a "hostility toward the foreign"—have here *wandered* or shifted. Instead, it now has an erotic love for being (what is true because *it is always*) and a hatred of becoming (what is false because it wanders). Of course, this argument should be held in suspicion given what comes later in the divided line. Many things associated with becoming have being, despite the fact that they change. Even in the rather static image of the divided line, becoming does not lack being entirely. However, here, the philosophical nature hates becoming and that which *wanders* and erotically loves that which *is always*. Consequently, Socrates here sets up a radical contrast between philosophy (love for *what is*) and necessity (that which *wanders*). Indeed, given his assertion above that there is "every necessity" that such a person will "yearn for the truth," it would seem that the opposition between necessity and philosophy is not only an ontological/natural opposition, but also one necessitated by reason, or logical necessity.

Despite the stated necessity of the opposition between philosophy and necessity, there are reasons offered in the text to suggest that natural necessity pervades the philosophical nature, qua philosophical. For example, we observe in these passages the introduction of the *erotic* love of *what is*. What appeared in book II to be an "impossible" (375 c) need for two simultaneously contradictory characteristics in the same person (a contradiction that brought to mind the nature of philosopher dogs) seems to have been further resolved here with the subtle insertion of erotic love. For, it is again "impossible" for "the same nature to be a lover of wisdom and a lover of falsehood" (485 c). Insofar as the lover loves all of something, insofar as he desires and strives for it to the neglect of other things, the lover must be in a way *unified* by his erotic desire for that thing. When the object of erotic desire is that *which is always*, one's entire being is unified by the desire for the satisfaction of becoming one with it. Here, desire (an epithet of necessity) unifies the philosophic nature, not knowledge or logical consistency.

Socrates then argues that the singular focus necessitated by erotic love for the pleasure of *what is* (a pleasure of the soul), forces one to turn away from the pleasures of the body; for, erotic vision sees (or finds relevant) only that which it desires. Curiously, for a pleasure of the body, Socrates offers the love of money, not love of sex, food, or satisfaction of "stinging," wandering, and ephemeral desires.[2] I suppose this particular qualification may be an allusion to the introduction by Cephalus of the "usefulness" of money for living a just life (330 a). But, it is nevertheless a curious example of bodily pleasure. In addition to a reference to Cephalus, we may have here an example of the theme of mediation, a frequent topic in much of the text (not least of which examples are evident in book VI's "light" from the sun which stands between the power of sight and the object it sees). Of course, money is always a mediator. One observes in life people *in love* with money. But is love of money ever a matter of being in love with money as such, in love with "all of it," as it were, to the exclusion of all other things as is love of *what is always*? Or is love of money always rather love for that which money is merely a mediating symbol? If the latter, then one is not in love with money in such cases, but one is instead in love with the power, honor, objects and mastery of others that money affords. In my view, this may raise the question of what mediates one's love for *what is always*, if anything. Is there anything that stands between intellect [*nous*] and *what is always*? Money stands between a particular desire and its object and light stands between the sense of seeing and the object of sight. What makes *what is always* accessible to human *nous*? Is there a mediator that affords access?

A further question might be posed about the exclusion of bodily pleasure from the philosophic nature. Is not *erōs* always intimately connected to the body *and* the soul? In the dialogues, *erōs* is the source of frenzy, passion, and other *movements*. There can be no movements, no wanderings without bodies. While *what is always* may lack movement and wandering, the *erōs* that drives one toward it certainly does not. Would there not be a corollary to the pleasure of the soul in the body? As we observed in the introduction, erotic desire is one of the ways necessity shows itself, qua erotic necessity. As such, necessity haunts the philosophical nature insofar as he remains erotically compelled by *what is*, even as—in the current formulation—the philosopher hates what wanders.

Necessity here hides on both sides of the definition. Given that the philosophic nature loves [*eraō*] *what is* (485 b), then *erōs* already subtends our relation to knowledge, to truth, etc. Therefore, necessity does too. Moreover, necessity may remain deeper, more visceral, more evolutionarily ancient than *logos* or even *nous*. To be sure, as we observed in the introduction, the *Timaeus* raises the same problem for us. When Timaeus begins his speech for the third time, the new beginning is necessitated by the need for an account of necessity which was *already* there before the *demiurgos* started composing (Plato 2001, 52d). If the philosopher loves the truth of *what is*, then it may be erotic necessity which marshals even the search for truth for the sake of its own ends.

In what we have observed above, Socrates sets up a superficial proportion that takes the following form. As the philosophical nature is opposed to necessity, so does *what is* oppose what wanders. The proportion serves as a kind of first measure for recognizing the philosophical nature. However, as we observed, *erōs* complicates and perhaps even dissolves the contrasting relation. The superficial proportion is repeated in a different form in what follows. As the philosophical nature is opposed to necessity, so too is free speech opposed to *oi polloi* speech. In the following paragraphs, we will consider how necessity complicates this proportion as well.

After giving articulation to the philosophic nature's erotic relation to *what is always*, Socrates adds another condition by which Glaucon may "judge a nature to be philosophical or not" (486 a). He urges Glaucon not to fail to notice [*lathē*] that the unphilosophic nature partakes of illiberality [*aneleutheria*]. This lack of freedom is quickly further illuminated as "small talk" or "trivial speech" [*smikrologia*]. "Trivial speech is most contrary to a soul that is likely to yearn [*eporegō*] for the whole in all things divine and human" (486 a).

The formulation strikes the reader as strange. What does small talk have to do with a lack of freedom? This question no sooner occurs to the reader than another one emerges. Socrates then suggests that a person with a philosophic nature concerned with "all time" and "all being" will not imagine that death is something terrible.[3] Given that the philosophic nature concerns itself with *what is always*, and given that he finds those things which come to be and pass away to be false and hate-worthy, it is not surprising that the philosopher on this model would find the transitions of becoming to be of little concern. Thus, he would display no fear of death. However, in the next sentences he places these two concepts (illiberality and fear of death) together in such a way that they appear to belong together. Unfree, cowardly natures are incapable of philosophy: "a *cowardly* [*deilos*] and *illiberal* nature . . . would not partake in true philosophy" (486 b, emphasis added).

While there are several crucial features of the philosophic nature as presented *in the argument* that Socrates does not possess (such as having knowledge), our protagonist in the dialogues does embody some of these qualities *in practice*. Certainly, Socrates exhibits courage in the face of death in the *Phaedo* (1998); further, he demonstrates a resistance to small talk in response to Polus' floral and empty explanation of the power of rhetoric in the *Gorgias* (1998, 448 c - 448 d). However, when we follow his activity, Socrates displays a certain freedom from the constraints of what we might call the superficial talk regarding the most important things that circulate in a political community, in the *oi polloi*. As an example, we may look at the beginning of the *Republic*, at the origin of the argument, when Cephalus, queried by Socrates about the usefulness of his wealth, responds that it is useful because wealth can help secure a just disposition insofar as it prevents a man from owing debts (to either gods or man) and, thus, ensures that he is not afraid to speak the truth rather than to lie to the one to whom he owes a debt. Cephalus' assertion ostensibly derives from the respected poet Pindar, whom Cephalus quotes to support his claim about justice (331 a).[4] This is of course the introduction of the primary subject that originates the *Republic*. When Socrates responds that this conception of justice is unacceptable, Polemarchus charges into the discussion to aid his father by quoting another poet. If Simonides is to be believed, then his father's conception is to hold; for Simonides said "the just is to render to each what is owed" (331 e).

To this assertion, Socrates claims to be baffled, asking Polemarchus what he thinks it means. The heir of the argument responds with an interpretation of the poet's words. Simonides is reputed to mean: doing good to one's friends and harm to one's enemies. It seems that no one quoting the poets to Socrates really knows what the poets mean. At the very least there is a significant gap between the poet's words and the interlocutors' interpretation of them. None of Socrates' interlocutors appear to have done the necessary interpretive work of thinking through these sayings of the poets. Each slings the quotations around in everyday speech in order to support conventional and normative traditions and notions, but no one exhibits the *freedom* from the traditions enough to ask what these sayings actually mean . . . except Socrates. Thus, perhaps it could be argued that this is a way that Socrates' practical activity displays a "liberality" *vis à vis* small talk. That's not to say that Socrates' relation to the poets and the repetition of the poets' sayings is one of rejection or denial. It is, rather, a loosening from their static and concretized everydayness, a certain kind of freedom from their easy circulation, a liberal hesitation through the act of the question. The question, indeed, is the measure of Socrates' liberal actions in speech. The question is that by which Socrates loosens and frees the straps that hold one's attention toward the dramatic narrative of the cave walls of *oi polloi* in which we are all always already absorbed. Therefore, in Socrates' practices, one observes a form of courage and liberality that belong together, insofar as they are both related to raising questions about the principal ideas that form the very bonds that hold a city and a soul together.

Such freedom and courage are of course dangerous for many reasons. To name only a couple of risks: by questioning, one must face the danger that a consequence of interrogating the poetic utterances that form the central concepts of a society will be the loss of the secure status of the concept under investigation. If the meaning of "justice" is placed into question, there is a risk that the bond that ties humans together within a polis may come apart. The myth of Gyges (359 d) is precisely an example of this loss. Once Gyges acquires the ring, he possesses the *freedom* to turn, to loosen himself from the bonds that weave him into the surrounding community. By freeing himself from the thoughtless acceptance of the meaning of justice, the bonds that weave him into the community are severed, enabling him to topple even the *archōn* governing his city. But further, with respect to the soul itself, questioning produces the risk articulated in the *Phaedo* (1998, 89 d)[5]—namely that one may become a misologist, and perhaps even, a misanthrope. In possessing the courage and liberality to raise questions about the most important ideas, one is in danger of losing the very ground that supports our most important concepts, insofar as that ground is replaced by a visceral cynicism that inhibits our ability to accept that the things we care most about (justice, beauty, truth, wisdom, virtue) mean anything at all.

As will be developed further in the coming pages, the discursive order of *oi polloi* reflects a form of necessity. It is the conceptual economy into which each human and citizen is born. While the proportion articulated at the beginning of this section wished to radically separate the philosopher and the *oi polloi*, we observe here that, in fact, the philosopher's free speech and the small talk of *oi polloi* cannot be so easily separated.

Socrates continues to elaborate the qualities of the philosophical nature in ways that contrast with necessity. After Socrates urges Glaucon to concede to the necessary qualities of a person who possesses a nature that enables him to "lay claim sufficiently and perfectly [*teleios*] to what is" (486 e), he summarizes these positive virtues: "a man could never sufficiently practice [the sufficient and perfect [*teleios*] analysis of *what is*] if he were not by nature a rememberer, a quick learner, magnificent,[6] gracious [*euxaris*], and a friend and relative [*suggenēs*] of truth, justice, courage, and moderation" (487 a). When Glaucon responds affirmatively, Socrates suggests that the city be turned over to such men once they have been "perfected [*teleioō*] by education and maturity" (487 a). However, before Glaucon can respond, Adeimantus[7] interrupts with a crucial question that takes hold of the dialogue.

In a certain way, the problem Adeimantus introduces raises a question about whether the theoretical presentation of the image of the philosopher king squares with the practical activity that Socrates, qua philosopher, performs. At the same time, it occasions a meditation on the difference between the seeming and the being of the philosophical nature. Adeimantus interrupts the discussion, on the one hand, by raising a doubt which imperils the entire argument, insofar as he asks whether Socrates' interlocutors have been misled as a consequence of their inexperience in playing the game of Socratic draughts (dialectic).

> ... because they lack experience at questioning [*erōtēma*] and answering, they are led astray a little by the *logos* at each question ... [and] just like the draughts players who are not skilled but are beat by the clever [*deinos*] ones ... , so too they are beat in the end, and have nothing to say, by this other kind of draughts, played with *logoi*, not with pawns (487 b-c).

Consequently, if this account of Socrates' method is true, one could argue that the practice of dialectic would be another proof of the advantage of the stronger—"the stronger" in this case is the one more skilled at dialectic—insofar as the one employing it, would get the better of the weaker. "Truth" would be measured by rhetorical strength, not being. Moreover, in addition to this doubt, Adeimantus adds a second: the theoretical image of the philosopher that Socrates has composed in speech contradicts the actual practice of philosophers in cities.

But, the truth [about the being of philosophers] is not affected by [this game of draughts]. . . . In *speech*, [the interlocutor] cannot oppose you at each question, but in *deed* he sees that those who, having set into motion in philosophy, . . . most become quite strange [*allokotos*], not to say completely malicious; while the ones who seem reasonable [*epieikēs*] . . . they become useless to cities (487c-d, emphasis added).

While Socrates manipulates the discussion so that the dialectic achieves a certain composition of the philosopher's appearance in *speech*, this does not affect the truth at all. For Adeimantus, the reality of the philosopher in cities appears at worst maliciousness and at best uselessness.

The two doubts that Adeimantus expresses are related. Why do people think that Socrates' method of questioning has deceived them? Precisely because they are somehow forced to give assent to assertions and images that do not appear to reflect their own experience of reality. Another way of posing the question, a question that is already interior to the dialogue as a whole, would be: do the method and images that Socrates employs do what they ostensibly claim to do: namely, do they clarify *what is* from *what merely seems to be*, or *what wanders*? Or, rather, does he utilize his discursive devices to (sophistically?) manipulate his interlocutors into believing in a novel appearance, in contrast to what is also just an appearance? In the current case, the being of the philosophic nature is made to appear *in a private soul* (the individual interlocutor's—Glaucon's) in contrast to its common appearance *in the city* (the *oi polloi's*)? The interlocutor offers an image of the *oi polloi's* conception of something, the conception of us all; while Socrates' images force the interlocutor to give expression to something novel, perhaps from out of his own soul. For instance, Glaucon gives expression to the appearance of justice through the image of Gyges' ring (359 d). While it does not exhaust the appearance of justice of our community (it is but one image of justice that Glaucon claims to be trying to resist), the image of Gyges' ring is nevertheless the one circulating in the community that has appeared in the poorly articulated speech of Thrasymachus. In response to this speech, Socrates marshals another speech to come to support another appearance of justice. His dialectical speech forces his interlocutor to reach inside, engage the appearance, and draw from himself another one. However, *at no time have we transcended the region of the appearance of things*. We've merely observed the birth of a new appearance from out of (or contrasted to) the appearance that we always already inhabit. Both of these examples raise Adeimantus' question: do the method and images that Socrates employs do what they ostensibly claim: namely, do they clarify *what is* from *what merely seems to be*?

Given the importance of this question, Socrates' response to the interruption is most curious; for, Socrates concedes that, to him, these hypothetical figures presented by Adeimantus speak the truth (487 d). Therefore, dialectic *is* a game of draughts "played with *logoi*, not with pawns" (487 b). And philosophers *are* at best useless, at worst malicious in cities. With this admission, Adeimantus then reveals his cards a bit more clearly. The hypothetical accusers are cast aside and he takes responsibility for the observation when he asks how they could give the power to rule the city to those whom "*we admit* are useless to cities" (487 e, emphasis added). Rather than answering with an argument, Socrates claims that the question Adeimantus asks [*erōtas erōtēma*] needs to be answered through an image [*eikōn*] (487 e). Socrates is indeed always "greedy [*glischros*[8]]" (488 a) for images, though it remains unclear why what is presented in the image (the famous ship's pilot parable) cannot be treated in the elenchic (question/answer) form. Perhaps the image makes the phenomenon immediately visible. Rather than requiring step by step progress to a conclusion (in which the interlocutor may be *misled*), the image shows the entirety at once. Rather than an abstraction into disconnected thoughts, the image, like a painting, already has everything in it for the viewer.[9]

Of course, however one is to interpret Plato's reasons for having Socrates present the image instead of a dialectical argument, the image remains nevertheless inadequate. One may wish to suggest that the inadequacy lies in the fact that images in the *Republic* do not have the metaphysical status of knowledge—by presenting images, we are in the cave, a world even "lower" than that of becoming and wandering things. Perhaps this is true. But the metaphysical status of images is not the doubt I wish to raise against the parable here. Rather than the form of an image, I am raising a doubt about the content.

The image paints a scene in which there exists a ship owner (analogous to the *oi polloi*), a group of sailors (analogous to the politicians) who vie for control of the ship by competing in the skill of rhetorical persuasion rather than by possession of the knowledge of navigation, and the presence of a "stargazer" (analogous to the philosopher) who possesses knowledge of how ships move successfully from place to place. The sailors crowd around the shipowner, each attempting to persuade the shipowner to allow him to pilot the ship. Around the endeavor of persuasion grows an entire system of honor that the sailors generate and maintain. Those that are successful in persuading the shipowner to bestow the honor of piloting are envied for their skill and cleverness. Even though they know nothing of ships, seas, or navigation, they are praised for the skill of acquiring rule (either by persuasion or force). In contrast to these sailors, the "true pilot" cultivates the art of sailing by attending to "year, seasons, heaven, stars, winds, and all of the things in the art" (488 d) of navigation, while ignoring the rhetorical/political maneuverings of his fellow passengers. For this reason, the political sailors laugh at the practices of the "true pilot," dismissing him as useless. Consequently, the image offers an explanation of how philosophers come to be judged useless to cities and Adeimantus appears convinced by it. However, does the image actually show this adequately? Are philosophers truly analogous to pilots of ships? And is the knowledge of navigation comparable to the knowledge of ruling a city?

This parable has often been cited as a presentation of Plato's suspicion of democracy (Rosen 2005). Insofar as democracies are steered by persuasion rather than knowledge, no one really knows or cares to which ports the city sails. As far as both actual and possible cities go, I fail to see that this phenomenon would be unique to a democracy. Indeed, given the argument that comes later regarding the necessary maliciousness of the philosopher, it would seem that all political regimes are unsuitable for the philosophical nature (497 a).[10] Regardless of the form of the city, one may ask what knowledge the philosopher possesses that makes him/her capable of steering the ship of politics. If *Socrates* is to be our example of a philosopher, then certainly, unlike the stargazer in the image, Socrates does not possess the knowledge for sailing the vessel of politics. Everywhere, whether the subject is rhetoric, justice, virtue, etc., Socrates remains *in search* of knowledge among his peers, without ever seeming to find any there and without ever being in possession of knowledge himself. It strikes me that this privation that animates Socrates' erotic strivings cannot be taken lightly. If, *instead of Socrates*, the philosopher articulated in the image is to be the character presented at the beginning of book VI and whose *nature* empowers her to be able to lay hold of "what is always the same" (484 b), while wanting nothing to do with the things which "wander (*planaō*) in what is many and various" (484 b), then the image is again inadequate—both metaphorically and literally. For, *this* philosopher cares little for the knowledge of the workings of ships *or* cities, both of which wander and vary. Thus, even though I do not "need to closely examine [*exetaxō*] the image [*eikōn*]" (489 a) in order to know what Socrates means, if I do (unlike Adeimantus) examine the image, then a gap opens up between the image and the phenomenon it is supposed to explain.

For me, here we observe yet another example of an inherent/systemic incommensurability expressed in the *Republic*—city and soul, theoretical argument and practical endeavor, erotic impulse and technological control, public and private, nature and culture, necessity and freedom, being and becoming. The *Republic* forces the reader to navigate the gap left open as the human attempts to join each figure into an unproblematic relation to its other.

As stated above, despite these problems, the image persuades Adeimantus (at least on the surface) that there exist corrosive and distorting forces that shape the reputation of the philosophic nature as one which is useless to cities. Consequently, Socrates has qualified the sense in which he assented to the truth of Adeimantus' second assertion. Presumably, given Socrates' words on the matter, it is not in fact true that the most decent philosophic natures are useless to cities; but rather, they are useless only insofar as cities do not use them. Or perhaps more accurately, they are not useless, but go unused. Nevertheless, precisely how this—their erotic passion for *what is* and their hatred for *what is becoming*—would be useful to cities goes unquestioned by Adeimantus.[11] So much for the philosophic nature's uselessness "to the many [*tois pollois*]" (489 b). What about the "*necessity* of the maliciousness of the many" [*tēs tōn pollōn ponērias tēn anagkēn*] (489 d, emphasis added)?[12]

In order to begin to address Adeimantus' second slander (*diabolē*) against the philosophic nature, Socrates abandons the use of parable and returns to the form of question/answer. He finds that it is necessary to repeat the original formulation of the philosophic nature and to acquire Adeimantus' assent: the true lover of learning, we are reminded, "strives" as much as possible for "what is." This object of his erotic love is so intense that he does not lose his passion for it. He finds it impossible to cease yearning for it until he grasps it with the appropriate part of the soul, "couples" with it, and, as a consequence of this union, "begets" intelligence and truth. "Knowing" results, soothing the "labor pains," "but not before" (490 b). As we mentioned in our analysis of the philosophic nature's relation to the body, the invocation of *erōs* appears to signal the moment that necessity reasserts itself into the argument. The presence of *erōs* forces the reader to question the simple opposition between *what is* and *what wanders*. But what about virtue?

The "slander" that philosophy is a practice that cultivates a maliciousness in its practitioners is a moral claim. The opposite assertion that the philosophic nature is "a friend and relative [*suggenēs*] of truth, justice, courage, and moderation" (487 a) is also a moral claim—as is obvious by the terms employed by Socrates. The field of morality, consequently, would be the locus upon which human self-possession originates—it would be the measure of *what is* for a human, a uniquely human activity through which one stands firm despite the surrounding storm and seizes *from out of oneself* a stability in ever-flowing *physis*. In other words, "truth, justice, courage, and moderation" are the mark of the *being* of self insofar as it distinguishes itself from *necessity*.

But Plato complicates this facile and overly simplistic distinction between necessity (as the ruling origin of *what wanders*) and virtue (as the ruling origin of *what is*) by employing the paradigmatic language of necessity—erotics—throughout his description of the virtuous (that is, "true") philosopher. Here, we understand that erotics lie at the foundation, qua condition, for the philosophic nature's desire for *what is*. If the condition for the philosophic nature's search for truth is desire, then *he does not originate it himself*. It is not a matter of virtue, but of necessity and, as such, the philosopher, qua philosopher, is subject to a necessity, to what *wanders*, even insofar as he seeks *what is*. Necessity guides both before and despite education, before virtue, before knowledge and before either reason or *nous* know what they are doing.

Using language from the tragic stage, Socrates then questions the need to repeat from the beginning the entire *chorus* of the philosophic nature. Instead, to address Adeimantus' second slander, he will concentrate on the sources of its corruption. What are the sources of corruption of the philosophic nature? To answer, Socrates appeals to what we might perceive as a *tragic necessity*. Exactly the same things that mark it as heroic, virtuous and govern-worthy, make it subject to corruption: "courage, moderation, and everything we went through" (491 b). Like the reader, Adeimantus thinks that this is "strange [*atopos*] to hear." In fact, it appears as though Socrates is demonstrating Adeimantus' original critique that he uses dialectic to force his interlocutors to accept an image in *argument* [*logos*] that is the opposite of the *reality or experience* of the thing itself (490 d). However, Socrates qualifies his argument in a way that seems to reduce the intensity of the contradiction.[13] To explain, he employs an analogy of the cultivation of a living/natural thing. "Every seed or growing thing," says Socrates, "whether plant or animal . . . the more vigorous it is, the more it fails . . . when it does not get the food, climate, or place suitable to it" (491 d). If one plants the most robust seed in infertile land, one cannot expect to cultivate a "virtuous" plant. The soil in which one plants something matters. The entire ecosystem lies in the background supporting the cultivation of organisms. By employing the language of growing things (*phyō*), of nature, Socrates again utilizes the analogy of necessity (the *wandering* cause) to attempt to illuminate something about the virtuous philosophical nature. The individual naturally gifted in "courage, moderation, and everything we went through" (491 b) will be easily corrupted by the surrounding ecosystem. By necessity, the superior qualities necessary for philosophy will lead him toward a comportment of exaggerated self-importance if the environment happens to be [*tugxanō*][14] conducive for such a cultivation.

> "If he happens [*tugxanō*] to be from a great city, is rich and noble in it, and is further, handsome and tall? Will he not be full of unlimited hope, leading him to mind the business of both Greeks and barbarians, and will he not, thereupon, exalt himself to the heights, mindlessly full of pretension and without sense [*nous*]?"
>
> "Indeed he will," [Adeimantus] said (494 c-d).

As quoted above, the maliciousness of the philosophical nature is true because it is *necessary* [*tēs tōn pollōn ponērias tēn anagkēn*] (489 d). Here we observe the operation of necessity upon the seed of the philosophical nature, especially because the philosophical nature is always already woven into a surrounding ecosystem that makes all the difference. Yet, as the passage above proclaims, this feature of necessity shows itself as a matter of *chance*. The reader will recall that, in the introduction, we argued that *tugxanō* remains one of the ways that necessity shows itself in the *Republic*. Here, we observe the same formulation to express necessity operating in the background as a wandering or a happening [*tugxanō*]. Yet, it remains the decisive element that occasions the emergence of maliciousness or virtuousness. It is not by decision that one finds oneself in a corrupted ecosystem, it is by necessity. One *happens* (*tugxanō*) to be planted in this or that field of cultivation. As such, necessity decides. The wind blows, the seeds are dispersed, and the ecosystem in which a seed *happens* to find itself settled necessarily determines much about the character that appears, insofar as the noble qualities that the seed possesses interact with the infinity of features of a surrounding environment.

The centrality of chance in the cultivation of either the virtuousness or the maliciousness of the philosophic nature is again emphasized by Socrates when he describes the need for divine intervention if the noble seed *happens* to find itself in unsuitable soil.

> If the nature of the philosopher . . . happens [*tugxanō*] upon a proper education [*mathēsis*], it will *necessarily* grow into every kind of virtue; but if it is not planted and cultivated in what is proper, it will grow into the opposite, unless some god happens [*tugxanō*] to help (492 a, emphasis added).

If, by the *wandering cause*, the seed of the philosopher happens to find itself planted in an educational ecosystem that is "proper," her noble qualities will sprout and flower. If, however, by the *wandering cause*, she has the bad fortune of being planted in unsuitable educational soil, her noble qualities will require the intervention of a god (again, by the *cause* of chance, the wandering cause) to change the course of growth. At what point in these descriptions of the philosophic nature have we transcended the framework of necessity, of the wandering cause?

Throughout these sections of book VI, *ostensibly*, Socrates has been giving an argument to distinguish the philosophical nature from the forces of necessity. The philosophical nature cares only for "what is" and hates "what wanders." However, as we observe in the passages above, *underneath* these claims, necessity appears to be smuggled back into the discourse by Socrates either consciously or unconsciously (if the latter, then consciously only by Plato). Moreover, necessity appears here in at least three ways: as erotics, as natural growth, and as chance. All three of these appear to be interwoven with each other, are there in advance of any philosophical nature and serve as a condition for the very possibility of the activity of the philosopher. In the full sense of the term, they are *a priori* to the emergence of the philosopher. Consequently, the argument opens up a difference between what the human being (in this case, the philosopher) consciously conceives of herself to be doing (insofar as she reasons and employs intellect) and what is really going on underneath her consciousness (by necessity). It strikes me that this opening gap may be meant to greatly qualify what Plato thinks human beings are actually capable of in terms of acquiring control over their motivations and actions. Even when it comes to noetically apprehending the truth of a thing—of intellecting *what is*—underneath what they take to be self-conscious freedom and choice, they are driven toward it unconsciously by the wandering cause.

None of this is brought into question by Adeimantus. Instead, Socrates' questions and Adeimantus' answers remain focused on working out the reasons for the necessity of the maliciousness of the philosophical nature. The argument takes an unexpected turn, however. Socrates asks Adeimantus if he agrees with the opinion of the many (*oi polloi*) that youth are corrupted by sophists teaching in a private (*idiōtikos*[15]) capacity (492 a). To respond affirmatively to this question would not be at all surprising. Indeed, Socrates himself seems to suggest such an interpretation in many of the dialogues. One need only reflect on Gorgias' influence on Callicles and Meno, for instance. However, here, Socrates does not allow Adeimantus to answer this question, but instead he himself responds in the negative:

"Is it not the men who speak in this way who are the greatest sophists, who educate . . . and produce [everyone] just the way they want them to be: young and old, men and women?"

"But when?" he said.

"When many gathered together in masses sit down in gatherings, courts, theaters, army camps, or any other public meeting space of the many, and with much uproar, censure some of the things said or done, and praise others, excessively shouting and clapping in both cases" (492 a—b).

According to the Socrates of book VI, the greatest sophists (*megistous sophistas*) are not the private teachers, but the *oi polloi*. The *oi polloi* are precisely constitutive of the ecosystem in which every human seed—whether excellent or mediocre—happens to find itself planted. That is to say, the original source of the corruption of the philosophical nature is public, not private. The soil into which human souls are planted are public speeches. These settings of discourse are not merely political in the narrow sense. The broader conception of political discourse includes assemblies and courthouses, to be sure; however, these speeches structure human life in all of its regions: theaters, army camps, schools, churches, social media and perhaps even within familial homes (these are not only settings of formal education—women and the old are included). As Socrates suggests here, in public spaces, the many manifest the political emotions associated with praise and outrage in order to carve out citizens with the same dispositions and opinions. In this way, the multitude churn and mold the youth in the model of *oi polloi* themselves. Socrates makes it clear that it is not only the Athenian democracy that is organized this way (497 b). The ecosystem of the human, *oi polloi*, is a feature of human necessity, not merely a free choice of political regime. It marks the incommensurability of the city and the soul, of the public and the private.[16] Even in the circumstances in which the many are emotionally engaged in the formation of souls after themselves, it is still a matter of necessity. For example, "the uproar of blame and praise" fashions souls in the manner of a visceral robotic response, not self-conscious decision or noetic insight.

Furthermore, since *oi polloi* constitute the necessary conditions for the growth of the seed, no individual human soul escapes formation by the many. Every kind of *private* education will be "swept away by such praise and blame" (492 c), and every soul in the ecosystem will "say the same things are beautiful and shameful, practice/pursue [*epitēdeuō*] what [the many] practice, and will be" (492 c) as *oi polloi* are. To this, Adeimantus replies, "The *necessity* [of this] is great" (492 d, emphasis added). Thus, Socrates argues that no private speeches (sophistical or otherwise) are able to overcome a seed's formative cultivation by the many. After he asks Adeimantus if he knows of any private speeches that will counter the many and prevail, Socrates asserts that "even to try is foolishness [*pollē anoia*]" (492 e). For, someone undergoing an education in opposition to the many "does not, has not and will not become a character with a different virtue" (492 e). Private education is not, has never, and will never produce human souls with a comportment toward virtue that is different from the many.[17]

These remarks again raise the question of the operation of necessity underneath human perception, volition and thinking. In this case, private speech makers self-identify within a city as opposing the *oi polloi*, of being in possession of a sophisticated method by which they challenge and exploit the public opinions and beliefs of the many. However, Socrates suggests here that the structure of necessity is such that claiming a right to a unique identity that is distinct from the surrounding political community is imaginary. It has never happened and never will happen. The political representatives of the many in the polis, the ones that Socrates earlier called the "greatest sophists" (492 b) are equally deluded. They perceive themselves as being identities somehow radically distinct from the "private wage earners" (493 a). But Socrates argues that the private wage earners educate in "nothing other than these opinions [*dogmata*] of the many" (493 a), even though they imagine themselves to be novel and innovative. A system of identity creation is cultivated in the city through which apparent oppositional identities are formed and engage one another in acrimonious and violent ways. However, the system and its differences are imaginary. Both camps *unknowingly* but *necessarily* marshal the same dogmatic concepts and both reinforce the broader, foundational structure of political conviction.

The "private wage earners," the sophists, do in fact have a special relation to the structure of conviction. They study *oi polloi* like a man who studies "the natural impulses and desires of a great, strong beast he is raising." (493 b). The sophist discovers which sounds make the beast angry and which make it compliant. "After learning all this by keeping company and spending time with the beast, he calls it wisdom and, having contrived an art [*technē*], starts teaching" (493 b). However, the private wage earner does not disclose to himself which of these angers and desires *are* noble or just, but applies these terms ("noble" and "just") from out of the public doctrine of opinion and belief. The passage anticipates the image of the cave. All participants in the games and competitions in the life of the cave (whether chained or free to cast shadows from above the wall—*oi thaumatopoioi* [514 b]) necessarily originate from the system of dogma below the earth. If the private wage earners are *oi thaumatopoioi,* they are not even aware that they too belong to a structure of necessity that folds them into itself. They falsely believe that they escape it.

What is the difference between "the private wage earner" and the philosopher here? The private wage earner educates in nothing other than the opinions of the many; that is to say, the sophist does not actually employ *private* speech (if there is such a thing). In other words, the sophist never transcends the field of *necessity*.

One might observe a similar conception of the contrast between private *logos* and necessity in book VIII's description of the oligarchic man—another wage earner. There, Socrates suggests that the oligarchic man has "bad desires." However, instead of persuading them with private speech, he suppresses them by necessity:

> When someone like this has a good reputation in business, seeming to be just, he holds down bad desires by force [*bia*], which are there, with some decent part of himself. He holds them down not by persuading them with argument [*logos*], but by necessity [*anagkē*] and fear, doing so because he trembles for his whole substance (554 c—d).

In the case of the oligarchic man, the ruling disposition of his soul reflects the ruling disposition of the city—that is to say, love for money. He has been fully appropriated by the order of *oi polloi* and his personal comportment mirrors the political one. The love for wealth both designs his activities and, somewhat paradoxically, his virtues. His actions are guided by the desire to preserve his wealth. If he feeds his "bad desires" in his contractual relations, he will lose his "reputation" among the *oi polloi*. If he were capable of "private speech" (translated here as "argument"), he might "persuade" his desires in accordance with what is best. However, he can only hold them down by force and necessity. By "necessity" here, it is not clear whether Socrates refers to natural or logical necessity. That is to say, it is not clear if what is meant is, for example, some sort of "if . . . then" logical determination: "if I take advantage of my client to earn more money, then I will be sued and may lose it." In this case, necessity shows itself in the force of the structure subtending the propositions. It is not private, free discursive persuasion; but rather it is an inherited motive force inscribed within the possible forms of discourse inherited by *oi polloi*, like the motive force that drives the syllogism from premise to conclusion. If, instead, he means natural necessity, it may be of the variety associated with instinctual fear—the order of animal necessity prevents the oligarchic man from satisfying his unjust desires because of, among other things, the punishment threatened by *oi polloi* for violating its laws. In neither case does the human being perform its activities by means of private speech, but rather, like a bee within a hive, through necessity.

To return to the private teacher in book VI, Socrates states that, insofar as the private wage earner "has no other *logos* about" justice, the good, or the noble than that of the *dogmata* of *oi polloi*, he "calls *the necessary* just and beautiful" (493 c, emphasis added). Here, we observe another explicit connection between the soils of discourse that constitute the ecosystem of the human seed and the field of necessity. By learning what makes the many angry and tame, sophists conceive of themselves as stepping outside of necessity, taking private possession of it, and forcing it to surrender to their own political desires; however, for Socrates, at no time have they transcended the structure of necessity, at no time have they actually uprooted themselves from the soils of discourse that constitute the ecosystem of the human seed. Necessity pulls their strings. The public is their private. Within the grip of necessity, they are neither capable of seeing that their private motivations, desires, and actions are always already determined by *oi polloi* (by necessity), nor are they capable of giving an account of how *necessity* differs from the *good*: "having never seen nor being able explain to someone else how much necessity and the good differ by nature" (493 c).

One is left with the impression that the philosophic nature differs from the private wage earner by being in possession of something truly private. Both the public and the private *in the polis* belong to necessity. The philosophical nature (if it exists) must lie elsewhere. Socrates argues that the *plēthos* (the multitude/the many) cannot distinguish the beautiful itself from the wandering beauties (494 d). As such, he explicitly brings the distinguishing feature of the philosophical nature (loving *what is*, rather than *what comes to be* and wanders) to bear on the difference between the private wage earner and the philosopher. Any person wholly enveloped in *oi polloi* is incapable of philosophy; for, "philosophy is impossible for the many [*plēthos*]" (494 a). Such a claim places the emphasis on the difference between the philosopher and the private wage earner precisely on their relation to *oi polloi*. Even though, by *necessity*, there are no human beings not always already cultivated by the *plēthos*, the philosopher's comportment cannot be reduced to the many's as is the sophist's. While the sophist only mirrors the comportment of *oi polloi* back to itself in a feedback loop of necessity, Socrates suggests that the philosophical nature exhibits something *truly private* in relation to it. In fact, this privacy (if it actually exists) remains the principal feature of the philosophical nature by which it *may* distinguish itself from the forces of necessity. The turn toward *what is* is not something a polity can do. That requires individuation and a private freedom from necessity. Every human finds herself planted in an ecosystem in which something like "the beautiful," "the just," and "the virtuous" appear and organize her life. In these conditions, *both* the preservers of the polity *and* the private sophists merely throw these terms around without wakefully distinguishing the beautiful itself from the wandering beauties. With respect to the question of justice, Plato has Cephalus and Polemarchus show us the consequences of this activity in both young and old men. Socrates' questions serve to individuate them and force them out of the flow of necessity. One might argue that the Socratic *aporia* does nothing else than uproot the seed from the necessary soil of discourse. This turn can only happen in an individual soul, not at the level of the city.

Given what we have said above about the all-pervasive features of necessity underneath the mere appearance of self-control and self-possession of the individual human, my parenthetical qualifications regarding the philosophical nature should not be taken lightly—if, indeed, it exists at all. One of the many difficulties with articulating the origin of such a privacy lies in the fact that this privacy does not emerge via private means. The turn does not emerge spontaneously within the soul, but rather one must be *pushed into turning* from outside of oneself, from some source that presumably does not lie within the order and origin of necessity. When the nature that naturally possesses "facility at learning, memory, courage, and magnificence" becomes necessarily shaped into the kind of soul that is "mindlessly full of pretension and without sense" and, consequently, has an exaggerated sense of self-importance (494 b-c), another person who exists *somehow outside* of this system must approach.

> "if *someone* were to come to a young man in this state [*diatithēmi*] and tell him the truth: that intelligence is not in him, even though he needs it; and, to get it, he must work like a slave. Do you think he will hear it through a shield of such evils?"
>
> "Far from it," he said (494 d, emphasis added).

Who is this hypothetical someone? Whence comes this hypothetical someone? From the *oi polloi*? Impossible: the many are folded into the structure of necessity. From the private wage earners? No, they merely mirror necessity. This person must come from outside of the region of the public and from outside of the region of the private teachers. That is to say, he must come from outside of necessity—from nowhere. The someone that approaches comes from *nowhere* and is, in fact, *no one*, because no place is outside of necessity and everyone is formed (both physically and discursively) by necessity. Such a person is, thus, *a-topos*: without place, strange.

The group composed of people that can become philosophers without corruption is very, if not impossibly, small. The number of humans born that possess the characteristics articulated above as pre-conditions for philosophy is already miniscule. However, given Socrates' assertions that we have analyzed above, those that escape the necessary corruption (by chance/necessity) in any of the existing cities reduce this small number much further, perhaps infinitely. Socrates lists a number of possibilities that, by the wandering cause of necessity (chance), the philosophic nature may avoid its own natural corruption. Each case appears to express a certain form of privacy *vis à vis* the city. The first example Socrates offers is of a "noble and well-raised character, held in check by *exile* [or flight/avoidance—*phygē*]." This exile enables the soul to "remain in accordance with nature with her [*philosophia*], without [*aporia*] corruptors"[18] (496 b, emphasis added). The origin of the exile is not clear; however, if we are to interpret the phrase *hupo phugēs katalēphthein* with its political meaning, one might argue that the source of alienation from the *polis* is external to the noble and well-reared disposition. It is *by chance* that the soul has the good fortune to be sent into exile before she can be corrupted by *oi polloi*. The source of the emergence of privacy is external to one's deliberative and noetic faculties. Plato's technical term for the external shock that engenders something like radical individuation and privacy, *aporia*, appears conspicuous here. Even though in the context presented by the passage it makes sense to translate it as an "absence" of corruptors, still, the presence of this crucial term must be a signal to the reader: our first example displays a person who has been exiled from and shocked out of the public into some sort of privacy, some individuation, qua exile.

Socrates provides further examples: a big soul in a small city that despises politics and is compelled to look out "beyond" (496 b); figures that come from arts outside of philosophy, despising their own disciplines, are driven toward *what is*; philosophical natures "cursed" by the bridle of Theages—or bodily illness—that serves as a prophylactic against joining with, and thus being corrupted by, *oi polloi*. The last case in particular seems to invoke the suggestion that necessity flows underneath the emergence of the uncorrupted philosophical nature; it is in fact *bodily* necessity, not knowledge or intellect, that saves the philosophical nature from itself. An external force of bodily illness chances to compel the philosophical nature toward *what is*.

Following these examples, Socrates includes his own form of private salvation: "my case—the demonic sign—is not worth mentioning, for it has come to be somehow in someone or noone before" (496 b). While Plato does not have Socrates offer details elaborating the features or functions of the demonic sign in this context, the reader finds an account in the mouth of Socrates in the *Apology*. Socrates's *daimon* is given as an example in the accusation that he makes new gods and does not believe in the old ones (*Euthyphro* 1966, 3 b). In his public defense, he states that it is precisely this that interrupts the flow of his activity and holds him back, especially in matters that involve *oi polloi*. From the *Apology*:

> Having begun [*archamenon*] in childhood, this is a certain voice that comes to me, and when it comes, it always *turns me away* [*apotrepei*] from what I am about to do, but never [*protrepei*] *turns me* forward. This is what makes me refuse the public things (1966, 31 d, emphasis added).

When the language of "turning" is emphasized in the translation, the image of the cave in the *Republic* immediately comes to mind. In his everyday life—in his natural and political necessity—Socrates is carried along through his activities and speeches upon the ship of public identity which glides along the waters of necessity. Suddenly, from outside of this system of movement, appears a voice that not only stops him, but causes him to anchor ship and turn away from what he is about to do. Here runs an obvious parallel between the daimonic voice of the *Apology* and the stranger that emerges from the shadows in book VII of the *Republic*. There, the stranger unfastens the cave-dweller from the binds that restrict his ability to *turn* his head, and then forces the citizen to *turn away* from the wall—the image of political/ discursive necessity. In any case, Socrates includes the *daimon* as another way that a philosophical nature may avoid necessary corruption. Again, it is a matter of external intervention, a chance occurrence of the wandering cause, that twists one loose from the public and forces a turn into a form of privacy. Consequently, the daimon shows itself as one of the hypothetical "someones" that we have analyzed above—it is someone strange that comes from nowhere, from outside of necessity, in order to cultivate the bloom of the private.

The infinitely small group of philosophical natures that have managed to escape the corruption of their natures live private lives of modest expectation, not celebrated intellectual achievement, grand discoveries, or political conquest and/or revolution.[19]

> After having seen the madness of the many, and having seen that no one doing the things of the *polis* does anything healthy . . . Taking all of these things into consideration, he keeps quiet and attends to his own things [rather than politics] . . . Seeing others filled with lawlessness, he is pleased [*agapaō*] if somehow he himself can live his life here free [*katharos*]of injustice and unholy acts, and depart [this life] with beautiful hope, graciously and cheerfully (496 c—e).

Such is the life of the philosophic nature in every regime that has ever existed. By chance or by some external necessity, they have the luck *somehow* to be twisted free from the *oi polloi* and released into a certain privacy, insofar as this is possible.

However, Socrates leaves open a window of possibility for a view outside of all existing regimes. If instead of an existing regime, the philosophical nature chanced [*tugxanō*] upon a proper one, "he would grow and preserve both the common things and the private" (497 a). But even if such a regime were really possible, the philosopher's integration into such a place happens by chance, by the wandering cause. Therefore, the cultivation of the erotic relation to *what is* in the philosophical nature in both actual and possible regimes first and foremost depends upon necessity (upon *what wanders*), not upon knowledge or intellect or anything resembling self-sufficiency or self-consciousness.

In this section of chapter 1, we consider our theme (the relation of the philosophical nature and necessity) by differentiating the law-giver and the guardian. For, it appears to me that the philosophical nature reflects the work of the law-givers more than the guardians. Yet, as we will see, the law-giver always originates his or her thinking about the law in the middle of a system already on the way—that is, already within necessity.

Socrates speculates that Adeimantus will next ask him what regime is the suitable one in which the philosopher might grow to save both public and private things (497 c). However, Adeimantus denies that this is his question. Rather he wants to know if the regime is the same as that they've already built in speech. One cannot help but wonder if Adeimantus is missing an opportunity to tie Socrates down here to an explicit assertion. Does Plato compose the dialogue here in such a way that the ebb and flow of conversational necessity happens to pass by a chance for an answer without Socratic qualification?

Whatever Plato's reasons for pushing Adeimantus past Socrates' invitation here, he has Socrates answer the question in a strange way. He says, "it is the same in the other ways [τὰ μὲν ἄλλα, ἦν δ' ἐγώ, αὕτη]" (497 c) [as the city that they have already built in speech] and in this way too . . . it would be *necessary* [*deēsoi*] that something always be present in the city having the same *logos* of the regime as you, the law-giver, had when you set down the laws" (497 c). Every edition of the *Republic* I have consulted translates this *logos* differently. In my view, these differences signal a disagreement or confusion with respect to how each translator wants us to interpret the passage. James Adam (1902) translates it as "reasoned theory," Shorey (1969) renders it as "conception," Jowett, as "idea" (1908), Sachs translates it as "rational understanding" (2007), Reeve, as "rational account" (2004) and so on. Therefore, I have left it untranslated. Still, in what follows, I'll attempt to pin down a more precise meaning and to connect what is named in this concept of *logos* to that of necessity.

In order to help us understand the meaning of the "*logos*" in this passage, both Reeve (2004) and Shorey (1969) point us to Stephanus page 412 a—b. There, in the relevant passage of book III, Socrates is developing the concept of education in the city—music and gymnastics. Just before, he observed that the person too narrowly interested in gymnastics runs the risk of becoming a misologist. "[The young man produced by such education] no longer makes use of persuasion through speech but accomplishes everything with force and savageness like a wild animal. And in ignorance and awkwardness, he lives without rhythm and without gratitude/gracefulness" (411 d-e). Socrates suggests that the education of our city, therefore, cultivates a sort of musical tuning of the soul. In fact, according to him, "some god" (411 e) did not give music and gymnastics to humans in order to encourage, on the one hand, the cultivation of the body with gymnastics, and on the other hand, the cultivation of the soul with music. Rather, both disciplines are for the sake of tuning *the parts of soul* to each other in a harmonious way; these disciplines create a balance between the "spirited" and the "philosophical" parts of the soul. "The person who makes the finest blends gymnastics with music and applies them to his soul in due proportion is the one whom we should most rightly say that he is the most perfectly musical and well harmonized. . . . Will we need such a ruler [*epistatēs*] in our city, Glaucon, if the regime is going to be saved?" (412 a-b). A requirement for a competent overseer is to have a soul well-tuned and harmonized by the education of gymnastics and music.

Is this a person with the same *logos* as the lawgiver in the passage quoted above (497 c)? Not necessarily. I would argue that the hypothetical guardians of the city fit the description of overseers (whose characteristics Socrates goes on to determine in the text that follows). But it strikes me that the lawgiver has a special, self-conscious, perhaps even dialogical *logos* of the law in a way that *transcends* that of the guardian's. That is to say, the guardian and the lawgiver have different relations to the law. The lawgiver establishes the educational curriculum with his/her/their opinion [*doxa*] as a consequence of the kind of discursive/dialogical *logos* that Socrates, Adeimantus and Glaucon are currently undergoing. In this case, they are the lawgivers and remain categorically different from the guardians. The preservation of that opinion is secured through the education of the guardians. However, insofar as the lawgiver originates the opinion and the educational curriculum, s/he has a different relation to the opinion than the guardian, whose soul is, in fact, *a product* of the opinion. The lawgiver(s), by contrast, is the well-spring of the opinion—indeed, perhaps it can be said that the lawgiver, qua originator, is not exhausted by the content of the opinion, while the guardian, qua product, is exhausted by it. One may further speculate that, as a product of the opinion of the lawgiver, the guardian's relation to the opinion is precisely not as opinion, but as fact. *The lawgiver, on the other hand, as originator, perceives the somewhat stochastic origin of the opinion in a way that the guardian does not.* To be sure, the opinion emerges from a dialogical *logos* that circulates around a problem that exists for the lawgiver. On my reading, the dialogical gathering together into a constellation of concepts around the problem defines the *logos* of the lawgiver out of which *grows* the opinion that Socrates names in the relevant passage above (497 c). It is therefore contingent upon a number of factors that affect the dialogue and, thus, the constellation of concepts—factors like the interlocutor and the questioner, the setting of the dialogue, the subject of the dialogue, among others. All of these factors affect the development of the opinion of the lawgiver, but not the educational system or the guardians that this educational system produces.

In any case, a hint given for the difference of relation to the *doxa* is found in book IV, among other places. In the discussion of courage there, Socrates says "a city too is courageous through a certain part of itself, through having in it a *power* [*dunamis*] that through everything *will save the opinion* about the terrible [*deinos*] things—the very things and sorts of things that the lawgiver passed on [*paraggellō*] in the education. . . . Courage saves opinion brought into being by law through education about what . . . is terrible" (429 b-c, emphasis added). In a similar fashion to my analysis above, this passage asserts that the educational system that is legislated and put into place by the lawgivers shapes and molds the guardians in such a way that the opinion will be preserved. Glaucon claims not to understand this formulation, so Socrates offers an image of what he thinks is something similar: dying fabric. Education shapes the guardians with the opinion of the legislators—not just about courage, but about everything—in such a way that it will be saved regardless of the pleasures or pains experienced in their day to day lives. In a similar manner, says Socrates, fabric preparations that good textile artisans perform ensure the color in the fabric will remain colorfast, regardless of what it is washed with (429 d - 430 b). However, the opinion of the lawgivers is only like the educational curriculum or the dye once it has been instituted, once it is no longer an opinion. Prior to that—or rather, *for the legislators*—it remains more fluid, open to questioning. In other words, in this state the opinion belongs to the region of dialectic. The evidence for this lies in the dramatic setting of the dialogue itself. The present opinion emerged from dialectical questioning and, qua opinion, it has the potential to be pulled back into the orbit of dialectical questioning, into the conditions that subtend the constellation of concepts out of which it grew. This is not the case for the guardians, who, in ideal educational conditions, hold the opinion within their fibers regardless of the detergent in which they may be washed. Indeed, the guardians are legally bound by the lawgivers' opinion to prevent innovation (422 a), the political equivalent of the bleeding of dyes.

A similar question must be raised to the one above regarding the hypothetical "someone" that steps in from outside of the structure of necessity to turn the philosophical nature. We must ask what this "something" is in the city that has the same *logos* as the legislators. As a reminder, I will quote the passage again: "it would be *necessary* [*deēsoi*] that something always be present in the city having the same *logos* of the regime as you, the law-giver, had when you set down the laws" (497 c). Long ago, Adam interpreted this passage to suggest that "the rulers must understand the *constitution* and not merely accept it on the legislator's authority, if the spirit of the original legislator is to survive his death" (Adam 1902, 34). As such, "having the *logos*" for him means "understanding the constitution." I'm not opposed to this interpretation; however, there are two reasons I think it should be modified. First, Socrates does not refer to "someone" that understands, but rather he says that "something" has "the *logos*." What has the *logos*? The constitution. Secondly, according to my reading above, I think that, by "*logos*," Socrates refers to the dialogical *logos*-conditions of the lawgivers and their constellation of concepts. This is not a "*logos*" understood as a hypostatized, static document. Thus, in my view, the term "constitution" in Adam's interpretation may be retained if we keep in mind the more originary meaning of "constitution": that is to say, the dialogical conditions by which the opinions emerge that *ground* the educational (and thus, political) regime. But what does it mean to say that dialogical *logos*-conditions of the lawgivers and their constellation of concepts must be present in the city if this *logos* is not the written, static constitution? Not only is this *logos* not a person, but it is also not a static, rigidified *thing*.

One might wish to say that the *Republic* is a constitution. Indeed, it is a written document that contains assertions with respect to the legal and educational organization of a city. However, it is not a formal constitution in any common sense of that term. Rather, it is a dialogical *logos* that concerns a meaning-horizon of justice, and this would be a central subject around which any constellation of concepts would circulate if the goal of the discussion were the articulation of a formal, static constitution, even if the *Republic* is not reducible to anything static—whether conceived in terms of a constitution or in terms of an interpretation. As such, it is the setting of the cultivation of a motive *doxa*. The *Republic*, therefore, may be described not as a constitution, but as *constitutional*, in the sense that it makes manifest a dialogical ground.

Moreover, the meaning-horizon made visible by the *Republic* relies upon a number of contingent, yet, necessary conditions. The dialogical *logos* that takes place around justice is occasioned (*tugxanō*) by the gathering together of Athenians and foreigners by a public, yet foreign festival. Its setting is the inaugural festival for the foreign (Thracian) goddess that the Athenians associated with Dionysus (insofar as her worship involved bacchic frenzy and *orgia*) and Artemis (insofar as she too was a huntress): Bendis. Her worship, its sacrifices, and all of her associations gather the lawgivers together and provide the ecosystem out of which grows the problem of justice that animates the entirety of the dialogue. With this festival as a backdrop, the conversation takes place despite Socrates' reluctance and despite his desire to return to the city—indeed, like a *daimon*, someone (a slave) *happens* to reach out, grab hold of his cloak and *stop and turn* him toward the dialogical ecosystem. With whom does the conversation begin? The aged Cephalus has reached an age at which he likely worries for the first time about how he has lived his life and what this will mean in the possible afterlife. With whom does the conversation proceed? Like the natural temporal order of necessity of both biological and cultural beings, Cephalus' son inherits the *logos*. Glaucon and Adeimantus are driven by the desire to push the argument further. Who are these people? What are their individual motivations for pursuing the conversation? All of this material and more constitutes the dialogical conditions out of which emerge the *logos* of these particular lawgivers. We observe an irreducible dialogical configuration that shapes the formation of the living opinion of the lawgivers. However, even in this short series of questions, we see that it is *necessity* in all three of the forms we have determined (erotics, natural growth, and chance) that has occasioned every feature of the dialectical *logos* out of which originates the ruling *doxa* of the *politeia*. None of the conditions of the discourse transcend the structures of necessity.[20]

Another question for our reading involves the philosophical status of this *doxa*. A number of the foregoing concepts are brought together in a problematic way shortly after Socrates asserts the necessity that there must remain something in the city with the same *logos* as the lawgivers. After subtly criticizing the teachers of rhetoric in Athens, Socrates suggests that it is natural to assume that *the many* would be suspicious of the present speeches constituting the laws of the *politeia* because *the many* have never seen "one or more" rulers "balanced" with virtue in deed and speech at the helm of the city. Further, *oi polloi* have never listened adequately to the sorts of "beautiful" and "free" speeches characteristic of the philosophical nature (who erotically loves *what is*):

> You blessed one, they have not listened sufficiently to beautiful [*kalos*] and free [*eleutherōs*] speeches that strive in quest of the truth for the sake of knowing and that 'salute from afar' the subtleties and eristics that tend toward nothing but opinion [*doxa*] and strife in court and in private company (499 a).

There are two features of this speech that cause alarm. On the one hand, if I am right to say that the streams of necessity have gathered this pool of discussants together in the Piraeus and have, consequently, shaped and determined the ecosystem of *logos* in which the dialectic takes place, then which speech (*logos*) from which interlocutor is "free"? The discourse of the *Republic*, therefore, would not count as an example of the production of speech of a philosophical nature that "strives for the truth for the sake of knowing" (499 a), insofar as this discourse, even if it is beautiful, is not "*free.*" The very mark of "free discourse" is its freedom from necessity. On the other hand, to what does the dialectical journey of our interlocutors in the *Republic* lead? It leads precisely to "opinion"—the opinion of the lawgivers regarding justice, courage, wisdom, beauty and the rest; the opinion with which the law is composed and the educational paradigm is generated and conducted; the opinion that must be preserved in the guardians. At what point do we achieve the *distance* by which we might "salute" at the many and the *doxa* that animates their lives in both public and private?[21]

Socrates confirms the priority of necessity (in the form of chance) when he claims that "neither city nor constitution, nor a man will ever become complete before some *necessity happens* to envelop [*anagkē tis ek tuchēs peribalē*] those few philosophers who are not malicious to take charge of a city . . . or a true *erōs* for true philosophy falls upon those who hold power from some divine inspiration" (499 b—c, emphasis added). If human beings are to achieve their *telos*, necessity must either envelop philosophers to take charge of the city philosophically (by chance), or necessity must erotically compel individuals among the ruling toward philosophy. I take the first example of necessity ([*tuxē*] chance) to emphasize a philosophy in the context of the public and the second example (*erōs*) to highlight the private. Thus, in both cases, whether publicly or privately, necessity—not knowledge, or choice, or a prior grasping of *what is*—holds the position of priority *vis à vis* the philosophical nature.

As we observed before, there appears to be a question about whether such a nature, the philosophical nature, exists. Among the concluding arguments that sought to address Adeimantus' objection and to flesh-out the necessity of the corruption of the philosophical nature, we find one that relies upon a fable-like construction. However, even in the context of a fable in which the philosophical nature is articulated as having an uncertain, merely possible existence, Socrates smuggles in the language of necessity as a kind of a ruling principle.

> If, then, in the limitless time passed, some *necessity* [*tis anankē*] constrained those at the foremost of philosophy to take charge of a city, or there even now is in some barbaric place . . . or will be later, we are willing to fight for the argument that the constitution we have described has been, is and will be when this Muse has become master of a city (499 c—d, emphasis added).

In this passage, one finds an appeal to an ideological ground for decision. Even if the philosophical nature does not have a concrete reality, we *ought* to do battle for its possibility, whether in the past, the present or the future. Here, philosophy is spoken of as a "muse," an entity which comes in from the outside, which is invoked, and fills the ecosystem with its essence—the erotic desire for *what is*. The relation of the muse to temporality proves curious here. From the point of view of the fable, we will do battle for the argument that, when the muse enters "endless time," it will have a transformative effect on the historicity of the temporal. Philosophy, the erotic comportment toward *what is*, rewrites time when it rules a city, such that the city has been, is, and will be. Erotic love is precisely one of those temporal interruptions that has the power to completely reshape the past, the present and the future. When one is struck with love, all the events of the past can still be organized in accordance with an historical narrative composed of propositions and assertions. Yet, even though the historical narrative before the event of erotic love is identical to that after it, the *meaning* of the past, present and future has been transformed. The meaning of those events is not contained in the historical narrative and its propositions: the event of erotic love lights up the meaning of those temporal narratives in a new way. Similarly, the lightning strike of the erotic love for *what is* also lights up the meaning of the narratives of the historical past, present and future. *Now*, the philosophical nature "looks at and contemplates things that are well ordered and always in the same state"

(500 c). The affairs of human beings "abusing and taking pleasure in quarreling with one another" (500 b) appear in a different light before and after the *Geistesblitz* of the soul. However, as the quoted passage exclaims explicitly, even this transformative rupture in the structure of time, this disruption in the field of necessity (what else organizes motive flow of the past into the future?), is from the beginning already *tis ananke*, "some necessity" (499 d).[22]

With the necessary and remarkable introduction of the philosophical nature into the field of time, Socrates speculates that, because this nature loves the "good order" of everything that is always "in the same state," (500 c), he will form himself after these self-samenesses by imitating them. The text offers reasons to doubt that imitating *"what is"* still carries the ontological status of *what is*. Indeed, one might wish to say that, qua imitation (compare book III), the copy of *"what is"* is precisely something that *wanders*. Nevertheless, in the passages that follow this self-composition of the philosophical nature (500 d - 502 c, ff.), we observe the argument in miniature of the constitution of our city. Once the philosophical nature creates himself through imitation and comes upon the scene, "some *necessity [ananke]* comes to be for him to take care to place what he sees there [the self-samenesses] into the comportments of humans, both in private and in public, and not only in himself" (500 d, emphasis added). As in other places in book VI, one would expect to find the language of erotics here. We are, after all, speaking about the reproduction of the forms of *what is* in the citizenry. However, instead, we find the language of craftsmanship, of *techne*: "do you think that he will be a bad *craftsman [demiourgos]* of moderation, justice, and popular virtue" (500 d, emphasis added)? There are at least two remarks to be made here. Firstly, *ananke* remains categorically different from *techne*. The beings that emerge by necessity come to be by erotics, by nature, or by chance. While necessity occasions *techne*, *techne* does not occasion necessity. Secondly, we observe here a fundamental distortion in the account of the emergence of cities, constitutions and peoples (a distortion that I think Plato is attempting to bring into view). Insofar as Socrates here presents the city in speech in miniature, the text makes manifest implicitly that, even when we think we are "crafting" a constitution, necessity is always already operating underneath. For, before the craftsman raises the hammer, "some necessity" (500 d) has already come to be. Are cities and souls technological artifacts? Or, rather, are these beings, like biological beings, entities that come to be, *wander* into existence as a consequence of erotic necessity? Further, does necessity fold the philosophical nature's urge toward "what is" into itself?

NOTES

1. This and other passages that describe the philosophic nature as hating falsity and lies obviously bring into question the early introduction of the "noble lie" *tout court*.

2. Charles Khan in his "Plato's Theory of Desire" points to the introduction of the "money-loving principle (*to philokhrematon*)" in book 4. He then cites the text in order to elaborate this principle: "by which we desire the pleasures concerned with food and begetting and the like" (Khan 1987, 83). However, he passes over the problem that this elaboration of erotic desire poses without comment: money-loving *is not* the same as the erotic love of a person, of sex, or even of food. People frequently disregard value and money in order to risk it for the sake of the satisfaction of their sexual and culinary proclivities. The erotic love of a person has often led to the total disregard for money, justifying the expenditure of great sums.

3. Another thread of consideration here would be how we are to attend to the dramatic feature of the disposition of the characters. Glaucon emphatically agrees by superlative (*ēkista ge*) that death will not be anything terrible to a nature of this kind. But one wonders if the two men understand the same thing by the philosophic nature. Glaucon certainly thinks death should not be worthy of consideration here, but he likely thinks this because of his concern for honor. It could be argued that his understanding of wisdom is still oriented toward honor. While Socrates' *erōs* is very much focused on wisdom for the sake of itself.

4. It is perhaps important that Cephalus' interpretation of Pindar seems at best to be a stretch. This, and Polemarchus' interpretation of Simonides that follows, appear to suggest that the poetic works that circulate and secure the conceptual economy of our big ideas are often slung around without any real reflection.

5. In the *Republic* book III, Socrates raises his fear of misology as well. However, in that context the fear is expressed in a way that is almost a reversal of the one in the *Phaedo*. In the relevant passage of book III, Socrates is developing the concept of education in the city—music and gymnastics. Just before, he observed that an education too narrowly focused on gymnastics runs the risk of producing a misologist. "[The young man produced by such education] no longer makes use of persuasion through speech but accomplishes everything with force and savageness like a wild animal. And in ignorance and awkwardness, he lives without rhythm and without gratitude/gracefulness" (411 d-e). Thus, rather than the cultivation of speech and questioning, misology in book III is rooted in excessive sport and cultivation of the *thumos*. At the end of book VII, misology returns in concept, if not in name, in relation to the practice of dialectic. "When they cross-examine many men and are cross-examined by many, they fall quickly into a great distrust of what they formerly believed. And from these things, both they themselves and the whole of philosophy are slandered by the other men" (539 b—c).

6. James Adam notes that *megaloprepēs* is meant by Plato to be the opposite of *aneleutherōs* and *smikrologos* (1902, 487 a). Stanley Rosen points to the connection to Aristotle's *Ethics*, highlighting the differences on this issue between Aristotle and Socrates' account in Plato. "'Liberality' has nothing to do with spending money (as it does for Aristotle) but refers to something that reminds us of Aristotle's 'greatness

of soul' (*megalopsuchia*). What I shall call Socratic greatness of soul has to do with speech, not deed, and with the erotic inclination toward comprehensiveness and depth of knowledge. . . . Socrates again applies what will later be a technical term in Aristotle's ethics: 'magnificence' (*megaloprepeia*). In Aristotle, the term refers to the proper expenditure of large sums of money on splendid public buildings and the like, whereas liberality concerns spending small sums in the proper way. For Socrates, on the other hand, the attributes in question are the mark not of a gentleman but of a philosopher, and so of someone who, in the just city, neither possesses nor spends money" (2005, 231).

7. Adeimantus' role in the dialogue appears to be interruption. He often interrupts to force a question raised by the conversation that Glaucon has not perceived or pressed. In fact, it was due to his question in book II about what Glaucon left out in the ring of Gyges that led to the censorship of the poets. Moreover, his interruptions often exhibit a skeptical view of Socrates' claims, just like in the current passage. Here, I have gathered together his interruptions in the *Republic*: In response to Glaucon's account of Gyges, Adeimantus interrupts with: "you don't think, Socrates, that the argument has been sufficiently stated?. . . . What was most in need has not been said" (362 d). In response to this accusation that Glaucon has left out the most important part, Socrates claims that Glaucon's speech had brought him to his knees. In a skeptical tone, Adeimantus replies, "Nonsense" (362 e). At the beginning of book IV, Ademinatus "interrupts" to ask "what would your apology be, Socrates, if someone were to say to you that you're not making these men happy . . . " (419 a). When, at the beginning of book V, Polemarchus asks Adeimantus if they will let Socrates go, Ademinantus replies "not in the least" (449 b). Then, he says to Socrates: "you are being lazy and cheating us of a whole section of the argument . . . " (449 c). In our current example from book VI, Adeimantus interrupts with perhaps the most damning contradiction to Socrates' image by suggesting that dialectic is deceitful and that philosophers appear weird, malicious, or useless (487 d). Here when Socrates responds: "do you suppose that the men who say this are lying?" Adeimantus says "I don't know." In the exchange that follows, Adeimantus' aggressiveness appears tamed. The next interruption is not really an interruption. In book VIII, after Socrates introduces the question "who is the man" corresponding to the timocracy, Adeimantus answers "someone like Glaucon." Socrates partly agrees and partly disagrees. He says that the timarchic man would have to be "more stubborn," "less capable of music, although he loves it," "a lover of hearing," but not "skilled in rhetoric," brutal "with slaves," tame "with free men," obedient "with rulers" (548 d - 549 a). Adeimantus agrees with Socrates' qualification. Adeimantus is the interlocutor for the remainder (the great majority) of the regime's decline into tyranny. Why? When Glaucon finally next takes over the argument (in book IX), Socrates is summing up the "worst man" (576 b). Then, Glaucon is the interlocutor for the remainder of the dialogue, even during the critique of the tragic poets (which had been the subject matter for Adeimantus in the previous books).

Many view the relation between Socrates and Glaucon to be the primary relationship in the dialogue. Often, it is interpreted in pedagogical terms (Brann 1966 and Sallis 1996). Adeimantus is then viewed as deficient in some way as an interlocutor

(Long 2007, 79; Sallis 1996, 400–401). For reasons that will become clear in the course of this text, I agree more with Stanley Rosen's observations of Glaucon's weaknesses and limitations (Rosen 2005, 12). Still, despite these limitations, Rosen observes that Glaucon's erotically compelled interruptions keep the dialogue *moving* (Rosen 1993, 466). I wonder if we might argue that Adeimantus' contributions *slow it down*; importantly, he stops Socrates, forcing him to further elaborate on things that Socrates wishes to pass over quickly. In doing this, he thoroughly changes the course of the discussion. For instance, his interruption marks the profound turn in the discussion toward the philosopher's relation to the good in the middle books of the *Republic*.

8. Shorey notes that *glischros*: "is untranslatable, and often misunderstood" (488 a). He translates it as "*strain after* imagery" (note, 1969, 488 a). Adam (1902) translates it with "greedy."

9. I doubt this conclusion given that Socrates' images are always complicated and palimpsestic, insofar as there are things kept hidden in his images—for instance, the current one is gathered together from many sources—"like the painters paint goat-stags by making such mixtures" (488 a).

10. "'Which of the regimes at hand do you say is suitable for it?' 'None at all,' I said" (497 b). In fact, the best chance a philosophical nature has of living well, is to mind his own business; for, "no one in city affairs does anything healthy" (496 c). Again, one must question how Socrates' example follows this advice. While he does not engage in politics, *per se*, his activity is not solipsistic. The ends of his questioning appear to have an air of both the private and the public.

11. Why is Adeimantus' skepticism assuaged by the image? His interpretation of poetry in book II seems driven by a desire for a total clarity and total correspondence between the things of the world and the speech employed to express them. Socrates seems to tailor his speech for Adeimantus when he says many of the events present in Homer are necessarily expressed with a "covert meaning [*huponoia*]" (378 d). Thus, in his censorship project with Adeimantus as interlocutor, Socrates states: "A youth cannot judge what is a *covert meaning* and what is not, but, at such an age, that which he takes into his opinions is hard to wash out and becomes unchangeable" (378 d-e, emphasis added). Why would Adeimantus not, therefore, insist on something without a "covert meaning"?

12. Why does Plato have Socrates draw these two statements regarding the *oi polloi* here? The effect is confusing. The reader recalls that Adeimantus first accuses the philosopher of being useless to cities and malicious. However, here it appears at first that Socrates is saying that, not the philosopher, but the many are 1) useless insofar as they don't use the philosopher and 2) malicious (necessarily). While it does become fairly clear that Socrates means the necessity of the majority of the philosophers, not *the majority*, qua *oi polloi*, the initial confusion and interpretation is supported by the fact that, as it turns out, the majority of philosophers educate *in nothing other* than the opinions of the many. Further, what is *necessary* about the maliciousness of the many/many philosophers? Why use the language of necessity? Throughout this argument there is the insertion of the language of nature: necessity, erotics, growing, rearing.

13. Socrates issues the imperative to "grasp the whole [*holos*] of it rightly, and it will appear clear to you and what was said will not appear strange [*atopos*]" (491 c). Might we read this in a tragic form? Namely, when we grasp the philosophic nature as a "whole," we observe that the very characteristics that make it great/just/noble, also make it corrupt/tyrannical/base. Moreover, Socrates asserts that the difference between the two relies on chance (*tugxanō*), upon finding oneself in a suitable environment. Is this the same as the philosopher searching for the whole of what is?

14. The reader will recall that, in the introduction, we argued that *tugxanō* remains one of the ways that necessity shows itself in the *Republic*. Here, we observe the way that necessity functions in the background as something wandering or just happening [*tugxanō*] and, yet, occasions the emergence of maliciousness or virtuousness.

15. The adjective "private" is introduced into the regime for the first time here in book VI (*idiōtēs*—the private person is used many times). Socrates last used the term *idiōtikos* at 345 e. He will use it again in book VI at 492 c, 492 d and in Book VII at 525 c.

16. One observes here a tacit engagement with Adeimantus' initial interruption in book II, the interruption that necessitated the censorship of the poets. The educational regime exists not only in the sacred texts, but in all the spaces organized by the *oi polloi*.

17. One is reminded here of a frequent claim about the *Republic* (See Brann [1966], Sallis [1996], and Howland [2004, 79]). Socrates is attempting to educate Glaucon. He is trying to turn Glaucon from his education by the many (who have "talked Glaucon deaf" (358 c)). Whether he is successful remains a question, but the setting of the *Republic* is precisely the location for such a turning—the Piraeus lies both inside and outside Athens. Like a philosopher dog.

18. The translation of the phrase *hupo phugēs katalēphthein* is controversial. Regardless of translation, pinning down the meaning of a soul which is held down/constrained/held in check by avoidance/flight/exile remains challenging (see Adam 1902, 496 b).

19. Compare Odysseus' choice of the private life in the "myth of Er" in book X of the *Republic* (620 c).

20. In his analysis of the "science of the good," Seth Benardete argues that the perplexity that engenders an investigation is never free from the perspective in which the perplexity first appears. What he calls "perspective," I am calling here "the conditions of necessity." The relevant passage from *Socrates' Second Sailing*: "Since no science can direct the acquisition of science . . . it is never the case that any perplexity is ever wholly free from the perspective in which it first comes to light as a perplexity and makes it a matter of concern" (1989, 165).

21. As we will show later, it may be the case that the *Republic* occasions in the reader some sort of freedom at the level of the private. It may generate the emergence of *nous* as a consequence of the *aporia* that the text engenders, for instance. But this would not be without qualification a freedom from necessity.

22. After this oracular paragraph, Socrates asks Adeimantus if he thinks that the multitude shares this opinion (the ideological commitment to the messianic potential of the philosopher). When Adeimantus expresses doubts, Socrates exhorts him to moderate his severity against *oi polloi*. It occurs to me that Adeimantus' disposition throughout the dialogue has been one of severity against the many. In fact, the censorship of the educational curriculum is necessitated by Adeimantus' critique of the poetry of education in book II. Given that Adeimantus does not interrupt the dialogue in a critical fashion after this exchange in book VI, one wonders if his earlier harsh judgment has been rehabilitated here.

Chapter 2

The Necessity of the Greatest Study: The Good

Continuing our exegetical analysis of book VI, this chapter considers the new beginning necessitated by the conversation of the interlocutors. The new beginning consists of a revision of the earlier education in two ways. On the one hand, room must be made for an education in "*logoi*," often translated as *speeches, concepts or arguments*. Of course, the education articulated earlier already included reading, writing, and the cultivation in the soul of the concepts that will govern the community: wisdom, courage, moderation and justice, among others. However, apparently, this education lacked the learning of "*logoi*" in some different sense that encompasses all of these concepts and propositions. I offer a reading that suggests that this extra-propositional *logos* might be dialectic. On the other hand (and related to the first), the necessity emerges in the conversation for the study of "the good." I suggest that the study of "the good" presents similar difficulties to that of "necessity" in the *Timaeus*. Like necessity, "the good" has subtended our conversation all along; and like necessity, "the good" has the same *a priori* relation to all of the central concepts that constitute the educational paradigm and the virtues present in the soul. In chapter 1, we observed that the *dramatic setting* of the dialogue functions as a productive ecosystem of necessity, an ecosystem that shapes and determines the arguments that emerge in the *Republic*. In chapter 2, we find that all the central concepts that constitute the educational paradigm (justice, moderation, etc.) do not exist in empty space or in a vacuum. That is to say, their meaning cannot be isolated to propositional/definitional articulation. Rather, these concepts belong first and foremost to another *ecosystem* of necessity—the good. For, it is this ecosystem of "the good" that necessarily gives them their most important meaning, not that meaning which one finds in their definitions. The new beginning of the conversation is a rebirth or fertilization that turns the discourse toward a new content ("the good") and a new form (dialectic). However, doubts are raised about whether either of these two offspring will be born in the conversation.

After he assuages Adeimantus' concerns by answering his critical question regarding the uselessness and maliciousness of the philosophical nature within cities (even though he seems to avoid the question about his deception via dialectic), Socrates turns the discussion toward giving an account of the "studies and pursuits" that "the saviors" will undertake to preserve "our constitution" (502 d). Of course, we have already observed Socrates and his interlocutors elaborate on the characteristics of the rulers as well as the philosophical natures. However, now Socrates says that it is necessary [*dei*] "to consider [what involves the rulers [*archōn*]] from the beginning [*archē*]" (502 e). Immediately, one wonders why it is necessary to begin again. What did we get wrong? What did we leave out of the account such that our new formulation must start over from the beginning? Should we abandon all we said about education earlier?[1] In book II, Socrates introduces the system of education into the "city in speech" by saying "like myth-tellers at leisure telling myths in a myth, let us educate these men in speech" (376 d). In what follows, he states that the best course of study is "gymnastic for bodies and music for the soul" (376 e). The reader will recall that Socrates already significantly revised this assertion when he argued in book III that "some god" gave music and gymnastics to human beings, not in order to use one for the soul and the other for the body. Rather, gymnastics too is for the soul; it balances music's effect on the soul with courage (411 e).

In my view, we observe in book VI a further revision that will animate the remainder of this book and encompass book VII as well. Shortly after the passage in which Socrates argues that there will have to be "something" in the regime with the same *logos* that the lawgivers had when they composed the city (497 c), Socrates repeats the word *logos* (498 a) with a meaning similar to the one we elaborated in chapter 1. However, this time it is in the context of asserting the appropriate time for the practice of philosophy in the span of a human life. He thinks that philosophical education should be undertaken in "the opposite [way to] what is done now" (497 e).

> At present, those who take it up at all do so as young men, just out of childhood, who have yet to take up household management and money making. Then, just when they reach the most difficult part they abandon it and are regarded as the most fully trained philosophers. By the most difficult part, I mean the one concerned with arguments [*logoi*] (2004, 497 e).

Even "at present," in a time in which the presence of philosophical natures is called into question, philosophy has a unique position within the educational curriculum of the youth. Initially, it inhabits something of a liminal space in between childhood and adulthood. Childhood has its own educational practices; in it you are indoctrinated with the *doxa* of the lawgivers, you are formed and cultivated into a certain political species of humanity. Normally, adulthood signals the emergence of practical life. The educational curriculum of the lawgiver's scheme for childhood (music and gymnastics) forms the soul, filling it with the concepts of justice, beauty, truth, courage, moderation, etc. Ostensibly, these prepare one for a productive, successful, adult life in the city. What need is there, then, for this interim education, the liminal period between the education of youth and the practice of that education in adulthood?

If one were to ask Thrasymachus (whom Socrates likely offends with the above assertion [498 d]), he would argue that this period in between the *becoming* of a citizen and the *being* of a citizen is when a young man may acquire the rhetorical skills to use these formative concepts in the *polis* in such a way that he may exploit *oi polloi's* conviction in them. For Thrasymachus' argument, it is a period in which one dwells between the *becoming* and the *being* of a citizen. The youth acquires a distance from himself, loosens himself from the strong unquestioned belief in the most sacred concepts of his city and learns how to exploit their organizational power so that he may get the better of his own (and even perhaps other) citizens. In other words, for Thrasymachus, this would be the time during which a youth may pay the fine to the private wage earners in order to learn the path of descent into the earth and retrieve the ring of Gyges. One can imagine that there are private wage earners without the same sort of malevolent commitments as Thrasymachus. To be sure, there exist sophists that seek to exploit this period between childhood and adulthood to cultivate in students the rhetorical skill to utilize the concepts communicated in childhood for the sake of flourishing in adulthood, qua *oi polloi*. However, in both cases, Socrates would say that all private wage earners abandon philosophy at the moment it becomes most challenging.

Socrates argues that all the private wage earners have students leave philosophy at the very moment it reaches its most difficult part: *logoi*. Obviously, the student learned to read and write in primary education. The difficult part does not involve *logoi* understood as learning the basic definitions of concepts or grammatical construction. Further, the private wage earners teach rhetorical skill and persuasion. Thus, it is clear that, *by logoi*, Socrates does not mean oratory or the stylistic use of language in public and private. What then does Socrates mean by *logoi* (497 e)?

Philosophy shares something with sophistry, insofar as it recognizes the existence of this liminal position between childhood and adulthood, between *becoming* and *being* a human, as a place and time in which everything is at stake. Perhaps, for both sophistry and philosophy, dwelling in the space in between childhood and adulthood means that the student loosens himself from the concepts of his city. As we wrote when considering the "liberal" characteristic of the philosophical nature, dwelling in this liminal space means being granted the occasion to free oneself from the static and concretized everydayness of a polis' most sacred concepts, a certain kind of freedom from their easy circulation, a liberal hesitation through the act of the question. The question, indeed, is the mark of both Socrates' and Thrasymachus' discourse—although, to be sure, Thrasymachus *questions* the legitimacy of the concepts of *oi polloi* in a sophistical assertion, while Socrates *questions* his interlocutor's understanding of such concepts in dialectical form—if, indeed, the *elenchus* is a form dialectic.[2] The question frees us from the everyday relation to the culture in which we are all always already absorbed. But the question also marks a kind of *new beginning*. The question interrupts the flow of necessity and signals an impasse (*aporia*) in a way that requires a regrouping and a reassessment—that is to say, a new principle of movement.

With the above formulation of the *logoi* (497 e), I think Socrates means that this event of liberation in which the question arises about our inherited conceptual economy is precisely the *beginning* of the *logos*, not the end of it. For Thrasymachus, liberation means the end of the dialogical search, it marks the moment when the concept no longer holds and anything goes. But, for Socrates, this event marks the beginning of the dialogical search, *a new beginning* generated out of the old. As such, the *logoi* that are "at present" abandoned, the most difficult ones, are the dialectical ones. The liberation that takes place while dwelling in-between occasions is dialectical *logoi*. Consequently, the "*logoi*" in the above sentence, "by the most difficult part, I mean the one concerned with arguments [*logoi*] (2004, 497 e), could as well be translated by "dialectic." During the special period in-between, private wage earners lead students into loosening themselves from their cities, perhaps to the point where the students are no longer strictly *oi polloi*, but exhibit something of the private *vis à vis* the education/legal system. However, they stop there. The philosopher, then, dwells in this space of the private in order to interrogate the meaning horizon of *oi polloi*. This practice is philosophy. As such, philosophy is not a "sideline practice"; it is rather the practice of a human being. To speak in Aristotelian terms, one might even say that philosophy is the principal *work* of the human being; that is to say, loosening oneself from the structure of formation, education, and *oi polloi* remains the exquisite "function" (Aristotle 1984) of the human being. Everything else is a sideline practice. Other living things build structures, gather into communities, communicate the presence of danger and need, perform agriculture and husbandry, engage in war, sacrifice themselves for others. The human being is the being that places herself into question and, as such, *may*[3] be capable of disrupting the flow of necessity in order to *begin again*.

In the course of a human life—that is to say, the course of human necessity—each human undergoes an education of his/her soul. The education plants the seeds of the *logoi* within one. But, for Socrates, this education does not exhaust the whole of a human life, qua human. The seeds must be watered, tended, pruned. Further, the blooms of the mature plant are both the same as the plant and also different. The plant blossoms insofar as it differentiates itself from itself and prepares to occasion the renewal and release of the offspring, the new seed. For the human being, qua human, the organic blossom of the rose mirrors the new beginning of the education of the rulers; for, "we must consider [what involves the rulers [*archōn*]] from the beginning [*archē*]" (502 e). The new beginning lies in engaging the hardest part, the dialectic of *logoi*. Dialectic occasions a turning toward and away from the concepts in a manner that forces a new, vital engagement in the life of the concept. Dialectic resembles *erotic necessity* insofar as it signals a rebirth. One is born and indoctrinated with a *doxa*; the human child receives itself from the surrounding educational atmosphere, qua *oi polloi*. Then, if the child happens to be struck with the occasion to be compelled (erotically) to turn and question herself and others, she may engender a free relation to the concept in such a way that a new beginning, a new life, a new vital relation to the concept blossoms. This resembles reproduction. Like a mother and father gathering together in erotics, they produce a new "concept," it is a new beginning from out of the old "gene pool." However, the "child" of the erotic movement cannot be reduced to either the mother or the father; it is something new. At the same time, it cannot exist without them either—it contains their DNA. As such, dialectic (questioning—*erōtaō*) may be like reproduction, but the offspring that this reproduction generates is of *logoi*.

An anecdotal example may prove instructive. Once upon a time, I lived in New York City. During a Saturday stroll, I accidentally stumbled upon the Guggenheim Soho branch of the more famous parent museum on the Upper East Side. At that moment, there happened to be an exhibit of a series of Andy Warhol's later work titled "The Last Supper" (1986). The exhibit consisted of 60 meditations on the celebrated Renaissance master work by Leonardo Da Vinci with the same name. The collection was diverse. Some pictures incorporated Leonardo's entire image, while others zoomed in myopically to individual features of the painting. In the latter, the viewer's attention was directed toward certain characters in the painting, or even relations between the figures. The effect was to force an interpretive stance on the part of the spectator by shifting the orientation, scale, or color. Of course, this distortive treatment denies the viewer the expected visual unity of Leonardo's perspective. However, it does something else too; it forces the viewer to forge a dialectical relationship with the painting. *Everyone* knows Leonardo's *Last Supper*. It is instantaneously recognizable. As a child, it probably hung as a reprint on a neighbor's wall or lie folded inside a coffee table bible inside a grandparent's house. Like everyone, I have walked past the image a hundred times in various settings in my life and, on those occasions, I thought . . . nothing. We know this image of Leonardo's so well that we do not know it at all. Until, that is, I happened to chance upon an exhibit that forced me in at least 60 different ways to turn and see the painting for the first time. Warhol tugged on the cloak of a flâneur, occasioning a new beginning with The Last Supper. Similarly, book VI is a point in the discourse in which what concerns the rulers "must be considered from the beginning" (502 e).

The new beginning for our analysis of the things that concern the rulers consists of the "greatest study" (503 e). We will eventually learn that the "idea of the good is the greatest study" (505 a), but at least initially, Socrates remains coy when asked what the greatest study is. It remains important that our new beginning, our re-turn toward the *logoi* concerning the rulers, involves "the good." The good is what has been left out of our account so far and its assessment will force everything that has gone before into a new light, just like Warhol's engagement with The Last Supper.

Socrates initiates this turn in the discourse by introducing a contradiction at the heart of the philosophical nature in a similar way that he did at the beginning of book VI and in book II's philosopher dogs. In this instance, too, he couches the philosophical nature in terms of natural necessity:

Philosophers must be set down as the most precise [*akribēs*][4] guardians . . . Then observe that you will likely have few. For, the nature we said must [*dein*] belong to them has parts which are seldom willing to grow together [*sum-phuō*]; rather its many parts grow [*phuō*] pulled apart [*diaspaō*] from each other (503 b).

Always or for the most part, the characteristics necessary for the philosophical nature are generated by *physis* in a way that is mutually exclusive. They "grow" apart rather than together. Socrates gathers the examples of these characteristics into two classes that exclude each other. However, we have reason to assume that the complexity is greater than this. In the first class, Socrates refers to those natures that are "good at learning, have memories, are quick-witted and sharp" (503 c), etc. These "quick" natures have obvious advantages; however, Socrates suggests that these same men are often "led forth by the quickness where chance [*tugxanō*] happens to direct, and all stability goes out of them" (503 c). In the second class, Socrates places those natures that are "stable" and "not easily changed" (503 c). These are natures that one "would make use of for their fidelity/loyalty [*pistos*]" (503 d). Moreover, in war, they are not likely to be easily "moved by fears" (503 d). But for the same reason, these natures are "hard to move" in their studies—"learning is hard [*dusmathēs*] for them, like becoming stupefied [*aponarkoomai*]; and they are filled with drowsiness and yawning when they must suffer through such things" (503 d). As Socrates suggests, these two natures appear to exclude each other. One is quick and easily moveable, while the other is slow and immovable. Thus, it will be rare to find humans with these contradictory natures growing together. It would have been necessary for two opposing seeds to have happened [*tugxanō*] to find themselves growing in the same plot of land.

In order to reveal the presence of these natures among us, Socrates argues that we must put the youth to the test. While we tested the natures already in primary education (e.g., 412 c), Socrates now introduces a new form of trial. "We let [the new test] pass then but speak of it now—[the potential guardian] must also be exercised [*gymnazō*][5] in many studies, if it will be able to bear the greatest studies, or whether it will be a coward, as some are cowards in the other gymnastics" (503 e - 504 a). In my view, Socrates introduces here a new education for the liminal period between childhood education and adulthood. The details of the education will be brought to light in chapters 6 and 7, but I will describe these "exercises" in a preliminary way here insofar as they relate to the greatest study. In book VII, we will observe the introduction of new forms of arithmetic, plane geometry, solid geometry, astronomy, and harmony. Yet, these disciplines are not identical to those with the same name that the city teaches children. Each of these new disciplines cultivates an *aporia* within the student in different ways. As such, the new studies that are conducted in the liminal period of human life introduce the phenomenon of "turning" and force *nous* to be called forth. Rather than simply employing the inherited concepts of "number" and "the one" (524 d), for instance, in order to perform a practical calculation, the new arithmetic generates an *aporia* so that one may for the first time ask what "number" and "the one" *are*. Each of these disciplines, therefore, teaches "turning" toward *what is*. Yet, they are only preparation for the more difficult *logoi*. The new studies prepare one for the primary study: dialectic. While the orientation of the first five studies is narrowed to specific regions of technical discourse, dialectic "endeavors to grasp *with respect to everything* . . . what each is" (533 b, emphasis added).

Thus, the new studies introduced here in book VI are initially intended to test the natures of their courage and ability to turn. With reference to book VII, one can perceive what sort of new beginning the new studies represent. The new studies engender a new comportment toward the *logoi* that one has inherited. Engaging the hardest part, dialectic occasions a turning toward and away from the concepts in a manner that forces a new, vital engagement in the life of these inherited concepts. A new radical relation is instituted that turns away from the *appearance/doxa* of those things toward the *being* of them, toward their *what-is-ness*.[6]

Here Socrates suggests that the central virtues possessed by the rulers (justice, moderation, courage, and wisdom) were not expressed with enough precision in the earlier books. Previously, the current lawgivers defined these concepts *vis à vis* the classes of humans in the city; they enacted them into law and encoded them into the educational system with the expectation that these virtues as expressed in the city were also those of the individual soul. That is to say, the tripartite division of the population of the city and the virtues belonging to each of these classes were supposed to mirror the tripartite division of the soul and the virtues belonging to each of these. However, already in book IV, Socrates explicitly raises doubts about this equivalence (434 d). Moreover, in the current passage of book VI, he refers back to these doubts to elaborate the problem that faces the present discussion. "Understand well, Glaucon," he said in book IV,

> "In my opinion, by following methods [*methodos*] such as these in [our] arguments, we will not get a precise [*akribēs*] grasp of this. There is longer and fuller [*pleiōn*] path [*odos*] leading to it. But perhaps we can speak in a manner that is worthy of what was being said and investigated before."
>
> "Must we not be satisfied with that?" he said. "It would be enough for me for the present."
>
> "Well, then," I said, "it should be sufficient for me too." (435 c—d).

Here Socrates expresses doubts about whether the organization of the soul mirrors the organization of the city. Moreover, he argues that the only way we can achieve a more precise grasp of the problem is by *a different method or path* than the one in which the participants are engaged in book IV. In what has gone before, our lawgivers have only presented an outline or sketch [*hupographē*] (504 d).[7] Thus, one presumes that this new method is dialectic—the longer and more difficult, yet apparently unavoidable route. In book VI, we find almost the same formulation.

> We were saying that in order to get the most beautiful look [*kateidon*] at [justice, moderation, courage and wisdom], there would be an other, longer way around [*periodos*] . . . [8] and you said that [the shorter approximation] was sufficient. And so the statements made subsequently were . . . not precise [*akribēs*] (504 b).

In this passage, Socrates recalls his earlier doubts about whether the virtues of the city are the same as the virtues of the soul. Moreover, he recalls these doubts at the very moment that the discourse has turned toward the greatest study, suggesting that the potential rulers must be tested in accordance with the new *methodos* to ensure that they are possessed of the sort of nature that is both quick and slow. However, there is an important difference between the two passages. In book IV, Glaucon asserted his satisfaction to hurry along with an abbreviated articulation of the argument. Further, Socrates conceded that he too would be satisfied with such statements. Yet, now, when we have reached a point in the argument where we must turn back, begin again, and take the more difficult path, Socrates says that he is not satisfied with the precision of the earlier *logoi* that came to light. And when Adeimantus, now, also tries to rush past the difficulty by replying to Socrates' doubts that, to both him and *the other lawgivers present*, those arguments were sufficient "within measure," Socrates chastises him. He replies that "a measure in such things that falls short at all of that which *is*, is no measure at all" (504 c). Given the context in which the interlocutors must work together to give an account of the sorts of exercises that would adequately test the seemingly contradictory traits of quickness and slowness in the potential rulers, it appears that they themselves have all already failed the test here. In both passages, first Glaucon, then Adeimantus (and, according to him, all the others), we observe the failure to exhibit the character of slowness and stability that would allow one to stop and dialectically pursue the longer path of *logoi* at just the moment that it becomes more difficult.[9]

Despite this important detail in the dramatic action of the dialogue, Plato has Socrates continue the discussion of the greatest study with his interlocutors. Adeimantus again proves to be a source of constraint on Socrates, asking "do you suppose anyone is going to set you free without asking what it is" (504 e)? Socrates emphatically answers in the negative. He "certainly" knows already that no one will let him leave without asking his opinion about what it is. This question, nevertheless, appears to him to be superfluous because, he says,

> At any rate, you have heard it not a few times. But now you are either not understanding or thinking to attack me again. I suppose it is the latter, since you have often heard that the idea of the good [*ē tou agathou idea*] is the greatest study, and that, by making use of [the idea of the good], the just and the rest become useful and beneficial (505 a).

Here, Plato has Socrates remind his interlocutors that they have already heard that the greatest study is the idea of the good. It strikes me that this passage may be interpreted in at least two ways. On the one hand, in the most superficial and obvious manner, the reader may interpret the passage to mean that Socrates himself is the source of these past statements. That is to say, Socrates has been incessantly repeating this claim for Adeimantus' whole life. However, I want to suggest another reading that links this claim with the renewal of the discourse. Perhaps Socrates' assertion here refers to an *a priori* that has been implicit both from the beginning of the conversation and for all of the interlocutors' entire lives. With respect to the dialogue itself, there has been a presumed conception of *the good* operating underneath the conversation from the very beginning. In some ways, the role of *the good* at this point in the dialogue resembles that of the concept of *necessity* at the middle point in the *Timaeus*. Each dialogue must begin again because the relevant concepts (*necessity* and *the good*) have been presumed all along without explanation.

In the case of the *Timaeus*, we observed in the introduction to this book that the dialogue's namesake employs the concept of necessity from the beginning without giving any account of it. Consequently, there is a great deal about the direction and conclusions of the conversation up to the point of the new beginning that is subtended by an unreflected and uninterrogated conception of "necessity." In fact, in the first half of Timaeus speech, one often reads some form of the phrase "it is necessary" to lend support to the assertion of claim after claim; yet, at no point does the hearer actually receive an account of what this necessity means until the new beginning (47 e - 48 a). On my reading of the *Timaeus* (see also Winslow 2023), it becomes clear with the new beginning that the concept of *necessity* remains an urgent priority in any argument which seeks to give expression to first principles of nature (indeed, necessity lies prior even to the demiurge). Without an account of it, all the individual forms and structures of the cosmos remain deeply and importantly ungrounded. For, the meaning of necessity subtends the conditions of organization of Timaeus' cosmos and therefore also the very being of each of the things *physei*. Namely, the demigurge, the whole, the world-soul, the gods, the animals, the humans, etc., are already dependent upon necessity before they begin their work or come into being. Recognizing this, Timaeus returns to the beginning to make necessity visible so that all that comes to be as a consequence of it can be seen *in the light of necessity*.

In my view, Socrates' claim about the idea of the good in the present passage can be read in a similar fashion. From the perspective of what is necessary for the present conversation, the laws and educational structures that have emerged in the conversation and have been put into place in the *Kallipolis* only have meaning insofar as they appear in the light of the good.

> By making use of [the idea of the good], the just and the rest become useful and beneficial. And . . . we do not know it adequately. If we do not know [*oida*] [the idea of the good] and know [*epistamai*] however much of the other things, you know that [the knowledge of the other things] is no advantage to us, just as if we acquire any possession without the good (505 a).

Like the phenomenon of necessity subtending all the beings of *physis* in the *Timaeus*, the discourse must begin again in order to give articulation to the idea of the good; for, without an account of that which envelops justice, moderation, courage and wisdom, these latter concepts are bereft of a ground thanks to which the knowledge of them has real meaning. Moreover, despite Socrates' apparent assertion to the contrary (see 493 c), the good is not only necessary, but in a certain way, the good resembles necessity. Necessity is a kind of sea in the waves of which *ta onta* find themselves. The beings come to have meaning by relating to each other, to other beings, and even to themselves *by means of* the currents that carry them along, the currents of necessity. So too, the good is an ocean into which justice, moderation, courage and wisdom sail along. Without this ocean, these concepts lose their meaning—they are suspended in empty space. Or rather, they *appear* to be suspended in empty space and the direction provided by the ocean's currents remains invisible without an account of it. However, unlike an actual ship, it is rare that when one sails upon the ship of justice that one is explicitly aware of the sea that carries the ship along; it is rare that one observes that this vessel of which one has knowledge only actually means something in relation to the currents through which one navigates. In the present passage, Socrates appeals to this necessity in arguing that we must renew our journey [*methodos*] and take the long way through the idea of the good. Thus, the greatest study, the idea of the good, remains intimately connected to the renewal of the discourse. It points to an expectation, a motive anticipation that was present at the beginning of the conversation, but nevertheless has remained veiled. Moreover, it is an anticipation which has already bestowed meaning on everything that has been said, though this meaning lies hidden in the previous discourse—its elaboration remains therefore urgent.

Like necessity in the *Timaeus*, the good in the *Republic* is necessarily operative already at the beginning of the dialogue. As a kind of *hypokeimenon*, it animates the discussion in advance, and it folds all of the conceptual developments of the argument into itself. However, there is another way that the good of the *Republic* is like necessity in the *Timaeus*. It is *a priori* not only with regard to the dialogue, but like necessity, the good is also prior to all the *ta onta* that come to be within it, including animals, plants, human beings, cities, and constitutions.

When one gets out of bed in the morning, in almost total ignorance, one is enveloped and occasioned by the forces of necessity. From the physics of the gravity that both enables and limits standing on the floor; to the biology of muscle contraction, breathing, and metabolism; to the sociology of cultural expectation and the human norms of time and work (for example), necessity is already there, occasioning and limiting the event of getting out of bed and starting the day. In the case of the good, Socrates offers an argument in favor of an equally all-encompassing force:

"This is what every soul seeks and for the sake of which it does everything, and it divines that the good is something but is at a loss [*aporeō*] and does not have an adequate grasp of what it is, and cannot trust it as it does the rest" (505 d—e).

Every soul does everything it does for the sake of the good. One is confronted here by a curious ontological principle—an *onto*logical principle that is not *being*, but the good. Prior to every sort of doing, the good is the end for which every doing is done. Like necessity, the good lies prior to every cell division, every metabolic procedure, every volition, every desire, every endeavor, every action, every thought. Insofar as the good is the for-the-sake-of-which of every doing, all living things, qua living, are occasioned and limited by it. The good is, therefore, the most architectonic force (*except perhaps for necessity*) and it already directs all functions in advance of their functioning. In addition, like necessity, the soul does not *know* the good, does not *think* it, does not *sense* it, but rather *divines* [*apomanteuomai*] that it is something. Both necessity and the good resist knowability, resist substance for the same reason. The good and necessity are all beings' conditions of possibility. If the good occasions every doing as its for-the-sake-of-which, then even the endeavor to come to know it *as a being* is already subtended by the good—the endeavor to know the good is already directed in advance by the good. Thus, one "divines that the good is something but is at a loss [*aporeō*] and does not have an adequate grasp of what it is" (505 e).

Among the comportments of human beings animated and occasioned by both the good and necessity is the opinion. In a certain way, opinion remains the source and point of departure for human inquiry, even in the current dialogical occasion. It is from the father (Cephalus) that we inherit the originary opinion that initiates the current inquiry. Cephalus is composed, like us all, of a gathering of shadow-like opinions that sometimes come into focus for elaboration, but most of the time recede into the background, organizing our world in latency (qua *lanthanomai*). Perhaps opinion is not adequate for the rulers of cities or the rulers of the soul, but it is nevertheless the *Ursprung*, the *archē*, and every *archē's* motive force is the good. In the sentiment of Heraclitus: both before humans have heard it [the opinion] and once they have heard it for the first time (Heraclitus 1906, 61). Socrates initiates this point of departure from opinion in the current inquiry by asking a series of questions about what the good is "in the opinion of the many" (505 b). With the agreement of Adeimantus, he argues that these opinions are inadequate and curiously employs the language of divination again. "I divine [*manteuomai*]" that no one will come to know the just and beautiful things before the good is known (506 a). Insofar as he only "divines," Socrates tacitly admits that he does not himself know (in the technical sense of knowing).

Nevertheless, he argues that, without a knowledge of the good that transcends opinion and divination, our guardians won't be worth much.

> "I suppose, at least," I said, "that just and beautiful things, if their relation to the good is not known, will not produce a guardian that is worth very much.... our constitution will not have been perfectly arranged until such a guardian who knows these things looks after it?"
>
> "Necessarily [*ananke*]," he said (506 a—b).

Even if the guardians have knowledge of justice, moderation, courage and wisdom, this knowledge might as well be lacking if they do not have knowledge of the good in which the former concepts come to have real meaning. Adeimantus follows this observation by appealing to its necessity.

However, following this assertion, Adeimantus poses a question that sounds a lot like Meno's in the *Meno*. In that dialogue, Meno asks Socrates if he thinks that virtue is something teachable, or acquired through practice, or, if neither of these, something that comes to humans through nature or in some other way (1903, 70 a). It is clear that Meno's question remains animated by the discourse of the *oi polloi*, whether in the form of private teachers (like Gorigas) or the chatter in the public assembly. For the rest of the dialogue, Socrates tries unsuccessfully to convince Meno to turn back dialectically toward the question "what is virtue?" instead of searching for and acquiring arguments useful for the competitions of discourse among the *oi polloi*.

In this moment of the *Republic*, the sophistication of Adeimantus' question exceeds Meno's insofar as he asks Socrates a "what is" question: "but now, Socrates, do you say that the good is knowledge, or pleasure, or something else?" (506 b). Yet, despite the shift toward the good's being, the question is similar to Meno's insofar as it fails to take up the problem in a way that would transcend opinion. It would seem that Socrates understands this and asks Adeimantus in response if, in his opinion, "does it seem just to you to speak about what one does not know as if one knew?" (506 c). Adeimantus argues that one ought to be willing to state what one "supposes." In light of the fact that, just a few paragraphs earlier, Adeimantus agreed with Socrates' assertion that everyone despises mere opinions about the good, his assertion here appealing to a moral obligation to offer an opinion comes as a surprise to the reader. In the context of Adeimantus' earlier agreement, Socrates claimed that, while many people are satisfied with an account of things merely "opined" to be just, moderate, courageous and wise, with respect to the good, "no one is content with what procuring only what is opined to be, but all seek the things that *are* . . . and all treat as unworthy the [mere] opinion [of the good] (505 d). Thus, Adeimantus seems to lose track of his own agreements in the argument. Socrates is equally shocked by Adeimantus' reversal of the former agreement and asks "What? . . . Have you not perceived that all opinions without knowledge are shameful? The best are blind" (506 c). For Socrates, therefore, the new beginning which leads to the long road of the greatest study does not consist of an answer to the question: is the good, in Socrates' opinion, knowledge, pleasure, or something else?

It appears as though the conversation about the idea of the good just might end there. However, Glaucon seizes control of the argument again by uttering an invocation to Zeus: "No, in the name of Zeus, Socrates," said Glaucon. "You are not going to drop it now when you are just at the end" (506 d). The interruption by Glaucon is pregnant with many curiosities. On the one hand, Glaucon strangely claims that Socrates is at the "end" of his elaboration. However, Socrates has just asserted that they have arrived at a subject that necessitates that they "begin again." If Socrates is to continue, therefore, the group is in fact at the very beginning of the conversation . . . again. For the reader, though, we are far from the beginning of the text and far from the end. In fact we are very near the center of the text. Thus, for Socrates, we are at the beginning of the argument, insofar as we must begin to flesh out what makes everything that has gone before meaningful. Yet, from the reader's perspective, the question about the idea of the good begins in the middle. And according to Glaucon's opinion, Socrates' speech is at its end. How might we untangle Plato's collision of perspectives in which each member of the discussion (including the reader) is lit up as being on different paths toward the idea of the good and, yet, in conversation with each other despite being in different positions on the path?

In any case, Glaucon, with the support of Zeus, provides a motive force for the conversation by insisting that Socrates go through the good in the way that he has gone through justice, moderation, courage, and wisdom. However, from everything that was said about the greatest study and the need for a new beginning to reach it, the reader already knows that this is not adequate and the good cannot be approached in this way. If this is not the true second sailing, one wonders on what journey Socrates and his interlocutors are now embarking. After all, it is not the necessary, long road and, further, it is still grounded in opinion.

NOTES

1. In contrast to a reading that would require us to abandon the earlier education, Adam argues that "Plato does not propose to supersede the earlier education in Music and Gymnastic, nor are the two schemes theoretically incompatible . . . We are clearly intended to suppose that the Rulers receive the moral as well as the intellectual

training, although in practice, no doubt, some modifications might be necessary, so long as the two proceeded simultaneously" (1902, 502 e). Still, Adam recognizes that there are scholars who disagree and suggest that the two educational schemes are incompatible: namely, August Krohn in *Der Platonische Staat* (1876). Charles Khan appears committed to conceiving of the *Republic* as a systematic whole (Khan, 1987). In contrast, David Roochnik argues for a dialectical interpretation—*Kallipolis* (books 2–4) is not the Republic, he argues (Roochnik, 2003). I agree with Roochnik. In my reading, the philosopher of book VI is incompatible with the laws of *Kallipolis*.

2. As we observed above in Socrates' use of images, he does not exclusively employ the question answer form. However, as we will consider in chapter 7, in the *Republic*, we never learn precisely what dialectic is.

3. The modal form is used here to remind us that it remains a question in our reading whether the philosophical nature exists at all.

4. The term *akribēs* is introduced in book I by Socrates when he asks Thrasymachus to clarify if by "ruler" and "stronger," he means that employed in common speech or in the "precise" [*akribēs*] sense (341 b). Now, Socrates suggests that the most precise characteristic of the guardians is being philosophical. We receive a further elaboration of this meaning of *akribēs* shortly after when Socrates argues that unqualified natures should not be allowed participation in "the most precise [*akribēs*] education, honor, or rule" (503 d). I interpret this to mean that those natures in whom the two contradictory natures do not grow together [*sum-phuō*] into a unity should not be allowed the dialectical education of the greatest study—they are denied the new beginning. There are multiple questions that this raises. If dialectic is not a side-line practice, but the most important practice of the human being, then the "city in speech" forbids this definitive action to all but a very few (if any) humans. What if the technological composition of a city, its laws, and education, stumbles here upon its limit? Can the most important features of human nature be achieved by pedagogical artifice? Or is there something arbitrary, something *necessary* (in *our* sense of the term) about these features that transcends the region of *technē*, of *nomos*, of *episteme*? The passage treating the growing together of characteristics is loaded with the language of *physis*, not *technē*. Further, the restriction recalls the problem at the heart of the *Republic*: are cities and souls really equivalent? (Socrates himself raises this doubt when he says "So, let's apply what has come to light for us there to an individual,

and if it is confirmed, all will be well. But if something different is found in the case of the individual, we will go back to the city and test it there" (2004, 434 e). For, perhaps it makes more sense *for a soul* to restrict dialectical investigation to the part that rules than *for a city*. Finally, it would appear that the lawgivers themselves fail this test. At 504 b, Socrates argues that the earlier arguments were inadequate, "not precise [*akribeia*]" (504 b). Adeimantus then replies that those arguments were to him and the other lawgivers present "[satisfactory] within measure." Chastising Adeimantus, Socrates replies that "a measure in such things that falls short at all of that which *is*, is no measure at all" (504 c).

5. Bloom (1991) appears to be alone in translating *gymnazein* here as "giving gymnastic." Shorey (1969), Reeve (2004), Griffeth (2000) and Sachs (2007) translate it as "exercise," while Sterling and Scott (1985) translate it as "test." Given the centrality

of gymnastics in both the education of the children and in the testing of their courage, etc., perhaps Bloom is right to keep our focus on Plato's use of this term. It's not just any kind of exercising/testing, after all.

6. That book VI and VII represent the initiation of the movement of turning away from appearance and toward *what is* remains a crucial part of the text. However, that is not to say that these books fully resolve the problems we have introduced regarding the primary education of the guardians. For, as we will observe later, the good is *beyond being*; even if, through the articulation of the divided line, the allegory of the cave, and the account of dialectic, Socrates and his interlocutors have given an adequate account of coming to know a noetic perception of *what is* (and there are reasons to doubt even this), they never transcend the question-frame of *being*. Yet, the good is beyond being and without the light of "the good" permeating the statement of *what is*, it is all quite meaningless (505 a).

7. What is the difference between a *hupographē* and dialectic? We are led to believe that the articulation of justice, moderation, courage, and wisdom were achieved in accordance with the way of a sketch. Yet, the longer route includes passing through the idea of the good in order to see what makes these have meaning at all. The longer route involves turning.

8. In addition to the correction articulated in this paragraph that it was a mistake to say that we would be satisfied, we have an important change in terms from the previous argument at 435 d. Earlier, Socrates used "*odos*" to denote the longer, more complex path. Now he uses *periodos*, which emphasizes the *circular*, rather than *linear*, journey one must take. Perhaps this change in shape signals how the two paths differ.

9. As will become evident in the arguments that follow, I am more sympathetic to Drew Hyland's reading of the failure of these interlocutors to take the "longer path," than Mitchell Miller's. Mitchell reads the shorter path taken as an "introductory account" (Miller 2007, 310). On this interpretation, the shorter path is not deficient, but simply an introduction to the subject matter that gets further *completed* in "later" dialogues. In Hyland's approach, by contrast, the shorter path is not merely too short, but also "deeply flawed." He argues that Plato calls on the reader to ask him/herself what was "problematic" or "misleading" about the path the interlocutors have already taken (Hyland 2011, 150).

Chapter 3

The Child of the Good: On Light and Desire

In chapter 3 our analysis turns toward the famous image Socrates presents of the "child of the good." As was already suggested in the previous chapter, both the articulation of the good and even Socrates' opinion about it were stated as unlikely given the constraints of the conversation. In this chapter, we consider Socrates' inadequate substitution. Moreover, we will highlight and elaborate on Socrates' emphatic caution: the image of "the child of the good" may deceive us. In the course of the interpretation, we offer a reading that suggests that the source of the deception does not lie in some arbitrary epistemological weakness, but in the ontological gap between *being* and the *good*. Further, we suggest that, for this very reason, we are deceived by all of the images of the central books of the *Republic* that are intended to illuminate the good: "the child of the good," "the divided line," and the "allegory of the cave." For, these images only get us as far as an account of being, while the good remains "beyond being." Finally, we suggest that despite this deception, the image of "the child of the good" provides a productive analogy for thinking about the good: just as light from the sun yokes together the power of sight and the thing seen, serving as a mediator between them and producing vision; so too does the "light" of *desire* from the *idea* of the good yoke together the faculties of the soul with the thing desired, serving as a mediator between them and producing action. *Desire* is what "lights up" something *as* good. This interpretation further complicates the radical separation of necessity from the good; for, *desire and love are features of the structure of necessity*.

Exhorted to continue with his opinion about the idea of the good, Socrates qualifies everything he is about to say by claiming that he might be incapable of an account and that, in his unbridled enthusiasm, he may expose himself to shame. In addition to the qualification of inability, he further distances his forthcoming discourse from the idea of the good by asking his hearers to enable him to abandon it: "let us set aside what the good itself is for now—for, it appears to me to reach beyond the present thrust [*parousan hormēn*] of my opinion about it now" (506 d—e). Whatever Socrates' opinion about the good is, we are asked to forget about hearing it; for, the current motive force of the argument forbids reaching his opinion. Here, *hormēn* [thrust] may mean something like *archē*. According to Socrates, the impulse driving the discourse forward, the necessity that guides the conversation along, rules over it in such a way that prevents the conversation from reaching Socrates' opinion about the good itself. What is the present thrust? Must it not be Glaucon's compelling urge—the urge that encouraged him to place the imperative on Socrates? In other words, the present thrust is to be found in Glaucon's desire to hear Socrates' account of the good through the same *methodos* through which we earlier approached "justice, moderation and the rest" (506 e). As such, the necessary constraints placed upon Socrates by Glaucon forbid the means by which we can reach not only the idea of the good, but even Socrates' opinion about it.[1]

Instead, Socrates will offer another image:

> "I am willing to articulate what appears to be the offspring [*ekgonos*] of the good and what is most similar to it, if for you it is desirable [*philon*], but if not, leave it alone" (506 e).

Here, rather than pursuing the idea of the good through the long path, Socrates casts an image on the cave wall. It is an image of the generation of natural beings. How would an image of the offspring of the good disclose something about the good? In my reading, the image betrays a relation between beings and the good in a way similar to that relation between beings and necessity: one may catch a glimpse of the good through the image of an entity that becomes visible thanks to it. That is to say, through the children of the good, the good becomes visible indirectly. It is, therefore, a reproduction of the good, but is itself not the good. One could, of course, say the same thing about justice, moderation, courage and wisdom in the text: they are *ekgonoi* of the good. Each of these beings is necessarily what they are thanks to the structure of erotic necessity that links them to their "father." But the good cannot be reduced to any one of them. Indeed, the debt these children owe to their father is even more profound than in the case of biological reproduction. For, in biological reproduction of animals, for instance, there exists a necessary debt between father (and mother) and offspring. The offspring owes its *being* to the parents. But in the current image, the offspring owes its *goodness* to the father. That is to say, the father bestows *legitimacy* upon the offspring. In this framework of paternity, the father generates the children (justice, moderation, courage, wisdom, the sun) but the children only gain legitimacy by participating in the light of the father's family name. It is justice in the genitive case, rather than justice in the nominative case. In the previous account of justice, moderation, courage, and wisdom, we observed these concepts in their bare propositions: "justice is minding one's own business," for instance. In these cases, justice appears in the *nominative* case—the proposition (and its knowledge) is an expression of the *being* of justice as dependent on nothing other than itself. However, as Socrates will say shortly, "the good is not being but is yet beyond [*epekeina*] being" (509 b). Therefore, insofar as justice contains the referent to the good, we can speak of it in the genitive case. It is the *ekgonos* of the good: like all legitimate proper names in Greek, the genitive contains a reference to the source of its legitimacy. In this case, the father is the good.

In response to Socrates' offer to speak of the child of the good, Glaucon uses the language of economic exchange, exhorting Socrates to speak of this merely derivative subject for the time being. Another time, he says, Socrates will pay [*apotinō*] what remains due of the account of the father (506 e). Plato has Socrates observe this reference to the cultural institution of money exchange and employ his own, drawing from it a metaphor that contains an interior contradiction: interest [*tokos*[2]].

> "I wish," I said, "it were possible for me to repay it and for you to receive it, and not, as now, just the interest. At any rate receive this interest and offspring of the good. However, take care that I do not in some way unwillingly deceive you by giving a fraudulent account of the offspring/interest [*tokos*]" (507 a).

On the one hand, Socrates reaffirms that he is unable to pay (that he does not in fact have the knowledge of the father). However, this time, he adds to this assertion that Glaucon is also unable to receive an account of the father of the child of the good (*if there is* an account in the form of propositional knowledge). The problem of *giving* an account of the good now appears to be not merely a problem of Socrates' lack of knowledge of it. His interlocutors are not prepared *to receive it* either, if it exists. Perhaps at least a part of the problem lies in Glaucon's economic understanding of the exchange. Socrates refers to his own contribution as mere interest, as *tokos*. Since the word *tokos* can mean both "interest" and "offspring" at the same time, it would appear that Socrates' metaphor draws attention to this distinction. Does Glaucon's use of an economic metaphor betray to Socrates that his interlocutor cannot receive the account? Not only are "interest" and "offspring" not the same thing, but they belong to different systems of production.[3] Of course, "interest" belongs to an economic system of production. It is a product of *technē*. Artifacts do not have a father (even if they have a maker) and are not, in fact, children. Moreover, what about the system of legitimation, the very mark of "the good"? How does "interest" become legitimated? Systems of exchange come to be as a consequence of the agreement of participants in the system to recognize the codification established by a ruling body of reference (a constitution) that is technologically crafted. Interest becomes established and legitimated in reference to this body of knowledge. Interest, therefore, can only be said to be legitimate insofar as it is quantitatively *correct*. As correct, interest is equal to the expected product secured by the technological system of economic exchange. That is to say, that interest is not a child of the good and *does not refer to the source of its legitimacy, qua good, but only to knowledge*. Like justice without an account of the good, the technological knowledge system of economic exchange cannot point beyond the limits of its own system of constitutive propositions. On its own, it floats in empty space—*apparently* ripped out of the ecosystem that gives it real meaning, real legitimacy. That is to say, the system is in the nominative case, not the genitive. But the *tokos*, qua offspring, has a father and belongs to the system that gives it legitimacy in a more profound sense. It is of the father. Further, while the origin of the production of offspring lies in erotics (that unique species of necessity), the origin of the production of interest does not, at least not directly. Does Glaucon grasp this essential difference? Given that Plato has him employ the language of money exchange and then has Socrates respond with this ambivalent image of *tokos*, it would seem that perhaps Glaucon confuses the difference between erotic and technological production.[4]

In any case, the image of the child of the good exhibits an essential ambiguity. It is to show something of the good, but indirectly. In the gap between the account of the child and the account of the father lies a source of misunderstanding. Socrates urges his interlocutors not to allow him to "unwillingly deceive" (507 a) them. But what would be the source of the deception? One is reminded here of Adeimantus' earlier critique of Socratic dialectic (which Socrates did not deny): taken question by question, one does not perceive that one is being deceived, but in the end one has assented to a global assertion that genuinely appears to one to be the opposite of reality. Is this the "unwilling deception" that Socrates means here? I do not think so. In my view the source of deception lies in the essential gap between *Being* and the *Good*.

Whether the problem is that the propositional account of the good is impossible, or the interlocutors have failed in some way to make themselves receptive to an account of the good, or the new beginning by which the long road to an account of the good was abandoned—whatever the reason, Socrates cannot give an account of the good, but must give an account of what he calls the child of the good. However, as I hope to show in the following paragraphs, the child of the good involves the *Being* of things. Thus, just like the previous propositional/definitional accounts of justice, moderation, courage and wisdom, the rest of book VI and book VII are animated by the question of *Being*—of the what-is-ness of things. And this direction of the discourse toward the analysis of being is necessitated by the imperatives issued by Glaucon and the interlocutors. But, as we have argued above, the being of things appears in the *nominative* case, not the genitive (the conjugation of the good). To repeat, in the case of justice, the proposition (and its knowledge) is an expression of the *being* of justice as dependent on nothing other than itself. However, the *good* is beyond *being* (509 b); it is the source of justice's legitimacy. One might suggest that the *good* provides the ecosystem in which the *being* of justice resides, even while it remains beyond the articulation of the definition of justice and its propositions. Knowledge of the what-is-ness of justice does not enable us to arrive at an understanding of the good—it can even distort and disguise the good (is there a better example of a disembodied knowledge of justice than the proposition "justice is minding one's own business"?)—but the good might be a kind of ecosystem of relations out of which sprouts justice, moderation, courage and wisdom such that they are legitimated as what they are.

In any case, Plato has Socrates warn his interlocutors (and us) that the coming account of the child of the good holds the potential to deceive. In light of our current analysis, there may already be a deception in the immediate exchange that follows. Socrates repeats what he says[5] we have already heard before several times; namely, that, on the one hand, "we both say and define in speech [*logos*] that there are [*einai*] many beautiful things, many good things, and so on for each of the things" [507 b]. On the other hand, in addition to these "many" things, "we also assert that there is a beautiful itself, a good itself and thus [something 'itself'] for all the things that we establish as many; and, again, according to one idea of each, we assign it as being one, addressing it as what each is" (507 b). Thus, Socrates repeats a version of the ontological formulation we have seen several times. In the account we observed at the beginning of book VI, there are the kinds of things that *wander*, that become, shift and turn. Then, there are the kinds of things that *are always*.

Socrates presents a dualistic ontological and epistemological paradigm. Of the things, we perceive the *many* things that wander with the senses [*aisthēsis*] and we grasp the ideas that always are with the intellect [*nous*]. However, Plato would often appear to present this dualistic paradigm as a problem with which the reader is intended to struggle. For example, in the *Timaeus*, we have a similar ontological organization. Timaeus presents a dilemma. On the one hand, of the things, there are those that wander. Fire, air, water and earth wander insofar as they are never fully present as what they are; instead, they are always on the way to something else. If you were able to stop time and take a snapshot of air, you would find that it is already on the way to water,

water already on the way to fire, etc. On the other hand, the things that always are never change. They are the measure of stability. While giving his speech, Timaeus discovers that this duality introduces a problem: how are the things that *wander* supposed to participate in the things that *are* if they are so radically opposed to each other in their being? In light of this difficulty, Timaeus introduces the "third thing": the *chora* (2001, 50 c—d). The third thing serves as the occasion for the formless to become formed into something graspable at all and for the form to come into being and pass away, or to become. Implicitly faced with the same difficulty now, it is not accidental that Socrates introduces another "third thing" in book VI of the *Republic*.

After reintroducing the dualistic ontological paradigm, Socrates adds that two forms of the being of things are further divided experientially by being associated with different faculties of the soul. "We say that the many things are seen but not thought [*voeō*], while the ideas are thought but not seen" (507 b). There is an unexplained emphasis here on the sensuous faculty of sight. The priority of sight becomes further reinforced with the claim that the divine "craftsman [*dēmiourgos*]" was "lavish" in his technological construction of the sense of sight (507 c) by requiring of it a "third thing." In fact, the introduction of the "third thing" is at least provisionally limited to the sense of sight. Socrates asks Glaucon if he can think of any third class of thing that is required for hearing: "not having recourse to a third thing the [faculty of hearing] will not hear and [the sound] will not be heard" (507 d). Glaucon responds that, "no," he knows of no medium, and Socrates also then affirms that he too supposes that "there cannot be many, if any, that need" (507 d) a third thing for perception to take place. Scholars have brought attention to this false supposition. Often, they come to the defense of "Plato's" "scientific" error here. Clearly, they say, the *Timaeus* shows us that Plato knows that the medium of air is required for sound (67 b). Moreover, Aristotle's *On the Soul* too points to the necessity of a medium for the faculty of hearing. Shorey, for example, writes off Socrates' hypothesis as literary caprice rather than scientific rigor: "the statement is true enough to illustrate the thought" (1969, 507c). Adam seems to take a similar stance in his reading: "Here . . . scientific analysis of perception is not proposed" (1902, 507 c). Thus, we are to forgive Plato this brief lapse in "scientific" precision. Of course, the literary image that Socrates is about to cast (the sun) lends itself to this limitation to the sense of sight. However, I question whether the mistake is not intentional for two reasons. First, it may be related to Socrates' warning earlier that he might unwillingly deceive us. There is something about the path of inquiry conducted via the concept of the child of the good (the sun) that will not adequately take us where we need to go—to the good. Secondly, Glaucon's ability to "be careful" that Socrates not "unwillingly deceive" him is now called into question. He gives a hard "no" in answer to Socrates' question, even though he does not yet understand what sort of thing the third thing might be, not even for sight. As far as he knows at this point, there are *no* things that require a third thing in order to be perceived. Only when Socrates then asks if he's noticed that *sight does require* a third thing, does he soften his "no" to "how?" Thus, Glaucon fails to observe the necessity for third things in anything involving perception until Socrates explicitly tells him that the third *is necessary* for the phenomenon of sight.

In response to Glaucon's question, Socrates exclaims that Glaucon knows that "sight will see nothing and the colors will be unseen" . . . if the third kind [*genos*] of thing remains absent (507 d—e). Light is the third kind of thing that Socrates mentions here. Light is precisely that which lights up the visible things such that the power of vision can see them. Without the light, vision sees nothing and things remain unseen. Light mediates the relation between the power of sight and the perceptible things which act upon it. Socrates employs the metaphor of a "yoke" in order to describe the function of light in sense perception.

> "It is no small idea [*idea*]
>   that yokes together the sense of sight and the power of being seen, a yoke more honorable than other yokes, if light is not without honor" (507 e - 508 a).

According to Socrates, light yokes together the perceptible thing with the power [*dunamis*] of sight. The Greek word employed here (three times in one sentence) can be used to describe the device that joins a team of horses to a chariot. But *suzeukis* can also mean the sort of being yoked together suggested in "wedded union." In the latter case, one might expect the production of offspring. The *ekgonos* of this sort of yoking would be perception, or seeing. Seeing is the offspring when light weds the perceptible thing with the power of sight. There is more than the power of sight and the thing potentially seen—the actuality of seeing comes third when the union of these two are occasioned by light. It is for this reason, perhaps, that it is more honorable by the measure of an "idea"[6] than the yoke joining horses to chariots. The kind of sense-making we call seeing is the product of the practice of this form of yoking. Light enables seeing to produce an *understanding* of the sensible field. Light is a yoke which, qua third thing, is productive of offspring (the offspring of the activity of sight). The seeing that light breeds remains a sense-making that opens up the world to us and limits it at the same time. It may be that *ideas* are yokes too.

The mediating substance, light, brings something to bear on the phenomenon such that things are meaningful as "visible." Yet, as was made clear by Glaucon's initial ignorance, most of the time we look straight through the light without seeing it. The light is there in between, shaping our perceptive experience of the thing; however, we fail to observe that we are looking *through* the light. We think, rather, that we have an immediate relation to the object of vision. As a medium, how does light shape our interpretation of the phenomena that we see?[7] Perhaps we can say that, in the region of perceptible beings, light provides the <u>as</u> structure of visual perception. We look through the light, as a medium, and it makes the thing visible *as* visible. The light makes it possible to divide the visible horizon into distinct things, qua visible. Different senses without reference to sight may have different sorts of borders between things; the mediation would provide different horizons of interpretation, such that different limits would appear, different principles for perceptual individuation. Touch, for example, might unify a thing, not by color, but by textures that for touch remain continuous across some things that for sight are merely contiguous and vice versa. The other senses equally hold the potential for shifts in such perceptual continuity/contiguity. However, sight remains the more readily available example because we can easily locate a divine origin from which the third thing emanates: the sun. Light emanates from the sun which makes the production of sight possible, as well as the kind of perceptual understanding that the sense-making of sight undergoes. We will extend this analogy to the *idea* shortly. Like the sun, *the idea* might also be understood as a source of light. That is to say, ideas may be understood as discursive entities that emanate a mediating light that makes beings appear in a certain way and with a certain meaning.

The third thing is a presentation of the revision of the dualistic ontological paradigm often associated with Plato. If we extrapolate from perception to being, what provides the <u>as</u> structure? What is the third thing in the region of knowledge and truth? Socrates begins to offer an interpretation of this through the image of a proportion.

> "This now," I said, "is what I mean when I say the offspring [*ekgonos*] of the good: that which the good engendered in proportion [*analogos*] to itself. As the good is in the intelligible place with respect to intelligence and what is intellect, so is this [the sun] in the visible place with respect to sight and what is seen" (508 b—c).

Here Socrates sets up a geometrical proportion between the father and the son, between the good and the sun. Further, the famous *divided line* and the *allegory of the cave* follow from this proportion, insofar as the organization of both the cave and the line are founded upon the fundamental distinction articulated here. The line divides the *beings* encountered (images/shadows, beings *physei*/beings *technei, mathemata,* and *eidē*) and the affections that the beings have on the soul (*nous* (but also dialectic), *dianoia, pistis,* and *fantasia*) into the visible and intelligible regions. However, in my reading, *we risk being deceived* by Socrates again here; for the proportion contains a false equivalence. While the good may light up both intelligible and visible things in a certain way indirectly (to be analyzed below), it does not illuminate them in a way that would enable a proportional comparison to the sun. For, the sun lights up visible things as *what they are* as visible things. Its light concerns the visible *being* of things. Yet, the good does not light up the things as *what they are* as intelligible beings. It does not light up the *what-is-ness* of the intelligible things as intelligible; rather, it is knowledge of *being* of the thing and its truth that does that.

On the one hand, the distinction between how things are seen in the light of the good and how they are seen in the light of being is obvious. The analogy between what is intelligible and what is visible works precisely because they are both modes in which beings appear *in their being*—even if one leads to intellection (and perhaps opinion) and the other to sensation. On the other hand, the false analogy is so rarely read as an example of one of Socrates' cautioned deceptions by interpreters of the good of the *Republic*, that it might be useful to appeal to Aristotle's famous example of perception and intellection in *On the Soul* to support our claim with something other than self-evidence. In that text, Aristotle argues that perception is the reception in the perceptive part of the soul of the perceptible form of the thing. The perceptible form (for example, color) is stamped upon the perceptive part of the soul without the material, just as if it were a form pressing into wax (2001, 424 a 20). Analogously, Aristotle suggests that intellectual perception is the reception in the noetic part of the soul of the noetic form of the thing. The intellectual form (the *ousia*/being of the thing) is stamped upon the noetic part of the soul without the material, just as if it were a form pressing into wax (2001, 429 a 15).[8] Thus, the analogy between what is intelligible and what is visible works precisely because they are both modes in which beings appear *in their being*—whether that being is perceptual or noetic. Socrates organizes the analogy between perception and intellection in a similar way.

> When [the soul] rests upon that which is lit up by truth and that which is, it thinks [*noeō*], knows [*gignōsko*], and seems to have intelligence [*nous*]. But when it rests on that which is mixed with darkness, on coming into being and passing away, it merely supposes [*doxazō*] and its vision is weakened, changing opinions up and down, and seems not to have intelligence [*nous*] (508 d).

On the one hand, there are noetic beings: the forms [*eidē*] of the beings. On the other hand, there is the [noetic part of] the soul. Like the sun and its light, there is a third thing that illuminates the noetic being and enables thinking, intellection, and thus knowing to occur in the soul. Therefore, so far, Socrates provides an analogy very similar to Aristotle's. The image of the child of the good gives rise to the following analogy: being's truth is to the intellect's knowing as the sun's light is to perception's seeing. In my view, there is no legitimate connection to the good in this argument.[9] Socrates is [perhaps "unwillingly"] deceiving his interlocutors here by producing an inadequate equivalence between the being of things and the good. At the very least, he's "leaving out a lot" (509 c); for, beings appear *good* through another *idea*.[10]

Given my focus in this section on the analogy presented as an image of the child of the good, I must necessarily neglect Socrates' addition of the phenomenon of opinion emerging in the soul as a consequence of its fixation on the wandering things as opposed to the unchanging things. However, in passing, I want to note that the passage is important *vis à vis* our earlier remarks regarding the possibility of the philosophical nature. If Plato is a tragic thinker (and I think he is), then the two options we are given here appear complicated when we picture the *actual activity* of the paradigmatic philosopher (Socrates) presented in most of the dialogues. We learned earlier that the philosophic nature is the one who loves and strives after *what is* and, thus, is the one *who knows*. However, we observed that, while Socrates certainly strives after *what is,* there is no indication in the dialogues that he actually consummates his erotic urge and *knows* anything except that *he does not know*. In my view, this raises the question of whether, for Plato, humans are capable of transcending the limitations of "resting on that which is mixed with darkness . . . " and thus of transcending the intellectual comportment of opinion.

In any case, we may now return to the idea of the good after this brief reminder of the problem of the philosophical nature. Again, beings do not appear good through the idea of knowledge, being or truth. The earlier books of the *Republic* presented "true" propositions of the being of justice, moderation, courage and wisdom. How they can be said to be good was precisely what Socrates claims in book VI was left out. This was the problem that necessitated the long path of dialectic. Beings appear *good* through another *idea*. To use our formulation from earlier: while knowledge (and its propositions) illuminates things as *what they are*, the good lights up things as *legitimate*.[11] Yet, Socrates' complex images—his *proportion*al relation between the good and the sun, his presentation of the *geometrical image* of the Divided Line,[12] and his *Allegory* of the Cave only get us as far as the knowledge of the *being* of things: the knowledge of the truth of the being of things is intellected/noetic.[13] The good, however, is "beyond being" (509 b).

Our reading must contend with one more problem that arises with respect to the relation between the good and truth/knowledge in these paragraphs; for it may appear that Socrates doubles down on his commitment to the idea that the images that follow the child of the good are adequate presentations of the good's relation to the order of knowledge. To this end, Socrates exhorts

Glaucon to "say that what offers the truth to the things known and gives the power to the one who knows, is the idea of the good" (508 e). Again, we have not established this relation in the analogy articulated above. Everything that follows from here (the divided line, the allegory of the cave) only gets us to knowledge, if indeed even this is a trustworthy claim. Rather than offering an argument, Socrates merely exhorts Glaucon to trust that the good provides the truth to things known. Socrates follows this exhortation with an addition that scholars have judged difficult to interpret in the manuscripts.[14] Following Adam, I translate the passage to say:

> Being the cause of knowledge and truth, think it [the idea of the good] as a thing known; but as beautiful as these two are—knowledge and truth—if you regard it [the idea of the good] as something different from them and still more beautiful than they, you will regard it rightly (508 e).

How is the good "a thing known," if we've been actively excluded from giving an account of it? In what way is the good "a cause" of knowledge and truth? I interpret this passage to say something similar to what we have argued about offspring [*ekgonos*] above. It warrants repeating here: the image betrays a relation between beings and the good in a way similar to that relation between beings and necessity: one may catch a glimpse of the good through the image of an entity that becomes visible thanks to it. That is to say, through the children of the good, the good becomes visible indirectly. It is, therefore, an offspring of the good, but is itself not the good. This is precisely what it means to say that knowledge and truth (as well as justice, moderation, courage and wisdom) are different from and less beautiful than the good; for, they are *ekgonoi* of the good. On the one hand, each of them "are" and owe this *being* to their father and mother. Each of these beings is necessarily what they are thanks to the structure of erotic necessity that links them to their "father" and "mother." On the one hand, they have being, but their goodness has not been established by the mere fact that they *are*. On the other hand, the good cannot be reduced to any one of them. Indeed, the debt these children owe to their father is even more profound than in the case of biological reproduction. As we argued earlier, in the biological reproduction of animals, there exists a *necessary* debt between father (and mother) and offspring. The offspring owes its *being* to the parents. But in the current image, in the ancient Greek context, the offspring owes its *goodness* to the father. That is to say, the father bestows *legitimacy* upon the offspring. In this framework of paternity,[15] the father generates the children (justice, moderation, courage, wisdom, the sun) but the children only gain legitimacy by participating in the light of the father's family name. It is justice in the genitive case, rather than justice in the nominative case. To frame this in the language of Socrates' proportional relation above, just as the sun provides the light that illuminates the visible thing as visible, so the *idea* of justice provides the truth that illuminates the just act as *being* just. The expression of this idea *through which* one perceives noetic beings in the world might be said to be knowledge of justice: for example, "justice is minding one's own business." But, still, it is only justice in the *nominative case*; it is merely propositional, having been uprooted from the structure of its legitimacy which is *beyond* the being of justice: the idea of the good.

In what way, then, does the idea of the good light up beings for us? Is there a third thing that makes beings visible, not as the beings they *are*, but *as good*? Socrates' explicit arguments in the *Republic* leave this question unanswered. However, I would like to offer an interpretation that links the good back to the structure of necessity. Earlier, we observed that, for Socrates, the activity of sight requires a third thing. In addition to the visible thing and the power of vision, sight needs the "yoke" of light to join the two together such that the offspring (seeing) can be cultivated. In the case of the idea of the good, in what way does it "light" up the things such that the soul perceives them as good? Is it not through "*desire*"? "Desire" is the third thing that makes it possible to recognize something *as* good. Even more, is it not *erotic* desire that causes the soul to seek union with the object judged good in order to generate its offspring? When I encounter some being in the world *as* something good, the model of perception changes from our earlier example. In that situation, there is the faculty of sight, the being in the world, the light, and then the offspring which follows this union: seeing the being in its visible nature. However, when I encounter something in the world *as* good, the system of perception involves 1) the being, 2) the faculty or faculties capable of love (book IX makes it clear that this is all three faculties), and 3) the light of desire which reveals the being to the soul as good. The "good" being does not merely appear *as* a being; that is to say, what becomes visible is not the being's substance (*ousia*) or its existence (if such a concept exists in Plato). Rather, it appears as *desirable*. In my reading, therefore, *the light of the good is desire and need*.

However, such a reading makes visible a problem already suggested many times in this book. If the light of the good is desire, then how does one distinguish the good from necessity? If desire is a species of necessity (as both the *Republic* and the *Timaeus* suggest), then not only the many are incapable of radically distinguishing one from the other, but the philosopher too.

What then is the offspring produced by the yoke of desire? Perhaps it can be said to be an activity in the Aristotelian sense. When a being is yoked or wedded to the faculties by the light of desire, it engenders an action; desire effects an *energeia* when an entity is lit up by it. By way of speculation, we might suggest that, as such, desire transcends the limitation of the faculties.

For, *erōs* stretches throughout the soul, through all the faculties and all the virtues.[16]

In response to Socrates' observance that knowledge and truth are not the good, Glaucon expresses his doubts that Socrates might mean "pleasure." To this curious hesitation, Socrates responds with the imperative of the verb *eufēmeo* [hush] (509 a), which apparently is employed in contexts requiring attention to the sacred. Adam (1902), Shorey (1969), Sachs (2007) and Reeve (2004) remain silent on this conspicuous use of a religious imperative. Bloom notes that the term means "'say something good' or 'use words of good omen.' It is primarily a word appropriate to religious observance" (1991, 464). Thus, he follows Shorey and translates the imperative with "hush." Sallis (in *Being and Logos* [1996]) and Benardete (in *Socrates' Second Sailing* [1989]) skip over this conspicuous response to Glaucon's negatively-stated hypothesis that Socrates might mean "pleasure" (1996, 408). However, the term *eufēmeo* warrants our consideration; for, it first appears at the beginning of the dialogue in a location of importance. There, the note first sounds out that initiates the dance of the entire dialogue; it takes the form of a question. Socrates asks Cephalus whether what "the poets call the threshold" of death is difficult to bear (328 e). In response to this question, Cephalus quotes a poet, Sophocles. Once upon a time, someone asked the aged Sophocles if he was still capable of sexual activity. He replied, "Hush man [*eufēmeo*], most gladly I escaped it as though I had fled from a raving and savage master" (329 c). Socrates uses the same term in response to Glaucon's question/claim regarding Socrates' intentions in determining the meaning of the good: "surely," says Glaucon, "you do not mean to say that it is pleasure" (509 a). As far as I have been able to find, *eufēmeo* is employed only twice in the entire dialogue. On the one hand, here, in response to this hypothetical inquiry about pleasure by Glaucon. And on the other hand, it is uttered by a poet (even if the utterance is not poetic) in the service of contradicting an interlocutor with respect to the regrettable loss of erotic pleasure. As such, both times that Plato has his characters employ the imperative, it is in response to the subject of pleasure, perhaps even erotic pleasure.[17]

In my reading, by placing this imperative in the mouth of Socrates in response to the insertion of erotic pleasure in the discussion, Plato invokes the earlier passage. As we have pointed out above, the figure of erotic pleasure haunts the dialogue. For my Plato, it remains an inevitable feature of human life, insofar as it belongs at the very center of all existence in the world. That is to say, *it is necessary and is ruled by the structure of necessity.* Whether or not Cephalus' actual words invoke doubts about his understanding of old age, death, poetry, the use of money, or justice in the reader, his actions do. Cephalus makes assertions about the meaning of justice by quoting Pindar

(331 a). However, he lacks the desire, the erotic urge, to dialectically investigate what these phrases actually mean.[18] He is happy to be freed from this necessity; Cephalus is already, for all intents and purposes, dead. It is, thus, too late for Cephalus. The loss of *erōs* means precisely that he is incapable of philosophical investigation. Therefore, Cephalus' remarks about erotics are not trustworthy. We inherit them (via Polemarchus) and must turn them over for ourselves, but only if we are filled with the desire to do so. Without this desire, we lack everything. That is to say, qua necessity, *erōs* has already animated our discourse and compels the speeches forward. *erōs* is contradictory, it resists reason. Is *erōs* destructive? Yes. Is *erōs* the origin of everything productive? Yes. *erōs* (and, thus, necessity) is contradictory and, therefore, tragic. Reason cannot fold it into itself, it cannot comprehend it—even as *erōs* remains the condition for the possibility of reason.[19] *Logos* remains one of the ways that humans are compelled (*anagkazō*), qua necessity (*anagkē*). If reason is a form of desire [Khan 1987], then the irrational (*erōs*) occasions the rational (*logos*). The problems engendered by *erōs* are not, therefore, eradicable by means of reason. If reason is a product of necessity, then necessity has already appropriated *logos* for its own ends. Nevertheless, even if *logos* turns out not to be a faculty that enables the human being to transcend its own finitude, the faculty of *logos* does enable (or compels—*anagkazō*) problem-solving within the region demarcated by finitude (something we must develop presently in our analysis of the divided line and the allegory of the cave). More importantly, with regard to philosophical matters, the light emitted by the convergence of *logos*, *nous*, and *aporia* makes visible human finitude and its limitations; and this vision, while not loosening the human from the grip of necessity, transcends the closed structure of hypotheses that circumscribes the world of science (509 b), the *mathematikē*. Again, this transcendence does not push the human beyond finitude, but perhaps makes it visible for the first time. Such a glimpse of the *being* of the human is, by itself, already a transcendence.

NOTES

1. Compare Seth Benardete in *Socrates' Second Sailing* when he refers to the circumstances of the *Republic*: that they "do not allow Socrates to pay his debt in full; and the image of the sun functions initially as a way of satisfying Glaucon without Socrates ever giving him his actual opinion about the good" (1989, 158).

2. The word *tokos* can mean both "interest" and "offspring." In book VIII, there is another play on this double meaning (555 e).

3. Aristotle emphasizes the double meaning of *tokos* in the *Politics*, suggesting that it is the form of the generation of money most contrary to nature. For him, money

came into being in order to exchange goods or labor for an equivalent quantity of money, but *tokos* is the generation of money from money—like parents generate children from themselves (Aristotle 1986, 1258 b).

4. Compare Sallis' analysis of the problem of *technē* in *Chorology* (1999) and *Being and Logos* (1996).

5. Even though Socrates claims that we have heard what he is about to say about the "the many things" and the "ideas," there are enough differences between this and earlier accounts to cause many scholars to "correct" what he then says. For instance, Adam writes that Socrates' use of the term *einai* can't be used in its technical sense because it would be inconsistent with the end of book V (1900): these many things "are" not, but 1) are opined to be, and 2) are classed among the wandering things—as we saw at the beginning of book VI. Further, Shorey writes that the "modern reader will never understand Plato from translations that talk about 'Being'" (1969). It may be important to remember that Socrates has just warned us about being deceived.

6. Plato has Socrates use the technical term *idea* here in a strange way. Like Shorey (1969), perhaps we should consider this a mere "loose use" of the term, rather than its technical use in the Platonic corpus. It may be "little more than a synonym for *genos* above." However, I'd rather take the risk of assuming that Plato wants the reader to recognize the term, especially insofar as the *idea* has an important role to play in this part of the dialogue. The idea too may emit light that makes beings visible, qua meaningful, in a certain way.

7. This question might animate the entirety of the work of the California artist James Turrell. Regardless of his own authorial intention, this question shapes my interpretation of his work. Moreover, his pieces occasion meditation on other mediating classes that shape our interpretation of objects.

8. On my reading of Aristotle, the metaphor of wax introduces its own problem; namely, insofar as form reflects the being of the thing, qua, *to ti en einai*, it is not static, but in a certain way processual. It is the *activity* that the thing does in order to be what it is. A form in wax implies stasis. See my "In the Life of Thinking in Aristotle's de Anima" in *Epoche* (2009, 13:2). Also, my "Aristotelian Definition and the Discovery of *archai*" in *Bloomsbury Companion to Aristotle* (2013).

9. John Sallis thinks that the good bestows oneness on things. "To say that the good confers truth means: the good confers, makes possible, that kind of showing in which something can show itself as one" (Sallis 1996, 409). As is obvious from my commentary above, I disagree with this reading. I think the good is missing from the analogy. In Aristotle's *Metaphysics*, *being* confers oneness in a fairly explicit way. It seems likely that, for Plato's Socrates too, unity is achieved by being. It is not clear at all how goodness would do that.

10. Seth Benardette expresses a similar sentiment when he writes "whether the beings are good is not disclosed with the disclosure of the beings" (1989, 163). However, unlike me, he continues to take Socrates' analogy seriously, rather than broken: "The good, then, is not manifest in beings that the good discloses (1989, 163). On my reading, the good is beyond being in a more radical sense.

11. Seth Benardete (1989, 163) also observes that whether the beings are good is not disclosed with the disclosure of the beings. On my reading, the good is not

disclosed by knowledge and truth. As will become clear, I think this is the "unwilling deception" Socrates mentions at the outset of his analysis.

12. Julia Annas also recognizes the problem by asking "where in the line is the Good, so stressed in the figure of the Sun? Reading the Line after the Sun we are naturally led to think that the Good is identical with the 'unhypothetical first principle' grasped by the person with . . . 'intellect.' But it does not fit into the scheme of the line very happily. It cannot be just one of the contents of EA [the noetic region]: but if not, where can it go?" (1997, 150–151).

13. In the first formulation of the affections of the soul, dialectic is included in the same region with *nous* (intellect) (511 b). However, in the recapitulation it appears absent-mindedly left out of the list. Does dialectic have some power that enables the soul to transcend the limits of being, to get beyond being to the good?

14. Adam changes the case of the participle *gignoskomenhs* to *gignoskomenhn* to make it agree with *aitian*; Shorey agrees that *gignoskomenhs* makes the passage "difficult" to interpret (1969).

15. A reviewer imagined that, with these and the following words, I am offering an argument *in support* of paternalistic practices and societies. Nothing could be further from the truth. I am simply referencing the ancient Greek practice of distinguishing an offspring as merely *being* from recognizing one as both *being* and *legitimate* (or "good") as an analogy for understanding Socrates' distinction between the mere *being* of justice, wisdom, courage, and moderation (in perhaps a definition) from the recognition that these things both *are* and *are good*.

16. Compare book IX in which Socrates revises the description of the tripartite structure of the soul to be "wisdom-loving, victory-loving, gain-loving" (581 c). Both Roochnik (2003) and Khan (1987) point to this revision as well.

17. As has often been suggested (see, for example, Roochnik 2003, 56), Glaucon is presented as a very erotic man, having both a lover (368 a) and a beloved (402 e). Thus, it might be said that erotic pleasure is the pleasure that he desires most.

18. Cephalus' comprehension of the poetry that he slings around in support of his claims is even more radically called into question by the words that he puts into Sophocles' mouth about old age. Few authors have presented old age as devastatingly sad as Sophocles in *Oedipus at Colonus* (1235).

19. Charles Khan argues in "Plato's Theory of Desire" that reason is a form of desire: "reason in the *Republic* is not only essentially desire but essentially desire for the good" (1987, 84). While I view Khan's refusal to allow a clean separation between desire and reason a very important contribution, I don't read the dialogue's presentation of the reason/desire relation in such optimistically systematic terms. In fact, I agree that Plato has Socrates introduce this reading, but in my view, with it, he introduces a problem/*aporia*, not a systematic "theory." Desire/erotics are a species of *necessity*. The claim that "reason is essentially desire for the good" says that "the good is essentially rational necessity." Such a reading reminds the reader of the problem that Socrates diagnosed in "the many" earlier in book VI: *oi polloi* can't distinguish "the good" from "necessity." If reason is desire and desire remains an expression of erotic necessity, then reason is necessity, not the good—that is, *if* necessity and the good can be radically distinguished at all. For these reasons, it strikes me that

Khan's *theoretical system* of Platonic desire remains doubtful whether necessity and the good can be distinguished or not. Still, as is evident from the current argument, I appropriate the claim "reason is a form of desire" with these qualifications.

Chapter 4

Necessity in the Intelligible Region of the Divided Line

In the previous three chapters of this book, we have foregrounded the characteristics associated with the articulation of necessity in the *Republic*. We observed that, in what might be called a linear interpretation of the arguments, the text produces a claim in which philosophy (and the good) are in opposition to necessity. However, by developing a reading of the dramatic details of the text in relation to others, we are able to offer reasons these might be used to call the linear argument into question. That is to say, the radical separation of the philosophical nature and necessity may be a challenge to the reader that was intentionally inscribed into the drama of the dialogue. Necessity—in the shape of *erōs* (erotic love), wandering movement, *tugxano* (chance happenings), and the ecosystemic origin of both concepts and living forms—was shown to condition the emergence of the philosophical nature in a way that renders a radical separation between philosophy and necessity problematic.

Moving from the image of "the child of the good" to the image of "the divided line," chapter 4 provides an interpretation of the intelligible region of the latter. Given the connection commonly made between necessity and natural law, one might expect to find the language of necessity more frequently in the region of the line representing the visible. However, it actually shows itself more in the description of the intellectual movements of the intelligible region. Chapter 4 offers an analysis of the intelligible line segment in order to understand how necessity functions in this famous image. From our analysis, we add an additional expression of necessity to the list above: necessity is articulated as a motive force. Moreover, it shows itself as *compulsion* or *force* not only among the things of *physis*, but also the things of thought [*dianoia* and *nous*]. One presumes that science and philosophy (which investigate what is intelligible) are free from necessity; however, as expressed in the image, both of these endeavors are ruled by necessity as by a motive force.

After Socrates asserts that the good "is not being, but is still beyond being, above it in dignity and power [*dunamei huperechontas*]" (509 b), Glaucon reacts as if Socrates, in referencing something that is "beyond being," might as well be talking about crystal healing. He offers a joke by punning on Socrates' last words: "Apollo, what a demonic hyperbole [*daimonias huperbolēs*]" (509 c). In response to the joke, Socrates reminds Glaucon, "you are culpable for compelling [*anagkazō*] me to speak my opinions about it" (509 c). Here, Socrates employs the language of *anagkē*, of necessity, to describe his relation to the discourse. Over the course of the first six books of the *Republic,* we have encountered this language frequently. The verb first appears at the beginning of book one when Thrasymachus presents his claim that "the just is for the use of the stronger, and the unjust is profitable and useful for oneself" (344 c). After making this claim, he tried to leave. However, the other men present "compelled [*anagkazō*] him to remain" (344 d). Like Socrates in many places in the dialogue, Thrasymachus is *compelled* to remain and speak. This is the first instance of the verb; however, even though the language of *anagkē* is not used there, one could point also to the very beginning of the text as an example of a similar exertion of *anagkē* on the dialogue, insofar as force is employed. After all, Socrates is prevented by force from returning to the city by Polemarchus' slave.

Here, at the end of book vi, Plato employs the verb again, having Socrates remind Glaucon that he is the origin of the force of necessity compelling his speech. When Glaucon commands Socrates not to stop until he has elaborated on the good's similarity to the sun (509 c), Socrates warns him that he will no doubt "leave out a lot" (509 c). The image that follows this warning is the famous "divided line." As one might expect from what was written above, in my reading, the most important of the things that might be missing in what follows is precisely the good.[1] However, one thing that is not missing is the language of *anagkē*. Necessity remains present even in the absence of the good.

Curiously, in Socrates' presentation of the divided line, the language of necessity seems to proliferate most in the region of *intelligibility*, not visibility.

> Look too at the sectioning of the intelligible section . . . in one section, using as images the things that were imitated before, the soul is compelled to investigate [*zētein anagkazetai*] from hypotheses and passes [*poreuō*] to an end, not to a beginning [*archē*]. In the other section it goes to the beginning [*archē*] without hypothesis, it moves from hypothesis without the images in the previous section, it makes its way [to the *archē*] with forms through forms (510 b).

The beings by *physis* and by *technē*, qua images, compel (*anagkazō*) the soul to investigate them on the basis of hypotheses that the soul somehow already has. One gathers beings/images together in accordance with the presumed organizational meaning contained within the hypotheses. The investigator organizes the beings into systems of knowledge, bodies constituted by propositions in accordance with the presumed hypothesis. One imagines a knowledge-system composed of syllogisms organized around a particular concept.

To take "life" (*bios*) as an example, the investigator begins with the "hypothesis," that is to say, the presumed answer to the question "what is life?" From there, the scientist proceeds to gather together beings under the heading of the meaning presumed in the hypothesis. One formulates a series of propositions that form the body of biology, starting from the hypothesis and moving from there out toward the "end" of the science of biology. Again, in this example, the science of biology is an ever-expanding series of propositions, beginning from the initial hypothesis (presumption) and *reaching toward* an all-encompassing system of knowledge (an end), whether it actually *reaches* it or not. However, at no time in this scheme has the investigator actually interrogated the presumption s/he already holds, the presumption that subtends all the work proceeding from the hypothesis containing the assumed meaning/answer to the original question "what is life?"

To perform the sort of analysis that frees one from presumption (or at least discloses one's presumption *as* a presumption), Socrates says that one moves not *forward* from the hypotheses to *the end*, but from the presumption (the hypotheses) *back* to the *beginning*, turning back to a starting point without hypotheses [*anupothetos*].

By sketching for Glaucon the opposing directions of movement in the intelligible region of the soul, Socrates has articulated the difference between scientific investigation and philosophical search. However, what remains remarkable is the presence of *necessity* in the intelligible part of the soul in both endeavors. Whether one starts with hypotheses and builds a system of knowledge or starts with hypotheses and turns back toward the beginning, the soul "is compelled to investigate [*zētein anagkazetai*]" (510 b). What is the status of intellectual freedom here? One might argue that both science and philosophy are thought to be the disciplines that are *free*. But from what are they supposed to free one? Precisely from necessity. Science is supposed to be the activity that enables one to step out of necessity in order to analyze its structure, for instance. However, in this preliminary sketch of the intelligible region of the soul, all the work performed in/by this region comes to be as and in accordance with necessity. One does not freely take up the subject of investigation; rather, one is compelled, or the investigation is necessitated.

Glaucon does not understand what Socrates means by the sentences we quoted above, so Socrates says, "try again" (510 c). He offers the discipline of mathematics as an example.

> I suppose you know that the men who are engaged in geometry, calculation and other such things assume the odd and the even, the figures, three forms of angles, and other things akin to these according to each inquiry [*methodos*] as known. They make these hypotheses and do not deem it worthy to give an account of them to themselves or others, presuming that they were clear to all. Beginning from them, they go ahead through what remains and end in agreement with the presumption toward which their investigation was set into motion (510 c-d).

Here, Socrates curiously refers to peripheral concepts that are presumed by the disciplines of "geometry, calculation and the like," not the ur-concept or ur-form that is presumed. One would expect to see "the measurable" or perhaps even "the earth" as the form of these disciplines. Instead Socrates offers examples of concepts without which, to be sure, the science of geometry cannot get off the ground, but which are nevertheless not the first presupposition. Still, the procedure is the same as that offered above: beginning from concepts the meaning of which is presumed to be understood by all, they make these hypotheses and ground their exposition upon them.

In the example of geometry, the investigator uses "visible forms." That is to say, s/he performs demonstrations with visible points, lines, angles, and circles, for instance, on a chalkboard. The arguments take these visible figures as points of departure. However, the arguments are not for the sake of this or that visible form. For instance, illuminating this particular visible circle and its tangent on the chalkboard is not the goal of the demonstration. In fact, the circle on the board only approximates the intended circle, which is not possible to draw on a chalkboard in its intelligible form. When a geometer performs a demonstration by drawing a circle on the board, she realizes that the circle is merely an approximation and that the characteristics of the universal circle that she seeks to illuminate with the demonstration are only suggested by the visible form. The geometer is interested in the universalizable claim being made about all idealized circles, not about the particular/visible circle on the board. "They make the statements for the sake of the square itself and the diagonal itself, but not for the sake of the one that they draw" (510 d-e). While human beings see the image of the circle and its tangent on the board, and this engenders imagination and trust in the soul, the intelligible property of the circle and the tangent is not visible. The universal statement of proposition 3.16, for example, in Euclid's *Elements* states that, if one draws a straight line (a tangent) at right angles to the end of the diameter of a circle, then one cannot draw another straight line between the circle and this tangent (Euclid 1956, 3.16). According to the divided line argument, such a claim is not based on trust or imagination (the affections of the soul associated with the visible). Rather the affection in the soul cultivated by this property of the circle and its tangent is thought [*dianoia*] (510 e).

We are then told that this is the form that Socrates meant by "intelligible"; it is a form that can only be thought, not seen. But it remains a presupposition. The beings [*mathematikē*] of thought [*dianoia*] are presupposed by the investigation to be totally transparent first beginnings. They are necessarily treated as if *everybody knew* what this form meant, and therefore, the researcher experiences no hesitation in using them as a first beginning. That is to say, it is a matter of *common sense*. However, Socrates argues that they are not transparently meaningful, they are only hypotheses.

In relation to this presupposed meaning of the form, we find the language of necessity employed again:

> [A] soul is compelled [*anagkazō*] to use hypotheses/assumptions in searching for it. It does not go to a beginning since it is unable to escape or rise out of its hypotheses. And it uses as images those things of which images were imitating the things below, and in comparison with which they are imagined [*doxazō*] to be clear and are honored (511 a).

This is a striking claim. Not only does the thought (*dianoia*) of the geometer and the biologist incorrectly presuppose the hypothesis as a first beginning, they do this *by necessity*; she is "compelled to use hypotheses." The *mathematicos'* thinking is necessarily appropriated and carried along by a wave of necessity originating and ending outside of the investigator. That is to say, the investigator does not freely start with the hypothesis. There is, rather, a motive force (necessity) originating elsewhere that appropriates the investigator and the investigation. Should we call the origin *common sense*? Common sense remains for us a given, a ground, to which we are shackled *necessarily*. It has already appropriated our sensuous and intellectual faculties in a way that conceals itself as a structure of necessity. We imagine ourselves free to think what we like, to investigate what we like, but common sense does not originate with any individual; it is that in which the individual first belongs, as individual. Before we ever come to think, we have already been enveloped within its meaning horizon. *Oi polloi* first makes thinking possible by placing us in a meaningful relation to a world, to others, to ourselves. As such common sense (*the many*), is a force of necessity; it forms the region of human endeavor. We think that we freely select a refined discipline to pursue and develop, but common sense has already made the beings of the world in their various regions *appear legitimately worth pursuing*. Indeed, as we observed earlier, *oi polloi* supports and celebrates endeavors that secure its presuppositions, while chastising and discouraging those that do not. Perhaps common sense remains the "internal" expression of this "external" origin of legitimacy; the internal, thus, connects one wave-length to the series of external waves to which it belongs.

If we combine this image with that of the cave of book VII, then we see the dramatic enactment of this merely geometric presentation of the *dianoia* line segment.

> And if there had been among them any honors, and praise for one another and there were prizes for the man who is sharpest at perceiving the things [shadows] that go by, and remembers best which [shadows] usually pass [*poreuō*] first, which later, and which at the same time, and from these things is best able to divine [*apomanteuomai*] what will come (516 c-d).

The beings encountered in the third tier of the divided line (the *mathematikē*) and the affections these beings have on the soul (*dianoia*) make possible an intellectual relation to the beings in the cave and on the cave walls. That is to say, a knowledge system comes into being that universalizes the relations between the beings. There are laws that govern the images passing by on the cave walls and these laws are "perceived" by *dianoia*. After having been initiated into the structure of the *oi polloi* . . . after having watched for years with one's fellow cave citizens the beings/images pass before one on the wall, the "soul is compelled to investigate [*zētein anagkazetai*] from hypotheses and passes [*poreuō*] to an end, not to a beginning [*archē*]" (510 b). The visible beings passing by on the wall are no longer treated as beings, but as images belonging to a knowledge system. A legal order is discovered that governs the shapes and sequence of the beings, an order that is communicable to those particularly skilled in such modes of thinking and research. The law is applicable to the passing beings as images that belong to what appears to possess greater reality: *mathematikē*. *Oi polloi* celebrates the accomplishment of such a system based upon their own presuppositions (they originate from puppeteers [*thaumatopoioi*[2]]), after all) and crowns the learned with laurels of achievement. Indeed, *these are* real achievements of *dianoia*. Anyone with eyes would recognize the world-historical accomplishment of the *Elements* and the *Principia*, for example, but Socrates suggests that they rest on hypotheses treated as beginnings (*archai*) rather than hypotheses that make the turn back toward the beginning possible. Indeed, one might argue that each presumes a different originating hypothesis. Each knowledge system, the *Elements* and the *Principia*, remains distinct precisely because they unfold from different originating presuppositions. Non-Euclidean geometry lends further credibility to this argument by the fact that it transforms the discipline by entertaining yet another originating hypothesis. Of course, this gives rise (necessarily?) to the question of whether there belongs a historical character to these paradigm shifts in hypothetical first beginnings.

Socrates follows the detailed presentation of *dianoia* with an elaboration of the earlier description of the final fourth tier of the divided line. Earlier, Socrates had described this segment of the line as the part in which the soul "goes to the beginning [*archē*] without hypothesis" (510 b). In the second articulation, Socrates more fully fleshes out the object and affection of this part of the soul. The object is an intelligible being that

> *logos* reaches with the power [*dunamis*] of dialectic [*dialegesthai*], making the hypotheses be not first beginnings [*archai*] but [true] hypotheses (like springboards) in order to go as far as that without hypothesis [*anupothetos*] at the beginning of the whole [*epi tēn tou pantos arxēn*]. Reaching this, it takes hold of it [*archē*] again so as to go down to the end (511 b).

Socrates has added the concept of the "power of dialectic" to the earlier articulation. Here we observe something resembling the common practice of Socrates. The fourth kind of being on the line is the form [*eidos*], not as hypothesis, but as beginning. Even though this segment appears in the image as a linear progression from the *mathematikē/dianoia* segment, it does not exactly reflect linearity in practice. If dialectic is the art of turning, then the being of the fourth segment is reached not in a linear fashion, but through a form of turning, a kind of discursive discombobulation. We observe this in the dialogues in practice when Socrates asks his "what is" questions. In the context of the *Republic*, we are already in the cave at the beginning. The entire divided line is represented in the cave, except (perhaps) for the fourth segment. The concept of justice emerges as a discursive assertion and appeal is made to the poets for discursive support. Socrates then *turns* the *logos* and places the self-evident concept of justice into question. Dialectic holds the discursive power to confuse and unhinge the self-evident hypothesis from its solidarity with common sense. Dialectic is itself a discursive power, a power owing its existence to the limited constraints of language and finitude, but a power nonetheless. As the quoted passage makes clear, dialectic remains a power that exploits the limits of language in order to reach back to the presupposition governing a knowledge system. On the one hand, it makes sense that the dialectical engagement with the presupposition may hold the power to make the presupposition evident—to disclose the meaning of the presupposition, qua presupposition. On the other hand, one perceives a hope and desire in Socrates' remarks that dialectic may hold the power to reach something more robust—a form that is not merely discursive, but is somehow ontologically secure and everlasting. I suppose that the interpretation to which one adheres depends upon how one understands the meaning of "at the beginning of the whole" [*epi tēn tou pantos arxēn*] (511 b). Does Socrates mean the beginning of the whole of all being? Some have interpreted it this way, suggesting that going back "to the beginning of the whole" means going back all the way to "the good." On this reading, Socrates gives the account Glaucon demanded from him; he provides the connection between the good and the likeness with the sun. To this end, Adam suggests that "after the idea of the good has been reached, the dialectician's conception of the *eidos* is accurate and complete" (1902, 71).

But what if Socrates means by "at the beginning of the whole" the beginning of a sequence of arguments constituting a particular science? That is to say, by arriving at the beginning of the whole, one has reached the conceptual presupposition upon which the knowledge system is based. In this way, one illuminates the formal character of "life," for instance, that subtends the system of a biological science.[3] If the latter, a further question emerges. Does the illumination of the form reveal the meaning of the presupposition? Or does it reveal "life," as such, prior to discourse and argument? In either case, a form is supposed to become intelligible by *nous* and precisely not by dialectic. Dialectic remains discursive. *Nous* is the power of the soul that grasps forms in their intelligibility (511 d); it is *aneu logou,* without *logos*.[4] It may be that dialectic places one in a compartment such that *nous* can receive the intelligible form, if one exists; but dialectic cannot "grasp" the meaning of the form. If the human being possesses the faculties to reach below the merely discursive and conceptual to something more robust and everlasting (if this something exists at all), then dialectic is the way the soul turns toward this being, and *nous* [intellection] is the affection of the soul that this being produces.

However, there is a way of reading the last line of Socrates' account of the fourth tier that raises doubts about whether the human has escaped the finitude of discourse by achieving the perception of this segment. He says that the soul here makes "no use whatever of anything sensed, but using forms themselves, through forms into forms, it also ends in forms" (511 c). But what if this strange sentence says nothing other than: using concept, the soul goes through concepts to concepts and ends in concepts too? In such a case, the soul never escapes the finitude and instability of discourse.

After Socrates gives his second account of the intelligible region within the image of the line, Glaucon appropriately finds the fourth segment, in particular, still confusing. He complains that he does not understand it adequately, but that he grasps [*manthanō*] that Socrates wants "to distinguish what is and is intelligible, contemplated [*theōreō*] by the knowledge [*epistēmē*] of dialectic, as being clearer [*saphesteron*] than that contemplated by what are called the arts" (511 c). Here in Glaucon's recapitulation of Socrates' second account, we have the formulation of the intelligible line segment for the third time in two pages. However, it is worth noting that each time the intelligible region and its affections are articulated, *it changes*. There exist differences between Socrates' first account and his second, to be sure; but Glaucon's recapitulation involves fairly significant discrepancies. Among several of these, we cite two here. First, Socrates refers to the "power [*dunamis*] of dialectic," while Glaucon speaks of the "knowledge [*epistēmē*] of dialectic." Power and knowledge are not only different words, they are conceptually and phenomenologically distinct. Second, Glaucon says that Socrates distinguishes the two segments of the intelligible realm by "clarity," while Socrates actually distinguishes them by their free-relation/unfree-relation to the hypothesis. The point I wish to make here is that as the intelligible realm comes to image in speech, the dialogue puts on display a certain inconsistency and ambivalence regarding it. To be sure, the same account may be understood by each participant (Socrates, Glaucon and the reader) in a different way. That would mean, of course, that insofar as the intelligible line segment comes to be in speech in the *Republic*, it is precisely not "intelligible," if intelligible means to be capable of either universal expression or consistent intellection across tongues, ears and minds.

Another feature of the intelligible line segment that is repeated in Glaucon's recapitulation for the third time in only two pages is our principle theme: *necessity*. "The beginnings in the arts [technē][or the sciences of the third tier]," he says,

> are hypotheses; and although those who contemplate them are compelled [*anagkazō*] to do so by thought [*dianoia*] rather than the sense perceptions, these men ... it seems to you, do not hold intelligence about these things, even though the things are intelligible with a beginning; and you seem to me to call the comportment [*hexis*] of geometers (and such [technicians]) thought but not intellect, as if thought is something between opinion [*doxa*] and intellect [*nous*] (511 c—d).

By quoting this passage, I do not intend to offer an interpretation or a critique of Glaucon's understanding of Socrates' account. Rather, I wish only to highlight the repetition of the force of necessity in the intelligible region's cosmology of beings and affections. It was important enough to Plato to have his characters affirm the force of necessity in the intelligible realm three times in two pages.

At the beginning of this section, we pointed to places in the text in which Plato has the dialogue participants exert force [*anagkazō*] on other interlocutors in order to undergo interrogation. As we showed there, the verb first appears at the beginning of book one when Thrasymachus presents his claim that "the just is for the use of the stronger, and the unjust is profitable and useful for oneself" (344 c); he tries to leave after pouring "a great flood of speech into our ears" (344 d). However, the other men present "compelled [*anagkazō*] him to remain" (344 d). That is to say, the members of the dialogue forced Thrasymachus to flesh out this radical claim. In my view, Thrasymachus, in asserting that justice is the advantage of the stronger, gives expression to what he thinks is a novel *hypothesis*. He intends to overturn the presumption that subtends the common opinion about justice. In doing so, Thrasymachus asserts an intelligible presumption that forces/compels the participants and the reader to "behold [justice] with thought, not sensation" (511 c).[5] Consequently, I think that there is some correlation between two things. On the one hand, the many dramatic events of the dialogue in which characters are *forced* to stay, to speak, to give accounts; and, on the other hand, the necessity which acts through the hypothesis in the intelligible line segment to compel [*anagkazō*] *Oi Theōmenoi* to behold the beings of the world through the lens of the hypothesis/presumption, to see the beings of the world organized in accordance with it.

NOTES

1. Adam (1900) comments that the only beginning without hypothesis is the idea of the good. For him, the line represents the ascent up to the good. But as my example of biology below indicates, on my reading, we only get to the *being* of the thing under investigation, not the good. In fact, Socrates' own example (510 c) from geometry reflects this as well.

2. At 235 b of the *Sophist*, Plato puts this same term into the mouth of the Stranger to describe the sophist.

3. Compare Shorey's note 5 to this passage. "παντὸς ἀρχήν taken literally lends support to the view that Plato is thinking of an absolute first principle. But in spite of the metaphysical suggestions for practical purposes the παντὸς ἀρχή may be the virtual equivalent of the ἱκανόν of the *Phaedo*. It is the ἀρχή on which all in the particular case depends and is reached by dialectical agreement, not by arbitrary assumption" (1969, 511 b).

4. Compare Adam's comment at 511 b (1900): "λόγος is not the faculty of reason [or intellectual perception], which is νοῦς." Also, see Aristotle's *Posterior Analytics* (100 b 9–13) and *Nicomachean Ethics* (1143 b ff. & 1142 a 25).

5. "διανοίᾳ μὲν ἀναγκάζονται ἀλλὰ μὴ αἰσθήσεσιν αὐτὰ θεᾶσθαι οἱ θεώμενοι" (511 c).

Chapter 5

Necessity in the Cave

In the previous chapter, we offered an analysis of the intelligible line segment in order to understand how necessity functions in this famous image. We observed there a conception of necessity as a motive force compelling thought in both of the intelligible line segments. In chapter 5, we carry this conception of necessity as a motive force over into the allegory of the cave. We argue that, while the divided line is a static image, the cave allegory serves to set that image into motion. Moreover, necessity shows itself as *compulsion* or *force* not only in the movements of humans out of the cave, but also in their return to the cave. Further, we suggest that the movement of the human soul into *aporia*—that crucial Platonic intellectual phenomenon—is achieved as a matter of compulsion [*anagkē*] or force. That is to say, *aporia* does not occur as a consequence of free action, but is exhibited in the cave as a matter of force/necessity.

To recapitulate and situate ourselves in the sequence of events leading to the cave allegory: Socrates told Adeimantus that the group had failed to take the longer route by which they might come in the argument to the most urgent study for the guardians, the greatest study, the study of the good. Despite this neglect, Adeimantus urges Socrates to articulate his opinions about it anyway. But Socrates asserts that opinions are ugly in comparison to knowledge and attempts to free himself from the task. However, Glaucon interrupts and demands that Socrates continue with his opinions, even if the road will be an abbreviated and misleading one compared to the road to knowledge. Socrates will later claim that this demand of Glaucon's is in fact a force of necessity: "you are culpable for compelling [*anagkazō*] me to speak my opinions about it" (509 c). The necessitating demand gives rise to a series of related images. The first is a visible metaphor (the sun) surrogate for the object of the greatest study (the good). As an example of a visible being, the sun is complex because, on the one hand, one cannot actually look at the sun without destroying the power of seeing. That is to say, the sun may not be a properly visible being since "seeing" it ruins the power of sight (Plato 1998, 99 e). On

79

the other hand, the sun is complex because it is the "visible" being that makes all vision of visible beings possible. The sun provides what is *necessary* for vision, for the perceptive soul to see. Yet, this necessary condition for sight remains outside of the perceptive grasp of sight itself.

Having obtained Glaucon's assent to this claim, Socrates argues that this resembles what the good does for the intellectual part of the soul. It provides the *necessary* conditions for the intellectual perception of knowledge and truth. As we saw in chapter 2, knowledge (of wisdom, courage, moderation and justice) without the good is not *legitimate* knowledge. The sun lights up visible beings for the power of sight; the good lights up intelligible beings for intellect. Socrates then tells Glaucon to noetically grasp [*noeō*] that "these two things *are*, one rules [*basileuō*] the noetic kind and place, the other rules the visible" (509 d). The faculty of sight and things seen are ruled over by the sun, while the faculty of noesis and things noetically perceived are ruled over by the good.

In my view, we observe the same problem here that we articulated in chapter 3. The "truth of being" rules over *noesis*, not the good; the good does not rule over noetic experience directly if at all, but is *beyond* it. Ignoring this problem produced by his own argument, Socrates introduces the divided line. It is with this next image that Socrates brings the visible into relation with the intelligible. Moreover, the image is geometrical. Before this image, there was not an explicit reason to think of the visible image as anything other than an analogy to make the intelligible intuitable. Now, however, Socrates unites them on the same continuous line and places them in proportion to one another: "take a line cut in two unequal sections, then go back and cut each section again in the same proportion [*logos*], the one of the visible kind, the other of the noetic kind" (509 d). Having completed this geometrical presentation[1] of the relation between the visible beings and their affections in the soul with the intellectual beings and their affections in the soul, Socrates begins book VII with "After this, " I said, "form an image [*apeikazō*] of our nature [*physis*] in its education [*paideia*] and lack of education [*apaideusia*]" (514 a).

The first line of book VII continues the thought from the previous book: "after this . . . " What is the connection? What work does the image-forming of book VII continue from book VI? In my view, the divided line may be Plato's way of disclosing the limitations of these sorts of human technological compositions. Despite giving intellectual and imaginative access to beings in a way that would not otherwise be possible, do *models* intended to represent nature, nevertheless, unavoidably deceive in some way? While the image plots the beings in accordance with a graspable rational order, it is an abstract, geometrical, two-dimensional, motionless depiction of the kinds of beings in the world and the soul that experiences them. Perhaps one could argue that the dialogue here makes visible two different forms of necessity: a logical one and a natural one.

By way of comparison, the dialogue *Parmenides* (where the term *anagkē* appears at least seventy times) seems animated by a similar question. I would argue that the problem made visible in the dialogue between Parmenides and the young Aristotle is precisely whether logical and natural necessity are conceptually identical and whether logical necessity can account for experience [*paschō*] (Plato 1996). A similar dilemma seems to animate the relation between the divided line and the cave allegory. Thus, after presenting the geometrical image, Socrates exhorts Glaucon to form another image, one "of our nature in its education and lack of education" (514 a).[2] Here and in the account that follows, we observe that Socrates charges Glaucon to cast an image through which they may see the divided line set into motion. In a way, then, the new image will allow the script of the divided line to be enacted on the stage. Interpreted in this way, the relation between the divided line and the allegory of the cave resembles that between the *Republic* and the *Timaeus*. If, indeed, the conversation in the *Republic* is the one that the interlocutors had that is mentioned at the beginning of the *Timaeus*, then the pairing of those two dialogues and these two images is similar. At the beginning of *Timaeus*, Socrates expresses a desire to see the city that was constructed in speech put into motion in accordance with its nature. He wants to see it at war and in negotiation with other cities. "It is as if someone who gazed upon beautiful animals somewhere, either produced by the art of painting or truly living but keeping their peace, were to get a desire to gaze upon them moving and contending in some struggle appropriate to their bodies" (2001, 19 b-c). The city in speech is too static and abstract to know if it is a good one. We wish to see it in motion. The divided line shares this characteristic. In this way, the cosmological speech of the *Timaeus* is to the *Republic* as the allegory of the cave is to the divided line. There are several important differences between the divided line and the cave allegory, but the existence of movement in the latter is certainly one of them.

What kind of movement? The image cast portrays the movement of our "nature," but not just any aspect of our nature; it puts on display our nature concerning [*peri*] education [*paideias*] and lack of education [*peri apaideusias*]. At first glance, the subject of the image appears rather straightforward: the movement we can expect to observe in the image will be from ignorance to knowledge. If *phyō* [to grow] in the word *physis* is emphasized, then the example may be seen in embryological terms. The nature of the human moves from ignorance to enlightenment like an acorn grows into a tree. But this simple understanding of the image is complicated by the fact that the movement is not unidirectional. The prisoner returns to the cave after having been released. Moreover, it is further complicated by the *practical* examples of the philosophical nature (qua Socratic practice) that we encounter in the dialogues. If knowledge is the measure of enlightenment, then our philosopher never grows into it, except negatively—he comes to know that he does not know.

Another way of interpreting *phyō* in relation to education [*paideias*] and lack of education [*peri apaideusias*] might be achieved by reference to the German Romantic conception of *Bildung*, or "formation," although without Romanticism's extreme optimism: "cast an image of our nature in its formation [Bildung] and deformation." As such, the image presents a picture of the human being and its cities in their uniquely human mortal existence. Such an interpretation may receive support by stepping back from the myopic analysis of the allegory of the cave and the divided line and looking at the movement of the dialogue as a whole. Once the dialogue is compelled into motion by the interlocutors, a city (a soul writ large) comes to be. Even though the city is technologically crafted, it resembles a living, organic being; for, it is *born* in speech, becomes educated through books III and IV, then comes to its full, functional maturity at the very beginning of book V. At maturity, in books VI and VII, the living being *turns* toward the structure of its formation in a dialectical and/or critical fashion. Like all organic beings, the city is a mortal being (546 a).[3] Book VIII articulates the city's descent into corruption and final obliteration. The origin of its decay is precisely the origin of its birth: *erōs*. That is to say, the force of erotic *necessity* originates all cities and all living beings. Yet, in the context of the *Republic*, erotic necessity is also the force that calculation fails to subdue, insofar as the rulers by necessity miscalculate "the nuptial number.[4]" Thus, on the one hand, *erōs* originates life, while also driving the living to risk this very life for the perpetuation of *erōs* itself. And, on the other hand, *erōs* not only originates the movement into life, but also, in originating it, contains the seed of passing away as well. Finally, in the myth of Er, book X casts an image of the motions that constitute this death as well as those by which a soul (a city writ small) passes back into life, movements—as we will analyze later—that are governed by the "spindle of necessity" (616 c). If we understand the cave allegory in the light of this larger erotic trajectory of the dialogue as a whole, then the imperative "cast an image of our nature in its formation and its deformation" appears to refer to the cycle of a nature through the lens of necessity. Individual organisms, individual humans, and the plural systems we name cities are caught in the wave of erotic necessity that constitutes the origin of their formation and deformation. While it belongs to human nature to strive toward the production of everlasting systems of knowledge, moral certitude, and political constitution, these systems and even this sort of human striving belong ontologically to the order of necessity. As such, by necessity, for *"everything that has come into being there is decay,* not even a composition such as this will remain for all time; it will be dissolved" in order to make way for the next "turning round of circles [of life]" (546 a), the next birth of conceptual order.

Moreover, human nature has its own form of cultivation and lack of cultivation, a form intimately connected with the appearance and perception of the beings articulated in the divided line. In it, Plato presents us with the mark of a specifically *human* finitude. The image cast portrays the undergoing/ suffering [*pathos*] of the movements of cultivation and de-cultivation. The beings of the divided line come to disclose themselves to us through *paideia*, but equally hide themselves as well. For the most part, scholars interpret the cave to be the space of the uneducated (*apaideusia*). In this interpretation, the human beings that reside chained to face the images on the cave walls are uneducated until someone comes along to drag them out of the cave into a state of education. The movement expressed by the allegory is interpreted, therefore, as one from an uneducated state to a state of education.[5]

In contrast to this hegemonic interpretation, I will argue that the image betrays the opposite movement. In fact, the order in which the events are articulated in the first line is precisely the reverse of the standard reading. Socrates exhorts us to "make an image of our nature in its education [*paideia*] and lack of education [*apaideusia*]." Certainly, even though scholars suppose the movement of the image to begin with "lack of education," there is no logical necessity for Plato to have Socrates name *paideia* first for this interpretation to remain relevant. Still, in what follows, I will offer an interpretation of the allegory as if Plato intends to present the image in the order articulated: that is to say, as though *paideia* is our nature in the cave and *apaideusia* is the movement out of it. That is to say, I will argue that the image presents the human being first in its enculturation. *Paideia* is a concept that names the movement in which the human being becomes one among the *oi polloi*. However, in my reading, being released from the cave somehow by a hypothetical someone, being *forced* out of the cave, resembles the experience of *aporia*. *Aporia*, I will argue, is precisely a form of *apaideusia*; and the whole of book VII, including the "higher studies," serves to illuminate the experience of *aporia*—an experience the articulation of which might be Plato's central contribution to the history of philosophy.

Our reading requires reformulating the first line of the cave allegory once again. However, this new translation of the relevant terms should strike one as familiar, at least in terms of the history of interpretation of the concept of *paideia*: "cast an image of our nature in its *enculturation* and its *deculturation*" (514 a). With this formulation, the cave image betrays the movement of the structures of *paideia*, of enculturation. It presents an image of the means by which a human being becomes appropriated by a surrounding community in accordance with its human nature. That is to say, if human nature shows itself as the way that the human works [*ergon*] and dwells on the earth, then it must be understood as a nature that is enabled by being enveloped in images and discourses; for the systems of images and discourses in which the human being dwells are those that reveal and organize the world to human beings and, thus, enable the work they perform to be the beings that they are.[6]

> "See humans as if they were dwelling in an underground cave . . . from childhood both their legs and necks are in straps so that they remain in the same place, only looking forward, lacking the power to turn their heads by the straps. Light for them is kindled by a fire far above and behind them. Between the fire and the bound humans is a road above, along which see a wall, having been built just like the screens that puppet-handlers [*thaumatopoioi*] set in front of humans and above which they reveal puppets."

> "I see," he said.

> "See too humans carrying objects [*skeuos*] along this wall, holding them above the wall, as well as statues of men and other animals made of stone, wood and all sorts of stuff . . . some carriers utter sounds while others are silent."

> "Strange [*atopos*] image, you speak of" he said," and strange [*atopos*] bound men."

> "They are like us." (514 a - 515 a).[7]

The human beings in this pitiful condition remain entombed in the earth with only an artificial light to bring color to their world. Moreover, their entire understanding of existence is determined by what appears and moves in shadows and images in front of them, mere projections of artificial compositions cast by the light. The artificial light is responsible for mediating the cave-dwellers' experience of these beings; it allows the beings to appear in a certain way. Evoking the description of the child of the good, this artificial light is a third thing that bestows a meaning that must be distinct from the propositional/definitional content expressed by the analysis of the beings themselves. This is crucial. If, in the competitions of prediction and analysis that take place in the cave among those that dwell there, someone were to offer a definition of the being moving across the cave wall, the artificial light and its contribution to the interpretation of the being remains invisible. The genus/species content of the definition does not contain a reference to the meaning bestowed upon the being by the artificial light.

Further, there are humans that exploit the artificial light and use it to organize the lives of the cave-dwellers. The shadow projections of the artifacts are in no way neutral appearances. Yet, not only beings originate in artifice for them, but their movements too are artificial. Their motion only mimics self-motion, insofar as it is determined and calculated by the *thaumatopoioi*. That is to say, the cave-dweller's understanding of nature (being born, growing, dying, changing in accordance with location and altering) remains wholly mediated by the artificial creations of these human beings that appear removed from the chains and restricted movements of their fellow cave-dwellers. The reader feels an immediate sympathy for the bound figures at the bottom of the cave. One imagines that Glaucon feels pity too; for, he replies that both the image and the prisoners are strange [*atopos*]. To Glaucon, the space of the cave appears to be *nowhere*. But then Socrates says: "they are like us." Thus, in effect, Socrates corrects Glaucon's judgment by suggesting that, in fact, the cave and its prisoners are *everywhere*—and we too are like them.

In what way are we "like them"? In my reading, Socrates' image above depicts our nature in its *paideia*—that is to say, in its enculturation. Our entire educational lives lie in the cave. We are prisoners of the cave insofar as the world becomes illuminated as a consequence of the conceptual economy into which we are born. Our parents and friends are mechanisms of enculturation; Religion too envelops us in a culture and bestows meanings upon the things that are revealed through its light; as we move through the formal education of primary school, we are further formed into *oi polloi*; insofar as we are compelled to participate in our city's laws and institutions, we become encultured; when we marry, as we raise our children, when we prepare for death, we are being educated in the cave and initiated into its world disclosure.

What about the space of the university? Would it lie outside of the cave for Plato? I have doubts. We are often inclined to locate the university (where one reads the "allegory of the cave") in a privileged position above ground and in a non-artificial light. However, for Plato, I would argue, the education that takes place in the university can in no way represent an ascent from the cave. The university appropriates its students and faculty through the mechanism of artificial enculturation too. Literary history, the study of poetry, the departments of history and philosophy, the labs of science and the chalkboards of mathematics—all of the university's disciplines come to have meaning insofar as they are means of lighting up objects in accordance with the artificial fire of the cave. The universities are the spaces in which the most sophisticated guardians of the conceptual economy into which we become encultured dwell. These comments are not intended as a screed against the contemporary university. My reflection here should not be read as a judgment about the "decline" of the university. Rather, they are merely descriptive observations without moral judgment of the kind of activity that every human soul undergoes as it becomes a citizen among *oi polloi*. The universities are the most refined of the sources of the artificial light of the cave. When Socrates references the "honors, praise for one another and prizes for the man who is sharpest at perceiving the things [shadows] that go by [on the cave walls], and remembers best which [shadows] usually pass [*poreuō*] first, which later, and which at the same time, and from these things is best able to divine [*apomanteuomai*] what will come [next]" (516 c-d), certainly he describes the life of many institutions in human life, but his example most clearly describes both the activity and the "light" that we observe emitted from the modern university. The university too lies inside the cave and is a mechanism of enculturation. We celebrate the cultivation of knowledge systems that come to light there and we bestow honors and praises upon the most sophisticated of those in the university that come to grasp what appears to be a *necessary* sequence in the order of shadows that pass before us. These scholars formulate methods of prediction that enable us to organize our lives around the shadows more securely. However, for Socrates, they never observe that the shadows and the forces that connect them to each other, that constitute their systems of knowledge, originate from hidden artifacts carried by *thaumatopoioi*[8] in an artificial light.

Of course, the *Republic* often makes visible the ways that poetry becomes employed as a mechanism of enculturation in all levels of education. As we observed earlier, everyone in the cave throws around the phrases of the poets in a way that attempts to appeal to them for support in argument, even though the meaning of the poem itself remains obscure and in need of interpretation. In fact, in the case of Cephalus and Polemarchus, the utterances of the poets are interpreted through the artificial light of the cave; they are appropriated to the argument in light of a very specific situation and discourse that is composed not only by the sayings of the poets, but by the festival of Bendis, by the political situation of the day, by the class circumstances of the interlocutors and their individual histories within the city, by the spirit of competition between Socrates and Thrasymachus, by the erotic sensibilities of Glaucon, among many other things—all of which are conditioned by the artificial glow from the fire that makes them visible. The utterances of the poets are constitutive and form many of the puppets that are used to cast shadows upon the cave walls and perhaps also the way the artificial light shines; however, the poets are not present to answer the interlocutors' questions. Their poems are rather a matter of constitutive inheritance, reaching a sculpting hand into the present from out of the past. They are a necessary condition for every level of education and for every station of personal and civic life. But they weave our identities together in a way that remains closed to us in all but the most rare events of human experience (*aporiai*).

Poetry is not the only constitutive discourse problematically employed as a mechanism of enculturation (both inside and outside of the university). In Plato's dialogue the *Sophist*, we learn that philosophy too remains one of the images that becomes projected on the cave walls in the light of the artificial fire. Having reached another impasse in the investigation searching for "the sophist," the stranger suggests that he and Theaetetus must risk appearing to commit "parricide" [*patraloias*] (1996, 241d). For, "it will be necessary [*anagkaios*] for us to put to the test the argument of my father Parmenides" (my translation, 241d). Consequently, the stranger will raise doubts about whether non-being *is not* and being *is*. The problem that necessitates this cross-examination of Parmenides is the discourses that involve image [*eikonas*], imitation [*mimema*], and phantasm [*phantasma*] (like the discourse called the *Republic*), all of which both appear *to be* and also *not to be*.

The most compelling [*anagkaios*] way to begin this pseudo-parricide is by calling into question precisely what seems most self-evident [*enargēs*] (1996, 242 b). To this end, the stranger begins by raising doubts about the quantity and quality of beings that we have been taught like children to believe exist by, not only the inherited discourses of Parmenides, but by those of all of the "most precise" [*akribēs*] (1996, 245 e) philosophers.

> Some sort of *muthos*, that's what each appears to me to have told us, as though we were children. One[9] tells us that the beings are three, that at one time some of them make war upon each other somehow, and at another time, when they've become friends, they have marriages and children and provide nurture for their offspring . . . And the Eleatic tribe in our regions . . . explains that "all things" . . . are in fact one.[10] Then, some Ionian[11] and later some Sicilian[12] Muses realized that it was safest to weave together both views and say that Being is both many and one, and that it is held together by enmity and friendship. The reason is that it continuously comes together in differing with itself—so say the more high-strung of the Muses. But the softer ones relaxed this constant tension and say that sometimes, under the influence of Aphrodite, the All is one and friendly, and at other times it is many and at war with itself through some strife (1996, 242 c - 243 a).

Here we observe the utterances of the most precise [*akribēs*] (1996, 245 e) philosophers presented like shadows on the cave walls, like myths presented to children. Every educated person knows these phantasms that are cast by the artificial light passing through the puppets of Parmenides, Heraclitus, and Empedocles. Moreover, every educated person is expected to be able to articulate them. Children go to school, listen to teachers, and repeat back to the teachers the "opinions of the philosophers" when they are required to take an exam. The children most precise at articulating these statements win awards and perform well on standardized exams. Young people attend university and receive a more sophisticated account. They use these sayings as a ground upon which to write essays. They take exams in which they parrot the sayings of Parmenides and Heraclitus. Exam question one: what was the principal argument of Parmenides? Answer: All things are one. Exam question two: what was the principal argument of Heraclitus? Answer: All things flow. Those students most adept at guessing what comes next in the glow of the artificial light win awards and funding to work at the most prestigious institutions. Enculturation involves not only the verses of the poets, but also the musings of the philosophers, the methods of the scientists, and the demonstrations of the mathematicians. Their concepts and/or systems float by on the walls of the cave as well. It is a question whether, for Plato, the philosophers attached to these *logoi* were ever outside of the cave; however, the *logoi* themselves are certainly not.

The stranger follows this rehearsal of "what seems most self-evident [*enargēs*]" (1996, 242 b) by claiming that, even though he has inherited all of these sayings, took the tests and passed the exams, he now realizes that he never understood a word of it.

> Do you, Theaetetus, ever understand what in gods' name they are saying? For my part, when I was younger, whenever someone would mention this thing that now perplexes [*aporeō*] us, namely Non-being, I thought I had a precise understanding of it. But now you see how far we've gone into an impasse [*aporia*] about it (1996, 243 b).

What does it mean to say with Parmenides "'all things,' as they are called, are in fact one" (1996, 242 d)? We have all taken a course titled "ancient philosophy," in which we read the extant poem of Parmenides. But "now" that we try to work through an interpretation of what "being" means in this light, we are "at a loss" [*aporeō*]. The stranger interrogates a kind of imaginary puppet of Parmenides in a passage which Heidegger thought suitable to choose as the originating sentence of his magnum opus *Being and Time* (Heidegger 1993): "since we've reached an impasse [*aporia*], you [Parmenides] make sufficiently apparent to us what in the world you want to point to wherever you utter 'being.' For it is clear that you've recognized these things for a long time, while we supposed we knew earlier, but have now reached an impasse [*aporia*]" (1996, 244 a). With Plato, we are perhaps in a unique position *vis à vis* the inherited philosophical tradition. Might we argue that, in fact, it is only with Plato that we hold and are held by such a tradition? We find ourselves in the cave, having inherited a tradition of discourses about being. Similar to the poetic tradition, the discourses envelop us, organize our institutions, our interactions, and stimulate research in the cave of human imagination. Such is the hermeneutical situation in which Plato finds himself. What then is Plato's contribution to this history? The theory of the forms? Platonism? Are these to be added to the discourses of the more precise philosophers and handed down as yet further contributions of content, filling out the body of the history of interpretations of being? The standard model gives rise to a narrative of a history of disagreement. Similarly, the history of science (to quote Canguilhem (2008, 26) can be interpreted as nothing other than a history of error. It seems as if something has been missed in the descriptions of the phenomenon of human philosophical thought if it is interpreted only to produce lists of alternative and mutually exclusive ontological paradigms.

In any case, I would argue that, rather than appending novel content to the tradition of ontology, Plato makes its *reception* central to his philosophical endeavor. The concept that Plato creates and contributes to the history of philosophy is not exactly a concept. Rather, he makes an *experience* [*pathos*] visible. An experience without which there is no philosophy and yet it is an experience that does not exist in any of the philosophical curricula in the cave: Plato's contribution to the received tradition is the experience of *aporia*. If books II, III, IV, and V contain the articulation of the *enculturation* that belongs to the cave of the *Kallipolis*, then book VII might be said to be the book in which the possibility of *deculturation* occurs, insofar as the book contains all the "sciences" which occasion a turn of the soul. That is to say, each of these sciences cultivates the experience of *aporia*—which does not produce a conceptual content, but rather an intellectual void, an intellectual void that is nevertheless intellectual. We observe precisely this phenomenon in the stranger's interrogation (quasi-parricide) of received discourses of Parmenides and the other most precise philosophers in which a form of the word "*aporia*" is articulated four times on one page. If we then extrapolate this *aporia* with respect to the received philosophical tradition from the *Sophist* to the cave allegory of the *Republic*, then, instead of interpreting the movement of the cave as one from ignorance to knowledge, we can interpret it as one from *paideia* to *aporia*, or from enculturation to deculturation.

Back to the cave. We are told that the condition [*pathos*] (514 a) of the cave is a matter of necessity. The cave-dwellers are "compelled [*anagkazō*] to keep their heads motionless" (515 a). As said before, they are "like us"; so a central part of what we suffer [*pathos*], qua a universal condition of human nature, is to be locked into a system of images (a system that includes beings, movements, and the artificial light that makes them visible). Moreover, being locked into such a system is not a matter of choice, but a matter of necessity. One imagines the situation of the human being in the cave in a similar way as a bee in a hive of bees or an ant in a mound of ants. Each bee's identity, its very meaning in the world, is determined by its relation to the hive—what is good, beautiful, virtuous, heroic, and valuable for the individual bee remains wholly shaped by what preserves the present and future of the hive. Further, the system that exhibits the meaning of, say, virtue or beauty is not a matter of individual achievement, choice, or collective vote, but is rather a matter of necessity. Like the bees, we are "compelled [*anagkazō*] to keep our heads motionless" (515 a).

To the list of consequences that follow from this claim about the way the world is disclosed to the cave dwellers, Glaucon repeats and reaffirms the origin of it in necessity: do the cave dwellers believe that they themselves are naming and discovering the beings passing by? "*anagkē*" (515 b); do the cave dwellers believe that the shadows are the truth of beings disclosed? "*pollē anagkē*" (515 c). The system of the cave appropriates the prisoners into its reality by preventing them from turning around and seeing the origin of the system, a system that is in fact constituted by artificial puppets illuminated in an artificial light, all of which becomes manipulated in accordance with the motivations of the puppeteers. But this mode of world illumination is said to be a matter of necessity for the human being. It is necessary insofar as it is part of the constitutive condition of the human being. That's why the articulation of the puppeteers and their artificial light needs to be thought more deeply; for, it is not as if one has a choice between choosing artificial light and, say, non-artificial light here. In the cave, there is nothing but artificial light. Moreover, the argument that the *thaumatopoioi* know the truth of the cave strikes me as too simple. They too are confined by the cave walls and restricted to its light, even if they have a freer relation to the puppets and the light.

The condition [*pathos*] of the human being inside the cave resembles the condition [*pathos*] of a bee in a hive. The analogy to the bee enables us to observe the connection between this condition and the natural necessity of the human being. The discursive structure [*logos*] that discloses the world to the human in the cave is not something, at least at first, that the human being possesses that enables him or her to escape the bonds of necessity. Rather, *it is precisely these bonds*. *Logos* in the cave is folded into the structures of necessity that constitute the nature of the human being. *Logos* is one of the mechanisms through which necessity operates in the cave. Since images are constituted by it, *logos* is the means by which the individual human being becomes produced as one among the many [*oi polloi*]. Therefore, the *logos* of the cave is not a tool used by an individual human being that distinguishes him/her from necessity. Rather, it is that *in* human nature (human necessity) by which an individual is appropriated by the hive.

However, before one seeks to argue that the image of movement that Socrates provides after this description of the prisoners who are "like us" is an unproblematic movement from human necessity to human freedom and/or knowledge/intellect, I think it is important to point out that Plato does not allow such a happily simplistic interpretation of the movement. The release from binds is not a release from necessity. As we argued earlier in our analysis of the various ways by which a soul gifted with all the spectacular qualities of the best human might be turned away from a life of corruption by the *oi polloi*, necessity pervades the experience of freedom from the system of constraint. As Socrates says:

> "Consider the release and remedy from both bonds and lack of circumspection [*aphrosunē*] if something such as this by *nature* [*physei*] should happen ... when someone is released and *compelled* [*anagkazō*] suddenly to stand up, turn his neck, walk up to the light and look. And, doing all these things, is both in pain and ... dazzled. ... What would he say, do you suppose, if someone ... were to *compel* [*anagkazō*] him to reply to questions about what [the old shadows are]? Do you not suppose he would both be at a loss [*aporia*] and also hold the things seen earlier to be truer than the things now shown?"
>
> "Much more" he said.
>
> "And, if he should *compel* [*anagkazō*] him to look at the light itself, would his eyes be pained and would he flee, turning back to those that he is capable to observe, and consider [*nomizō*] these to be clearer than the things now shown?"
>
> "Just so," he said.
>
> "And if," I said, "someone should drag him by *force* [*bia*] through the jagged, steep ascent, and did not let him go until he had dragged him out into the light of the sun, would he not be pained and irritated at being dragged?" (515 c—e, emphasis added).

The cave-dweller does not release himself. Freedom from the constraints of the discursive system of the cave is not achieved as a consequence of an internal act of will or of reason. Moreover, the movement of release does not arise from the educational system by which the cave-dweller has been encultured, not even at the level of the university. Rather, it is described to occur "by nature [*physei*]" (515 c). Precisely how the procedure is by nature remains unexplained. A hypothetical someone appears from outside the system of the shadows and releases the cave-dweller from his binds. The release originates externally to either the individual cave-dweller's rational/intellectual capacities or the system of education the cave-dweller undergoes. Further, the cave-dweller's new free relation to the system of education comes about as a consequence of *necessity*, insofar as he is "*compelled* [*anagkazō*] suddenly to stand up, turn his neck, walk up to the light and look" (515 c). Clearly, one can use the language of freedom in conjunction with this act of release only with a very strong qualification: the cave-dweller *is forced* [*bia*] *to comply* and would rather not undergo the terrible suffering that his new-found "freedom" engenders: "he is in pain . . . dazzled . . . at a loss . . . hold the things seen earlier to be truer than the things now shown" (515 d).

Thus, the source of release and ascent remains obscure.[13] At first, it appears that the shoes of the hypothetical someone who releases the prisoners could be shown to fit a Socrates. To be sure, across the dialogues, it is mostly Socrates who poses the questions that engender the *aporia* within his interlocutors—indeed, against his interlocutors' will. Socrates is *compelled* to *compel* his interlocutors into *aporia*. But that is *all* he does. It could be argued that the Socratic *elenchus* remains only ever a negative endeavor—the positive accounts of virtue, beauty, justice, etc., that occur after the aporetic moments are conspicuously unconvincing and/or incomplete (justice is minding one's own business?). The remaining "habituation" (516 a ff.) in which one becomes *at home* in the non-artificial light of the good never occurs in the dialogues. The motion in the cave image, therefore, betrays yet another gap between the practical example of the life of the philosophical nature (*if* Socrates is a philosopher) in the dialogues and Socrates' arguments and images about it.

After giving an account of this period of aporetic disorientation upon ascent from the cave, Socrates says that the sojourner grows habituated [*sunētheia*] to his new light conditions and gradually becomes capable of seeing the beings in the light again: "at first . . . the shadows, after that . . . the images [*eidōlon*] of humans in water, as well as other things, later . . . the things themselves. From these things . . . the things in heaven" (516 a). The sojourner that escapes the cave grows *accustomed* to his new environment and, consequent to this habituation, he is able to cultivate a familiarity [*gnosis*] and a sense of anticipation, of expectation, with regard to the coming and going of the things in the new light. In many ways, the new relation to the light and the objects in the light are similar to those of the cave. Understanding in both the *topos* of the cave and the *topos* above ground requires habituation, making oneself at home; that is to say, one must find one's way into familiarity and *Heimlichkeit* through the becoming of experience and time. This is precisely the same manner by which the prisoners become encultured. Through visual experience and pedagogy, the systems of the cave become familiar, predictable and consistent. However, there are at least two important differences between the structure of habituation in the cave and that out of the cave.

On the one hand, the beings (puppets and statues) that generate the shadows in the cave are technological artifacts, while those that generate shadows above ground are natural beings. Artifacts are understood as images or, rather, as *imitations* of natural beings. One may presume that there is an ontological difference between the two. To appeal to Aristotle, technological objects imitate natural motion. However, while beings generated by *physis* contain their own form and possess a principle of motion within themselves, technological objects do not. Their form lies in the mind of the craftsman and their principle of motion lies outside of themselves (for example, Aristotle 1984, 1140 a 1–20). Nevertheless, given emphasis on the mechanism of habituation, Socrates does not elaborate precisely why what is seen above is different from what is seen below from the point of view of habituation.

On the other hand, the source of light is an important difference. As one passes by the artificial light in the cave on one's assent along the road, one can look directly at the source of artificial light and perhaps even see how it is that the *thaumatopoioi* manipulate and organize the way the shadows are cast upon the wall. However, given the limitations of human visual finitude, the same relation to the source of light is not possible above ground. That is to say, despite Socrates' assertion (516 b), one cannot stare at the sun. Without mediation, one cannot peer directly at the source of the way the natural beings appear in the light. Socrates does not call attention to this fact and Glaucon does not contradict Socrates. Quite the contrary, Socrates says, "then finally I suppose he would be able to look at the sun, not its phantom [*phantasma*] in water or some other place [*en allotria edra*], but itself by itself in its own space [*xōra*], he would behold it as it is" (516 b). And Glaucon replies with our thematic concept: "'*anagkaion,' ephē*." However, again, human beings cannot look at the sun. It is a matter of human finitude, of human necessity. In the *Phaedo*, Plato has Socrates articulate this fact while explaining his "second sailing" (1998, 99 d) via *logoi* after he failed to reach the desired destination by investigating material *physis*. There, he says,

> "Well then after these experiences [with investigating material *physis*]," said he, "since I had had it with this way of looking into beings, it seemed to me I had to be on my guard so as not to suffer the very thing those people do who behold and look at the sun during an eclipse. For surely some of them have their eyes destroyed if they don't look at the sun's likeness in water or in some other such thing" (1998, 99 d—e).

Here, in the *Phaedo*, Socrates contradicts his character's claims in the *Republic*. If a human being looks at the sun, the power of seeing is destroyed. In fact, the only way one can look at the sun is through things like appearances in water or *through technological artifacts* that distort the power of the sun so that it can be "seen." One must, in fact, look at the source of the light above ground through the medium of "some other place [*en allotria edra*]" (516 b). It remains unclear precisely what one would see even if one were able to sustain one's gaze. What content, what knowledge does extreme, blinding light contain?[14] In any case, it strikes me as very important that, if *Phaedo*'s Socrates is right, then in the world outside of the cave, the things that are lit up by the sun are mediated by a source that is inaccessible to human modes of apprehension. As we observed earlier, the light is a third thing—something that remains most often unseen. We perceive the thing in the light, but most of us remain ignorant of the light in which the thing appears. In the phenomenon of sight, we have 1) the power of sight and 2) the thing seen; however, the light is a mediator between the two. As a mediator, it shapes the thing seen in important ways that remain invisible to the viewer. Moreover, the source of the light is itself not exactly visible. Sure, one can point toward the region of the sky containing the sun and indicate the source. However, what does one see if one looks directly at the sun without mediation? If one tries to look at the sun as a source of the light in the way one looked at the artificial light in the cave, qua mediator, one destroys one's ability to see. Thus, in both cases—looking at the sun and not looking at the sun—the source of mediation remains hidden (*lanthanomai*). But perhaps one would reply that the sun is only a metaphor . . . is only a "child of the good"? As such, the image remains inhibited by the limitations of sight. Surely, the source of intellectual illumination does not blind the human being intellectually? While we can all agree that the human is subject to a visual finitude, her capacity for intellect remains infinite, does it not?

Comparing the knowledge of causes in the cave to the knowledge of causes in the upper world reveals something interesting regarding intellectual finitude that is also borne out in the *Timaeus*.[15] Given that the objects of knowledge and the light that illuminates them are all in some sense human artifacts, it may seem as though the knowledge systems inside the cave are actually more intelligible than those outside the cave. The ones inside the cave were made by humans and, as such, they are technological creations. Once one understands the system of the cave, the possibility of analysis emerges. The puppets can be compared to their blueprints. The causes of the fire's generation can be studied through the means of practice, so that its flame may be reproduced, its colors altered, its intensity adjusted. Further, those who utter the sounds, carry the puppets, and alter the light—the *thaumatopoioi*—can be interrogated. However, the beings outside of the cave are creations of *physis*. Nature is not an artisan that composes her beings in accordance with readable blueprints—even as we apply human technological concepts in our efforts to render the phenomenon visible as something familiar, as a *technē* (for instance, through the application of concepts like "codes," "scripts," "dna" and "rna" that seek to convert the phenomenon of protein production into a familiar linguistic system). Rather, natural beings compose themselves. Even if we want to think of the composition in an ecosystematic way, there too there exists no "artisan." Consequently, there exists a gap between the technological knowledge systems we contrive to comprehend nature and the comprehension of nature. Most often, the systems we employ "work" for a period of time, but the gap eventually necessitates a shift and produces a history, a "history of error" (Canguilhem 2008, 26). In any case, all of this raises the question of whether gaining access to knowledge systems is really what is happening in Socrates' description of being habituated to the world outside.

One may wish to appeal now to Socrates' claim that the knowledge systems in the cave are based upon "opinion," not knowledge, while the ones above ground are based upon knowledge. But the truth of this claim hangs upon the certainty secured by looking at the sun (or the good), the source of the light that makes the beings "appear." Earlier, in his analysis of the child of the good, Socrates articulated a difference between knowledge and opinion grounded upon the light from the sun: "When [the soul] rests upon that which is lit up by truth and that which is, it thinks [*noeō*], knows [*gignōsko*], and seems to have intelligence [*nous*]. But when it rests on that which is mixed with darkness, on coming into being and passing away, it merely supposes [*doxazō*] and its vision is weakened, changing opinions up and down, and seems not to have intelligence" (508 d). If this measure means that looking at beings in the light of the sun without a comprehension of the source of light, then even up above, one only grasps the beings with opinion in their becoming, not in their being with knowledge. John Sallis suggests that this distinction articulates not two different regions of beings (in the manner the divided line presents it), but two different *modes* of perceiving the same thing: "on the one hand, a mode of showing in which what shows itself shows itself *wholly* . . . and, on the other hand, a mode of showing in which what shows itself is also *concealed* . . . i.e., mixed with darkness" (1996, 406–407, my emphasis). I am not convinced that the beings above the cave present themselves "wholly." Insofar as they are mediated by the light of the sun (which cannot be perceived), they remain by some measure *concealed*. Without the certainty provided by knowledge of what lies behind the blinding light of the sun, we are left with only opinion. There remains something mixed with darkness in the perception of the beings outside of the cave.

Thus, the release from the bonds of the cave and the movement of ascent to the world above is not a release from necessity. As we saw in the divided line, the transition from the visible region to the intelligible region was a matter of *anagkē*, insofar as what one encounters in the visible compels [*anagkazō*] one to investigate by means of hypotheses. These investigations are of *mathematike* which compel one into thought; however, they proceed from presumed principles and create systems of knowledge based upon those presumptions. Now, in the allegory of the cave, we are given an image that portrays the movement that transitions one from the visible region up [*anabasis*] (517 b) to the noetic region, from the region of the *eikones* to the region of the *eidē*. This movement too remains a consequence of being compelled [*anagkazō*] insofar as the sojourner is forced to take leave of the cave and to maintain his gaze upon the entities in the upper region.

In his concluding remarks composing the image of the cave, Socrates exhorts us to liken the visual segment of the divided line to the interior of the cave and the exterior of the cave to the intelligible segment. But he adds a signal qualification to the image he has just painted: who knows if it is true? Perhaps a god.

> Likening the place made manifest [*phainō*] through sight to the dwelling place of the prison, and the light of the fire in it to the power of the sun, and the going up and the beholding the things above to the soul's path up to the intelligible place, you will not miss my hope, since you desire [*epithumeō*] to hear it. A god perhaps [*pou*] knows if it happens [*tugxanō*] to be true. In any case, these phenomena appear [*phainō*] to me in this way. In the knowable [*gnōstos*] realm, the last thing to be seen . . . is the idea of the good . . . the cause of all that is right and beautiful in everything (517 b—c).

Earlier in this book, we have appealed to other dialogues (for instance, *Timaeus*) that point to *chance* as one of the ways that necessity shows itself. We observed that the *Republic* articulates the emergence of the philosophical nature to be a matter of necessity, especially insofar as a promising nature *happens* [*tugxanō*] to find itself in a suitable soil for philosophical growth. To our surprise, we found that it therefore depends on *chance* (one of the categories of necessity) in order to come into being. Here, Socrates repeats the verb in relation to the truth of the image he has presented. Of course, Socrates warned us multiple times to pay close attention so as to avoid being deceived. But Socrates raises explicit doubts about the truth of the image he has presented; for, are there truths that are presented by chance? Perhaps, if necessity takes hold of one's tongue and speaks through one, qua a god or a muse. But then, truth means something other than the result achieved by holding oneself close to an independent rational capacity and following it through to the end.[16] Instead, truth would be revealed by the arbitrary whims of a god that *happens* to take possession of one. Shorey points to this passage to challenge those readers who assign to Plato a certain kind of metaphysical Platonism: "Plato was much less prodigal of affirmation about metaphysical ultimates than interpreters who take his myths literally have supposed" (1969, 517 b).

While there may exist many reasons to doubt the truth of the image, I wish here to focus on the question of whether seeing the beings above the cave amounts to truth and knowledge insofar as these concepts are understood to denote a grasp of the being/knowledge of the thing rather than the becoming/opinion of the thing; for, the possession of the truth of something means that the bearer of such truth has transparent, everlasting knowledge (*epistēmē*) of the being in question. Perhaps most importantly, when one leaves the cave, one does not escape the things mixed with darkness—the source of opinion (508 d). Because of the blinding light, one is at first *only* able to make out the "shadows [*skia*]" and "images [*eidōlon*]" of things; these are precisely entities mixed with darkness and therefore subject to opinion.

Eventually, as a consequence of habituation [*sunētheia*], says Socrates, one is able to make out the "things themselves [*auta*]" (516 a). However, the things themselves are made visible only as a consequence of the light of the good. We have already asserted that the only content in the argument that secures the presence of the good in this sequence of Socrates' images is the term "the good." At no point do we receive a convincing argument linking "the good" to knowledge or truth in the images. In fact, as we have observed, we receive an argument precisely *against* this: Socrates argues that "the good" is beyond being. To intellectually perceive [*nous*] the being of a thing is to know the truth of it. But "the good" remains conceptually distinct from and, in fact, "beyond" being. Consequently, even if we are habituated to see the things themselves [*auta*], what we see is still mixed with darkness, still images, appearances in water, and shadows; for we have not and cannot look upon the good to determine how the good's light shapes the things that appear in it. Insofar as the things still appear mixed with darkness, they give rise to opinions, not knowledge. As such, the things themselves still appear as images. Consequently, if someone asks "how much time do we spend looking at images and reflections, and how interesting is this?" (Annas 1997, 149), it would seem that one must reply: in the allegory of the cave, we spend *all* of our time looking at images. Moreover, Plato might be said to only ever present images, indeed, interesting ones.

Another way to frame this difficulty would be to say that beings appear in the light of concepts. Concepts are a third thing between the perceiver and the thing perceived. Concepts provide the light that allows them to appear to the human perceiver. Insofar as the beings appear in the light, the concept emitting the light remains obscure. Perception sees through the light and interprets its relation to the thing as one of immediate presence. The thing is present in the light for perception. However, what remains unperceived is that the light *mediates* the relation between the perceiver and the thing itself. The concept that emits the light remains latently unseen, uninterrogated. For these reasons, I do not think that anything in the cave allegory transcends the third tier of the divided line. In the divided line, hypotheses are starting points in two ways. One begins by taking the hypothesis for granted, by assuming it. For example, the thing itself in this scenario might be *a living thing*. The relevant concept, therefore, is life. Perception sees the living thing as metaphysically present before it. The life of the living thing *appears* immediate. However, it *is* precisely mediated; the concept that allows the thing to appear *as living* is the concept "life." The concept goes uninterrogated as thought [*dianoia*] gathers the living beings together into a system of "biology," a system mediated through an uninterrogated concept—a presumed answer to the question "what is life?" The movement from the hypothesis depicted in the fourth tier of the divided line turns its sights precisely upon the concept, the source of the light in which the living thing appears to one *as* living. According to Socrates, the ultimate concept is the good. Ultimately, then, all the beings are lit up by it and appear in its light. Perhaps we can also say, insofar as the good is beyond being, that all the other concepts too are lit up by the good. The form/concept of "life" lights up the *being* of the *living* thing as a proposition, but life is legitimated by "the good." In my reading, not only do we not gain a glimpse of the form of "the good" in the image of the allegory of the cave, but we do not even achieve a clear noetic vision of any form (the being and its affection in the fourth tier of the divided line). All of this is mixed with darkness and, thus, only gives rise to opinion. But a god perhaps knows if this happens to be true.

If leaving the cave means to gain a vision of the good without mediation, there is no outside of the cave.

Before we transition to an analysis of *anagkē* in Socrates' account of the studies that prepare one for dialectic, we must first offer an interpretation of one additional moment of necessity that appears in the cave allegory. I refer here to the fact that the human being that escapes the cave for a time is compelled [*anagkazō*] to return to it. In the image itself, the return is presented as hypothetical: "if such a one were to go back down again and sit in the same seat . . . " (516 e). When he returns, his eyes are not accustomed to the darkness; consequently, he does not see very well and cannot participate with success in the shadow games that *oi polloi* play. He is, thus, the object of ridicule and the example employed when people speak of the corruption that happens if one tries to go up, out of the cave. If he tries to loosen those around him, *oi polloi* kill him (517 a). However, shortly after he presents this image, Socrates reveals that the return to the cave is nevertheless necessary [*anagkē*]. In fact, the law-givers themselves must do what they can to ensure not only that the philosophical natures ascend to the greatest studies, but they must also compel them to return to their seats in the cave.

> "Our work as law-givers," I said, "is to compel [*anagkazō*] the best natures to go to the greatest [study], to see the good and to go up and when they have gone up and seen . . . not to allow them what is now allowed."

"What?"

"To stay up there," I said, "and not go down again among those bound ones and share their labors and honors, whether lowly or more serious ones" (519 c—d).

It is a matter of necessity that the law-givers ensure that the philosophical natures do not do what they are likely to want to do: that is to say, remain above. As Socrates said earlier, "do not be struck with wonder that those reaching that point are not then willing to do the business of humans, but their souls are always eager to spend [*diatribein*][17] their time above. To be sure, that is likely [*eikos*]" (517 c—d). After witnessing the forms of the things and the form of the good, the philosophical natures must not be allowed to follow their personal inclination or desire; rather, they must be *compelled* to return to their seats in the cave. This strikes the reader as cruel, especially given the grave risk of a likely persecution and horrible death. It appears that the only positive personal benefit of such a life in the cave would be knowing that what the surrounding community holds as most important is in reality foolish. But, only a Thrasymachus could take pleasure in a life led with this knowledge. Certainly, misology and misanthropy are to follow. Would an uninformed life of the bee in the hive not be better? After all, the humans in the cave do not appear to suffer in any great way as a consequence of their ignorance. Glaucon echoes some of these concerns in his reply: "we will do them an injustice, and make them a difficult life when a better life is possible" (519 d)?

The point of going up to see the good was to provide legitimacy to the virtues of the soul. Wisdom, courage, moderation and justice only obtain their legitimacy when they are informed by the vision of the good. Without it, wisdom, courage, moderation and justice are only presumed opinions. As in our analogy with bees, without the vision of the good, these virtues are what they are for the hive. Yet, when the vision of the good is achieved by those who are capable of achieving it (the philosophical natures), we "do them an injustice" by making them return to the hive and live life in accordance with the city's opinions about the virtues or risk being the object of ridicule or being put to death.

Socrates chastises Glaucon for forgetting "again"[18] that, from the point of view of the law-giver, the only concern is the happiness of the city as a whole, not of any particular class. The law that binds the parts of the city together produces happiness in the city, on the one hand, by persuasion and, on the other hand, by force, compulsion or necessity. Socrates says,

> [the law] tries to generate [welfare] in the city as a whole, joining [*sunharmozō*] the citizens by persuasion [*peithō*] and compulsion [*anagkē*], and making them give to each other the profit that each is able. And it [the law] creates such men

in the city not to turn in order to let them take [*trepō*] whichever course each wants, but in order to use each to *bind* the city together (519 e, emphasis added).

Certainly, law conceived in this manner betrays a utopian vision of the function of justice in a city (and perhaps a soul). More than the earlier articulated definition of justice as "minding one's own business," we are reminded here of Aristotle's analysis of justice in book V of the *Nicomachean Ethics* (Aristotle 1984) as that which binds the citizens of a city together. If justice is violated, if this bind is broken by some act of injustice, then the law occasions the application of penalty to bring the perpetrator back in line with the community and restore the bind that has been severed. Nevertheless, it is not "truth" and/or "knowledge of what is" that preserves justice, or happiness, or well-being in the city; it is law conceived as persuasion [*peithō*] and force [*anagkē*]. Where did the law come from? Not the philosophers that have seen the good. But from our law-givers, Socrates, Glaucon and Adeimantus. There is no indication that any of these characters have been released from the binds of the cave, ascended the path, and become blinded by the light of the good. In fact, instead of going up, our interlocutors have only gone down (to Piraeus). To be sure, Socrates himself claims not to know what the good is. Thus, the law of the *Kallipolis* persuades and compels without this grounding.

As such, the law appears as the principle of order *inside* of the cave; it gathers the citizens together—despite their differences in function—and bestows upon them a unity and recognizable identity. In this way, the law in the *Kallipolis* resembles the law that governs a beehive or an ant mound. That is to say, from this point of view, the law of our aristocracy resembles the law of *necessity*. The reader will recall that the law established by our law-givers does not allow for innovation (422 a, 424 b). Thus, we must ask: does the release from the binds in the cave already represent a violation of justice in the cave? If justice "binds" the citizens together, is the release from these binds an injustice in some way, insofar as the release loosens the philosophical nature from his bind to the other citizens and frees the philosophical nature from the necessary constraints of the law? Moreover, given that innovation of the law remains forbidden, one must wonder what contribution of content the philosopher kings will bring with them back into the cave to enable the city to live in a state of wakefulness rather than "a dream" (520 c).

In addition to compulsion, the law-givers must also engage in persuasion with the philosophers to keep them in the cave and ensure that they seek to rule. They must whisper "just things" into their ears while also "compelling" [*pros anagkazō*] them both to take care of and guard the others (520 a). Socrates offers these words of persuasion as an example of how the law-givers might speak to the philosophical natures:

For yourselves and for the rest of the city we have generated [*gennaō*] you like leaders and kings in hives [*smēnos*]. You have been better and more perfectly educated and are more capable of participating in both [the upper and lower lives]. Thus, you must descend . . . into the common dwelling place of the others and grow accustomed to gazing [*theaomai*] at the dark things [again]. For, growing accustomed, you will see countless times better than those there, and you will know each of the images and that from which it is an image, because you have seen the truth about the beautiful, the just and the good things.[19] (520 b—c).

These words serve as an example of one of the many problems with those readings that interpret Socrates' statements in the dialogues as the arguments of Plato. Here, Socrates speaks as a law-giver. His stated goal is persuasion, not truth-telling argumentation. I find it striking that the "knowledge" of the good supposedly achieved in the vision above the cave is not compelling enough, is not self-evident enough to ensure that the philosophical natures descend into the cave to complete the art of turning. Rather, they require persuasion and compulsion—perhaps *a second noble lie*. The philosophical natures need a Solon, a law-giver, or a law in order to persuade and compel them to return to their seats in the cave. That is to say, it is not a free will informed by the knowledge of being and the good that completes the turn, but an *external force of persuasion*. Necessity is what Plato puts into the mouth of Socrates here—not a propositional assertion. It was an external force that initiated the turn away from the binding law, and it was an external force that compelled the soul out of the cave; but it was equally an external force that compels the soul to turn back down.

In addition, our metaphor of the social insects returns insofar as Socrates seeks to persuade the philosophers that they are "leaders and kings in hives [*smēnos*]" (520 b). What sort of city is a hive? What kind of leaders rule it? Interpretations of apian imagery in the dialogues have been diverse and contradictory. Among them, some have suggested that the traditional image of the product of the bees, honey, is exploited in the *Republic* by Socrates in order to "strengthen his critique against poetry" (Liebert 2010, 97). In this reading, the apiary "sweetness" of poetry is a grave danger to political and moral stability. Others have read into Plato's use of traditional bee imagery the paradigm of virtuous moral order. For example, Lidia Palumo writes that when Plato "specifies that the swarm is one of bees, the reference is always positive, referring to an ordered and virtuous group (Palumo 2022, 15). She further elaborates this point in a footnote: "the σμῆνος can be good or bad but a bee σμῆνος is always positive because bees' industriousness and its product, honey, is evoked. This is what makes the bee σμῆνος an orderly and virtuous group" (Palumo 2022, 15). She, thus, reads the hive image in Plato to be the metaphorical example of a model virtuous city. In addition, she points to the hive as an originary example of vice as well; for, the drone [*kēphēn*] becomes associated with many vices in book VIII.

The ancient Greek world understood the organization of the hive in a somewhat different manner than we do. Along with the other "gregarious" insects, Aristotle gives an account of the *smēnos* in *History of Animals*. For him, it is composed of king bees, worker bees and drone bees. The worker bees do all the work. "They first build cells for themselves; then for the so-called kings and the drones. For themselves they are always building, for the kings only when the brood of young is numerous, and cells for the drones they build if a superabundance of honey should suggest their doing so" (Aristotle 1984, 623 b 33–624 a 5). It does appear from this description that, for Aristotle and for the ancient Greeks, the hive resembled a social organization more than a reproductive organization. For Aristotle's world, the hive was ruled by a king. It was not until the end of the 17th century that Jan Swammerdam described the reproductive function of the queen in his *The Book of Nature* (1758). While the hive may provide for the kings and the drones, this generosity is not without limit. With respect to kings, even though they seem always to need a king to preserve the hive, the worker bees "kill most of them without mercy, especially kings of the inferior sort" (1984, 625 a 15). The worker bees, the guardians of the hive, appear to know what they need when it comes to being ruled. Further, the hive's tolerance for the drones, who are "devoid of sting and lazy" (1984, 624 b 26) is limited as well. If the hive runs low on honey, the guardians "eject" the drones (1984, 625 a 21). Nevertheless, in contrast to Palumo, I see no evidence in Aristotle for suggesting that drones do not belong by nature to the hive. If drones represent to the Greeks laziness and vice, then, by their very nature, hives *possess* drones. *To be* a successful hive means *to have drones*, except in conditions of extreme need and colony collapse. That is to say, ridding the hive of its vice (the drone) is an exception engendered by weakness. This comparison between a drone-filled wealthy bee colony and an unhealthy, impoverished one on the verge of collapse immediately calls to mind the difference between the city of pigs and the city of relishes.

If a hive is a collective of organisms that act as one—a form of multicellular organism—then it does not operate in accordance with philosophy, intellect, or the sight of what is and the good. Rather, the hive operates in accordance with *necessity*. In a way similar to Socrates' assertion regarding the law's binding relation to the philosophical nature, each organism in the hive performs its work for the sake of the whole. The worker bee is not free to suddenly decide that the life of a drone or a king would be preferable to the life of a worker bee. Even more, the worker bee is not free to abandon the hive and pursue a life as an individual after she has somehow recognized that the habits and practices of the hive are arbitrarily assigned and that the hierarchy and meaning produced by these practices is not grounded in a universal truth. The law of necessity rules the hive, not the philosophically achieved truth. As far as the bee flies in search of blooms, it never climbs out of the hive. Consequently, here in book VII, I would argue that Plato employs the image of the *smēnos* in order to call attention precisely to the difference between a bee hive and a polis. Are bees really like humans and are cities really like hives? If the philosophical nature, with its vision of what is and the good, is to play a role, then apparently not. However, with what we have seen so far in books VI and VII, we have been unable with certainty to distinguish the examples of the philosophical nature from the nature of necessity. Thus, it may be that Plato's comparison with the hive places emphasis on this question of whether we are trapped in our necessity, like the bee is trapped in hers.

NOTES

1. While the divided line is stated, it cannot be said that it has actually been drawn. Unlike, say, the figures in the *Meno* with the slave boy, this figure cannot actually be drawn, or it contains a falsity. As John Sallis says: "The line which he instructs Glaucon to draw . . . cannot, strictly speaking, be drawn. We should not too easily dismiss this conflict as a mere accident" (Sallis 1996, 415). The reason it cannot be drawn is because sections B and C are equal and thus not "increasingly clarifying." Julia Annas too observes that the line cannot be said to "illustrate an increase in clarity": "the equality of DC and CE suggests that Plato is not interested in having each section of the Line illustrate an increase in clarity over the one before" (Annas 1997, 149).

2. I think it is important to maintain the language of image [*eikōn*] here. Reeve (2004), Griffeth (2000), and Shorey (1969) translate the term with "compare"; but in my view this hides from the reader the presence of "image" in Socrates' imperative, a crucial term in both the divided line and the cave allegory. To provide context via a comparison of other instances of the verb in the dialogue: one finds it in book III where Socrates speaks of the kinds of things appropriate for a sensible man to imitate: "when he comes upon someone unworthy of himself, he will not be willing to form himself seriously in the image [*apeikazō*] of an inferior, unless it is a short time" (396 d). Thus, the *image into which one fashions* oneself is important, even if it is only, in fact, an image. Again, in book III, Socrates employs the term in order *to fashion* a certain way of life into the *image* of the panharmonic mode of music: "would we to liken [*apeikazō*] that food and way of life to melodies and songs written in the pan-harmony . . . we would make a correct likeness [*apeikazō*]" (404 d-e). Again, one best organizes one's soul in accordance with the image of a particular mode, while avoiding others. Then, in book IV, Socrates uses the term again to convert an abstract presentation of courage in the soul into an image. "I am willing, if you wish" to form an image [*apeikazō*] of "what it seems to me to be like" (429 d). In book V, we find it mediating the image of the city to the image of the body: "likening [*apeikazō*] the

well-managed city to a body relative to the pain and pleasure of each part" (464 b). Later, in book VI, Socrates compares the "image" [*eikōn*] of the piloting of ships to the image of current cities: "forming an image of the statesman now ruling to be the sailors we related, you make no mistake" (489 c). In the divided line, Socrates uses the term to describe what happens when one is compelled to use the things in the visible tier as images in the intelligible: "it uses as images the same things from which images are formed [*apeikazō*] by the things below" (511 a). Finally, in book VIII, we find the word used again to describe the act of fashioning oneself into the image of something else: "the young form themselves in the image [*apeikazō*] of their elders" (563 a). In all but one of these cases, "compare" seems to me to be too weak to convey what is going on. Given the prefix *apo*, perhaps "cast an image" would be an alternative rendering of the verb in many of these instances. In any case, the proliferation of images appears to be the most significant feature of human perception, whether visual or intellectual.

3. This claim comes from the Muses. Socrates invokes the muses to tell us how the city will "be moved" and how faction will arise. The muses speak to us in a "tragic" style: "It is difficult to move a city put together like this. But, since passing away belongs *to all that comes into being*, not even a composition such as this will remain for all time, but it will be dissolved. And this is the dissolution: Not only to plants in the earth but also to animals upon the earth comes to be a bearing and barrenness of soul and bodies *when life-cycles for each join together a revolution of circles*" (546 a, emphasis added). The mortal character of the human city plays an important part in Claudia Baracchi's reading of book VIII and the decline of the city (Baracchi 2002, 76).

4. "Although they are wise, those you have educated to lead the city, will, with calculation with sensation, not happen [*tugkanō*] upon the right moments for fertility and infertility, but it will pass them by, and they will at some time generate children when they should not" (546 b).

5. Adam, for instance, writes that the "The simile of the Cave presents us with a picture of the life of the uneducated man" (1900, 514 a). More recently, Jacob Howland writes "In its depiction of these three types of souls and of our initial condition of *apaideusia*, and in its identification of philosophy with education, the Cave provides a playbill for the larger educational drama that unfolds over the course of the *Republic*" (1993, 133). Often, one encounters the language of moving from an unenlightened state to one of enlightenment (Annas 1981, 253; Brann 2004, 101), but it is not clear to me what "enlightenment" means in this context; for, as will become clear in what follows, unlike Cornford, I do not think, that the person rising out of the cave apprehends "first principles of reality and truth" (Allen 2013, 191–192).

6. Here we borrow the concept of *to ti en einai* from Aristotle (For example: Aristotle 1924, 994 a 18).

7. N. Smith (1997) argues against received interpretations of how it is that Socrates means that the cave dwellers are "like us." "I will argue," he says, "that in saying that the prisoners in the cave are 'like us,' Plato was making the point that the conceptions most of us employ in governing our lives and those of others, were actually to be understood as images of images" (smith 1997, 188). I agree with this sentence

except for his introduction of the qualification "most of us." Socrates (not Plato) says that the cave-dwellers are "like us" not "most of us." If one felt the need to change the formulation at all, it would be better to change it to "all of us." But, it appears that Smith excludes Socrates from the cave-dwellers (something Socrates never does) and argues that the cave-dwellers are those in Socrates' company (Smith 1997, 188).

8. Again, at 235b of the *Sophist*, Plato has the stranger use the term *thaumatopoioi* to describe the sophist. I am not confident, however, to claim that the "makers of wonder" in the cave are simply the common sophists of the dialogues. As we observed before, Socrates argues that they educate in nothing other than the opinions of the many.

9. In Harvard's translation, Harold Fowler notes that this probably refers to "Pherecydes and the early Ionians" (1921, 244d).

10. One may guess that these discourses are those of Parmenides.

11. It seems likely that this refers to "Muses" involved in Heraclitus' writings.

12. While this appears to refer to the "Muses" speaking through Empedocles, it nevertheless seems odd to unify the thought of Heraclitus and Empedocles here and in what follows in the quotation.

13. Rachel Barney (2008) helpfully provides an interpretation of the perplexing role of necessity in the ascent from the cave. She suggests that one might expect that the form of beauty would initiate an erotic desire to coax, persuade and seduce the cave dweller to turn toward knowledge of the forms. However, Plato has Socrates use the language of *anagke*, of compulsion, not desire. Therefore, she asks why. After considering different ways the reader might interpret the meaning of necessity here, she concludes that "we should therefore understand necessity in the Cave as simply what overcomes resistance" (Barney 2008, 11). Like me, she considers *eros* to be a species of necessity (Barney 2008, 13). However, she appropriates Diotima's speech in the *Symposium* to make the further argument that love is the love of beautiful and, therefore, good things. Consequently, for Barney, we can still argue that the dweller of the cave is moved by *eros* because it is a being-compelled by erotic desire for knowledge of forms. In my reading, Diotima's speech is a purification and simplification of a much more complex *eros*. Indeed, hers is not the last word. Alcibiades interrupts the tranquility in the figure of Dionysus to announce that *eros* will not be constrained or controlled by reason or knowledge. In many ways, the relation between Diotima's and Alcibiades' speeches resembles that between the Knight's and the Miller's tales in Chaucer's *Canterbury Tales* (1970). After *eros* is lifted to the pedestal of nobility in the Knight's tale, it rebels and insists that the irrational and the vulgar belong to it as well. My argument differs from Barney's insofar as, for me, *eros* and necessity make visible human finitude more than human transcendence.

14. Drew Hyland too raises this question: "if we do look directly and sustainedly at the sun, it causes not more lucid visibility of the world, but blindness!" (Hyland 2011, 157)

15. See my "Difference in Plato's Timaeus" (Winslow 2021).

16. Julia Annas opens her analysis of the cave with: "the person with knowledge . . . is the person who thinks things through where others remain unreflective" (1997, 143).

17. It is worth pointing out that, according to the Liddel, Scott, Jones, *diatribein* not only means "to spend time," but seems even more often to mean "to waste time," "to fritter away time," "to put off by delay."

18. The two forgotten moments occur in book IV and book V. In book V, Socrates asks Glaucon if he remembers when "I don't know whose speech chastised us for not making the guardians happy" (465 e - 466 a). After Glaucon says that he remembers, Socrates argues that they were making the city as a whole as happy as possible, not any one group within it (466 a). The unknown origin of the argument was Adeimantus': "what will your apology be, Socrates, if someone were to say that you are not making these men happy?" (book IV, 419 a). Socrates responds that "it would be nothing surprising if they are even the happiest. But we are not looking to distinguish the happiness of any one group in founding the city, but to the city as a whole" (420 b). Thus, Socrates has made this claim twice to the group as a whole, even if Adeimantus was the first interlocutor. Adam disputes the notion that Glaucon has forgotten twice (Adam 2009, II, 102).

19. I find this passage confusing for additional reasons. If you have seen the truth, it is of the singular. It is the good, not the good *things*. That is to say, the vision of the good, if it exists, is a vision of the singular manifestation of "the good." It is not plural. Yet, the adjectives employed here *are in* the plural. For me, this "slip" in terminology raises a question about the truth regarding the singular vision of immobile things outside of the cave?

Chapter 6

Necessity and the Highest Studies

In chapter 6, I will offer an analysis of how the figure of necessity appears in the so-called highest studies, those studies that prepare the guardians for dialectic (chapter 7). In my reading, the highest studies are distinguished from the ones in the early formation of the education of *Kallipolis* by occasioning an *aporia* regarding the primary concepts that provide the ground of each of their subject matters. The new studies are *the one*, *plane geometry*, *solid geometry*, *astronomy*, and *harmonics*. In their practical application, each study develops a particular dimension of the cosmos, allowing the production of a cosmological mathematical system. *The one* obviously works at the first dimension; plane geometry is the region of the second; the third dimension emerges from solid geometry; the movements of solids in space are described by astronomy, and harmony articulates the ratios that movements obey. However, in the setting of the "new studies" (perhaps the "theoretical application") in which each study occasions an *aporia*, we observe a "wandering cause" in the primary concepts. That is to say, there exists some irrationality or incommensurability in each of the dimensions. Insofar as the "wandering cause" is another name for necessity, then, as I argue, it is necessity that occasions the *aporetic* turns in each case.

Earlier we argued that Plato's signal contribution to the history of philosophy via the dialogues has been the elaboration of the concept/experience of *aporia*. Even though Socrates' explicit comments present an optimism regarding the possibility of the philosophical nature successfully enduring the gaze into that *which is* (and even the brightest part of that *which is*, the good) (518 c), no character in the dialogues actually undergoes this experience, especially not the character most occupying the position of the philosopher: Socrates. Instead, the dramas yield *aporias* with respect to what the characters thought they knew.

Perhaps the *Meno* offers a limited and interesting exception to this rule; for, one may wish to argue that the slave boy in the *Meno* rightly turns toward *what is* (the being of the square). And indeed, the dramatic comparison of a slave being led to knowledge, while the sophisticated aristocrat (Meno) appears incapable of it, remains a most important theatrical scene in the dialogue.[1] However, while the slave boy proves capable of being led to disclose to himself, on the one hand, the reasoning behind a square that equals sixteen square feet (1990, 83 c) and, on the other hand, the reasoning behind a square that equals nine square feet (1990, 83 e), Socrates makes clear that the slave boy remains incapable of finding his way to what he wanted: that is, the square that equals eight square feet (1990, 84 a). In fact, having exhausted whole numbers, the slave is *at a loss* of where to go next. Geometrically reaching eight square feet will require a completely new path that remains inaccessible to the slave boy without Socrates' external guidance. Despite Meno's acceptance of the claim to the contrary, it appears that Socrates performs something like *teaching* here.[2]

However, according to the drama, it would seem that Socrates engenders something more important in the slave boy than the proposition that leads to the knowledge of how to arrive at an eight square feet result. Socrates tells Meno that the slave boy no longer believes that he knows something that he does not know—he is in *aporia* about it (1990, 84 a). Meno agrees that *aporia* is a better condition than believing that one knows while not actually knowing (1990, 84 b). When one attends to the dramatic details, *aporia* again takes the center stage. Moreover, the interaction with the slave boy does a lot more than it was originally supposed to do—namely, address the paradox of learning. Articulating these excesses will be relevant for our elaboration on the experience of *aporia* in book VII of the *Republic*. To name three questions that emerge from the exchange:

Firstly, with respect to the most obvious goal, it responds to Meno's antecedent question. Socrates gives Meno an answer to his Gorgias-derived sophistical paradox: how does one come to know (or search for) something if one does not know what one is trying to come to know at all (1990, 80 d)? Socrates' so-called solution to the paradox is that what one seeks to know already inhabits one; it is inscribed on the "immortal soul." Meno readily concedes. However, except as a metaphor, this answer emerging from the surface argument is not satisfying[3] and, further, it is also not an answer that can possibly be grounded on reason or knowledge.[4] The answer articulates a more phenomenologically relevant meaning when taken as a metaphor or *image* rather than an argumentative assertion. If the experience of *anamnesis* can be said to reflect a particular relation between an individual and the source of his/her discourse, then a different interpretation (inspired by Aristotle) may take shape. In this reading, the conceptual economy into which a human being is born exists before birth, before incarnation. In fact, one might say that it is precisely the work of *paideia* to fold a child into this system of discourse—to inscribe the surrounding conceptual economy onto the soul of the child. As such, *paideia* is much more than the formal curriculum articulated in books two through five. Fundamentally, insofar as *paideia* appropriates the child to the conceptual economy of his/her city, it bestows an identity on the child. It is not because the child sprouts autochthonously from the soil of Athens that she displays herself as obviously Athenian. She shines out as Athenian because she reflects the conceptual economy that governs there. Her identity lies in the way she speaks, the habits she cultivates, what counts to her as just, noble, beautiful and good. Moreover, insofar as *paideia* appropriates the child to the surrounding system of discourse, it gives to the child a world, a conceptual world through which the beings in that world are meaningful and become interpreted. Read through this light, the "immortal soul" can be seen as precisely the environment of discourse into which a child is born, that exists both before and after the incarnation of individuals. The human being is the being with *logos*. However, the *logos* does not originate with the child. No child invents her conceptual relation to the world; rather, she is appropriated to it. For human beings, therefore, there is a relation from the beginning between *logos* with a capital *Lambda* and a lower case *lambda*. The relation is complex, since not only do individuals become appropriated by the *Logos*, but they can (if rarely), qua *lambda*, effect change in the *Logos* as well. The greater *logos* world always already exists; thus, insofar as one becomes appropriated by it, the forms are inscribed upon one's soul through *paideia*. However, this does not mean that the form becomes expressed in the individual in an unproblematic, perfectly clear way. As we have seen, *everyone* slings around the concept of "justice," a concept everyone has as a consequence of having been appropriated by one's surrounding conceptual economy. However, as we have seen in the case of Polemarchus, even though the meaning of justice, for example, appears obvious to us, we discover, when we are interrogated about it, that we do not know what we mean. *Anamnesis*, whatever it is, involves the interrogation of the concepts in the conceptual economy that inhabit us. Even though they inhabit us, there nevertheless remains a distance between their form of existence there and their form of existence in us, between *Lambda* and *lambda*, between public and private. The appearance of *aporia* in the interlocutor is the appearance of the recognition of a natural (and, thus, tragically complicated) division between these polarities, and the appearance of a condition for the possibility to *turn* between them.

Secondly, regardless of the quality of persuasion of the *argument*, the *dramatic* exchange with the slave boy unquestionably puts on display the endeavor of engendering *aporia* in the interlocutor. In my reading, one of the consequences of the slave boy exchange is the invitation to compare the *articulation of paradox* and the *experience of aporia*. Of course, Gorgias' paradox necessitates Socrates' example in the slave-boy exchange (1990, 80 d), and Socrates appears critical of the intentions of the paradox from the beginning: "do you see what a controversy you are conjuring up?" (1990, 80 e). Yet, one could argue that Meno, ostensibly, suffers the *paradox* and the slave boy suffers the *aporia*. Why are these two events *not* expressions of the same phenomenon? Does paradox not sting like a torpedo fish? From a certain point of view, they are the same. The paradoxes of Zeno and Gorgias lead one to perplexity. Socratic *elenchus* also leads one into perplexity. From the point of view of *proposition* and assertion, they are indistinguishable. However, from the point of view of *comportment*, they differ radically. Meno's ambition in employing the paradox is to trip up Socrates. For him, paradox is a weapon. However, when Socrates leads the slave boy into *aporia*, the *elenchus* is embodied in a comportment that holds itself toward the slave in a way that seeks to shift the comportment of the slave toward the matter at hand—despite its privative result, *it is productive* insofar as the recognition that one does not know what one thought one knew has been achieved.[5] The paradox employed by Meno does not hold itself in this way. Consequently, we see that more than the *content* of the argument itself, the *comportment* one holds in employing the argument is at stake in the exchange. The experience of *aporia*, therefore, empties one of content, loosens one so that, qua comportment, one is rendered capable of turning.

Thirdly, in addition to revealing that the central problem facing Socrates in the exchange is that Meno appears incapable of undergoing *aporia*, but only paradox, attending to the dramatic details shows that the exchange brushes up against our central theme: necessity. Even if we allow the slave boy to have disclosed certain logical properties of the square and to have consequently achieved a kind of knowledge of its being and a pathway toward its full conception, we still have the problem of the meaning of this kind of knowledge. The achievement of this particular knowledge reflects the unique features of the geometrical form, which betray a dependence upon logical necessity in a very explicit and particular way. As we see in the *Parmenides*, the dialogues frequently raise doubts about the equivalence of this form of necessity and what we have earlier called "natural" necessity. The being of a mathematical entity—a square—(knowable in accordance with logical necessity) and the being of, say, a human being, a tree, or justice (knowable, if at all, in accordance with ontological necessity) might express two "beings" with very different "ways of being." The former exists as a technological artifact, while the "human being" and the "tree" *are* in accordance with natural necessity. By which of these two modes of necessity something like "justice" exists is not in any way clear from the dialogue; moreover, this might be one, if not *the*, question of the dialogue: does human finitude limit understanding to technological artifacts and the logical necessity that produces them? If so, then to which kind of necessity does "justice" belong? Is it *merely* a human concept? Or does it arise by natural necessity like trees, humans . . . and even, perhaps, cities? Thus, when viewed through the lens of *necessity*, even the example of knowledge provided by the *Meno* raises questions about human finitude *vis à vis* the possibility of knowledge. The emphasis is placed, rather, on the experience of *aporia*.

ARITHMETIC

Because the slave boy exchange in the *Meno* raises these three questions, it remains instructive for our interpretation of book VII. In this chapter, I wish to provide an analysis of the studies that are said to "generate" (521 c) the human beings that the law-givers will "compel" [*anagkazō*] to guard the city (521 b). According to Socrates, these studies represent "how [the lawgivers] will lead them up to the light, like certain men are said to have gone up from Hades to the gods" (521 c). The reference to the cave is obvious. Just as the prisoner released from binds will "turn" his eyes away from the wall and toward the entrance of the cave, the new studies will occasion what Socrates calls a "turning" (521 c) of the soul. A few pages later, the turning of the soul is brought into connection with that natural disposition of the philosophical nature articulated early in book VI (hatred of wandering and erotic love of being). The new studies engender the possibility of "turning the soul itself from becoming to truth and being" (525 c). In our analysis of book VI, we suggested that the text itself raises doubts and questions about the possibility of this philosophical nature, especially insofar as Socrates is to represent it.

However, at the beginning of the new studies we have reintroduced a concept and goal of the new studies that raises new questions: the studies, when practiced in the correct way, not only cultivate a turn in the philosophical nature toward what is, but they also *necessarily* help prepare the guardians for war. This should not come as a surprise. After all, from the beginning of his exchange with Glaucon and Adeimantus, Socrates argued that in abandoning the city of pigs, composed of bare "necessities [*anagkē*] . . . houses, attire, shoes" (373 a) . . . we were transgressing the limit of the necessary [*anagkē*]" (373 d) and planting the seed of war. For, by including "relishes, myrrh, incense, flute-girls, pastries . . . painting . . . embroidery . . . gold, ivory, and everything of the sort" (373 a) in the *Kallipolis*, we were incorporating "the genesis of war" (373 e) into it as well. Thus, somehow, preparing oneself for the practice of philosophy, for the vision of *what is* and the good, requires the same studies that prepare one for war.

Indeed, the new studies are distinguished from the old ones precisely by this *comportment*—the act of war and the turning toward *what is*. One might argue that the content of the objects of the previous studies and the new studies is the same. What distinguishes them is precisely the comportment. To take an example from the first new study, the study of number: the practical application of number by the educated members of a society utilizes the same number; however, the soul holds a different disposition toward number in the new studies. As Socrates argues, those who are going to participate in the greatest things in the city must engage in "calculation [*logistikē*—the first of the new studies] and hold themselves to it, not like the private/amateurish [*idiōtikos*] do, but rather until they come to the contemplation of the nature of numbers with intellection itself, practicing it not for buying and selling like merchants or tradesmen, but for the sake of war and for the ease of turning the soul itself from becoming to truth and being" (525 c-d). Salespeople, cashiers, craftsmen, engineers, architects, computer scientists, physicians, chemists, physicists, etc., despite their differences in training and facility with mathematics, use number in a practical fashion—they operate with a presumed conception of number derived from their primary education (until that conception breaks down). If the conception of number breaks down, as it sometimes does in physics, mathematics and perhaps other disciplines, then they no longer contemplate number in accordance with their training, but intellect is called forth, the soul turns in its being away from *what wanders* toward *what is*—away from the familiar images of number passing by on the cave wall/chalkboard, toward *what is*. Philosophy is, thus, not a *discipline* but a *comportment* toward what we already "know." At the introduction of the first new study, Socrates relates the experience to the sensuous faculty of soul.

> "[Socrates:] Certain perceptible beings do not call thought to examination because perception suffices to judge them, and there are others which in every way engage thought in this examination, since perception gives nothing sound.
>
> [Glaucon:] You obviously mean distant appearances, or shadow paintings.
>
> [Socrates:] You have not understood my meaning at all" (523b).

Socrates here describes how, in certain rare and unplanned occasions, sensuous encounters engender thought. The faculty of sense encounters beings that it cannot "examine," cannot comprehend, and that stupefy it. In such circumstances, thought is then "in every way" forced into being. In my reading, by having Socrates initiate his analysis of the new studies with this experience of human life, Plato situates *aporia* at the very center of the objective of the new studies. Socrates relates a phenomenon that demonstrates the transcendental organizational role that stupefaction plays in the emergence of *nous*: it is a condition for the possibility of thinking as such. Glaucon's reply draws upon merely empirical examples of the confusion of the faculty of sense. As such, he fails to grasp the *necessary* structural organization in which thinking becomes pried from its complacent rest in common sense, in the presumed (but not *thought*) concepts of the earlier education.

When, in the pursuit of its practical life, sense stumbles upon something it does not recognize and for which it has no reference, *nous* is called forth. That is to say, all the practical disciplines occasion philosophy, insofar as they are compelled [*anagkazō*] into the philosophical nature in the way that we have seen throughout our analysis. Except, now war is added. The aporetic experience of losing the content of the meaning of number and then undergoing a noetic turning toward number as number is somehow instructive "to men of war" (521 d), according to Socrates. But is not the discipline of war, *strategy*, a practical science like engineering or architecture? Does it not count the same presumed conception of number? Why is war distinguished from these and placed alongside philosophy and the turning toward *what is*? This question will have to be bracketed for now.

In the current preliminary description of the first new study, Socrates' appeal to the faculty of sense as an origin of *aporia* is strange.[6] In the dialogues, *aporia* is normally reached as a consequence of some discursive failure, not sensuous failure. In the current dialogue, of course, the conversation pursues "justice." It seems reasonable to argue that justice is a concept that does not lend itself to perception by bare sense. Perhaps the question of how it is that one *perceives* what human beings call justice is already a central question of the dialogue. A reference to the original lines that called for the composition of a city in speech makes this clear: "Perhaps there would be more justice in the bigger city than in a small, singular soul and it would be easier to examine" (368 e). If *nous* only emerges as a consequence of an *aporia* that engenders a turn of the soul and a journey out of the cave and *aisthēsis* is incapable of perceiving discursive concepts, then with what "faculty" does one perceive justice in one's everyday life (whether correctly judged or not)? Even if the crowd's perception of an unjust or just act is not informed by a noetic perception of justice, the act nevertheless appears to it *as* "just" and consequently motivates an action—punishment or praise. How do *oi polloi's* judgments translate into perceptions in the souls of individuals?

Further, with the introduction of *aisthēsis*, we are provoked by another question: is there really a structural similarity between an *aporia* generated by the sensuous encounter with something sensuously perplexing and one generated by something discursively perplexing? Perhaps this sensuous encounter Socrates describes is not exactly what we today would call empirical—the latter assumption indeed appears to be the mistake that Glaucon makes in his interpretation of Socrates' words. As quoted above, Glaucon says that, by referencing perplexing sensuous beings, Socrates means distant appearances and shadow paintings. To this, Socrates replies: "you have not understood my meaning at all" (523 b). Consequently, with Glaucon, we may need to rethink what occurs in Socrates' sensuous encounter here.

Because Glaucon failed to grasp Socrates' words regarding the failure of sense and the invocation of *nous* in the experience of *aporia*, Socrates offers an image to make it clearer to him: fingers. The image strikes one as comical. Socrates says that each of the three fingers when observed closely looks like a finger and none of their differences (size, color, etc.) "compels [*anagkazō*]" the "soul of the many [*oi polloi*] to question" the being of the finger (523 d). We have seen this language before. It may be useful to recall our observations. In the "divided line," we read that the first tier of the intellectual region of the soul becomes activated insofar as

> [A] soul is compelled [*anagkazō*] to use hypotheses/assumptions in searching for it. It does not go to a beginning since it is unable to escape or rise out of its hypotheses. And it uses as images those things of which images were imitating the things below, and in comparison with which they are opined to be clear and are honored (511 a).

Not only does the thought (*dianoia*) of the geometer incorrectly presuppose the hypothesis as a first beginning, they do this *by necessity*; she is "compelled to use hypotheses." The *mathematicos'* thinking is necessarily appropriated and carried along by a wave of necessity originating and ending outside of the investigator. That is to say, the investigator does not freely start with the hypothesis. There is, rather, a motive force (necessity) originating elsewhere that appropriates the investigator and the investigation. Should we call the origin *common sense*? Common sense remains for us a given, a ground, to which we are shackled *necessarily*. It has already appropriated our sensuous and intellectual faculties in a way that conceals itself as a structure of necessity. We imagine ourselves free to think what we like, to investigate what we like, but common sense does not originate with any individual; it is that in which the individual first belongs, as one among the many.

Here, with the three finger example, Socrates gives an account of the comportment toward the "finger" of *oi polloi*, of common sense. In this case, the soul of the many—the many that resides in each human, qua human—is not compelled [*anagkazō*] to ask what a finger is. S/he does not experience perplexity [*aporia*] regarding fingerness, the *what is* of finger, but is rather "compelled" to make judgments about fingers with a presumed, uninterrogated discursive concept. Thus, insofar as there exists no sensuous perplexity [*aporia*] in an encounter with these fingers, "it is likely that [these three fingers] would not awaken the intellect" (523 d—e). Rather, one is compelled [*anagkazō*] by common sense to allow common sense's discursive concept of "finger" to rule over one's judgments.

Aporia shocks the soul in such a way that intellect [*nous*] is shaken awake; otherwise, intellect remains asleep and the soul rests in common sense/*oi polloi*. The example of the experience of perceiving "fingers" fails to prod intellect (*o nous*) from its slumber. What will wake him? Socrates begins to answer[7] this question by reference to the kinds of beings that sense senses: quantities, qualities, etc. With respect to bigness and littleness, thickness and thinness, and softness and hardness, for instance, Socrates suggests that sense perceives them insufficiently (523 e - 524 a). He then describes the process by which the insufficiency yields an *aporia* and a noetic awakening.

> "Firstly, the *aisthēsis* appointed to the hard is also compelled [*anagkazō*] to be appointed to the soft; and it messages [*paraggellō*] the soul that the same thing is perceived by it as both hard and soft"
>
> "Just so," he said.
>
> "Therefore, it is necessary [*anagkaios*]," I said, "in such things that the soul be at a loss [*aporia*] as to what *aisthēsis* means by the hard, if it says that the same thing is also soft . . . ?"
>
> "Yes, indeed," he said . . .
>
> "Therefore," I said, "it's likely that in such cases a soul first summons calculation [*logismos*] and intellect [*noēsis*] and tries to examine whether each of the things reported to it is one or two." (524 a—b).

How are the eyes of intellect opened in the first study of number as number? In this example, Socrates suggests that the soul receives simultaneously contradictory sensations associated with a particular sense. In the case of sight, for example, the soul necessarily receives both bigness and smallness because, by natural necessity, sight has the power to perceive both. There is something sensuously second-order here, however. When does sense relate bigness and smallness at the same time? With respect to the finger example, one compares the size of one finger with another, the size of two fingers with one, or one compares any combination of size that is possible. Some fingers are bigger/smaller than others. This is not perplexing. It is only when one acquires some intellectual distance that the ring finger, for instance, becomes perplexingly both small and big at the same time—big in relation to the little finger, but small when compared with the middle finger. According to Socrates here, it is only with such an observation that one might undergo perplexity. That is to say, it is only in the case that a being may be in violation of some anticipated and presumed principle of noncontradiction that the soul reaches a *cul de sac* of *aporia* while receiving sensations. When one takes a step back from the immediacy of the sensuous encounter and suffers the realization that the middle finger is both small and large at the same time, only then does perplexity emerge. However, is there a sensuous origin to the measure of noncontradiction? Or is such a measure already reliant upon the framework provided by *oi polloi*, by common sense—which is, as we have observed, a necessary condition of every human being, qua human?

Whatever the answer to this question, Socrates claims that the origin of the first of the new studies (number or *the one*) lies in this sensuous experience of suffering a contradiction and its resulting perplexity. After such an *aporia*, it is "likely" that *noēsis* (and *logismos*) will be called forth to solve the question of whether the being that exhibits this contradiction is "one or two" (524 b). Socrates then extends this phenomenon to include the philosophical movement of turning. When sense suffices to judge the being without contradiction and perplexity, there is no turn "toward being" (524 d—e, 523 b). However, when the sensuous experience gives rise to opposing impressions within the same being at the same time, then, apparently, the turning movement is *necessarily* initiated.

> "a soul would be compelled [*anagkazō*] to be at a loss [*aporia*] and to inquire [*zēteō*], to arouse into motion within itself thinking [*ennoia*] and to question what the one itself is. Thus the study of the one would lead and turn the soul toward the contemplation of what *is*" (524 e - 525 a).

The study of the one does not arise as a product of a disciplinary regime. One does not move from arithmetic, to geometry, to trigonometry, for instance, to *the one*—it is *prior* to any given mathematical system in both senses of the term. It emerges, according to Socrates, as a shock to the *sensuous* system *vis à vis* common-sense concepts that have become unreliable. The awareness of the one as an object of investigation comes to be when what a person had thought was self-evidently "one" shows itself as containing within it both a unity and a manifold. As such, the phenomenon violates an ontological principle of noncontradiction. It is not merely that something cannot *be said* to be and not be at the same time and in the same respect; emphasis is placed rather on the challenge this presents to a being's *being*.

We observe the claim in a more explicit way in book IV, when Socrates considers the difficulty of fleshing-out whether the soul is one or many. Socrates states that this "is difficult" to know (436 a). For, the soul appears to *learn* with a part of itself that is different than that by which it *desires*. And it appears to *desire* with a part different than that by which it is *spirited*. If it has three parts, the singular soul is, in fact, many. To begin to investigate whether the soul is one or many, Socrates invokes as a guide what has been called the first formal articulation of the principle of contradiction.[8] Socrates says,

> It is clear that the same thing is not willing to do or experience opposite things in relation to the same thing, in the same respect at the same time. Thus, if we should find this [opposition] happening in these things, we will know that they were not the same one, but many" (436 b—c).

Later, in book IX, we observe the remarkable unification of the soul through *erōs*, one of the ways that *anagkē* manifests itself, such that erotic being appears to be the kind of being that bestows ontological unity on the parts of the soul. There, the soul becomes reformulated in terms of its pleasures: the wisdom-loving, victory-loving, and gain-loving parts of the soul. However, here, I wish to emphasize that it is not merely a logical inadequacy, a logical contradiction that calls forth *nous*. Rather, an ontological contradiction surfaces that summons the intellect. This is true of every *aporia*.

In the case of the *first* study which results from the *first aporia*, the unity of the being of any being is in question. The human undergoes the experience of *aporia* when he "sees the same thing at once as both one and an infinite plurality [*apeira to plēthos*]" (525 a). As one conducts one's daily life, beings show themselves in accordance with the unproblematic presentation of common-sense concepts: the plant is one plant, the dog is one dog, the human being is one human. However, it may be that at some unpredictable moment the human appears to the viewer as more complicated than this. For instance, the singular human being is a multicellular organism composed of approximately a trillion individual cells. One might ask oneself the question: am I one or *about* a trillion? If I am one, what is the principle of my unity? Moreover, at any given moment, that same human being may harbor many more trillions of "foreign" organisms: bacteria, archaea, single cellular nucleated organisms and viruses—many, if not all, of these "foreign" organisms interact directly or indirectly with their host in a way that remains constitutive to what and how the host *is*. In this way, the soul "sees the same thing at once as both one and an infinite plurality [*apeira to plēthos*]" (525 a). While there is no guarantee that such an experience will force the common-sense conceptual regime to break down into *aporia*, the experience occasions the possibility that one will find oneself at a loss and that thinking may awake from its slumber to investigate what is meant by this unity, by the one.

Presumably, there remains the possibility that, instead of *the one*, the intellect could be directed to investigate what is meant by this "infinite plurality [*apeira to plēthos*]." However, conspicuously, the latter more problematic possibility goes unstated in the text. One can imagine that, if *nous* pursues the latter option, it would turn toward the perhaps impossible intellection of infinity and becoming, not "the one" and being. Still, the possibility that a singular thing may be constituted by an unlimited multitude is nevertheless a stated possibility among the two poles the contemplation of which yields noetic activity. What would it mean if, not unity, but rather an unlimited multitude were constitutive of the being of any/every given being?

I would contend that this possibility represents a latent challenge by Plato to Platonism's "being" and its knowledge. Moreover, the challenge lies at the very inception of the new studies; it is among the first study's founding gestures. It may be that the figure of an unavoidable necessity in the form of *the wandering cause* already haunts *the one* (the foundational study that provokes the intellect to turn away from the shadows floating by on the cave walls). Moreover, this complex *archē* holds consequences for each new study that follows; for, each of the following new studies adds a new dimension to the one prior to it. That is to say, in my reading, Socrates' studies constitute a kind of knowledge system of the world—starting with an indivisible point (the one), moving on to two dimensions (plane geometry), three dimensions (solid geometry), out beyond geometry and the earth (astronomy), and toward the harmonic movement of the whole (harmonics). Later, I will develop this suggestion into a more concrete interpretation. For now, I simply wish to highlight the fact that, if the "wandering cause" is already latently [*lanthanomai*] placed by Plato at the origin of the world-system he has Socrates create, then this Socratic knowledge system too is subject to *wandering*.

The ghost of the wandering cause is not the only clue we receive in the first new study to the presence of a virus in the system at the very beginning of its articulation. There exist gaps in the argument to which we should call attention. One such gap involves the relation between sensation and common-sense discursive concepts. Why does Socrates begin his analysis of the new studies in the experience of sensation? We have already drawn attention to the fact that Socrates' reference to sensation for the first *aporia* has been controversial in the literature for precisely the reason that judgments of things like quality and quantity are not bare sensations, but involve discursive concepts already. But, if Socrates is building a system of knowledge grounded upon *the one* (a kind of originary point of intelligibility upon which everything else intelligible is grounded) there are important reasons to begin his analysis in sensation. Sensation may represent for common sense the originary encounter with the beings in the world. If the beings in the world first become available to the soul through sensuous perception, then intelligibility needs to be linked to it in some way—even if sense represents only confused or contradictory encounters with becoming and shadows. But I would argue that it is precisely the gap between the sensuous encounter with beings and the experience of the opposition between the discursive concepts of "the one" and an "unlimited multitude" that is at stake here at the beginning of the first study. Leaving aside the question of whether either can actually be *thought*, it is certain that neither "the one" nor "an unlimited multitude" can ever be *sensed*. They are both discursive concepts. Perhaps Plato has Socrates leave a gap because it is unbridgeable. In that case, the gap is *necessary* because the perception of the one and the experience of sense are precisely incommensurable. To employ an analogy, "the one" is the square and "the immediately sensuous" is the square's diagonal. The incommensurable (*alogos*) diagonal lies latent in *every* square and constitutes it, but it cannot be made intelligible; that is to say, the attempt to make it intelligible is merely a contrivance, an artifact, a *technē*. This necessary gap at the origin lies in the fact that, for the human, there was never a purely sensuous beginning from which to start with pure sensation: discursive concepts were already proliferating and entangling sensations from the beginning. One cannot begin with the sensuous "one," qua sensuous, because it is already a discursive concept, even in mathematics.

Having considered the challenges facing the origin of the system of knowledge Socrates is creating with the new studies, I wish to offer a few concluding speculations regarding the experience of *aporia* in the one. If a human being operates with a presumed conception of "the one" derived from his/her habituation in the education of *oi polloi*, then the first new study represents the means by which the soul will turn away from this shadow conception of the one toward the being of it. That is to say, the new study places the human being in the experience of *aporia* regarding the first condition of the intelligibility of beings—that they are one. On reflection, the question "what does it mean to be one?" appears to generate an *aporia* on its own without all the talk about the sensation of fingers. Appealing to Aristotle's *Metaphysics* (Aristotle 1924, 1006 a 30–1006 b 11), we see him struggle with the *aporia* in his efforts to give articulation to the singular something. For Aristotle, if something is to be intelligible, it must *be one*. Otherwise, it is a "heap," and a "heap" is unintelligible. Aristotle argues that a being's being is not visible to sensuous perception. Rather, these are the being's secondary substances. For him, a being's *primary substance* is that which makes a being one. It is *what something keeps on being in order to be the being it is* (Aristotle's famous neologism: *to ti en einai*). However, how does one distinguish this singular something from something else? That is more of a challenge for Aristotle. For instance, one may define a leopard as a member of the panther family having the specific difference of spots. One articulates a leopard's genus and species. In doing so, one offers a definition that expresses the being of the leopard. However, this definition does not name *one* thing. It names many things. In fact, it names all the leopards in the world. For Aristotle, insofar as a "leopard" possesses matter, it has become differentiated into *one* leopard; however, this strikes the reader as unsatisfying, since matter is precisely unintelligible (Aristotle 1924, 1045 a 30–1045 b 7). Can the human being *speak* of the one in a way that gives expression to the singular? If it is to be a first beginning, *the one* always already remains a deep problem.

As we have argued above, while the ghosts of the wandering cause and of necessary gaps haunt the argument, Socrates nevertheless minimizes these differences and employs *the one* in an effort to provide a ground for a knowledge system of the being of things. An *aporia* generated by the perception of a thing in its unity and its unlimited multiplicity turns the soul away from the visible presentation of a thing in its becoming, its wandering, toward the intellection of a thing in its static, stable, dependable being. The one becomes a mathematical measure of a being's being. "Thus, you see, friend," I said, "that this study runs the risk of being necessary [*anagkaion*] for us, since it seems to compel [*pros-anagkazō*] the soul to use the intellect itself on the truth itself" (526 a—b). If the experience of *aporia* pushes the intellect to seize hold of one which remains stable, secure and everlasting, it may ground a system of knowledge. Consequently, the truth lies in a being's being. But if, instead, the experience of *aporia* forces the individual out of a common-sense conception of the one provided by the *oi polloi* and the individual is subsequently not confronted by a legitimate *one* upon which to seize hold but rather finds herself *necessarily* confronted by an indefinite multitude, then truth and being are separated from each other. Truth means something else. Socrates presumes the first alternative, while Plato remains silent.

PLANE GEOMETRY

After giving articulation to the study of the first dimension of being in arithmetical and geometrical terms—the one, the point, the number—Socrates suggests moving on to the next dimension: the study coming after (526 c) the study of *the one*. Glaucon correctly divines that Socrates means "geometry," suggesting that we are moving from investigating the being of "the point" to the being of "the line" or "the plane." However, Glaucon's assumption about the usefulness of such a discipline indicates that he has not yet understood how the new studies differ from the old ones. He points to geometry's practical utility in acts of war: "positioning an army, taking possession of places, arraying the troops in line, and in all other formations armies make battles and on marches" (526 d). While war was distinguished before from practical pursuits in a way that was not made clear, one can certainly turn/comport oneself toward it in a practical manner. Ever war and victory obsessed, Glaucon so far sees only utility in the service of these. To redirect Glaucon's gaze, Socrates argues against the notion that the most important function of geometry is its usefulness in war. Rather, he says,

> "The great and more advanced [geometry] aims to make it easier to catch sight of the *idea* of the good [*katidein tēn tou agathou idean*]. And we say that this aim is found in all things that compel [*anagkazō*] the soul to turn toward the happiest of what is" (526 d—e).

In the setting of the new studies, geometry is not employed for the sake of improving architecture, developing more effective machines, or even for arraying an army in a way that will enable it to defeat the enemy. While geometry may be useful for such endeavors, Socrates argues that the most profound effect of the study of geometry lies in its capacity to turn the soul. In the early study of mathematics, *oi polloi* inscribed the discipline of geometry upon the soul of the youth for the practical reasons that Glaucon states. It is useful for the youth of a city to be educated in mathematics because it positions the city to outperform other cities in the endeavors of economy, technology and warfare. However, once "educated" by *oi polloi*, the human remains capable of a turning of the soul *vis à vis* those geometrical concepts that *oi polloi* have folded into her. Socrates here states that, in the new studies, the soul might turn toward the discipline that is already written on the soul in a new way, in a more profound and important way than mere practice. Geometry, he suggests, can *compel* [*anagkazō*] the soul to turn toward the idea of the good [*hē tou agathou idea*] and the happiest of being [*to eudaimonestaton tou ontos*].

However, a number of questions emerge for us regarding the work of plane geometry in the new studies. First, as we have seen before, the turning of the soul occurs as a consequence of an *aporia*. However, the articulation of the *aporia* associated with plane geometry remains conspicuously absent from Socrates' description. If it is to compel us to turn, there must be something already built into the discipline that floats by on the cave walls that is capable of shocking us out of our complacent acceptance of the common-sense geometrical conceptions, something which, when made visible and brought into question, is capable of loosening us from our binds within the discipline. What does one encounter in plane geometry that engenders this experience? Socrates does not say. In our analysis of *the one*, we made reference to the square of plane geometry. Constitutive of every geometrically composed square is a diagonal that remains incommensurable (*alogos*) with its four sides. That is to say, insofar as every square contains within itself this incommensurability, there is something irrational built into the geometrical form. As the shapes pass by on the cave walls, this incommensurability goes unobserved. But, similar to the sensuous encounter with a singular being in arithmetic (which revealed itself as both one and infinitely many at the same time), the geometrical square displays *both* a rational stability to the being of the plane (to the second dimension), *and* something indefinite and irrational. Perhaps we can say that when an encounter with the square invokes this contradictory experience, *aporia* may result, necessarily forcing *nous* out of its slumber to confront the necessary irrationality in every rational two-dimensional form.

The figure of necessity as we have traced its meaning elsewhere appears in (at least) two ways here. On the one hand, if incommensurability can be understood as synonymous with the "wandering cause," then the irrational complexity that haunts the square and plane geometry finds its origin in necessity. Necessity, therefore, lies latent in the composition of the universal square, even the most rationally constituted one. However, this is not a necessity understood in the modern sense which is commensurable with reason and something like a Newtonian force law. Rather, this is a necessity understood as *the wandering cause*: a necessity that will not succumb to reason and that cannot even be excised from the rational system of Euclidean plane geometry. In the context of common sense and the practical application of the geometrical system, the contradiction can be ignored as the image of the square passes by on the cave walls; however, if the stranger's hand reaches out of the darkness and *compels* the viewer to look, an *aporia* may result. The instability of the faculties forces a turning of the soul to think philosophically—that is to say, the kind of thinking that emerges from a loss of confidence in one's own knowledge subsequent to having been emptied by an *aporia*.

With this last observation in mind, if, as Socrates suggests in book VI, necessity and the good are at odds (493 c), then geometry as a whole appears to lean more toward necessity—a logical one at that. The second sense of necessity shows itself here, insofar as a logical necessity appears to govern the propositions of geometry. Namely, propositions necessarily compel assent insofar as they rest on composed/crafted assumptions (the common notions and postulates of Euclid's book I [Euclid 1956, 154–155]). In geometry, the movement that governs the argument *necessarily* leads to the conclusion. Yet, this resurrects the question of whether the new studies operate in accordance with logical or natural necessity. As we observed in our analysis of the slave boy exchange in the *Meno*, the being of plane geometry cannot transcend its status as somehow an artifact, or a contrivance. It must be posited as a technologically crafted *image or model* because there are in fact no entities that exist in either one or two dimensions. Even if one wanted to argue that, for Socrates, a shadow or image exists in two dimensions and has a position among the things that *are* in the linear progression of being on the divided line, still, the shadow has the least quantity of being of any being and (based on the argument offered in books VI and VII) cannot serve as a standard of *what is*. Indeed, adding to the technological character of the current image, the being of the two dimensional square resembles what we today would call a two dimensional blueprint—which is of course not actually two dimensional. Thus, we may wish to ask if the *technē*-logical necessity governing the new study of geometry relies not on the being of nature, but rather on the being of *technē*. In the latter case, would the expression of the geometrical form be limited to a mere *model* of the phenomenon one wishes to know? Models *approximate* their objects and systems. Are Plato's natural forms not necessarily *more than* their technological reflections?

In addition to the problem of the lack of a description of the cause of *aporia* and the ambivalent expressions of necessity in plane geometry, another question emerges for us from the passage quoted above. How, precisely, does geometry force [*anagkazō*] a turn toward *the good*? As in our analysis of the idea of the good in the *sun analogy*, the *divided line* and the *allegory of the cave*, I would argue that here too Socrates' words do not touch upon a phenomenon in plane geometry that discloses the good. Insofar as plane geometry makes visible a relationship between, say, two angles that hold universally, then geometry compels [*anagkazō*] the soul to witness something that "is" in the way that Socrates has defined being. In proposition 1.15 (Euclid 1956, 277) of his *Elements*, Euclid argues that, if two straight lines cut each other, then the vertical angles that they form will equal one another. The demonstration does not claim to name the truth of a singular instance, but rather asserts something that holds universally. The being of the two angles is demonstrated to be equal always and this will never "wander." Consequently, the equality of the two angles will never be subject to movement, change or metamorphosis. In the context of plane geometry, this is what Socrates means by "what is." However, at no point do we receive an argument about the goodness of the conclusions of geometry—like in the divided line, we only reach knowledge of its objects' geometrical *being*, not its principle of legitimacy or its goodness.[9] In fact, from the argument, its principle of legitimacy lies in its necessary conclusion. Thus, the turn toward universality in geometry appears to be grounded upon a proposition's expression of *logical* necessity or the accuracy of its *technē*, not the good.

SOLID GEOMETRY

What study comes after plane geometry? As the drama of the new studies unfolds, there is something of a controversy that emerges. A gap opens in the drama insofar as the correct sequence in the presentation of disciplines is not followed: initially, Socrates posits astronomy as the study that naturally follows plane geometry. Then, after an interesting interruption about Glaucon's obsession with utility, Socrates corrects the order by turning toward solid geometry. Why does Plato have Socrates produce this rupture in the argument? Does the structure of the conversation reveal that, for Plato, there exists a natural gap between plane and solid geometry? Is there a way that moving from the second dimension to the third dimension requires a leap?

We will return to this question in the context of our analysis of Socrates' presentation of solid geometry. For now, we will consider more closely the content of the disruption; for, the gap in the argument is punctuated by Glaucon's response to Socrates' suggestion that astronomy comes next in the order of studies.

"Shall put astronomy in third place? Or what do you think?"

"Indeed, it seems right to me," he said. "A better perception of seasons, months and years belongs not only to agriculture and navigation, but also to military strategy" (527 d).

Again, for the third time, Glaucon reveals that he does not understand the field of investigation of the new studies. Glaucon is still one among the many. In some sense, he is still a prisoner in the cave, a prisoner to common sense and *oi polloi*. It may be the case that Plato shows this fact in two ways through the disruption of the correct order of the argument. On the one hand, Glaucon fails to observe Socrates' endeavor to build a system from the ground up: starting with the first dimension, moving to the second, and now expecting to develop the third. Instead of asking if the study of astronomy concerns the third dimension that should come next in Socrates' argument, he immediately agrees with Socrates, confirming for the sake of astronomy's usefulness to farming, navigation, and warfare. On the other hand, Plato shows Glaucon's thought still belongs to *oi polloi* by having Socrates humorously chide him regarding this fact. Socrates says:

"You amuse me [*ēdus ei*] . . . you are like someone fearing the many [*oi polloi*], not wanting to appear to prescribe useless studies. It is not easy, but hard, to trust [*pisteuō*] that in the soul of each there is an instrument [*organon*] that, by studies such as these, is purified and lit up, but destroyed and blinded by other endeavors. It is an instrument more important to save than ten thousand eyes (527 d—e).

Glaucon's mind still belongs to the *oi polloi*—which is to say, he continues to perceive everything through the lens of common sense. Moreover, it is not easy [*phaulos*], but rather difficult [*chalepon*] to believe [*pisteuō*] that these studies are for the sake of the cultivation and purification of *nous*. In other words, it is immensely difficult to allow doubt to surface regarding the common-sense notions of *oi polloi* in order to make space for intellect to awaken. We see this over and over in the dialogues: characters resist Socrates' attempts to dislodge them from their common-sense notions that at first appear so credible, to make them suffer *aporia* regarding them, and to empty them so that they are left with only themselves.

Socrates then gives Glaucon three options for carrying on the conversation. There are hypothetical interlocutors among whom Glaucon must choose to engage. Either he is to speak to the ones who share in the opinion about the human need to bracket the hive mind of *oi polloi* and cultivate noetic perception or he is to speak with those whom Socrates believes Glaucon's words have represented so far: those that believe all of this philosophical talk "is saying nothing" (527 e), or finally, he is to speak only with himself, "for his own sake" (528 a). The options provided offer an illuminating reflection on the interruption. Obviously, Socrates' imperative excludes the option of choosing to speak with and as *oi polloi*. However, the other two options are less certain. Perhaps "those for whom this seems good" (527 e), or those encouraging the cultivation of *nous* are somehow still somehow operating as *oi polloi*. One can imagine circumstances in which dialectically engaging with people who share in common beliefs about the cultivation of *nous* might not yield a noetic insight, but only confirmation of a common-sense opinion. For example, while there is a way that discussing Heidegger with Heideggerians is certainly useful and illuminating, it may be the case that dialectical engagement with a community that already agrees about the foundational questions only confirms common belief rather than something more radical. The new studies aim to acquire distance from both forms of common opinion. The text seems to suggest that "speaking to neither [of these two] but for your own sake" (528 a) is the appropriate comportment to hold toward the subject matters of the new studies. The question, of course, is whether it is actually possible to speak only for oneself. Or are the discursive conditions of speech *necessarily* already bound up with communities in a way that precludes the latter comportment. In any case, as one might expect, Glaucon chooses "*mostly* [*pleistos*] for my own sake to speak, to question, and to answer" (528 a, emphasis added).

In addition to raising the question of whether Glaucon understands the subject matter and goal of the new studies, the interruption *via* the mistake also *dramatically* positions a gap between the first and second dimensions, between plane geometry and solid geometry. Once Socrates acquires Glaucon's assent to speak, not in a way that pleases *oi polloi*, but in a way that reflects a frank answer emerging from himself as himself, Socrates shines a light on the mistake for Glaucon. He appeals to Glaucon's passion for military pursuits and says "go back [*anage*][10] a bit. For, what we took to follow geometry just now was not right" (528 a). As we have already pointed out above, the study that comes after the study of the second dimension ought to be that of the third. Perhaps someone would want to argue that astronomy belongs to the analysis of the third dimension, but it is not the place where one would naturally begin; for, astronomy is not simply the solid, but "the solid in orbit/revolution [*periphora*]" (528 a). Thus, Socrates argues that

> "the right way takes the third dimension (*auxē*[11]) next in order after the second, and this partakes of the dimension of cubes and depth" (528 b).

The interruption in the discussion stands between the second and the third dimension. Why does Plato insert this gap in the argument? In my reading, we observe a clue for one of the reasons for this in Glaucon's response. "But Socrates," he says, "it seems not to have been discovered [*euriskō*]" (528 b). Earlier, we wondered if the transition from the second dimension to the third required a leap. On the one hand, as we have just indicated, Plato produces a gap in between the second and the third dimension in their *presentation*. However, on the other hand, we observe here a reference to a *conceptual* gap between the two dimensions. Glaucon claims that the path between the second and third dimensions has not been "discovered" yet. There is disagreement in the literature about how to interpret this line. On the one hand, Shorey argues that the assertion should not be "pressed." He ignores the fact that the assertion is in the mouth of Glaucon and simply argues that "Plato only means that the progress of solid geometry is unsatisfactory" (1969). Adam asserts that, by the passage, Plato does not mean that the study of solid geometry had not yet been invented, but "he only means that its problems had not been discovered or solved" (1902). Both commentators suggest that the passage may refer to the Delian problem. Reference to this problem may help illuminate an interpretation in line with what we have developed so far—that is, interpreting whether there is a clear rational connection between the second and third dimension in the new studies.

In his *On the E at Delphi*, Plutarch references the Delian problem as originating from an oracle that the Delians received at Delphi. The story goes that the people of Delos were suffering from a plague that had been sent to them by Apollo. When they consulted the oracle at Delphi, they were told that the plague would be lifted if they doubled the size of the altar at Delos (a cube). According to Plutarch, they enlisted the help of Plato who told them that the god was actually enjoining them to study geometry (Plutarch 1935, 211). Whether or not Plutarch's anecdote is true,[12] geometrically doubling the altar (the cube) baffled mathematicians for centuries. While the historical literature is full of disagreement regarding the successful discovery of a solution to the problem, in 1837, Pierre Wantzel proved that the solution employing

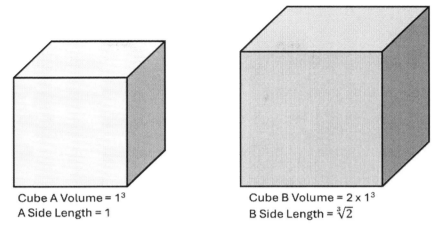

Figure 6.1. Cube doubling, ratio of volume to edge length of a cube, the starting cube is the unit cube with edge length.[13]
Created by the author based on an image by Petrus3743

the Euclidean method of a compass and straightedge is impossible (Wantzel 1837, 366). Why? Because doubling the volume of the cube requires an irrational quantity that cannot be constructed.

In the problem of doubling the area of the square with the slave boy in the *Meno* (considered earlier), Socrates uses the irrational diagonal to effect the change (1990, 84 a). However, there is no constructible line in the cube upon which to compose a line equaling the cubed root of two. According to ancient sources, Plato commissioned the celebrated mathematicians Archytas, Eudoxus, and Menaechmus to find a solution to the problem for the Delians. However, instead of pure geometry, they employed mechanics. Consequently, as the story goes, Plato rejected their efforts (Zhmud 2006, 84). If, in the new studies, the endeavor of solid geometry is taken in its purity, then one would expect the student to stumble upon the problem. Of course, the practical problem of doubling the cube only occasions the real problem, the real occasion for thought. What is baffling is not the mechanical problem of doubling a cube. Rather, it lies in what the pursuit of the problem reveals about the nature of solid geometrical objects. It is the disclosure of an irrationality, a wandering cause, that always already haunts the cube, an irrationality that reason cannot subdue except by employing "irrational" numbers (which are precisely irrational). For modern humans embedded in our own *oi polloi*, the use of irrational numbers has lost its radical character. The irrational number has been appropriated by common sense and no longer shocks the intellect out of complacency. For us, an irrational number is simply a slightly awkward rational number. However, the cubed root of 2 (1.259921...) remains a quantity with an infinite number of digits in its decimal representation and cannot be "grasped" unless one artificially ends the digits in an approximation, the equivalent of a *model*.

Perhaps, for Plato, what the new study of solid geometry shows is that an operation as "simple" as doubling a cube remains *necessarily* impossible because these entities are not fully compatible with human reason. If Apollo had asked the Delians to increase the volume by eight times, then we would have had a rational number by which to calculate the volume of the cube because the cubed root of eight is two. Of course, the entire number series cubed (x^3) produces this rational ground: one cubed, two cubed, three cubed, etc. However, everything in between these is subject to the *wandering cause*, qua irrationality; that is to say, all of it is subject to *necessity* in one of the ways that Plato has presented it to us. Might we suggest that necessity as a "wandering cause" already subtends even the cubed number series? Everything in between the series is irrational, to be sure, but these also belong to the number series, even if they remain mostly hidden from view. As such, we might compare the whole of nature to the image of a farm and reason to the life inside the farm house. The numbers in the cubed series are like windows that occasion and provide vision outside of the house onto the workings of the farm; however, the walls, the floors, and the ceilings (everything in between the windows) conceal from reason all the rest of what is going on outside. As the image portrays, might it be that, for the most part, beings exist thanks to the wandering cause, infinity, and unintelligibility, while *reason believes it* is the standard of the beings that *are* in the world?

In summary, the new study of geometry occasions an *aporia* that enables *nous* to wake up and turn the soul toward the being of the solid in a way that transcends the merely practical consideration of, say, doubling an altar. But, as in the case of the one and the plane, that is not to say that solid geometry in the new study enables the soul to rest in unproblematic confidence in the knowledge of three-dimensional beings. Moreover, it does not release the soul from its bind to necessity in such a way that enables it to acquire a pure vision of the good.

ASTRONOMY

After Socrates corrects the mistaken order of the analysis and the study of the solid takes its rightful position prior to the study of the solid in motion, the discussion returns to the next in order: "Then" I said, "in fourth place, we should put the study of astronomy, assuming that the study now let go [geometry of the solid] will exist if a city seeks it" (528 e). Astronomy, the study of three-dimensional entities in motion, will follow the geometrical study of three-dimensional beings.

Yet, Glaucon makes yet another mistake of presumption that Socrates feels compelled to correct. Moreover, again, astronomy remains the subject matter of the mistaken presumption:

> "You chastised me, Socrates, just now for praising astronomy vulgarly. Now, just as you approach it, I too will praise it. For, it seems to me that it is clear to all that astronomy compels [*anagkazō*] the soul to look up and leads it there away from the things here" (528 e - 529 a).

With the wound to his ego still smarting, Glaucon attempts to reclaim his dignity by anticipating Socrates' coming words about astronomy. In his first praise of astronomy, Glaucon referred to its practical usefulness.[14] Now, he believes he defends the discipline because it is theoretical. He appeals to the reputation astronomy has to everyone [*pas*] of urging those that partake in it to an intellectual life. Astronomy, he suggests, turns the soul upwards and astronomers contemplate the everlasting features of the heavens. Again, despite Socrates' caution regarding following the opinion of *oi polloi* in the new studies, Glaucon appeals to common sense: what is obvious to everyone. Socrates quickly dismisses Glaucon's argument and contrasts the opinion of *everyone* to *his own* opinion.

> "Perhaps it is clear to everyone except me," I said. "For, to me it does not seem like that . . . in the manner the ones now leading into philosophy practice [*metaxeirizō*] it, it makes them look down" (529 a).

In contrast to Glaucon's interpretation of his words, Socrates does not think that the current practice of astronomy satisfies the conditions that mark the new studies. Even if the mathematical contemplation of the stars does not necessarily have a use or concrete practical aim, that does not mean it engages the intellect in the manner we have described above. With this caveat, Socrates expresses the concern that the visible things of *becoming* mask themselves as intellectual things of *being*. By the *new* study of astronomy, Socrates does not mean undergoing the experience of wonder when one lies face up on the ground under the night sky. Moreover, he does not mean the kind of mathematical analysis that tracks and predicts the motions of the stars for purely theoretical means. Aristophanes' Socrates in the *Clouds* is comedically presented as engaged in this sort of theoretical astronomy.[15] Adam suggests that Plato has this in mind when he has Socrates present the present argument that distances Socrates' position from both practical and theoretical astronomies—the theoretical ones are still based on vision (1902, 529 b).

But, it seems to me important, given the dramatic details of the content of Glaucon's mistakes clarified above, that both of these mistakes are predicated upon their connection to *oi polloi*. For instance, early in the articulation of the new studies, Socrates argues that the analysis of the one is predicated upon an experience for which perception does not already have a concept (inherited by *oi polloi*).[16] If we substitute the word "visible" for the word "perceptible" [*aisthesis*] in the relevant passage, then we have an articulation of the problem in the same language of Socrates' second critique of Glaucon's conception of the work of astronomy: the problem of an astronomy based on vision. Vision is one of the functions of perception, after all. As Socrates said: "certain [visible] beings do not call thought to examination because [vision] suffices to judge them, and there are others which in every way engage thought in this examination, since [vision] gives nothing sound" (523 a). Vision stumbles upon something in the sky for which it does not already have a concept. The new study is therefore predicated upon precisely the failure of vision. This experience may generate an *aporia* that occasions the emergence of *nous*. In the new study of astronomy one is required to lose oneself, qua common sense, regarding *both* the practical use of astronomy for navigation at night, etc., *and* the theoretical assessment of, say, the orbit of Venus (in, for example, Ptolemy). Perception finds itself comfortable and at home by being in possession of the foundational concepts for these (the wanderer Venus, the concept of the eccentric circle, the concept of the epicycle, the system of Euclidean geometry, etc.). The mathematical calculation of the movement of Venus does not generate an *aporia* and a consequent emptying of the self. The new study of astronomy that turns the soul away from what becomes toward "*what is* and the invisible" (529 b) requires the experience of the loss of common-sense concepts—whether these are practical or theoretical.

What occasions the destabilization of common sense in astronomy, of the study of the three-dimensional beings that move? Socrates does not say. However, in what follows, there are ambiguous arguments involving movement. When Glaucon asks Socrates to explain further what he means when he says that "it is necessary that astronomy be studied contrary to how they now study it" (529 c), Socrates speaks not of visible stars, but of the invisible movements of the things in which the visible things are moved (nested movements of visible things in intelligible things?):

"On the one hand, these manifold ornaments [*poikilma*] in the heavens, since they have been worked in various colors [*poikillō*[17]] in the visible, lead one to hold that they are the fairest and most precise [*akribēs*] of such things. But on the other hand, they fall far short of the true ones: those movements [*circular movements*] in which the really fast and the really slow [*rectilinear movements*] are moved in true number and in all the true figures with respect to one another, and move the things that are in them, which indeed, are grasped by *logos* and thought [*dianoia*], not sight" (529 c—d).

Socrates argues that the stars and planets that are visible in the sky are mistakenly taken by us as the most beautiful and the most precise [*akribēs*]. In chapter two, we showed that *akribēs* is often brought into an antithetical relation with common sense. Whatever *akribēs* means for Plato, he uses it in opposition to the common understanding of *oi polloi*. For example, in book I, Socrates uses the term when he asks Thrasymachus to clarify if by "ruler" and "stronger," he means that employed in common speech or in the "precise" [*akribēs*] sense (341 b). Here, "precise" is used to suggest that common speech interprets the glittering entities that move across the sky to be the most beautiful and the most "precise"entities—that is to say, the most *philosophical*, most *theoretical*, the *truest* entities. However, as Socrates conceives of it, *oi polloi* are wrong. This sort of claim is neither difficult to understand nor surprising. What follows is more of a challenge to interpret.

In contrast to the visible entities in motion, Socrates argues that what is truly beautiful and truly precise are the movements, not the sparkling visible objects. Thus, it appears that, by remaining focused on the visible objects, *oi polloi* lose access to the truth which lies, rather, in their invisible movements. What does this mean? Not the beings in movement, but the movements themselves are beautiful and precise? This is a problematic claim. In book VI (485 b—c), recall, the philosophical nature is distinguished from other natures by his "hatred" for movement and motions insofar as these belong to becoming. The erotic love for *what is* was contrasted to the hate for *what wanders*. It is possible, perhaps, to make the claim that Socrates appeals here to some aspect of movement that does not "move," some Newtonian force law, for example—or, alternatively, a geometrical form that harnesses motion and brings it under the reigns of being (the circle, for instance).

The tradition[18] has largely interpreted the passage on the model of the theoretical geometry articulated above. That is to say, the tradition reads the passage as an affirmation of an abstract mathematical assessment of the heavens in the fashion of the geometry of the movements of, say, Venus through the constellations. As such, Ptolemy's *Almagest* would function as a kind of culmination of astronomy in the model of the new study. However, at least two problems emerge with this interpretation.

On the one hand, as Shorey suggests, "by this way of speaking, Plato . . . disregards the apparent difficulty that the movement of the visible stars then ought to be [already] mathematically perfect" (1969, 529 d). If the movements are beautiful and precise, the movement of the glittering Venus must also trace a path that is beautiful and precise. I do not wish to appropriate Shorey's hypothesis that Plato disregards this problem. Why not assume instead that Plato intentionally inserts the problem? In fact, one might wish to argue that such a contradiction is already a source for *aporia* and a call to *nous*. However, as will become clear shortly, I think that there is a more profound *aporia* occasioned by the passage.

On the other hand, if the Ptolemaic elaboration of the path of Venus in the sky is the model the traditional interpretation has in mind, then it relies upon an *unquestioned* concept at its foundation—namely, the concept of circular motion. In Ptolemy, we begin with the concept of circular motion and then force the appearances to adhere to it through the other discourses inherited by the surrounding *oi polloi* (epicycles, eccentric circles, Euclidean geometry, etc.). The concept of circular motion is "abstract," to be sure; however, it is a concept that already originates with the *oi polloi* in which Socrates and Glaucon were born, even if its culmination in the system of Ptolemy had not yet been elaborated in their time. As such, the traditional interpretation of the new study of astronomy does not exceed the third segment on the divided line.[19] To speak in terms used in the text during the elaboration of the divided line, it would seem that "circular motion" would be one, if not the, concept that serves as a starting point for forming hypotheses that constitute the body of propositions of an astronomical system of knowledge. In beginning with "circular motion," one proceeds with a presumed concept. The noetic turn occurs when the concept of "circular motion" that grounds the hypotheses of the knowledge system itself becomes called into question. In this case, the turn that takes place from the third tier (the *mathematikē*) to the fourth tier (the *eidē*) is marked by the urgency of the question of the being of "circular motion," its *what-is-ness*. In Ptolemy, for instance, it can be argued that we presume its *being* in the manner represented on the third tier.

What in the new study of astronomy occasions the turn to the fourth tier? Again, Socrates does not say with any detail. However, as stated before, a reading may develop from out of what Socrates says about *the motions* in which the appearances reveal themselves. Or, as he says, "those movements [*circular movements*] in which the really fast and the really slow [*rectilinear movements*] are moved . . . and move the things that are in them" (529 d). Given the hermeneutic situation of ancient Greek cosmology, perhaps we may appeal to Simplicius' formulation in order to find a way into the subject matter of astronomical *aporia*: "by hypothesizing what uniform, circular orderly motion will it be possible to save the appearances relating to planetary motions" (Burnyeat 2000, 63).

As is well known, ancient Greek cosmology observed two different kinds of motions in the heavens: circular motion and rectilinear motion.[20] In my view, these are understood to belong to two different ontological forms, two different forms of being. In the context of Aristotle, circular motion belongs to the order of being that *always is* (Aristotle 1998, 265 a 24). According to him, it betrays a form of motion that does not have a beginning and does not have an end (Aristotle 1998, 265 a 13). Circular motion has something in common with those Aristotelian concepts *ousia* and *energeia*. That is to say, circular motion belongs to the same order of being as a being's *being* and its primary *activity*: the *work* that it performs to be the being that it is (*to ti en einai*).[21] For Aristotle, the primary activity that a being performs to be what it is does not begin at one moment and end at another. While for Aristotle, there are individual dogs, it is not the *ousia* of a dog that makes it an individual. The *ousia* (and its *energeia*) is the same one that was present in the father of the dog. There is something everlasting about the activity and the work in the dog that transcends what makes a dog an individual. Unlike the categories of, say, *quality*, *quantity* and *place*, the work of the dog, qua dog (the dog's *ousia*, its form) does not change, does not begin, and does not end.

In my view, the circular motion that occasions the movement of the constellations around us must be thought in similar terms. It has a different ontological status than other sorts of motion. In particular, it differs in its being from rectilinear movement—the movement that occurs that has a beginning and an end, the movement that appears to belong to wandering, to becoming, to change. In my reading, when Socrates suggests that the truest and most precise beings in the cosmos are not the visible stars, but rather "those movements [*circular movements*] in which the really fast and the really slow [*rectilinear movements*] are moved . . . and move the things that are in them" (529 d) are the truest and most precise, he is referring to circular motion. Moreover, he articulates a relation circular motion has to rectilinear motion.[22] There are several consequences that follow here.

First, circular motion is accorded a status of *being*. This is not unproblematic. In earlier passages, Socrates associated that which moves with wandering, change and becoming. Now we are confronted not only with a movement that *is*, but also this being of movement is said to be the truest and most precise. The claim does not compel a question from Glaucon; rather, he agrees.

Second, circular motion lies at the origin of all motion. In a way that is not made clear,[23] the passage suggests that circular motion secures a dependable reality for the other metaphysical forms of motion. Without the connection to circular motion and its being, the wandering motions do not possess reality. The planets (the wanderers), are moved in a manner that speeds up and slows down; they move forward and sometimes backward through the constellations. As such they appear to exhibit the kind of being of rectilinear motion. Consequently, it could be argued that they are not knowable—what would it mean to know something that becomes one thing at one moment and something else at another? In the case of rectilinear motions other than the planets, the problem is even more pronounced. The motion of a falling leaf may not possess *being*, since it becomes for a moment and then *is not at all*.

As Socrates says, "if someone, gaping up or squinting down, attempts to learn something of perceptible things, I would not say that he learns—for such things hold no knowledge" (529 b). Thus, it may be that, when Socrates says that there are "movements [*circular movements*] in which the really fast and the really slow [*rectilinear movements*] are moved . . . and move the things that are in them" (529 d), he may mean that there exists a circular motion in which and thanks to which rectilinear movements are and in turn move the things contained in these movements. It may be that, here, Socrates alludes to a narrative of circular motion in which the latter provides a kind of dependability to rectilinear motions so that they can be measured and, thus, to some degree "known."

Finally, a further consequence of the passage interpreted through the model of circular motion contains the source for an *aporia*. The motion that belongs to *circular motion is a motion that does not move*. In book VIII of his *Physics*, Aristotle seeks to show that circular movement can be continuous, complete and infinite. According to him, rectilinear movements cannot be continuous because (among other reasons) they turn back upon themselves (Aristotle 1998, 261 b 27). If you trace the path of Mars across the heavens, you will see it move forward, slow down, stop and then perform a motion in retrograde. Motions that stop and contain contraries cannot be called continuous, complete and infinite (Aristotle 262 a 15).

> Motion on a finite straight line, if it turns back upon itself, is composite and two motions, but if it does not turn back, is incomplete and destructible (Aristotle 2001, 265 a 21).

On the one hand, the motions of the wanderers in the sky are not continuous or complete because they turn back upon themselves and travel in the opposite direction. On the other hand, motions along a straight line, even if they do not reverse directions, are also not continuous or complete because they are destructible. Rectilinear motions have a beginning and an end; moreover, each of the limits that mark a rectilinear motion's finitude has a different cause.

However, according to Aristotle, circular motion is continuous, complete, indestructible and produced by one cause. Moreover, while rectilinear motion has a beginning, a middle and an end, circular motion does not. These temporal limits are indeterminate. Even geometrically, the points that compose a circle can be marked as limits only arbitrarily. "Each of them is alike a beginning, a middle and an end, so that the moving thing is both always and never at a beginning and an end" (Aristotle 2001, 265 b 1). It could be argued that this quality alone is enough to shock the soul and startle the intellect into wakefulness. The observation that something is always and never at a beginning and an end ought to produce a question leading to the meaning of the very being of circular motion: what sort of motion *is* circular motion if it remains both always and never at a beginning and an end? To make such a claim is, of course, one way to say that *circular motion is a movement that never moves*. But Aristotle makes an even more explicit observation about this contradictory character that belongs to circular motion. "The sphere is in a certain way both moving and at rest, for it holds the same place . . . and since [the center] always stays still, the whole is in a certain way both always at rest and continuously in motion" (Aristotle 2001, 265 b 5–10). With the concept of circular motion, the soul stumbles upon an entity that forces reason [*logos*] to say that the thing it has encountered requires a formulation that leaves it at a loss [*aporia*].

Earlier we asked how the new study of astronomy generates an *aporia* in the student such that *nous* may be called forth into action. What is it about the first principle of astronomy (the study of three-dimensional entities in movement) that can cause a turn in the soul. Here, we observe that, when we embark upon an investigation of the primary hypothesis of astronomy (circular motion), it occasions a turn from the third tier (the *mathematikē*) to the fourth tier (the *eidē*). This turn is marked by the urgency of the question of the being of "circular motion," its *what-is-ness*. Although Socrates does not mention it here, the turn toward the question of the being of "circular motion" and its relation to the order of motions underneath it is precisely a turn toward the question of at least one of the senses of "necessity" we have explored in the *Republic*. The study of the order of motions of every three-dimensional entity in the cosmos is of course a study of necessity. What governs such motions if not necessity? An *aporia* involving the meaning of the concept of circular motion would occasion a turn toward the question of the intelligibility of the three-dimensional beings that move.

As is well known, in order to solve the problem produced by the *aporia* of motion, Aristotle *hypothetically* poses the possibility of an unmoved mover to stabilize the sequence of motions, prevent infinite regress, and ensure the intelligibility of the cosmos (Aristotle 1998, 258 b 16–259 b 20). For him, *if* the motion of three-dimensional beings is to be intelligible at all, the unmoved mover must exist. But what if this hypothetical first principle that secures the unity, coherence, and everlastingness of circular motion does not exist for Plato? In that case, do we find ourselves in the situation of a less optimistic Platonic tragic-comedy? What if, in the Platonic dialogical form, we have a presentation of the tragic-comic drama of reason [*logos*] that unfolds in human life? What if, on the one hand, the platonic dialogue puts on display characters living within a narrative drama of the imagination that depicts the human in its technological endeavor to render the world known in its being; and, on the other hand, Plato *esoterically* presents the operations of *necessity*—with its arbitrary (wandering), erotic, irrational, and externally determining modes of being—that actually ground the technological compositions and systems of reason? The *aporia* occasioned by the concept of circular motion would be an *experience* that marks our way into this intuition. In book X, the connection of the motions of all of the three-dimensional entities in the cosmos to necessity is made explicit in the *image* of the "spindle of Necessity" (616 c). We will analyze the image more closely in chapter ten; however, it is worth noting here that the intelligible order depicted by the image occurs precisely as an image, not an argument. Moreover, the disclosure of the order of necessity is presented by Socrates through a mythological figure in the context of a myth, not a scientist or a philosopher using demonstrations. Finally, the revelation of the system of necessity appears *after death*, not within the limits described by the life of reason—appearing, rather, in a setting unavailable to human sensuous or intellectual perception except in the form of a *mythos-logos*.

HARMONICS

After Glaucon observes that the task Socrates sets for astronomers "is many times the work than what is now assigned to astronomy" (530 c), Socrates suggests that such difficulty must be sought in all of the disciplines that the lawgivers prescribe. He asks Glaucon if he knows of any additional study that should be suggested. However, Glaucon remains at a loss regarding what study is missing from their growing system. In response to Glaucon's negative answer, Socrates further expands the cosmological aporetic system by adding an additional form of movement. Provocatively, Socrates states that there are many forms of movement; *if* all of these forms are recountable at all, he says, only a wise person would be able to do it (530 c—d). The reader is struck by the possibility that the interlocutors are leaving potentially important movements in the cosmos out of consideration. Moreover, they do so by necessity given a gnoseological lack shared by perhaps everyone. It may be that movement exceeds full conceptual grasp. Indeed, it may be that it is impossible for human *logos* to comprehend all of the forms of movement. Nevertheless, Socrates claims that it is possible to name at least one additional study of movement, insofar as there exists an "antistrophe" of astronomy (530 c): harmonics.

Why is the study of harmony an antistrophe to astronomy? Immediately after the claim, Socrates says:

> "it seems likely [*kinduneuō*]," I said, "that as the eyes have fixated on astronomy, so the ears have fixated on harmonic motion [*phora*], and these two kinds

of knowledge are sisters [*adelphē*], as the Pythagoreans say and we, Glaucon, admit it. Do we not?" (530 d).

Like the current class of astronomers who employ the eyes to track the movements in the sky, the current class of those that study harmonics employ the ears to track the movements of the air.[24] However, those that employ the ears make the same mistake as those that employ the eyes (531 a): they rely upon what discloses only the unknowable, wandering features of vision and hearing.

Glaucon mistakenly interprets Socrates' critique to represent strictly empirical analysts of the movements of sound: "you speak of those useful men who torture the strings . . . twisting them on pegs" (531 b). But Socrates does not mean these. Instead, as in our example of Ptolemaic astronomy, he means the formal mathematicians: the Pythagorean analysis of harmony. "I stop the image [now] and say that I do not speak of these but rather those [the Pythagoreans] whom we said we are going to question now about harmony. For, they do the same thing as astronomers: they seek the numbers in audible concords [*sumphōnia*] but do not ascend to problems" (531 b—c). Consequently, as in the new study of astronomy, the new study of harmony does not focus on the analysis of empirical harmonies. Moreover, we do not place our attention on working out the mathematics of the motions of harmony. This sort of education already occurs in the early education of the youth. Rather, in the new study, we allow the "problems" of harmony to arise. That is to say, we look for what occasions *aporia* in the movements of harmony.

In response, Plato has Glaucon say that this new study is "demonic [*daimonion*]" (531 c). Does he mean that it is divine? Or perhaps impossibly superhuman? Or requiring the intervention of a god? It is not clear. Moreover, as we have observed in previous accounts of the new studies, Socrates does not offer an example of a problem that might invoke *nous*. If we turn to the *Timaeus*, I believe we may locate an example.

A problem of the order of presentation constantly haunts the monological cosmology presented in the *Timaeus*.[25] After Timaeus has given an account of the construction of the body of the cosmos by the *dēmiourgos*, he admits to having misrepresented the order of construction (Plato 2001, 34 c). The soul would have been constructed "prior to the body" (Plato 2001, 34 c). Thus, he must begin again, and tell the tale explaining how the *dēmiourgos* manufactured the soul of the cosmos. In the first part of the account of this construction, Timaeus describes the composition of what might be called the basic soul material from which the *dēmiourgos* will piece together the soul of the cosmological whole (Plato 2001, 35 a-b). The passage is notorious, having provoked disagreement among the earliest commentators, and the confusion continues to this day.[26] To summarize briefly, the carpenter of the cosmos mixes sameness, otherness, and being together; the product of this mixing is the material out of which the *dēmiourgos* will compose the soul (Plato 2001, 36 d–37 a). It is this subsequent composition that I would like to analyze to locate a Platonic *aporia* in the new study of harmonics.

Taking the single mass of soul stuff, the *dēmiourgos* divides it in accordance with a geometric progression, generating the following two series: 1, 2, 4, 8 and 1, 3, 9, 27 (Plato 2001, 35 b–36 b). Plutarch tells us that, already with Crantor, the double progression is depicted in the form of a Lambda (Taylor 1928, 137–8).[27]

It is important to note that the two series are composed of four terms: "a double tetractys," which forms a series of "exactly 7 terms" (Taylor 1928, 137), each terminating at the third power, so that the series proceeds 2^0, 2^1, 2^2, 2^3 and 3^0, 3^1, 3^2, 3^3. Or rather: 1, 2, 3, 4, 8, 9, 27. Taylor posits a number of philosophical and mathematical reasons for this geometrical progression: one of the most important (for any interpretation of the birth of nature) is that increasing from the zero power to the third gives us something like a

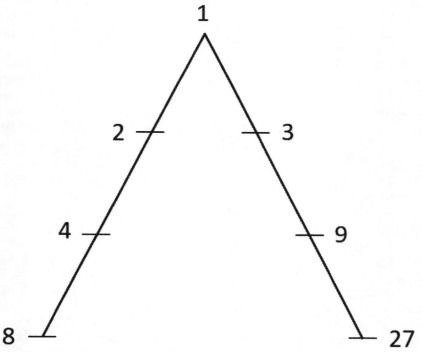

Figure 6.2. Representation of the double progression.
Taylor 1928, 137

movement from a point to three-dimensional entities, both even and odd in number (Taylor 1928, 137). Additionally, Cornford lists ten different phenomena for which the tetractys may be symbolic, including "*Magnitudes*: point, line, surface (i.e., triangle), solid (i.e., pyramid),; *Simple Bodies*: fire, air, water, earth . . . ; *Societies*: man, village, city, nation . . . ; *Seasons of the Year*: spring, summer, autumn, winter; *Ages*: infancy, youth, manhood, old age," among others (Cornford 1937, 70). Further, the series will prove to have musical significance, and it is this characteristic which is most relevant for the new study of harmonics in the *Republic*.[28]

After fixing these fundamental terms, the *dēmiourgos* continues to divide the soul stuff in the two series, by "filling up" the gaps in between each term with harmonic and arithmetic means.[29] Simplifying and combining the two series, we have: 1, 4:3, 3:2, 2, 8:3, 3, 4, 9:2, 16:3. 6, 8, 9, 27:2, 18, 27.[30]

By "filling up" the series in this way, the *dēmiourgos* is generating a sequence of intervals of 4:3, 3:2, and 9:8 in the series. From this observation, we perceive that the technician of nature, the carpenter of the cosmos, is crafting a soul in the form of a musical scale; for, the ratio 4:3 corresponds to the perfect fourth, that of 3:2 to the perfect fifth, and 9:8 to the major second. To complete the filling of the gaps that resulted from this last insertion, the *dēmiourgos* fills the remaining 4:3 intervals (Plato 2001, 36 b).

However, a subtle difficulty reveals itself: "And since there arose from these bonds new intervals within those he already had, he went about filling up all the 4:3 intervals with intervals of 9:8, leaving in each of them a fractional part" (Plato 2001, 36 b). I want to argue that this "fractional part" (the ratio 256:243) is an example of an *irrational* gap that forces itself into the narrative in this section. In ancient music theory, it was called the *leimma*, or "remainder," and it roughly corresponds to our semitone.[31] As Taylor demonstrates (Taylor 1928, 140–1), the *leimma* constitutes an irrational fraction; thus, in order for music to sound beautiful, to remain harmonious, it must contain an *irrational* interval. Ian Leask comes to a similar reading when he suggests that "The problem . . . describes an ineliminable discrepancy between what 'should' happen, mathematically, when a string is subdivided, and what actually occurs, sonically; accordingly, 'rational correctness' has to be tempered to achieve 'aural correctness.'"[32]

For a Pythagorean committed to the doctrine that all things are made of perfect numbers, the discovery that an irrationality haunts the beauty of harmony would be quite disturbing. Indeed, one of the tales about Hippasus claims that he was expelled from the Pythagorean society for revealing this destabilizing secret to the public (Taylor 1928, 141).[33]

To apply this harmonic irrationality to book VII of the *Republic*, there are two reasons for *aporia* in the new study of harmonics. On the one hand, an irrationality subtends the harmony which exists among the movements of all the three-dimensional entities in the cosmos. As in the example of doubling the volume of the cube in solid geometry, there is a quantity in the movement of harmonic relations that is not knowable. It, therefore, does not have a "what-is-ness." On the other hand, we observe that the *dēmiourgos* constructs the soul with a *necessary* gap; that is to say, the musical soul that he builds for the cosmological animal contains an irrational incompleteness. If the soul is the principle of movement for all living things, then the movement for all things depends in some way upon this irrational incompleteness, insofar as all things exist within the cosmological animal and remain moved directly or indirectly by its soul. Since the soul is the first principle of movement, all the movements of this divine carpenter's nature (erotics, generation, metabolism, locomotion) *necessarily* harbor a space of need or lack in the form of irrationality.

Thus, while the fifth new study, the study of harmonics, occasions an *aporia* which forces *nous* out of its slumber, it does not appear to be "useful . . . for the investigation into the beautiful and the good" (531c)—unless, of course, the vision of the beautiful and the good is not achieved by the disclosure of the being of something, its "what-is-ness."

NOTES

1. As he indicates (1990, 82 e), Meno is capable of learning the properties of the square. He displays the fact that he knows that the slave's first assumption is wrong. My suggestion here is that Meno shows that he is incapable of achieving the *comportment* that the slave is capable of achieving. However, the slave reaches the comportment of *aporia* regarding the being of the square, while Meno fails to reach it with respect to the concept of the being of virtue, justice, or teaching/learning, etc.

2. In her *Turning toward Philosophy*, Jill Gordon argues that the concept of the immortal soul and its corollary the endeavor of recollection "solves the difficulty brought up in Meno's challenging dilemma" (Gordon 1999, 37). I'm sympathetic to her reading. However, in this and the paragraphs that follow, I indicate that I have doubts that Socrates' arguments "solving the dilemma" are convincing. Moreover, I think the dramatic details Plato provides illuminate this. Further, while I agree with S. Montgomery Ewegen that readers like Gregory Vlastos (Vlasos 1971, 7–8) are likely wrong to dismiss Socrates' claims not to teach as "disingenuous, or as 'mere' moments of Socratic irony" (Ewegen 2020, 6), I do think that Socrates' practice here, despite his argument, depicts a difficulty: Socrates *is leading* the slave boy in a way that is not engendering recollection, but introducing something new that the slave boy did not have in advance.

3. Aristotle attempts to provide a more convincing argument in his *Posterior Analytics*. For an analysis, see Winslow 2013. "Aristotelian Definition and the Discovery of Archai" in *Bloomsbury Companion to Aristotle*. Bloomsbury Publishing: New York.

4. Jill Gordon argues that "the story of recollection is Socrates' direct response to Meno's challenge . . . the story will . . . show that learning is possible—and this it does. . . . Recollection explains the learning process in a manner that saves inquiry and learning from Meno's skeptical challenge" (Gordon 1999, 34). For reasons articulated in this paragraph, I do not agree with Gordon's very optimistic reading. In my view, the problem is articulated, but not solved.

5. Compare the close of the *Theaetetus*. As a consequence of their discussion producing nothing but "wind eggs," Socrates says to Theaetetus: despite this, "you'll be less severe with those who are around you and gentler, being moderate and not supposing that you know things you don't know" (Plato 2004, 210 c).

6. The literature often reads the use of the language of sensation in this passage as an instance of Plato's imprecision in terminology. For instance, Adam wrote that "Strictly speaking, of course, *aisthēsis* by itself does not, and cannot, present us with a judgment of any kind. It merely furnishes a particular sensation, which is referred to our mental picture of the objects in question, and the resulting judgment is not *aisthēsis*, but *doxa*, which is, according to Plato, a combination of mnēmē and *aisthēsis* . . . But in this part of the dialogue, Plato's argument is in no way affected by his imperfect analysis of the psychological process involved in such a judgment as 'This is a finger'" (1902, 523c). Shorey argues that the precise meaning of *aisthēsis* "is not to be pressed" (1969, 523c). Given that the *Republic* is a crafted dramatic work (not lecture notes, as with, say, Aristotle) over which Plato was reputed to have labored until the end of his life, an apology for his imprecision seems hasty. Perhaps it is better to assume that Plato has Socrates use the perplexing term *aisthēsis* at this moment with intention.

7. It is worth noting here that there exists a gap between the argument above in which the soul fails to grasp what "a finger is" and the argument below in which the soul's contradictory experience with sensuous opposites leads to a failure to grasp what number, unity or "the one" are. Plato has Socrates omit the link between these two arguments.

8. Adam asserts that this is the earliest "explicit" statement in Greek of the principle of noncontradiction (Adam 1902, 246).

9. Another question that emerges from the relevant passage that I will only pursue in bare form in a footnote here is: why does Socrates use the language of "happiness"? The study of geometry in the new studies forces [*anagkazō*] the student to turn toward "the happiest of being [*to eudaimonestaton tou ontos*]" (526 e). Some scholars have sought to minimize the significance of the use of the term. Shorey, for example, writes "once more we should remember that for the practical and educational application of Plato's main thought this and all similar expressions are rhetorical surplusage or 'unction,' which should not be pressed, nor used e.g., to identify the idea of good with god" (1969, 526 e). By this religious reference, he has in mind 19th century attempts to use this passage to identify "the good" with god (Adam 1902, 118). In those cases, translators translate the *eudaimonia* with "blessedness." While I agree with Shorey that identifying the good with god (especially a christian god) is excessive and problematic, we should not try to minimize the use of the term in this context. In my reading, the passage in the drama remains the most explicit and detailed assertion of

geometry's role in the new studies. It strikes me that Plato has Socrates use the term at this moment in the drama for a reason and that, perhaps, it should be emphasized if for no other reason than to elicit a question or a doubt on the part of the reader.

10. To obtain a sense of *anage* used in militaristic language, commentators suggest comparing the passage to Aristophanes' *Birds* (1938, line 383): "draw back a little." See Adam (1902), Shorey (1969).

11. Reeve (2004) and Shorey (1969) translate *auxē* with dimension, but Adam argues that this is a mistake. "It is better (with Schneider) to translate *auxē* by 'increase' than by 'dimension'; for *auxē* always implies something increased, and in the phrases *deutera auxē*, etc., this 'something' is the point. Among the Pythagoreans, who probably originated these expressions, the line was regarded as an *auxē* of the point, the plane of the line, the solid of the plane" (1902, 122). While I am translating *auxē* throughout with dimension, the idea of progression (and its potential failure) is secured when we understand that each dimension is an "increase" upon another.

12. According to Leonid Zhmud, Plutarch's interpretation is derived from Eratosthenes' dialogue *Platonicus*, a work he observes is a complete fiction. Further, Zhmud points out that the problem of the doubling of the cube was not set for Plato by the Delians, but arose in the mid-fifth century (Zhmud 2006, 84).

13. The author of this image is Petrus3743. Permission to use is governed by creative commons: CC BY-SA 4.0 <https://creativecommons.org/licenses/by-sa/4.0>, via Wikimedia Commons.

14. In his analysis of the idea of academic disciplines in Aristophanes' the *Clouds*, Jacques Bromberg points out that, in Xenophon's *Memorabilia*, Socrates praises geometry and astrology (the way to navigate at night and organize the seasons) for their practical uses, but suggests avoiding (theoretical) astronomy as a useless endeavor. Bromberg compares these statements of Xenophon's Socrates to Aristophanes' Strepsiades, who expresses similar concerns in the *Clouds* (Bromberg 2012, 88). Myles Burnyeat also points to Xenophon's Socrates as contradicting the Platonic one on mathematics insofar as he criticizes the non-practical concern with mathematics in "Plato on Why Mathematics Is Good for the Soul" (Burnyeat 2001, 4).

15. "As he was investigating the courses of the moon and her revolutions, then as he was gaping upward a lizard in the darkness dropped upon him from the roof" (Aristophanes 1853, lines 171–173).

16. The earlier passage reads: "certain perceptible beings do not call thought to examination because perception suffices to judge them, and there are others which in every way engage thought in this examination, since perception gives nothing sound" (523 a).

17. This is an important word in the *Republic*, especially in the context of the elaboration of democracy. However, it occurs throughout the text (365c, 399e, 426a, 557c, 558c, 559d, 561a, 568d, 588c, 604a, 605a, 616e). Moreover, in book X, during the description of the motions determined by the *spindle of necessity* in the myth of Er, the term *poikiloma* is used to describe the largest whorl (616 e). We will return to the spindle of necessity in our analysis of book X; however, for now, I wanted to highlight the fact that, when the *motions* of the cosmos are considered, Plato has Socrates utter

the term *poikiloma*. Shorey speculates that the use of *poikiloma* here may signal the complexity of heavenly movement (1969, 529 e).

18. In regard to this passage, Myles Burnyeat points to Simplicius' disputed story that Plato tasked mathematicians to "save the appearances" in order to affirm this interpretation of the purpose of the new study of astronomy. "I would emphasize that the challenge is there *de facto* in the texts regardless of whether we believe the popular story retailed by Simplicius, that Plato set this problem to the mathematicians of his day: 'By hypothesizing what uniform, circular, ordered motions will it be possible to *save the appearances* relating to planetary motion?' (*Commentary on Aristotle's De Caelo*, 492.3 1–493.5) Even if Plato said nothing of the sort, the *de facto* challenge remains" (Burnyeat 2000, 63, emphasis added in the quote by Simplicius). In my view, with the reference to "save the appearances," Simplicius has in mind something like the system of Ptolemy. Zhmud (1998) disputes Simplicius' historical claim that Plato tasked mathematicians with this challenge.

19. Plato reveals a further difficulty in the language that he has Socrates choose to employ regarding the mode of access to such mathematical realities: *logos* and *dianoia* (the faculty of the third tier). These belong to the *mathematikē* of the divided line. While they may turn one away from merely "trusting" in the beings that are by *physis* and *technē*, they do not turn one toward *what is*, and they do not awaken *nous* (the faculty of the fourth tier).

20. As an example, one may point toward Aristotle's *Physics*. At the end of the *Physics*, Aristotle hypothesizes that locomotion is the primary form of motion; it is prior to alteration and increase/decrease (Aristotle 1998, 260 a 20). Moreover, of the locomotions, circular motion is prior to rectilinear motion. Some things are put into a particular locomotion from a state of rest. That is to say, some motions are a movement from rest to motion and then to rest again. Some motions, therefore, are composite motions and contain contraries (Aristotle 1998, 261 a 27). Moreover, you might say that these motions have at least two causes: a) what causes a thing to move and b) what causes the thing to rest again. These motions are, thus, rectilinear. But there is a motion that only ever continuously moves and has only one cause. This motion is the circular motion (Aristotle 1998, 265 a 13).

21. See Winslow (2007, 51, 99).

22. There are several places in Aristotle where this assertion is made. In *On Coming to Be and Passing Away*, Aristotle offers an account which speaks of the relation of circular motion to things which come to be and pass away through the medium and double-interactive movement of the sun. "Since the change caused by motion has been proved to be everlasting, it necessarily follows, if that is so, that coming to be goes on continuously; for the movement will produce coming to be uninterruptedly by bringing near and withdrawing the 'generator' . . . It is not the primary motion which is the cause of coming to be and passing away, but the motion along the inclined circle; for in this there is both continuity and also double movement, for it is essential, if there is always to be continuous coming to be and passing away, that there should be something always moving, in order that this series of changes may not be broken, and double movement, in order that there may not be only one change occurring" (Aristotle 2000, 336 a 10).

144   Chapter 6

23. Often, commentators hypothesize that Plato's fuller argument for this appears in the *Timaeus*. Burnyeat argues, for instance, that the rhetoric of the *Republic* is tailored for an audience untrained in mathematics and, therefore, the more sophisticated account is given to the more adept audience of the *Timaeus*. In addition, this appears to be Burnyeat's understanding of Plato's use of the dramatic characteristics of the dialogues: the audience's lack of sophistication necessitates "the imagery and the panoply of persuasive devices that enliven the long argument" (Burnyeat 2000, 8), while the Timaeus does not need "the images or other rhetorical devices of the *Republic*" (Burnyeat 2000, 66). I do not agree with this assessment. We have seen many examples of obviously weak/questionable arguments in the *Republic* that it seems unlikely Plato held. Instead of merely pedagogical manipulation to persuade a readership of specific philosophical assertions, I think the form the dialogues take are necessitated by the subject matter and the interlocutors. Moreover, there are many images and rhetorical devices in the *Timaeus*, starting with the concept of a *technologically crafted* cosmos. It is precisely this image that strikes the reader as question-worthy and doubtful.

24. For a mechanical/technological description of the sense of sound, one may appeal to *Timaeus*: "Let us posit sound as the blow transmitted through the ears by the action of air upon brain and blood and reaching all the way to soul; the motion produced by this blow beginning in the head and ending around the seat of the liver is *hearing*; and insofar as the blow is swift, the sound is high-pitched, and insofar as it's slower, lower . . . " (Plato 2001, 67 b). Of course, the poverty and even comic character of this mechanical description is immediately evident. It is like saying that marbles charged with energy bouncing onto retinas is *seeing*, or the increase of heart beat consequent to receiving images of one's beloved is *falling in love*.

25. John Sallis develops a reading of these relatively frequent new beginnings that occur in Timaeus' speech (Sallis 1999, 97–8).

26. Both Taylor and Sallis provide an account of the traditional interpretations (see Taylor 1928, 105–6; Sallis 1999, 65–70).

27. Plutarch 1976, 1027 c—d.

28. Cornford argues that "these considerations are concerned with theories about the nature of number" and "have nothing to do with music" because "no one, setting out to construct a musical scale, would start by arranging the terms" into the two series articulated above (Cornford 1937, 68). Apparently, the issue for Cornford is the curious composition of the scale, which would expand to four octaves and a major sixth. For Cornford, there is thus no reason to flesh out an explanation of such a scale in the "science of harmonics" (Cornford 1937, 68). Rather, he believes Plato organizes it in this way because he needs seven numbers in order "to space the seven planets at distances corresponding to the terms" (Cornford 1937, 68). It may be true that the passage explores the nature of number and that Timaeus needs to include the seven planets (we see this in book X of the *Republic* too), but the claim that, consequently, the series has "nothing to do with music" seems extreme.

29. These are represented in the text by the phrases "a mean that exceeds one extreme and is exceeded by the other by the same *fractional part*, and another mean that exceeds one extreme by a *number* equal to the amount by which it is exceeded

by the other extreme" (Plato 2001, 36A). Cornford offers helpful examples of these means: "If we take for illustration the extremes 6 and 12, the harmonic mean is 8, exceeding the one extreme (6) by one-third of 6 and exceeded by the other extreme (12) by one-third of 12. The arithmetic mean is 9, exceeding 6 and falling short of 12 by the same number, 3" (Cornford 1937, 71n. 1).

30. A more detailed explanation of the way the *dēmiourgos* constructs the series can be found in Taylor and Cornford, as well as in Kalkavage's notes to the *Timaeus* (see Taylor 1928, 136–46; Cornford 1937, 66–72; and Kalkavage, "Music," appendix A of Plato 2001, 146–50).

31. Cornford and Kalkavage helpfully adapt Timaeus' diatonic scale based upon tetrachords to a series of notes in a modern octave, showing the relation between the major tones and the semitone (see Cornford 1937, 72; and Kalkavage, "Music," pp. 146–50).

32. In the last section of his essay, Leask recognizes that Plato's account (Leask conflates Plato with Timaeus) is qualified by the fact that it is a "likely story" (Leask 2016, 25). However, he quickly writes off this qualification by claiming that "even if the *Timaeus* carries a warning regarding its own claims . . . it is still prepared to *make* these claims" (Leask 2016, 26). Firstly, I do not think that the qualification is removed just because Plato is prepared to have Timaeus assert an interpretation. Secondly, I think it matters that Timaeus is the one making the claims. If Leask did not conflate Plato with Timaeus, it would be harder to blur the distinction between the one making the claims (a character in the dialogue) and whatever interpretation is possible for readers from the dialogue itself, as a whole.

33. See Iamblichus' *Life of Pythagoras* (1818, 47–8).

Chapter 7

Necessity and the Song [*nomos*] Itself (Dialectic)

Continuing our close analysis of book VII, this chapter will offer a reading of the practice of dialectic, a practice whose name is sometimes conceived to be interchangeable with that of philosophy. To begin, I will provide a brief survey of the relatively recent history of two opposing interpretations of dialectic. On the one hand, there is a tradition of interpretation that reads the Platonic text to present dialectic as *dialectikē* (a method, or a technological tool); and on the other hand, there exists a tradition of interpretation that understands the practice of dialectic to be a less formal, but serious discussion or conversation—that is to say, *dialegesthai*. While these two traditions do not exhaust the history of interpretation of this central concept in the Platonic dialogues, the articulation of them helps me to situate my own reading. To that end, I appropriate Gadamer's reading of Plato (with some qualifications) when he asserts that the real task of dialectic can "only be to activate for ourselves wholes of meaning" (Gadamer 1980, 5). With this aim in mind, I offer an interpretation of dialectic that relies on its formulation in the *Republic* as a song. The animating question becomes: how are we to understand dialectic as "the song itself," especially insofar as the five earlier studies serve as a "prelude" to this "song"? The answer to this question allows us to perceive a conception of dialectic that is both a *logos* and a *techne* (indeed, music remains both of these), a *logos* that takes a very different form than the linear and logical variety. It is in this way that dialectic shares something with the movement of necessity; for, all three—natural necessity, music and dialectic—*move* in a particular way. We will observe how they move in a *circular* fashion, rather than a linear, technological one.

Following the fifth new study, Socrates says that, if the inquiry leads to conclusions regarding how the new studies are related [*sungeneia*] to one another, then the inquiry has not been a labor without profit (531 d). However, if this common origin of birth is not made manifest, then it is without profit.

According to Socrates' *explicit/exoteric* statements,[1] the new studies share an ability to technologically present mathematical forms that *are*. In each case, they cultivate a turn toward the *what-is-ness* of their subject matter. Given that each new study builds upon the earlier one so that every study seizes hold of "what is" in each mathematical dimension (and also "what is" in the movements of the entities of those dimensions), Socrates appears to be gathering studies together into a kind of cosmological system of knowledge of what admits of being. That is to say, *according to the argument* of Socrates, the student of the new studies comes away with a knowledge system that secures something stable, consistent, and intelligible at each dimension of the cosmos until s/he reaches the whole. It is an optimistic vision of what human reason may achieve. Of course, even before our analysis in the previous chapter, one might reasonably have doubts that a knowledge system that only grasps onto what presents itself in being through the reductive method of these mathematical sciences could be conceived as exhaustive, or anything but a technological model (indeed, perhaps technological models cannot even be said to have being except in a problematic way). However, as I have shown in the previous chapter, even within the technological models of each new study, there exists some feature that is not capable of being brought to *what-is-ness*, some irrationality that provokes a kind of wandering within the mathematical entities that appear *to be*. Therefore, *according to the drama* of the new studies, each one reveals an incommensurability, an irrationality, or something that wanders within the concepts inherited by the new studies that, first, cultivates an *aporia*, and second, prevents the reduction to and isolation of *what is*. In my reading, this quality shows how the studies are akin [*sungeneia*] to one another according to the drama. That is to say, the drama makes manifest that, for Plato, what wanders (natural necessity) may subtend and haunt human knowledge in a way that is unavoidable. As necessity allows for the weaving together of the argument, the argument's undoing already lies latent underneath—indeed, the latter too belongs to necessity.[2] The drama reveals the wandering features that lie latent within the exoteric argument. In this way, Plato discloses the necessity of finitude lurking in human knowledge systems.

But these five studies are only preparatory. They are but a "prelude to the song itself" (531 d). As is made clear in the paragraphs that follow, by "prelude," Socrates means that these studies prepare the student for the most architectonic study: dialectic. Instead of engendering the experience of *aporia* and the invocation of *nous* with respect to only the inherited concepts relevant to mathematical dimensions of cosmology, dialectic concerns itself *with all* of the inherited concepts of the *oi polloi*, including justice, virtue, beauty, the good, etc. The student of dialectic experiences *aporia* not only with regard to the received conceptual economy of our cosmological disciplines, but "regarding everything [*peri pantos*]" (533 b). Insofar as the first five studies "train" one for *aporia*, they are a prelude to the song itself.

The concept of dialectic has been the subject of perhaps the most commentary of any concept in the platonic corpus. In what must be admitted to be an overly-simplistic summary, I will quickly survey two competing interpretations (perhaps even *presumptions*) of dialectic that animate much of the scholarship on dialectic of the last century or so. Providing a certain ecosystem of interpretation of dialectic will allow me to situate my reading in relation to those. For, in my view, despite (the character) Socrates' assertions regarding the power of dialectic, the new studies (culminating with dialectic) put on display a *tragic* conception of philosophy ("tragic" understood in the ancient Greek manner). While other disciplines—involving the *mathematike* on the divided line—build systems of propositional knowledge like hives of bees make systems for the production of honey, the *practice* of dialectic in the dialogue makes visible that these same human knowledge systems rest on unsecured and shifting principles. Further, the force that moves the soul into dialectical engagement is *not* the *being* of these first principles (whether critically assessed or presumed), but rather necessity. While, certainly, the aporetic character of the five new studies carries over into the practice of the "song itself," I will argue that there remains the possibility for a *positive* consequence of dialectical/philosophical activity: dialectic is a *creative* endeavor. In contrast to the conception of dialectic conceived as a technical method, I will argue that dialectic's/philosophy's creative movement reflects the movements of music and, therefore, the movements of *physis*.

Engaging the literature, I will place in two categories two chains of analysis that have tried to hold secure the meaning of dialectic in the dialogues: those that interpret dialectic as a logical/scientific *technē*, (qua *dialektikē*) and those that interpret dialectic as a moving conversation (qua *dialegesthai*). By employing this terminology to describe the tradition of interpretation of dialectic, I adopt, with certain amendments, David Roochnik's schema in his *Beautiful City* (2003). With regard to the tradition of *dialektikē*, some interpret the dialogues to present dialectic as something like a scientific method that guides the inquirer. Adam, for instance, is compelled to describe the method this way:

> [The dialectician] begins by offering a *hypothesis* on the subject to be discussed, and then proceeds to test his *hypothesis* by the conclusions to which it leads. If these conclusions are untenable, the original *hypothesis* is cancelled or annulled, and a new suggestion takes its place, only to suffer the same fate. The process is repeated again and again, until at last we reach an *archē* which will withstand every test (1902, 176).[3]

While there are differences between this presentation of dialectic and the one described in book VI, Adam's interpretation tracks Socrates' display of the *image* (which is, of course, *neither* a logical argument *nor* an example of dialectic) of the divided line, in combination with certain suggestions in book VII (533 c). This interpretation would correspond to the understanding of dialectic as a technical means by which human beings may glean dependable knowledge of the being of things (and, indeed, the knowledge of the good) from the blur of wandering in the world. To conceive of dialectic as a *technē* finds justification not only from the text's description of it as "the art [*technē*]" of "turning" (518 d), but also in its very etymology.[4] John Lyons argues that the suffix "*-ike*" indicates *technē* (1967, 143). The adjective *dialektikos* describes someone who is "skilled in argument." This particular skill is named *dialektikē* (Roochnik 2003, 133).

Because the dialogues appear to be "deliberately cagey" (Ferrari 2000, xxx) about how dialectic "achieves the feat" (ibid.) of reaching the *archē* of the being of things and, indeed, the good, scholars have been left with no choice but to speculate about how to understand the technical procedures of dialectic. For, the dialogues themselves do not give a consistent account of the process across the corpus. Even within a singular dialogue, say, the *Republic*, the relevant term translated as "dialectic" is often not *dialektikē*, but rather *dialegesthai*.[5] In an effort to massage the corpus to present the logical/technical practice of dialectic in a consistent fashion, many claim that Plato's conception of dialectic undergoes a progressive development from the supposedly "early" dialogues to the supposedly "later" dialogues.[6] Among those influential interpretations that are animated by a developmental view, one may point to Terence Irwin (1977) and Gregory Vlastos (1991). However, Kneale and Kneale utilize the developmental view in order to cast suspicion upon *Plato's understanding* of dialectic conceived as a *technē*/logical method. They claim that an understanding of the method moves from *elenchus* to one like that articulated above in Adam (the *Republic's* account), and then to the method of division and collection "illustrated in the *Sophist* and the *Politicus*" (Kneale and Kneale 1984, 9; cited in Roochnik 2003). Yet, according to them, despite the development, Plato himself remained confused about the matter until the end; thus, to their disappointment, they suggest that a coherent account of dialectic conceived as a logical tool does not exist in Plato (Kneale and Kneale 1984, 9).

David Roochnik remains highly skeptical of the search for what he calls the "technical meaning of dialectic" (Roochnik 2003, 139). To do so, he believes, scholars must "construct elaborate, and therefore highly speculative, chronological interpretations" (ibid.). Among those that adhere to a technical understanding of dialectic in a most "delightful manner" (2003, 139) is Gilbert Ryle. According to Roochnik,

Ryle argues that as Plato matures, major changes occur. First and foremost [among these changes], the Theory of the Forms takes center stage, and the dialogues cease to represent active question-and-answer debates, becoming more like *theoretical treatises*. This change is explained by Ryle's most speculative leap. He accounts for "the alarming disappearance of the Socratic Method" (1966, 152) . . . by arguing that Plato was legally prohibited from practicing dialectic (Roochnik 2003, 140, emphasis added).

Because of his commitment to the conception of dialectic as a technological tool, Roochnik thinks that Ryle resorts to "highly speculative, chronological interpretations" (ibid., 139); asserts that late Plato adopts a more theoretical, rather than a dramatic, style; perceives an intellectual progressive development across this chronology; and imposes an unfounded historical claim in order to further solidify his reading. The narrative of "Plato's progress" is a common one in the technical interpretations of dialectic. As Roochnik writes, "the attempt to chronicle Plato's progress, focusing—as Stenzel (1964), Ryle (1966), Robinson (1984), and Kahn (1996) each do—on the development of his conception of dialectic is a time-honored approach to the dialogues" (2003, 140). However, Roochnik believes that a presumption regarding the meaning of philosophy lies latent in this approach. Namely, philosophy is a technical subject. In the movement from the conversational/dialogical question and answer in the so-called early dialogues to the method of division of, for example, Plato's *Sophist*,[7] the perception of "progress" in this movement only makes sense if one is committed to the idea that philosophy is a technical affair in advance.

Like Roochnik, Francisco Gonzales views the technical interpretation of dialectic with suspicion. He argues that every study of Plato presupposes a conception of philosophy when it approaches the dialogues. "Since the dialogues normally identify philosophy with 'dialectic,' these questions also concern the nature of dialectic. What kind of a process, what form of argumentation, is dialectic? What can this process achieve? What is the nature of the knowledge possessed by the dialectician?" (Gonzalez 1998, 1). Gonzalez believes that each interpreter brings his own conception of philosophy to the text, a conception that Plato may not share. Such presuppositions dramatically shape the interpretations of those readers that view dialectic through the lens of a technical method. For instance, Gonzalez points to Richard Robinson's *Plato's Earlier Dialectic* (1941). According to Gonzalez,

[Robinson] treats dialectic as a purely formal method of constructing arguments . . . [and defines] dialectic in total abstraction from the content of Plato's philosophy . . . One finds in Robinson's book no interpretations of whole dialogues, but only detailed analyses of passages taken out of context . . .

Robinson has presented us with *the bleached skeleton of dialectic* (1998, 2–3, emphasis added).

By ignoring the dramatic setting and the actual practice of dialectic in the dialogues, Gonzalez thinks that the technical interpretation often strips the flesh and blood from the bones of dialectic. Moreover, as Jill Gordon has argued, depriving the literary and dramatic features of the dialogues of importance has enabled the developmental/technical interpreters of dialectic to bracket the distinction between Plato and Socrates. "Argument-focused thinkers treat Socrates as a mouthpiece for Plato" (Gordon 1999, 4). Terence Irwin (1977) uses the names "Socrates" and "Plato" interchangeably. Gregory Vlastos (1991) devotes a great deal of space to distinguishing between the presentation of the historical person "Socrates" in the dialogues and the "Socrates" who speaks for Plato. Such presumptions already betray an unjustified application of the meaning of the phrase "philosophical discourse" to Plato. As Roochnik suggests above, in this model, the commentator understands "philosophy" as a technical affair in advance. Further, these scholars reveal the prejudice that, for them, the *treatise* is the only serious philosophical form (Gonzales 1998, 4–5). For, the conversion of the dialogue into a technical argument naturally takes the form of a treatise. Even those that wish to recognize the importance of the dialogue form in all of its complexity "cannot keep from talking about 'Plato's argument,' 'Plato's view,' and what 'Plato endorses,' which [Michael Frede (1992, 201–203)] apparently gleans from what Socrates says" (Gordon 1999, 4). Thus, for Gordon, in the technical tradition of interpretation, the conception of dialectic is derived often from narrowed readings of the dialogues,[8] becoming stripped of its surrounding body composed of literary and dramatic features that Plato himself has crafted for it.

Dialectic is further removed from the natural platonic ecosystem of the dialogue by artificially finding ways to locate the voice of Plato in the arguments of Socrates in the service of converting the drama into a more manageable, more "philosophical" treatise. However, few, if any, of these developmental/technical readers of dialectic would apply the same procedure to the literary works of Shakespeare or Tolstoy. No one thinks that Pierre is the mouthpiece of Tolstoy or that, as Gordon writes, Richard the III is the mouthpiece of Shakespeare (Gordon 1999, 4–5). No one argues that "Tolstoy says" that freemasonry is the path to human enlightenment. Why, then, should we claim that "Plato says" virtue is a matter of divine dispensation?[9]

These latter critics of the technical interpretation of dialect often seek to give expression to "dialectic" and "platonic philosophy" in a way that takes seriously the form of presentation that Plato chose. That is to say, they offer interpretations in a way that incorporates an analysis of the literary and dramatic characteristics of the platonic corpus. Only in this way, they argue, does what is meant by the phrase "platonic philosophy" appear.

Gordon thinks that among the things that come to the fore when the form of dialogue is taken into consideration are the extra-logical characteristics of language and persuasion. "Dialectic is more than a logical method of pointing out inconsistencies in the interlocutors. There is an emotional side too" (Gordon 1999, 20). In particular, Gordon points out the production of shame in Socrates' interlocutors. Undergoing dialectic causes Thrasymachus to blush. In the *Gorgias*, Callicles suffers shame. Plato has Alcibiades articulate his shame in *Symposium*. "Shame plays an important role in the psychological dimension of dialectic. It works on a personal, existential level to compel interlocutors to reflect more deeply about who they are, what they believe, and how they choose to live their lives" (Gordon 1999, 28). Thus, ignoring the literary/dramatic characteristics of the dialogue in order to isolate a technical dialectical method through which one may purge arguments of inconsistencies misses a great deal of what Plato includes in the concept of dialectic.

Much of the contemporary work that takes the dialogical dimension of platonic dialectic seriously was foreshadowed by the analyses of Hans George Gadamer, Leo Strauss and Jacob Klein.[10] Because it suits my purpose here, I will utilize the example of Gadamer. For his part, Gadamer often appears to accept certain aspects of the genetic and esoteric traditions of interpretation. For instance, despite the developmental prejudices this implies, he affirms the chronological ordering of the dialogues, referring to the *Lysis* as "among those dialogues which are quite properly considered to belong to the early period" (Gadamer 1980, 1). And, even though he privileges the "literary dialogues" over the "indirect [esoteric] tradition" (Gadamer 1980, 126–127), Gadamer does recognize a "doctrine of ideas" (Gadamer 1980, 4), Further, he gives weight to the account of an unwritten doctrine in Aristotle (Gadamer 1980, 130).

Still, Gadamer emphasizes the dialogical/discursive character of the dialogues in order to counter those interpretations that search for a logical technique taught by Plato. "No one could seriously contend that the ability to think correctly is acquired only by a detour through logical theory" (Gadamer 1980, 5), he writes. In fact, he confirms that, as we have discussed above, we find "all manner of violations of logic—false inferences, the omission of necessary steps, equivocations, the interchanging of one concept with another" (ibid.). The path of thinking undergone by the characters in the dialogues does not show itself as a system of Euclidean geometry, a discussion "*more geometrico*" (ibid.), but rather as a "live play of risking assertions, of taking back what we have said, of assuming and rejecting, all while proceeding on our way to reaching an understanding" (ibid.).

Here, dialectic is understood as *dialegesthai*, as discussion. As such, it is employed to gain access to an entire reservoir of meaning. It does not simply strip away the periphery of the inquirer's view in order to isolate the meaning and logical coherency of a proposition; but rather it brushes up against a broader discursive *field of relations* in which such a proposition has meaning at all. As Gadamer writes: "the real task can only be to activate for ourselves *wholes of meaning*, contexts within which a discussion moves—even where its logic offends us" (ibid., emphasis added). Perhaps it could be said that there exists a discursive field around every proposition, and dialectic remains a mode of discourse that holds the potency to make this horizon visible to the human being.

Indeed, as is clear from my analysis of the new studies in the previous chapter, I think that, if there exists a methodological tool in Platonic dialectic at all, then the tool is the *question* and the question's aim is to cultivate *aporia* in the interlocutor and the reader. In my view, the method of division within the so-called late dialogues shares this aim, despite the absence of Socrates and his frequent form of engagement—the *elenchus*. As we have seen, the procedures of dialectic in the *Sophist* and the *Parmenides* do not lead to satisfactory propositions any more than the Socratic question and answer regarding the meaning of courage, virtue, love or justice. Against the geneticists/developmentalists, I would argue that we do not observe a progressive evolution of dialectic from early to late. Rather, Plato may be exploring the different discursive ways that the human being finds him/herself in *aporia*, the different ways in which *logos* shocks the human being into the awareness of the broader "wholes of meaning" (1980, 5) in which the human finds him/herself, qua human.

On this reading, what the different procedures of dialectic do is open up the beehive; they strip the individual bee of the political structures of self-evidence. This forces him out of the hive and, simultaneously, leaves him without the hive's foundational common sense. It is a move into a certain kind of confusion and a certain kind of isolation, not *certainty or knowledge*. The concomitance of confusion and isolation might be another way of phrasing what Deleuze called "philosophical modesty" and "stupidity" (both of which he derives from book VII of the *Republic*).[11] Through dialectic, one becomes *an idiot*—with all of the etymological baggage that term carries [*o idiōtēs*]. It is an isolation and alienation from the cave games and *oi polloi's* competitions grounded on the proposition and common sense. Despite the *negative* circumstances in which one finds oneself, the isolation is *positive*, insofar as one may gain a view of what Gadamer calls above "wholes of meaning, contexts within which a discussion moves" (Gadamer 1980, 5). Jill Gordon asserts that "dialectic is the Socratic existential stance" (Gordon 1999, 19 and 41). If, by "existential," she means that dialectic produces not so much a propositional content or a formal linear argument leading to knowledge, but rather the intellectual shock of *aporia*, then I agree. Dialectic is about the comportment one holds to what it is that one thinks one knows. As such, it is existential, rather than propositional or substantive.

I think it is precisely through the concept of the "wholes of meaning" that Gadamer differentiates dialectic/philosophy from sophistry in the Platonic dialogues. Awareness of the constellations in which meanings circulate, in the best of circumstances, forces one to lose the self-evidence provided by the hypotheses (in the third tier of the divided line) and the body of propositions upon which they stand. Becoming an idiot through dialectic/philosophy broadens one's vision in a way that may recall Bergson's description of the opaque "fringe" that surrounds the bright and clear "nucleus" of intellectual perceptions.

> The feeling we have of our evolution and of the evolution of all things in pure duration is there, forming around the intellectual concept properly so-called an indistinct fringe that fades off into darkness. Mechanism and finalism agree in taking account only of the bright nucleus shining in the center. They forget that this nucleus has been formed out of the rest by condensation, and that the whole must be used, the fluid as well as and more than the condensed, in order to grasp the inner movement of life. Indeed, if the fringe exists, however delicate and indistinct, it should have more importance for philosophy than the bright nucleus it surrounds (Bergson 1944, 53).

Dialectic makes visible the *fringe* that surrounds the propositions (or bright nucleuses) that constitute our knowledge systems in the cave. When the fringe becomes evident, there is of course risk. When one loses the self-evidence of the bright nucleus, one loses a lot. The possibility of a nihilistic relation to the very existence of a nucleus appears. In my reading, this is what Gadamer means when, quoting Aristotle's *Metaphysics*, he writes "the difference between dialectic and sophism consists only in the *proairēsis tou biou* [*choice of life*] . . . i.e., only in that the dialectician takes seriously those things which the sophist uses solely as the material for his game of winning arguments" (Gadamer 1980, 8). When one becomes aware of the fringe, there are (at least) two ways that this perception can determine one's comportment, one's "existential stance" (Gordon 1999, 19). The dialectician "takes seriously" the condition of the aporetic rupture, whereas the sophist exploits the fringe in order to succeed in "his game of winning arguments."

As is clear from my remarks, I find Gadamer's account of dialectic compelling. However, there is at least one feature of his interpretation that, in my view, lacks textual support. When he suggests that, in practice, dialectic shows itself as a "live play of risking assertions, of taking back what we have said, of assuming and rejecting," I agree. Yet, when he adds to this "all while proceeding on our way to reaching an understanding" (Gadamer 1980, 5), I am less convinced. Of course, everything hinges on the meaning of the term "understanding" (which is a technical term in Gadamer's philosophical vocabulary). The notion that the interlocutors arrive at a convincing "understanding" by the time the conversation reaches the end of the dialogue seems to me to be highly doubtful. In this case, by the phrase "convincing understanding," I mean an understanding that there is reason to say that Plato would affirm exhaustively defines "justice," for instance. But when one attends not simply to the arguments, but to what actually happens dramatically in the dialogues, one must admit that this dialogical/communal "coming to an understanding" never takes place. Do the characters *agree* periodically? Yes. Many interlocutors participate in the elenchic dialogues by assenting to Socrates' questions. On the one hand, when considering what often appears to be a conclusion regarding the meaning of certain concepts (justice, virtue, etc.), participants frequently agree with Socrates' definitions. Yet, there are reasons to doubt that Plato shares the commitment to these conclusions; for, neither Socrates nor the other characters are the author, Plato. On the other hand, it is part of the very movement of the conversation that Socrates elicits an affirmation on the part of the interlocutor. However, often—especially toward the end of discussions—they appear to be replying "yes" to his questions simply to encourage Socrates to come to an end. Thrasymachus openly admits to this (352 b and 354 a).[12] And, by the time we reach book X's arguments for the immortal soul, Glaucon appears to have given up his own dialogical responsibility. Certainly, there is no way to honestly come to an agreement or an understanding when one's "existential stance" prevents one from answering frankly.

Instead of meaning that the characters reach an understanding (and their agreement is a sign of this), perhaps Gadamer means that *the reader* is the interlocutor that arrives at *understanding*? But, Plato does not give the reader satisfactory answers to the questions raised by the dialogues, questions like justice, rhetoric, virtue, sophistry or any of the ostensible subjects of the dialogues. Each articulated conclusion is haunted by some ambiguity, some dialogical discrepancy, some contradiction with another part of the dialogue. Consequently, these privations preclude the agreement of the reader; they force the reader to recognize that some lack stands in the way of the claim to a more formal experience of understanding. That is to say, Justice is not *understood* by the end of the *Republic*. Moreover, not even dialectic is *understood* by the end of the *Republic*. The text offers many reasons for the reader to believe that what Socrates calls dialectic in the *Republic* has neither been clearly defined nor even conducted.

In his account of dialectic as the culmination of the new studies in book VII, Socrates inserts an important division between the first new studies (all of which treat a particular dimension of the cosmos mathematically) and dialectic. He asks Glaucon if the men who are clever at these mathematical disciplines are dialecticians [*oi tauta deinoi dialektikoi einai*] (531 d). Glaucon replies in the negative, qualifying his answer by suggesting that he has known only a few. By what measure can Glaucon make this qualification? It is not clear. For, the "long road" of dialectic required to answer the interlocutors' questions was not taken (435 d and 504 b). Given that "a measure in such things that falls short at all of that which *is*, is no measure at all" (504 c), the answers achieved by Glaucon's and Adeimantus' discursive journey so far are not satisfactory. They have not been supported by the "long road" of dialectic, but only by images and allegories. Therefore, Glaucon has not undergone the full dialectical voyage and, presumably, remains even incapable of giving an account of what dialectic is. Still, this fact does not stop him from applying the imaginary measure to his experience with other humans in his judgment about those who practice dialectic and those who do not.

If Glaucon does not know what dialectic is, he remains incapable of giving an account of it. Up to this point, Glaucon has been able neither to give nor to *receive* an account of dialectic. On the one hand, Glaucon has not received a dialectical account because Socrates said that the road to complete its articulation is too long (435 d and 504 b). On the other hand, Glaucon has not received an account of dialectic because the form in which it appeared was through the medium of an image (the divided line and the allegory of the cave) and precisely not through dialectic. Finally, in a few paragraphs, Glaucon is going to ask for an account of the song itself: "go on to the song itself and go through it like we went through the prelude. Thus tell what the manner of the power of dialectic is" (532 d). However, Socrates refuses Glaucon: "'you will not be able to follow, dear Glaucon,' I said, 'not because I lack the eagerness'" (533 a). The passage has been interpreted in wildly different ways.[13] But whatever his reasons, Plato makes it clear that the character Glaucon is unable to give or receive an account of dialectic.[14] Perhaps if one cannot give a dialectical account of dialectic, one cannot give a dialectical account of anything.

Remarkably, the ability to give and receive an account of what one knows is precisely the content which Socrates employs to formulate his next question, a question which to a certain extent seeks to define dialectic. He asks if "people who are not capable of giving and receiving an account will ever know anything of what we say they must know?" (531 e). Thus, one of the concepts of which Glaucon can neither give nor receive an account is precisely the concept dialectic—the activity by which one gives (and receives) an account of what one knows.

In an effort to further determine the meaning of dialectic, Socrates places it in relation to the earlier images of books VI and VII; moreover, he does this through the figure of music. Earlier, he had argued that the five new studies were a mere "prelude to the song [*nomos*] itself" (531 d). Now, dialectic is said again to perform a song [*nomos*].

> "Glaucon," I said, "is this already the song [*nomos*] itself that dialectic [*dialegesthai*] recites? It is intelligible, but may be[15] imitated by the power of sight. We said that sight attempts [*epikeireō*] to look at the living things themselves and at stars themselves and then finally at the sun itself. So too when someone attempts [*epikeireō*] to find the being of each thing itself through dialectic [*dialegesthai*] by means of argument [*logos*] without all of the senses . . . with intellect he takes hold of that which is good itself, he comes to be at the end of the intelligible realm just as the other comes to be at the end of the visible. . . . Do you not call this journey [*poreia*] dialectic [*dialektikē*]" (532 a—b).

Here Socrates appeals to the earlier images of the divided line and the cave. We are given an analogy in order to grasp the "journey" [*poreia*] of dialectic, an analogy between two incommensurable regions (the visible and the intelligible; the elemental and the formal). If we work through what vision does, suggests Socrates, then we *may* catch a glimpse of the movement of dialectic (*if* vision does in fact imitate intellect without qualification). In the cave allegory, we saw that, as the prisoners leave the cave, their eyes are overwhelmed by the brightness of things. First, they must look at the shadow-images of things and their reflections in water; then, as their eyes grow accustomed to the light, they "try" to look at the animals themselves and the stars themselves, not merely the reflections and imitations left in reflective things. Moreover, once they have looked at the things bathed in the light, they turn their attention to the origin of the light and cast their eyes upon the sun (risking the destruction of the power of sight).

In the current passage, Socrates qualifies the image further. There exists a world of beings around us in the form of *logoi*. These beings are taken as given, but like the visible beings in the cave, they are lit up in a particular way, by an artificial light. On this level, there is no reason to believe that the things that are constituted by the *logoi* are distinct from what shows itself as visible.[16] The one comes with the other for human beings. However, they have different ontological statuses and these are incommensurable. Further, they have different sources of illumination. Thus, we approach the former *without the senses* by means of "*logos*." That is to say, the beings around us that are discursively constituted are approached by discussion, questioning, and argument. As already noted in our analysis of both book VI and the cave allegory of book VII, *logos* simultaneously possesses a public (*oi polloi*) and a private (*o idiōtēs*) sense. The cave dwellers are like us. We too find ourselves in a cave already constituted discursively in advance. The beings floating by on the cave walls have discursively constituted meaning for us. We are appropriated to this meaning horizon and we take it for granted as common sense. It is only when someone somehow comes from somewhere to loosen us from our binds that it occurs to us that these meanings are discursively constituted—that is to say, their status as simple common-sense facts falls away. They can be interrogated and perhaps, in this condition, the human being is even *compelled* to interrogate them.

For instance, see a flag of heraldry fly into battle on the cave wall. We approach the flag of heraldry without the senses to determine *not* how it is constituted in the light of the sun (its colors, patterns, materials) but how it is constituted by *logoi*. For, these are the structures that leave their traces on the cave wall that the flag symbolizes; these are the structures about which the rules of battle are constituted, the rules by which human beings win praise and honor; these are the structures that govern the histories that recount the great and cowardly deeds that are disclosed for all to see in the flying of the flag. To reference the passages by Gadamer and Bergson above: we investigate the horizon of discourse that bestows meaning upon the flag. We investigate the "*fringe*" of discourse around it. The meaning of "the flag" remains a kind of condensation of this "fringe," a hard nucleus supported by a cloud of electrons, a central node that shines out brightly against a background network, a mushroom pin emerging from a bed of rhizomal mycelia.[17] This is why vision and dialectic are incommensurable in the *Republic*. While Bergson observes a fringe and nucleus in visible beings too, it might be argued that, for Plato, the visible more readily gives itself to perception (though this of course contains nothing knowable) without a fringe than the intelligible gives itself to intellect (at least this is implied in the analogy given in the current passage). Certainly, for the platonic dialogue, symbol objects like "the flag" are planted in discursive mycelium networks of *oi polloi*. The flag stands out as a mark of possession, identity, victory; but these too only have meaning insofar as they circulate in a particular conceptual network. In my reading, dialectic may concern itself with these networks; it uncovers and illuminates the fringe.

In addition to offering the analogy between the approach to the disclosure of things through "argument" (*logos*) and through vision, in the current passage Socrates seeks to further determine the meaning of dialectic through another analogy: music. What does the journey from the vision of the shadows of things in the light, to the things in the light, to the origin of the light have to do with music? How is this *poreia* musical? There are many things said in the *Republic* about dialectic that relate it to music. For instance, in the current passage, the new studies articulated so far are all called a "prelude" [*prooimion*] to dialectic, the "song" [*nomos*] itself.

The term "prelude" [*prooimion*] has occurred at strategic places in earlier parts of the dialogue, each instance appearing in moments which define justice.[18] First, at the beginning of book II, Socrates relates that, after engaging with Thrasymachus' assertion that the just is nothing other than the profit of the stronger (338 c), he thought that he "was delivered from the argument. But it appears as though that was only a prelude [*prooimion*]" (357 a). Presumably, this means that book I serves as a prelude to the work as a whole, containing all its themes in brief. That is to say, by the word "prooimion," Socrates means something like what Aristotle says in his *Rhetoric* when he writes that "the prelude [*prooimion*] is the beginning [*archē*] of a speech, as the prologue [*prologos*] in poetry and the prelude [*proaulion*] in flute-playing; for, all these are beginnings [*archai*] and create the path [*hodopoeisis*] for what follows" (Aristotle 1959, 1414 b). The prelude, then, is conceived by Aristotle as a kind of ruling origin [*archē*], containing the themes that will become explored in more detail in the work that follows it. Perhaps we can argue that the dialogue form, too—just as the play, the musical piece, and the speech—possesses an *archē*, a prelude that introduces themes, concepts and stylistic tropes that will animate the work. The first prelude of the *Republic* contains all of these. Moreover, as a dialogue, it not only contains the abstract concept of justice in the form of a proposition; but it also puts on display the souls of most of the characters (some of whose histories would be known to Plato's contemporaries), introduces movements and settings that shape the arguments of the dialogue (the need to descend from Athens into Pireaeus, the festival of Bendis, the foreign host) and expresses many of the dialogue's difficulties and questions which inform the problem of the meaning of justice: erotics, old age and death, youth, power and law, poetic education, discursive and biological inheritance, necessity and, especially, the ambiguities of discourse. In other words, the prelude offers all of the features of the *ecosystem* in which the problem/question of justice circulates in the dialogue.

The second instance of the term prelude [*prooimion*] arises in Glaucon's mouth. After Socrates determines what virtues will be cultivated in each of the classes of the city and in each of the parts of the souls of the citizens, they complete the account of the organization of the virtues by considering in which class the virtue of moderation belongs. But, moderation [*sophrosunē*] "does not act" the same way as the other virtues (432 a). Rather, it "has been stretched throughout the whole from top to bottom of the entire scale, making the weakest, the strongest and those in the middle . . . sing the same chant together" (432 a). In addition to these musical metaphors, Socrates uses the term "harmony" to describe the effect that moderation has on the *polis* and the soul. Moderation is the virtue that puts the citizens in relation to one another in such a way that if their correctly-tuned activity were audible, it would resemble the sound of a harmonious chord. The citizens are all in the correct key together, even as they emit different notes.

Having employed the musical metaphors to describe the conclusion of the organization of the virtues in the city, Socrates says that what justice is should now be visible. He engages with Glaucon playfully and urges him to hunt for it, lest it slip away and disappear into obscurity. Still, Glaucon remains at a loss. Socrates relates that he himself then "saw it and said: "Hurrah! Glaucon. Maybe we have happened upon its trail . . . and it will not flee from us" (432 d). Indeed, it has been "rolling around at our feet from the beginning and we did not see it . . . As those searching for something that they are already holding" (432 d- e). It is here, just after Socrates' musical metaphors describing moderation, that Glaucon invokes the term "prelude" in relation to the long conversation already undertaken in which we looked for justice as though we were searching the house for car keys that lie unnoticed in our hands: "A long prelude [*prooimion*] . . . for one desiring to hear" (432 e).

Whether or not we are to believe that Plato has the character Glaucon self-consciously reference Socrates' metaphors from music, it is clear that, through the musical metaphor he himself employs, we obtain a new picture of the concept of justice as something that can conduct a discussion from afar. Justice is capable of action at a distance. That is to say, justice can be understood here to have been a kind of condition for the possibility for the entire discussion so far. The first prelude contained the explicit discursive conditions for the discussion about justice: the ecosystem of supporting conceptual, dramatic, poetic, political, and biological features we indicated in our account of that prelude. However, this second prelude references something deeper about the *necessary* operation of justice itself. Like a prelude, some conception of justice has been operative already at the beginning in a way that was not explicit to us when we began. Some justice has been subtending our discussion already and has somehow made it all possible. We had not yet heard this prelude, but it was already structuring everything we had to say from the beginning. Indeed, "we had looked at moderation, courage, and practical wisdom, so it seems to me that this is what is left in the city. It furnished the power by which all these others came to be" (433 b). The *phenomenon* of justice has the quality of being in operation in an unconscious way and this unconscious operation of justice makes it possible for the *concept* "justice" to become an explicit question, theme or problem for us.

In addition to the new insights into justice, the announcements of these two preludes each mark what appears to be a different understanding of the movements of discursive progress (*dialegesthai*). Instead of a linear/logical form, there is expressed a musical form of discursive progress. Each announcement seems to signal the close of one verse and the beginning of another. For instance, the prelude that engaged Thrasymachus' assertion regarding justice, is started anew in the persons of Glaucon and Adeimantus. However, what follows the exchange between Socrates and Thrasymachus is not a linear progression that leaves the previous argument behind in a way that one might expect from the logical presentation of a modern philosophical argument or even in the movement of a rational syllogism. Rather, it is a *repetition* of the same themes; it continues to carry the entire ecosystem of book I along with it. This is composed of tropes and themes which persist, animating and shaping the discussion as it shifts and turns and becomes planted in new settings: the bodies and minds of the new interlocutors (Glaucon and Adeimantus) within the dialogue *and* each new reader outside of the pages of the dialogue. That is to say, the first prelude gives rise to a new beginning; book II is an original new birth, *and* it is a repetition of themes.

Such movement immediately reminds us of the movement of music and makes clear the reason for the musical metaphor. The gap between books I and II is the space in which we are able to return to the beginning of the melody, but with different lyrics. We circle back around to the new verse, but these original words are generated within the same musical body as the melody that accompanied the first verse. Each verse has the same melody and rhythm. It is perhaps in the same key, but contains different lyrics. As such, the dialogical form of disclosure is, like a musical progression, not linear, but circular. That is to say, *it turns*. Like music, dialectic too is an "art of turning." With respect to the connection between dialectic, music and the art of turning, one is reminded of the *Phaedo* in which Socrates relates that he had been visited by dreams that commanded him to "make music and work at it" (60 e). Since "philosophy is the greatest music" (61 a), he pursued it his entire life.

What does it mean to say that dialectic is the *art of turning*? How is philosophy musical? Dialectic *turns* toward those discursive structures (like Justice), on the one hand, whose comprehension belongs to a finite ecology (the content of prelude 1), and, on the other hand, that, like necessity, form the *necessary* semantic link between all the propositions based upon it (prelude 2): a condition for the possibility of any science of politics (in the case of the concept of justice). In the context of the divided line, the dialectical comportment emerges out of the soil that serves as the discursive origin for the images on the cave wall, the things (both technological and physical), and the sciences which organize both of those things into sciences. All of these are like a prelude to the song itself, insofar as they serve as the ecosystem out of which dialectic emerges (if it does). Additionally, another prelude for the song of dialectic is the link that *necessarily* binds together the propositions of any given science on the third tier: the presumed meaning of justice that is already animating the science in advance, but is not itself even perceived by the science that presumes it. This reveals itself as a necessary force for the production of science, for the production of linearly progressive knowledge systems. Yet, the human needs dialectic then to turn back critically and listen to the meaning articulated in the prelude and/or originate a new verse, a new movement.

In the manner of the previous paragraph, I wish to suggest that, insofar as these three "preludes" contain the themes and tropes of the "song" itself (dialectic), we receive something of an account of dialectic when we attend to the musical metaphors. That is to say, even though Glaucon, Adeimantus and the rest of the interlocutors have neither given nor received an account of dialectic in the course of the conversation, the dialogue's *dramatic* presentation of dialectic as the *art of turning* is nevertheless illuminating. I turn now to recapitulate each prelude's relation to dialectic.

Firstly, the movement of dialectic is musical and song-like insofar as it is organized in advance by a prelude that contains its musical modes, its key (or, to mix metaphors, its genomic structure): that is to say, its themes and tropes. Dialectic may be born from a question (What is justice? What is virtue? What is a sophist? etc.), but that question is born from a preexisting discursive ecosystem, just as book II of the *Republic* is born from the discursive conditions of book I and the entirety of the *Republic* is born from the conversation that took place "yesterday." To some extent, the "turning" that dialect performs is always a *turning back*, a repetition of this discursive horizon. Like the movements of a song, dialectic may be conceived as at once a turning back *and* a new beginning. For instance, book II turns back to the themes and melodies of book I and performs them anew, in a new beginning, with new lyrics and perhaps a new musical mode. The relation between book II and book I is already dialectical, insofar as book II is a new verse, chanting new lyrics, in the key of book I. One perceives this movement more in the allegory of the cave than in the divided line. In the cave allegory, one might argue that the emergence of the question releases the prisoner; however, the question emerges as a consequence of something already floating by on the cave walls. We begin where we are in the middle of a discursive world already underway. The prisoners are like us. The question emerges in the cave. The prisoner *turns*, leaves the cave, sees whatever he sees above, and then *returns* to the cave. The movement of the cave allegory is not linear, as we have already suggested above; but rather, it is *strophic*. It turns and begins anew, although perhaps in the same key and meter as already provided by the ecosystem out of which the question emerged. If the movement of dialectic is present in the *Republic*, it is present in this way: dramatic movement turns back upon itself in the course of discussion and reinscribes itself anew in novel settings and bodies.

In the third instance of the term prelude, the movement of dialectic is said to betray a musical, song-like structure insofar as it is preceded by the five new studies which are described as its "prelude" (531 d). On the one hand, as we argued in the previous chapter, the five new studies turn the soul toward *what is* in each region of inquiry for which each is responsible. However, the possibility of turning is occasioned in each case by the arrival at an *aporia* in the region, an incommensurability and irrationality that prevents the *mathematikē* from moving forward, and forces and compels a turn toward the primary hypotheses which subtend the *mathematikē*—Socrates describes this turning as dialectic.

> "A certain other path methodically [*methodos*] tries to grasp, about everything, the being of each thing. But all the other arts . . . while they dream about being, they are incapable of seeing it awake. As long as they use hypotheses and allow these hypotheses to remain undisturbed, they remain incapable of giving an account of them. For, if the *archē* is not known, then the end and the things in between are intertwined by what is not known. What contrivance will ever generate knowledge from such a concession?. . . . Therefore, the dialectical way alone moves in this manner: rescinding hypotheses in order to secure/establish the *archē*" (533 b—d).

Dialectic returns to the beginning, destroys the hypothesis, and begins again. At the beginning of this chapter, we argued that what the new studies have in common, what makes them akin to one another, is the ability to reveal some incommensurability, some irrationality in their subject matters that leads the inquirer to *aporia* with respect to a hypothesis. In my reading, this is how they are a *prelude* to dialectic. Dialectic produces a loss of confidence in the hypothesis that subtends the technological systems of the *mathematikē* and the ethical and political systems of *oi polloi*. That is to say, as stated earlier, while the five mathematical studies generate *aporia* with respect to their specific regions of cosmology, dialectic generates *aporia* "with respect to everything."[19]

In the second instance in which the *Republic's* metaphors link dialectic to song, the movement of dialectic is musical and animated by a prelude, insofar as something compels and organizes its movement in accordance with some necessity, something that is not immediately consciously graspable in the movement. Like justice in the *Republic*, there is something which compels one into the intellectual stance in which one finds oneself, something that "[provides] the power by which all these others came into being" (433 b). One searches for it, even though it is already in one's hand. There are reasons to argue that the dialogue suggests this condition for the possibility of a dialectical orientation toward oneself is "the good." Perhaps this is right.

However, even if it is the good, it compels *necessarily*, raising a question about Socrates' radical separation of the good from necessity in book VI.

The reason I have disrupted the order of the appearance in my recapitulation of the three preludes' relation to the movement of dialectic will now become obvious. For, at this time, I wish to return to the elaboration of the content of the second prelude. Indeed, it strikes me that this prelude most discloses the operations of necessity underneath dialectical movement. Moreover, insofar as necessity subtends certain aspects of the art of turning (that uniquely human form of movement), one is able to see that the musical character of dialectic inscribes dialectic within a horizon of finitude, human finitude, *vis à vis* knowledge.

In advance of inquiry and questioning, by necessity, the human being is already subject to the organizational/formal powers of the concepts that compel inquiry. Consequently, rather than a traditionally understood *method* (like the so-called scientific method) which presumes the existence of an abstract tool that remains separate from the inquirer and which mediates and organizes the whirl of the manifold into a coherent order, dialectic may be understood as a *comportment* into which human beings are freed to turn in relation to the various movements in and out of the cave. To be sure, dialectic must be conceived to involve (at minimum) the aporetic shock—which is better understood as a comportment (or existential stance) than a tool or procedure.

Moreover, for these reasons, I have doubts that, for Plato, dialectic and/or philosophy is an ability that human beings possess that will enable them to completely transcend their limitations with respect to the knowledge of being (or the good). In fact, the latter prejudice and aspiration seems to guide the technological endeavor of the third tier on the divided line—which is to say, the acquisition of knowledge and the organization of the world through technical means and in technical light. Human beings are compelled to pursue *mathematikē* through a linear logical method by which they seek to transcend their inscription within *physis*. Their movements are determined necessarily as linear in advance. For example, one observes this necessity in the very structure of the syllogism, insofar as there exists a necessary direction in advance in which one is compelled from premise to conclusion. Prior to the articulation of a premise, prior to the assertion of a proposition, there exists a necessary direction and motive force which compels the movement of the knowledge system and, yet, remains outside, compels from outside of the propositional inquiry. This logical necessity is perhaps the first unreflected hypothesis of all of the *mathematikē* and it has been "rolling around at our feet from the beginning" (432 d).

Still, the technological composition of human knowledge systems belongs to the human being as its necessary juncture with the world. Humans do not choose to compose such knowledge systems any more than the bee or the ant choose to organize their worlds in accordance with instinctual systems of social and architectural order. As argued earlier, I read the first three tiers of the divided line as being governed by *oi polloi* and common sense. Thus, the necessary technological knowledge systems are crucial to the human being's mode of being in the world and remain an important way in which the human being moves in the world in accordance with its nature. As such, conforming to the articulation of the third tier of the divided line (its structure of hypothesis and argument), human beings are *compelled*, necessarily, toward an articulation of the world in the order of knowledge systems that are linked together in a linear fashion through a sequence of propositions. Even though Socrates argues that sciences of the third tier only "dream about being" because they "use hypotheses and allow these hypotheses to remain undisturbed" and, thus, "they remain incapable of giving an account of them" (533 b—c), it seems as though some of the commentators on Plato discussed above attempt to find in the dialogues just such a composition of dialectic. However, in my reading, like Oedipus' drive to know, the structure of necessity that organizes human life in accordance with the three lower tiers of divided line guides the human being's urge to master its surrounding world through the application of technologically constructed knowledge systems.

However, when we attend to the musical and turning movements that subtend the narratives of the dialogue, one may wish to express a sentiment similar to that of Tigerstedt, who wrote that "a bewildered naive reader is nearer to the spirit of Plato than the learned scholar who calmly and confidently constructs a system of platonic philosophy. The offspring is ours. . . . In fact, *our interpretation of Plato is not a reproduction but a creation*" (Tigerstedt 1977, 100, emphasis added). This is precisely what appears in the dramatic dialectical movement of the *Republic*, even if the technical arguments surrounding dialectic do not provide anything precise and even exclude the possibility of such provision. When we consider the way that the dialogue turns musically, we observe that the narrative moves in a manner that we may wish to call dialectical, even if the characters are not conscious of this fact and are not actively applying a logical "method." The new beginnings that are cultivated in the *return* to the question of justice through the *art of turning* are original repetitions or, as Tigerstedt writes, "creations." Even for the reader, the experience of a return to the *Republic* after an absence bears out this musical motion: one encounters the same characters, the same setting, and the same words, yet something new is always revealed—something one was searching for; and yet, in previous readings, one did not realize it was already in one's hand from the beginning. But this requires an aporetic relation to the dialogue. One thinks one knows the *Republic*, as if it were a static being. However, the reader is always changing and, thus, approaches a different text each time. The aporetic encounter with the text occasions the "generation" of the new form, the new hypothesis, the new reading. And in addition to generating a new reading of the *Republic*, perhaps the new reading reveals something about what the reader has become since necessity has unwound her path between encounters with the text. The reader may imagine that she approaches the *Republic* as a free thinker, but necessity has already placed her before it within a certain attitude and framework.

Consequently, necessity is operational in an unconscious way in *both* forms of *technē*: the technological logic of the third tier *and* in the musical "art [*technē*] of turning," dialectic. Both forms of movement are *technai*. However, the musical movement of dialectic proceeds in a different way. As we have written, while technological system-building moves in a linear fashion in accordance with a logical necessity, music moves in a circular or spiral manner in accordance with the structures of natural necessity articulated above. Within the order of the song, the verse returns to the beginning and begins again. As such, the movement of music resembles the movement of *physis*. For, this is precisely the biological movement of living things. The relation between parent organisms and offspring is not linear, but circular. The parents of sexually reproducing organisms come together (by the erotic order of necessity) and produce offspring. Dialectic resembles this reproduction insofar as the child is a repetition of the parent organisms; however, the child is not reducible to the parents—it is an original. The child expresses *both* a repetition of the parent organism *and* a new beginning. The cycle of reproduction moves in this musical way.

I will conclude my analysis of the operations of necessity in the activity of dialectic by reference to the dialogue *Timaeus*. This dialogue is explicitly connected to the *Republic*, even if Plato joins the two in complicated and confusing ways.[20] Moreover, it offers an illuminating example of these two necessities (logical and natural) placed beside each other in the very same speech precisely in relation to the body of presentation.[21] For, on the one hand, Timaeus offers a monological, linear discourse animated by the presumptions of logical necessity insofar as it betrays a technological prejudice: the cosmological order that Timaeus self-consciously describes comes to be technologically insofar as it is "constructed" by a divine craftsman without erotics, like a house is crafted from lumber. However, at the same time, Timaeus' speech betrays a musical movement, apparently without his awareness, that comes back to the beginning and then begins anew. That is to say, if the character Timaeus is to be trusted to say what he actually thinks, his speech indicates that he believes he is giving a linear, monological argument in which the cosmos is composed like an artifact of human construction. However, Plato composes the drama such that, when the reader attends to the dramatic events of the dialogue, she perceives that the monologue *turns* like a dialogue and must return to the beginning and begin anew three times.

Toward the beginning of the *Timaeus*, Socrates expresses a wish to see the city that they have composed in speech (in the *Republic*) filled with a principle of movement, of nature. For, without this, the city in speech is immobile, abstract, merely a long definition. To see if it is truly beautiful, one needs to see it move in a way appropriate to its nature: Socrates wants to see it at war and negotiating with other cities in speech (2001, 19 b–c). The participants require a *logos* of *physis* in order to accompany the *logos* of the *polis*.

Because the person expected to give this speech about nature does not arrive, Timaeus is chosen to fill in for the missing interlocutor (2001, 20 a). To satisfy Socrates' desire, Timaeus attempts to generate a speech on the birth of nature in the form of an analytical, technological *logos*, a kind of technological artifact that requires a model and a linear presentation without gaps, failures in organization, lacks, or needs (2001, 28 a). But, despite Timaeus' best efforts, the speech is rife with all of these things. Further, these failures necessitate that the narrative continually restart from new positions. As Sallis has suggested, Timaeus must frequently begin again (2001, 30 c; 34 b; 48 b), generating a new discourse each time from new and neglected starting points (Sallis 1999, 97–8).

In my reading, Plato occasions a double interpretation of Timaeus' speech, dividing its content from its form. By doing so, he inscribes within the narrative a double interpretation, the second of which overwhelms the first. From the point of view of the first interpretation (that of content), Timaeus offers an analytical *logos* that necessarily follows a technological model. As I have shown elsewhere (Winslow 2021), the content of the *logos* of this cosmos lacks the movement of erotics, the movements of generation and growth; that is to say, it remains incapable of disclosing the life of living things (precisely those things it is tasked with articulating). Failing to supply this content, it does not provide the conditions for satisfying Socrates' desire to witness his *politeia* (also constructed in speech as a technological artifact) perform its motions in accordance with its nature and desire. As I suggest, it appears as though the reason for this lies in the limits of human, analytical modes of knowledge production—these require the manufacture of models, arborescent schemes of logical definition, and linear presentations without gaps, all of which approach the articulation of the existence of growing things, but seem constrained and unable to express them.

Yet, there is an additional, perhaps opposite reading, when one attends to the form of the discourse. I argue that despite Timaeus' self-conscious attempts, the speech does exhibit the movements of the life of living, growing things. That is to say, despite giving rise to a tragic gap and/or neglect from the point of view of content, human *logos* nevertheless, shows itself as partaking of the motion of animality from the point of view of the *dramatic form of presentation*. Timaeus consciously offers a linear analytical *logos*; but the unconscious form betrays a biological spiral, continually turning back upon itself in order to generate the new. Each time there is a new beginning. What has been articulated "before," is reinscribed and reborn in a new discourse, an offspring of the previous one. In my view, insofar as Timaeus' speech continually begins anew, it exhibits the movement of *physis*. Just like the offspring's relation to its parents, the *logos* is the same, yet different.

Consider a biological example: the generation of offspring and species does not reflect a linear or arborescent progression. If DNA, qua form, were merely repeated in the offspring—generating a linear line—one would witness a mirroring of the form, qua mother and father, in the offspring. But, in fact, the relation is much more complicated, even in the case of cloning. There are many examples one could offer here but allow me briefly to appeal to a popular, though illuminating one. In the documentary sequence "If By Chance We Meet Again," in the radio series *This American Life*, the host, Ira Glass, relates a story about a Brahman bull named Chance. To his owners, Chance was like a pet. He was the gentlest bull they had ever seen, desiring even to cuddle with the family. They were devastated when he died. Assuming that merely repeating his form (DNA) would enable Chance to be reborn and retake his beloved position in the family, he was cloned. However, necessity is the "wandering cause" (2001, 48 a). And the space of origination in which the elements meet the form (*chora*) is not empty, indifferent space. She contains powers as a differentiator; and what emerged from her was an entity that looked identical to Chance but was, in fact, an original. "Second Chance's" biological constitutional horizon (what we might call his epigenetic horizon) was original and originating. He proved to be far more violent and unpredictable than Chance, even goring a member of the family. Thus, the family had to suffer the loss of Chance once again, though this time while staring into a mirror of his living face. Offspring are not mirrors of their genetic predecessors. They are originals. That is to say, like Timaeus' discourse, they begin again. The movement of biological organisms is therefore spiral-like; it turns back upon itself and begins again. It remains the same but different. Each offspring repeats its father (and mother), to be sure, but originates something new as well. With respect to his speech, perhaps we can say that Timaeus himself is a *chora*: his speech originates within a gap filled with need in the first line of the dialogue. That is to say, it begins in a space of differentiation, animated and organized by the seeds planted by a previous discourse (the *Republic*), which has itself been planted by previous discourses (by Pythagoras, Empedocles, etc.). But nevertheless, the speech stands as an original and is differentiated from those seeds; it is not a mirror of them but an offspring—both in terms of the content of the speech and in terms of it being an utterance occasioned by Timaeus' original body. One might wish to argue that it is in this way that Timaeus's speech, despite being a monologue, nevertheless turns back upon itself like a dialogue, *dialectically* returning and circling back to the beginning and originating itself again, from a new position.

Finally, if it can be said that an account of the principle of growing things asked for at the beginning of the dialogue shows itself in this circular movement of biological generation/differentiation, then the form of Timaeus' *logos* of the cosmos, qua technological artifact, reveals this movement implicitly, even if not explicitly. Indeed, the dialogue enacts the distinction between *physis* and *technē* in a way that makes it impossible to draw a clean line of separation. Perhaps there is no better way to show this difficulty than in music; for music is both a *logos* and a *technē*. And yet, it moves in the same way as generation. Each new verse turns back upon itself in an originating way. The second verse repeats the first, but it nevertheless remains irreducibly new. The form of Timaeus' "song (*nomon*)" (2001, 29 d), therefore, performs the movement of a living principle, even if the lyrics do not sing it.

NOTES

1. As is clear from other remarks in this book, I take seriously Stanley Rosen's (and others') observation that, often, Socrates' arguments are in the body of a "sort of satire whose exaggerations teach the opposite of what they say" (Rosen 1993, 460).

2. With a similar sentiment, Claudia Baracchi argues that book VIII marks the organic decline of the city, despite its stable, rational, and calculative composition. When Socrates invokes the Muses, the tale told is one of a return of life, of life forcing itself upon the technological discourse: "what emerges in this discussion is an irrepressible return of life, an irruption of life in the midst of the discourse aiming at controlling it. This irruptive movement eventually undoes the politico-eidetic construction . . . [the politico-eidetic construction] is above all, in its passion for mastery, life-denying" (2002, 78).

3. Another influential example (an example that sees itself as correcting Adam's presumptions at least in part) would be that of Richard Robinson. In his *Plato's Earlier Dialectic* (1941) he sets forth a reading of dialectic that strips away the dramatic details in favor of the logical assertions. Isolating the logical formulation enables him to develop a platonism which is a philosophy of the proposition. However, it must be said that he begins the book by asserting a certain hermeneutic principle of reading. After listing five fallacies that famous readers of Plato have committed that distort Plato's intention, he argues that "these five errors are only errors when our aim is pure interpretation. From another point of view they may be valuable devices" (Robinson 1941, 4), He then cites Plotinus as an example of this positive development of creative reading. Further, writing in a time before the so-called continental/

analytic divide, he cites Bergson to support the observation that interpretation of Plato is asymptotic: "The interpreter must try, as Bergson put it, to restore by a long and roundabout process the single direct impression that Plato intended. Such a procedure can only be an endless approximation" (1941, 5).

4. While I am sympathetic to Shane Ewegen's argument in his *The Way of the Platonic Socrates*, I think we must be cautious when making claims about *technē*. That is to say, I am not sure that one can say, as Ewegen does, that "Socrates' way shows itself to be as far as possible from a technique, from a *technē*" (Ewegen 2020, 6). Even though the concept of dialectic changes over the course of the dialogues—prompting the "geneticists" (Tigerstedt 1977, 25) to try to establish a chronology of the dialogues—one can very well argue that dialectic plays an important role in whatever "Socrates' way" is (Gonzalez 1998, 13). And, as I indicated in the quoted passage above, Socrates' refers to dialectic precisely as a *technē*. It seems to me that the questions facing us are: what does Socrates mean by *technē* in this case? And why does Plato put the term in his mouth? With Ewegen we can say that he does not likely mean what appears in the concept of, say, a Cartesian method, to be sure; but dialectic nevertheless remains a *technē* in Socrates' mouth.

5. "Glaucon," I said, "this is the song [*nomos*] that dialectic [*dialegsthai*] recites?" (532 a).

6. E.N. Tigerstedt gives a useful historical overview of the "genetic" or developmental tradition of interpretation in his *Interpreting Plato* (1977, 25–51). See also Francisco Gonzalez' "A Short History of Platonic Interpretation and the Third Way" in *The Third Way: New Directions in Platonic Studies* (1995).

7. Further, as is clear from the interpretation of the *Sophist* offered above, I do not think the views and conclusions of the Stranger are Plato's views and conclusions.

8. In my too-cursory treatment, I am omitting commentary on the esoteric tradition of interpretation. However, as has already been suggested by Tigerstadt (1977, 64–74) and Gonzalez (1995, 7; 1998, 5), the esoteric tradition still asserts the existence of a technical system of philosophy in Plato. They argue that it existed outside of the dialogues. Therefore, they minimize the importance of the dialogues in Plato's "system" of philosophy.

9. For a sustained critique of the notion that Socrates is the voice of Plato, see Gerald Press. 2000. *Who Speaks for Plato?* In particular, Debra Nails. "Mouthpiece Schmouthpiece" in the same volume.

10. A bibliography of this tradition would include: Stanley Rosen (2005), Eva Brann (1967), Drew Hyland (1968, 1995), John Sallis (1975) and Charles Griswald (1981).

11. See *Difference and Repetition* (Deleuze 1994, 130 and 180).

12. "Feast on the argument . . . for I am not going to contradict you, in order not to aggravate these others here" (352 b) And "Let these be your feasts, Socrates, for the rites to Bendis" (354 a).

13. To my mind, one of the more interesting accounts of this passage is in John Sallis' *Being and Logos*. In his interpretation of the divided line, Sallis argues that the line is a complicated image. The line depicts beings in their relative clarity and degree of truth. Each being can show itself in the manner of each segment of the line.

However, it becomes more complicated when one considers that the divided line is itself a being. It too can show itself in these four ways (Sallis 1996, 439). In accordance with his interpretation, at the highest level of the line, what shows itself as the line is "showing as such" (Sallis 1996, 440). The *presupposition* that subtends our encounter with the line in a) its image, b) its physical/technical appearance, and c) in the science of demonstration and showing is d) "showing as such" (Sallis 1996, 440). That is to say, what *showing* is in its being still needs elucidation. For this reason, Sallis thinks that the entire "discussion between Socrates and Glaucon does not attain the level of episteme or dialectic but remains at the level of upward-moving *dianoia*" (Sallis 1996, 441) in the third tier of the line. Consequently, Sallis argues, "Socrates refuses to comply with Glaucon's request: in the *Republic* dialectic . . . is seen only from the perspective of *dianoia*" (Sallis 1996, 441), not *nous*.

14. Drew Hyland suggests that we cannot claim that this is an example of the master (Socrates) denying his student (Glaucon) an account. Rather, Hyland argues that, insofar as Socrates admits that Glaucon would only be seeing the good as *it appears* to Socrates, "Socrates is not in a position to insist upon the truth of what he would say" (Hyland 2011, 163). Nevertheless, as will become clear, I do think that there are reasons to suggest that Glaucon (as does any and every human interlocutor) exhibits necessary limitations as an interlocutor, and these limitations necessarily determine the outcome of the conversation in both positive and negative ways.

15. Reeve (2004) does not translate *mimeomai* here with the optative mood. Shorey (1969) does maintain the optative mood, but adds many additional things to support his interpretation. In my view, this grammatical choice generates further distance between vision and dialectic. It may even raise doubts about vision's ability to imitate dialectic at all.

16. See Sallis 1996, 439.

17. These descriptions are not intended as empty floral adornments of my prose. I am appropriating terminology and metaphors quoted earlier in the text by Bergson, Deleuze and Gadamer in order to make concrete a possible interpretation of the relation between language and dialectic.

18. For a reading of politics from the perspective of these preludes, see Christopher P. Long's "Socrates and the Politics of Music: the Preludes of the *Republic*" (2007).

19. My assertion is not without difficulties. The explicit argument that Socrates is making in the relevant passage continues to orient dialectic toward the disclosure of *what is*. We have already argued in previous chapters that, dramatically, it fails to achieve this disclosure in the contexts provided by the dialogues, not only in the *Republic* but also in the other dialogues. This raises a question about whether such an accomplishment is possible on Plato's view. Moreover, Socrates is about to introduce a problematic change regarding the highest region of the divided line, the segment in which we locate the things which Socrates names *eidē* and which generate the affection in the soul of *noēsis*. In the first formulation of the affections in the soul, he placed *noēsis* in relation to *eidē*. Intellection was articulated as the affection in the soul by the encounter with *what is*. However, in book VII, he places *epistēmē* in relation to *eidē*. "It will enough, like before [*hōsper to proteron*], to call the first part knowledge [*epistēmē*]" (533 e). Again, "before" it was not called "knowledge";

it was called "intellect." Do we take it as an oversight on Plato's part? Is the significant difference articulated by, say, Aristotle between "intellect" and "knowledge" not a difference recognized by Plato? In my reading, it seems more likely that Plato has Socrates introduce a mistake and/or difference in order to force the reader to raise a question about the equivalence. After all, what *actually goes on* at the fourth segment of the line has been in question all along.

20. On the question of the *Timaeus'* relation to the *Republic*, there is a long and complicated scholarship that has yielded no definitive conclusion. For instance, from the perspective of dramatic date, Proclus argued that the relation of the *Republic* to the *Timaeus* was chronologically sound: the conversation of the *Republic* occurred the day after the festival of Bendis, and that of the Timaeus occurs on the lesser Panathenaea (referred to in the passage at 26 e), two days later (see Proclus 2006, 26.10–20 & Plato 1902, 327 a—b). However, these dates have been disputed (for instance, by Eva Brann, "The Music of the Republic" (1966, 14), insofar as it appears that the lesser Panathenaea did not occur for another two months. Eva Brann's position appears needlessly extreme: she asserts that because the dates are disputed "there is no reason whatsoever to conclude" that the conversation in the *Republic* is the one to which the *Timaeus* refers (1966, 14). A.E. Taylor held the view that the conversation in the *Timaeus* did occur three days later but not on the Panathenaea (Taylor 1928, 45). However, Francis M. Cornford advised abandoning the notion that the conversation occurred three days after the festival of Bendis (Cornford 1935, 20–1). Claudia Baracchi offers an interesting interpretation of the question by focusing on the difference between the *Timaeus'* abstracted/schematic reconstruction and the *Republic's* living/spontaneous discourse (Baracchi 2002, 146–47). Thus, there are many ambiguities about the connection between the two texts, not only with respect to dramatic date and dramatic form but content as well. Gilbert Ryle lists some of these (Ryle 1966, 230–231). Further, perhaps most importantly, both the order and content of the speeches, remembered in Socrates' recapitulation in the *Timaeus*, vary from those presented in the *Republic*; yet, the participants all agree emphatically that nothing was left out or was different from the previous discussion (Plato 2001, 19 b). Given these ambiguities, must we not read the distortion as intentional and, thus, part of the interpretative task?

21. I offer a detailed reading of these elements in the *Timaeus* in my "Difference in Plato's *Timaeus*" (Winslow 2021).

Chapter 8

On Bastards and Orphans

Let us take a moment to briefly recapitulate the senses of necessity that have emerged for us in the *Republic* so far. In our interpretation of book VI, we cast necessity in the shape of *erōs* (erotic love), wandering movement, *tugxano* (chance happenings), and the ecosystematic origin of both concepts and living forms. Then, in the images of the divided line and the cave allegory, we further saw how necessity shows itself not only in the foregrounded ways, but also as *compulsion* or *force*. With respect to the cave, we observed that necessity (as compulsion) drives the movements of humans not only out of the cave, but also back into the cave. Further, we suggested that the movement of the human soul into *aporia*—that crucial Platonic intellectual phenomenon—is achieved as a matter of compulsion [*anagkē*] or force. That is to say, *aporia* does not occur as a consequence of free action, but is exhibited in the cave as a matter of force/necessity. With our analysis of dialectic in chapter seven, we observed that, when one draws an interpretation of dialectic from the dramatic movements of the dialogue as a whole, one observes a similarity between this movement and the movement of natural necessity. That is to say, the biological movement of necessity (from parent to offspring) is circular; dialectic (and musical verse) was postulated to be a form of *logos* that shares this circular form of movement with natural necessity.

In order to conclude my analysis of book VII, I will offer an interpretation of those humans whom Socrates names as the source of the bad reputation of philosophy in cities: bastards and orphans. Calling to mind the accusation of Adeimantus in book VI, Socrates suggests that when dialectic is in the hands of such people, the result is "uselessness" and/or "maliciousness." However, as I argue in this chapter, the figure of the bastard in human nature is more universal than this. Moreover, it is precisely dialectic which runs the risk of rendering a human being "useless" or "malicious." Consequently, I argue that there is a tragic necessity that subtends the human endeavor of dialectic: it is *deinos*. That is to say, dialectic is both *wonderful* and *terrible* at the same time.

Immediately after the articulation of the new studies and the role of dialectic in philosophical education, the dialogue returns again to the question of the philosophical nature; for, according to Socrates, the task before Glaucon, the law-giver in this instance, is the distribution of the new studies to the ruling class. However, a discrepancy in the account of necessary characteristics emerges quickly. Socrates asks Glaucon if he remembers what sort of men were selected. Glaucon emphatically replies "How [would I] not?" (535 a). Socrates then recapitulates the qualities that belong to the relevant nature, but with one variation.

> "The most stable [*bebaios*] and most courageous [*andreios*] must be chosen and, as much as possible, the best looking [*eueidēs*]. In addition, one must seek for men who have noble and virile characters, but also hold in their nature that which is useful for education."[1]

"What kinds do you distinguish?" (535 a—b).

Curiously, Socrates has just begun to recapitulate the qualities that the philosophical nature must possess, but he has added one without Glaucon noticing. Namely, he has added that the philosophical nature must be as good looking (*eueidēs*) as possible. Moreover, Glaucon has missed this detail just after Socrates has asked him if he remembers the qualities they must possess. In book VI, Socrates had used the term *eueidēs* [good looking] to describe the exceptional youth in a city of whom *oi polloi* would try to make use, but it was not one of the natural traits needed for the philosopher. Even if it were a requirement, Socrates' famously less desirable appearance would exclude him from such studies. Further, earlier in the dialogue (book III), Glaucon himself had qualified Socrates' argument that the musical man would love only harmonious souls *and bodies* by arguing that "if there were some defect in the body, he would abide it and would be willing to welcome him" (402 d). To this correction in his argument, Socrates concedes. Here, however, Glaucon stays silent on the matter, indicating he does not remember.

In the current passage, Glaucon's memory is further brought into question. As if to send a smoke signal to the reader, Plato shows that, despite having emphatically affirmed his memory, the character Glaucon indicates that in fact he *does not remember* the previously stated list of qualities.[2] In response to Socrates' declaration that these natures will possess qualities that are most "useful for this education" (535 b), Glaucon asks Socrates what they are. As Socrates goes on to elaborate the characteristics that he and Glaucon (and Adeimantus), as the law-givers, have already determined (485–487) and repeated (490 c), the ability to remember figures prominently among them. Therefore, missing the discrepancy and failing to remember what he himself asserted and/or consented to as the necessary qualities of a philosophical ruler strike me with the impression that, through these exchanges in this passage, Plato reveals that Glaucon does not have a good memory and, therefore, does not possess all of the natural qualities necessary to receive an education in dialectic (at least if these are, in fact, the qualities necessary for a philosophical nature).

Socrates reacts to Glaucon's question with the following answer: "eagerness [*drimutēs*] at studies, you blessed one [*ō makarie*]" (535 b). This vocative address (*ō makarie*) he often reserves as a response of surprise, criticism and sometimes even hostility.[3] Early in the dialogue, in book I, Plato has Socrates use the phrase many times in reply to Thrasymachus. For instance, when the latter asserts that Socrates will be unable to overpower him in argument, Socrates employs the address: "nor would I attempt it, you blessed one [*ō makarie*]" (341 b). In relation to Glaucon, Socrates utilizes the address in book IV when he playfully chastises both himself and Glaucon for being negligent in failing to observe that justice had been evident all along: "apparently, you blessed one [*ō makarie*], it has been rolling around at our feet from the beginning (432 d). In addition, Socrates employs the phrase with Adeimantus, exhorting him to tame his anger at the many: "you blessed one [*ō makarie*] . . . do not accuse the many in such a way" (499 d). Further, Socrates avails himself of the phrase to address both Adeimantus and Glaucon when he declines to attempt to offer an account of the good in book VI. He says "disgracing myself, I will have to pay a penalty be an occasion for laughter. But, you blessed ones [*ō makaroi*], put aside for now what the good itself is" (506 d—e). In the context of describing the characteristics of democracy, Socrates also uses the phrase. Democracy, says Socrates, is the most beautiful regime. Three times in one sentence he implements the crucial term found all over the dialogue: *poikillō*, or "many-colored" as a feature of democratic social organization:

> "It happens that this is the most beautiful polity: just like a many-colored [*poikilos*] garment embellished [*poikillō*] in all bright colors, embellished [*poikillō*] with all characters [ēthos], it would also appear [*phainō*] most beautiful. And many perhaps . . . like boys and women beholding sparkling [*poikilos*] objects, would judge this to be the most beautiful polity."

> "Indeed," he said.

> And, you blessed one [*ō makarie*]," I said, "it is useful to search for a constitution" (557 c- d).

In this passage, Socrates appears to be disturbed by Adeimantus' lack of attention. Whatever Socrates thinks about the many-colored characteristics of a democratic regime's social organization, it seems that Adeimantus should have been possessed by a more lively, less formulaic reaction. Perhaps because Adeimantus himself lives in such a regime, Socrates expected to elicit from him a shock and intellectual vivacity. Consequently, *ō makarie* remains an expression of his exasperation and frustration with both Glaucon's and Adeimantus' indifference or failure to undergo *aporia*.

Given that these uses of the phrase are not reducible to one another, one can argue that *ō makarie* is said in many ways, for Plato. However, on my reading, the way he wields the phrase in this moment of book VIII most echoes his use of it in the quoted passage above in book VII. That is to say, Socrates expresses his frustration with both Glaucon's and Adeimantus' failure to remember in a way that even resembles a swear or an outburst. According to the passage, Glaucon's limitations are directly related to his "nature." He may be among those possessed by "the most stable and most courageous" (535 a) nature, but perhaps he lacks the nature that animates the "lover of learning," and is not "an inquirer, but hates the work in such matters" (535 d).

In the recapitulation of the natural characteristics of the nature suitable to receive the philosophical/dialectical studies, we find, therefore, steadfastness, quickness of learning, good looks, an eagerness and love for these labors, and a good memory. Socrates then employs metaphors surrounding the social organization of sexual reproduction. He introduces the human social distinction between a bastard (*nothos*) and a legitimate offspring (which we have previously connected to a certain conception of "necessity" and "the good" in book VI). It is an interesting metaphor to bring to the argument. Given that we are asking about natural characteristics, why add a socially-composed concept to measure this nature? After all, other animal natures do not appear to us to formulate such a distinction. In ancient Athens the term names not only offspring between unmarried citizens, but also those between an Athenian male citizen and a foreign, non-citizen female (Kamen 2013).[4] Socrates points back to book VI in his defense of philosophy in the face of Adeimantus' attack against the pervasive maliciousness of its practitioners. Here, Socrates argues that failing to make the distinction between the bastard and the legitimate child is the reason for philosophy's current bad reputation.

> "The failure now, and the dishonor that has fallen upon philosophy which we discussed before, is that men who are not worthy engage in it. Not bastards, but the genuine should engage in it" (535 c).

Are we to read this passage to say that non-citizen foreigners have taken up philosophy and, consequently, cause the dissolution of the discipline? What is a "bastard" for Socrates in this instance?

The term bastard [*nothos*] first appears in book V. As one might expect, it is introduced while the composition of the controversial laws of reproduction are being formulated. There, Socrates suggests that when a man and a woman of reproductive age breed[5] without being united by a ruler of the city, the offspring must be considered a bastard: "we shall say that he is appointing a bastard [*nothos*], an unhallowed and unholy child to the city" (461 b). In this case, therefore, the concept of a bastard is imposed on a citizen by a technologically crafted legal decree. However, I do not think that Plato has Socrates use the term in this sense here in book VII.

In book VI, Plato has Socrates use the term again in a decidedly different way, but still with an emphasis on its reproductive connotation. In his defense against Adeimantus' slander against the philosophical nature (that is, it is useless and/or malicious), Socrates recapitulates the agreed upon natural characteristics that necessarily govern the philosophical nature: he is possessed by an erotic love for *what is*, a love this nature does not lose until he grows close to it, seduces it/is seduced by it, couples with it and, consequent to this erotic coupling, begets intelligence and truth. Only then do his erotic urges become satisfied—when his desire culminates in the production of an offspring of the truth of *what is* (490 b). Of course, as we argued in our analysis of book VI, the paradigmatic example of the philosophical nature (Socrates) does not achieve the satisfaction of his desires in any of the dialogues. Moreover, we observed then that the philosophical nature is wholly appropriated to the forces of necessity insofar as he is *erotically* driven into his activity and does not freely choose it. It is, in fact, his *nature*. But, here, our attention narrows to the manner that Socrates' words help frame the way he uses the term "*nothos*."

Socrates continues by prodding Adeimantus' memory—he references the additional natural traits previously agreed upon: "you surely remember that courage, magnificence, facility at learning, and memory went along with them" (490 c). Because Adeimantus introduced the slander against the philosophical nature, Socrates recapitulates the "nature of the *true* philosophers again" so as to define "what it must *necessarily* be" (490 d, emphasis added). The reader will remember that the origin of the corruption of this nature is exactly the same as the origin of its authenticity: these same natural traits. "The most surprising thing of all to hear is that each one of the things we praised in that nature destroys the soul that has them . . . courage, moderation, and everything we went through" (491 b). Like the life of plants, the ecosystem in which one finds oneself planted at birth plays a crucial role in the manner in which these natural [necessary] traits become cultivated. The soil and environment of the human being, we argued, is *oi polloi* understood broadly. The philosophical nature, therefore, becomes *bastard* or *true* in accordance with the ecosystem in which it is planted. It is a matter of necessity, that is to say, of necessity understood both as chance [*tugxanō*] (492 a) and as the rules of growth that determine in what sort of environment a child becomes planted and how it will fare. Indeed, even the child born outside of the politically recognized institution of marriage remains a matter of necessity, insofar as it is natural necessity that binds her to events unfolding prior to her generation.

Socrates confirms this analysis by suggesting that, when a human being that possesses these natural qualities appears as a youth, *oi polloi* "will want to make use of him" (494 b), and take advantage of his rare traits. Socrates asks Adeimantus if it is possible that such a man will philosophize. Adeimantus answers "not at all" (495 a). Therefore, as we suggested before, it remains a question whether the world has ever seen a philosopher on the model of Socrates' definition, especially if we are to add that, not only must he have been erotically compelled to seek *what is*, but he must have coupled with it and produced "true" offspring (490 b). For, the activity that human beings perform and the sort of things to which they give birth, qua human, are equally subject to the language which characterizes them as "bastard" and "true." Bastard men give birth to bastard offspring: "what things are such people likely to engender? Are they not bastard and trivial? Necessarily [*anagkē*]." (496 a). These offspring are, of course, not only biological "things," but also discursive things that emerge bastard or true.

Curiously, Socrates appears to switch back and forth between the father and the offspring in these passages in a way that is not altogether clear. Sometimes the orphan (*orphanos*) or bastard (*nothos*) is spoken of as the human being who improperly consorts with philosophy (495 c; 535 c; 536 a). However, sometimes he speaks of the bastard as *the child* of the improper coupling with philosophy (496 a). Namely, there is a fundamental ambiguity here between the human *animal* and the human *thought* that comes to be from the former entity's erotic activity.

Whether we want to argue that the child or the father came first, Socrates claims that bastard practitioners of dialectic are responsible for the bad reputation of philosophy.

"These [legitimate] men, for whom philosophy is most suitable, go thus into exile and leave her abandoned and *unconsummated* . . . while, after them, other unworthy men come to her—like an *orphan* [*orphanos*] bereft of relatives[6]— and disgrace her. . . . Those who have *intercourse* with her, some are worthless and the many worthy of many bad things" (1991, 495 b—c, emphasis added).

Here, Socrates substitutes the image of the *bastard* for the image of the *orphan*, both of which are conceptually related insofar as both are examples of human beings that find themselves severed in some way from their fathers. But from what father are these paramours of philosophy severed? Again, the language employed here about philosophy and its practitioners reflects the movements of sexual reproduction. Like the biological world, the passage suggests that philosophy generates in the manner of living beings (that reproduce sexually). In contrast to this, one might place technological production—which certainly also *compels* in accordance with *desire*, but not with *erotic desire*. With the language of a bastard severed from the father, does Plato wish to have Socrates' words here give articulation to a conception of a philosophy performed not through erotic desire, but through some sort of other, perhaps technological desire? If so, perhaps one can offer as an example Thrasymachus' application of the thought "justice is in the interest of the stronger." The thought is produced and applied as a teaching for the sake of integrating students into a political and social regime in a way that will help them succeed in the life of *oi polloi*. Consequently, the bastard or orphan would be characterized in the following way. The bastard *thought*, thus, would carry the connotation of an idea generated for the sake of some utilitarian end. The bastard *philosopher*, thus, would carry the connotation of a human motivated by the application of such a thought. Of course, as with Thrasymachus, the desire of such a philosopher would be more complex than the desire simply to teach the idea and watch it proliferate. However, the idea and its craftsman appear compelled by motivations other than for the sake of the erotic production of novel ideas.

So much for the meaning of "bastard" and "orphan" in these passages. But, who is the missing father? According to Socrates, these orphans and bastards seek to take advantage of the honorable position of philosophy among *oi polloi*; for, "in comparison with the other arts, philosophy holds a greater rank, even as it suffers the [ways we have elaborated]" (495 d). The ark of the father has long been missing from the temple, but the sounds of the old prayers still echo on the walls. Bastards "see that this *xōra* has become empty, but full of beautiful names and ornaments. Like those fleeing from prisons to temples, these people too are pleased to escape the arts [*technai*] into philosophy, those who happen to be the most refined in their low art" (495 c—d). With the articulation of this constitutive absence in the activity of dialectic and reproduction of philosophy by bastards (probably understood here as sophists), I perceive a way of interpreting how the father might be understood to be absent from these bastards and orphans.

A contemporary example may be instructive. For the most part, philosophy and dialectic are conceived as if they were departmental disciplines in a university. In most institutions of higher learning, there exists a variety of *technai*, a plethora of arts and sciences; and philosophy happens to be one among them. As such, philosophy is conceived as producing a particular system of knowledge, one that is distinguished from the others by its subject matter (as each of the others are distinguished from each other). But it is conceived to perform the same sort of activity: knowledge production. In the contemporary world of philosophy, that knowledge production shows itself for the most part as a philological enterprise. Philosophy departments have experts in particular thinkers, historical eras, or thematic regions who are tasked with, *finally*, getting a thinker or a thought "right." They are animated by the goal of the cultivation of a linear development of the tradition of philosophy, so that it may be codified, cataloged, judged against a backdrop of other philosophers, and a canon can be established, confirmed, or challenged. One is reminded here of Gadamer's reflections on aesthetic experience in *Truth and Method* (2010). Does the discipline of art history, for example, ever encounter the work of art? Is the experience of the work ever made manifest by the gathering together of the philological details of the work and the integration of the work into a system of historical knowledge? Or is it possible to engage in all of that work in a precise and perfect way and still never "see" Goya's *Hombres leyendo*? In the case of the experience of the work of art, whatever happens in the vision of the *Hombres leyendo* is the connection to the father. But I suppose it could be argued that the discipline of art history may be orphaned from this experience.

In the case of philosophy, what if the activity in university departments trades in only "beautiful names and ornaments"? And the parent is missing from the temple? We have already observed Socrates argue that sophists educate in nothing other than the convictions of *oi polloi* (493 a). In a certain way, this is precisely what most, if not all, universities do—including philosophy departments. Inside of the hive, in our small region next to the conveyor belts of knowledge production, we professors (in whatever discipline) imagine ourselves to be novel and innovative. A system of identity creation is cultivated in the university through which apparent oppositional identities are formed and engage one another in acrimonious and violent ways. However, the system and its differences are imaginary. Both camps *unknowingly* but *necessarily* marshal the same dogmatic concepts and both reinforce the broader, foundational structure of the opinions that guide the system of knowledge production. That is to say, we may wonder whether we, the practitioners of these disciplines in universities, ever suffer an *aporia* regarding our subject matters and make a turn away from the third tier.

What if, for Plato, philosophy is, in fact, not a discipline at all? To be sure, Socrates claims that dialectic is the most important *study*—the other studies are only a prelude to its song. "We have situated dialectic above the studies [*mathēma*] like a coping stone, and that no other study [*mathēma*] could rightly be set above it" (534 e). Dialectic is further stated to be *the study* oriented toward the disclosure of *what is*. One can interpret these sentences as the assertion that dialectic is in fact the methodological discipline for such a disclosure. However, it seems worth repeating: at no point in the dialogue do we observe this disclosure and nowhere is a method for such a disclosure articulated by Socrates.

As we have already suggested, the positive accomplishments of the conversation are, rather, *aporia* and, sometimes subsequent to this, *turning*. While these characteristics of dialectic are not present so much in the linear development of the argument of the *Republic*, they consistently appear in the images given by Socrates and the drama undergone by the interlocutors. In the previous chapter, we set out to understand how dialectic could be described by Socrates as a *technē* if it is not a scientific method, a procedure, or a "low art" (in the words of the quotation above [495 d])—activities of the soul that belong to the third tier of the divided line. We observed that dialectic, like music and biological reproduction, betrays a movement in contrast to system building. Appropriating the examples of musical and organic movements, we interpreted dialectic through Socrates' description of it as an "art of turning"; it returns to the beginning of systems of knowledge and renews itself. As such, dialectic is inherently both destructive and creative. Like the creative production of the coupling of a father and a mother, the offspring are irreducibly novel. While other disciplines—involving the *mathematikē* on the divided line—build systems of propositional knowledge like hives of bees make systems for the production of honey, the *practice* of dialectic in the dialogue makes visible that these same human knowledge systems may rest on unsecured and shifting principles. Therefore, the practice of philosophy is foreign to the work typically performed in the educational institutions of *oi polloi*. It must appear as something different, perhaps even something hostile to the producers of systems of knowledge.

From the point of view of natural characteristics, we saw that the bastard and the true offspring may in fact be identical insofar as each is "by nature a rememberer, a quick learner, magnificent,[7] gracious [*euxaris*], and a friend and relative [*suggenēs*] of truth, justice, courage, and moderation" (487 a). They may be physiologically and spiritually the same. However, I would argue that, insofar as one receives some sort of vital recognition from the father and the other does not, what distinguishes them is their capacity to receive the shock of *aporia* and *to turn*. Why this is a matter of recognition from a biological source, I'm not sure; however, it does appear that the connection to the father is neither cultivated in an institution nor passed on by a mere genetic trait. Perhaps we can say that the capacity *to turn* lies in human nature, even if it is not a natural characteristic that is easily fit into a filing cabinet organized by genus and specific difference. It is also not a study, at least if by "study" we mean an academic discipline or a system of knowledge of the *oi polloi* (neither of which transcend the third tier of the divided line). If philosophy (and dialectic) is grounded in the experience of *aporia* and *turning*, then, first and foremost, it is a *comportment*, a comportment into which a human may, by chance [*tugxanō*], find him or herself. It is what makes us comic and it is what makes us tragic. We inherit what we are from the poets, but we can become skeptical of even what we are and what we have inherited. This is the curious way that human nature becomes distinguished from other kinds of natures, like the bee or the ant that we also resemble. We can become alienated from the structure of inheritance that makes us what we are. We can become, to some degree, private [*idios*].

But perhaps this interpretation is already a technological appropriation of the thought of the father, an attempt to situate human life in a stable meaning-horizon: a meaningful cosmos in which the human has a significant place. There exists also the possibility that Plato employs the language of erotics and biological reproduction in order to emphasize that the human is inscribed within finitude even as he attempts to escape it. If in fact there are no ideas that are generated through a principle of nature but every human thought is a technological artifact, then human beings are always limited and there is no such thing as a novel idea. Or, if there are novel ideas, they do not come to be as a consequence of human craft and knowledge, but emerge spontaneously as a consequence of an ungraspable and tragic [*deinos*] necessity (like the principle of originality that subtends the novelty of a newly born child), not human will. On this reading, despite Socrates' optimistic presentation of the mechanisms of human knowledge production, he is forced to use the language of biological and sexual reproduction—that is to say, the language of necessity—in his struggle to account for a study and a method to transcend human *technai* (*mathematikē*) and human finitude.

Therefore, in his recapitulation of the persons who will receive the studies leading to dialectic, Socrates affirms some combination of the formerly stated naturally given qualities. The potential pupils will be possessed by such qualities, but in such a way as to be genuine rather than bastard or orphan. When Glaucon now in book VII admits that he does not understand the way Socrates uses these terms, Socrates gives a few examples through the lens of the necessary virtues. Glaucon appears to find them helpful. However, it seems likely that Plato intends them to remain ambiguous to the reader. With respect to "truth" (which might be a reference to the "natural" characteristic of wisdom), Socrates re-employs an activity that one might argue is associated only with human nature, one that has already been invoked multiple times in the dialogue: lying. How a human being incorporates the activity of lying discloses something about whether they are bastard or orphan.

> "Regarding truth," I said, "we will think a soul maimed that hates the willing [*ekousios*] lie [*pseudos*], bearing it with difficulty and being very angry when others lie, but contentedly receives the unwilling [*akousios*] lie and, when it is taken to be unlearned, is not irritated but tolerates [its lack of learning], like a wild animal, defiling itself in lack of learning [*amathia*]?" (535 d—e).

By the phrase "willing lie," it appears that Socrates means the straight-forward signification of lie—the sort of lie perhaps a used car salesman might tell you about the quality of the car you are about to buy. The salesman *knows* the car has been a lemon for the former owner. However, he willingly tells you otherwise to encourage you to buy it. Every human soul, including the bastard, would react with anger at the disclosure of the lie. A willing lie articulates *what is*, but knowingly articulates *what is* in a way that *it is not*—that is to say, falsely. It may be that only human beings do this. Because human beings always have a mediated relation to the beings in the world through the *logos* of *oi polloi*, they can articulate *what is not* as if it were *what is*. But what is an unwilling lie? Glaucon passes by the opportunity to ask what the difference is between a willing and an unwilling lie; however, there is a similar, though not exact, presentation of the difference earlier in the dialogue (book II).

While Socrates is purging the newly founded city of the unsavory deeds conveyed by the poetic tradition's accounts of the gods and heroes of ancient times, he asks Adeimantus if the gods are capable of lying to us. That is to say, he wants to know if Adeimantus thinks that "they make it seem to us that they appear in manifold shapes, deceiving [*exapataō*][8] and bewitching" (381 e). In response to Adeimantus' ambiguous answer to the question, Socrates invokes the concept in a way similar to that involuntary lie in book VII. He says,

> "You know that all gods and human beings hate the true lie [*alēthōs pseudos*], if that expression can be used?"
>
> "What do you mean?" he said.
>
> "[no one] voluntarily [*ekōn*] is willing to lie about the most supreme things to what is most supreme in himself. Rather he fears holding a lie there more than anything."
>
> "I do not understand yet," he said. . . .

"I mean that to lie and to have lied to the soul about the beings, and to be unlearned [*amathēs*], and to have and to keep a lie there is what everyone would least accept [*dexomai*]. They hate a lie in such a place the most."

"Very much," he said. (382 a—b).

Here, Socrates uses similar language to describe the relationship to the lie as we find in book VII. Adam interprets this passage to refer to the moral "doctrine" that vice is involuntary insofar as it derives from ignorance (382 a). While I do not wish to disagree with Adam on this point, I think both the passage in book II and the passage in book VII point more directly to an ontological difficulty the human being faces regarding the modes in which the world appears to him or her. As suggested above, there is a way that the human being can voluntarily exploit the loose connection between the *logos*/discourse and *what is* in order to satisfy some desire. That is to say, the human being can voluntarily lie. However, this ability is derivative. Socrates says that this sort of lie, the lie in speeches, is "a kind of imitation of the pathos in the soul" (382 b). It is derived from the very condition of human existence. While he makes a distinction between "real" lies and lies "in speeches," it is not possible to truly separate *logos* from lies. It is in fact *logos* that makes both lies possible.

For the human being, there is a necessity to engage with the world through the unstable structures of *logoi*; and this means that there always already remains the possibility that discourse mediates that relationship in a false way. Lying is first and foremost an ontological problem, not a moral one. To be one among the many means precisely that one inhabits a cave. The shadows and images that float by on the cave walls bestow upon the inhabitant an understanding of the world and of oneself. What is wise, courageous, moderate, just, beautiful, divine, and good first become visible inside the cave. Moreover, the discourse in the cave is not voluntary. Becoming one among the many is not voluntary. Rather, a condition of finding oneself at all is finding oneself already a member of *oi polloi*. Consequently, it remains the case that the answers to the most important questions, the most sovereign beings, exist as images in the most sovereign part of the soul—that part of the soul by which one would claim knowledge and through which one would pass judgment on those beings around one. But images and opinions can be false. For instance, one may judge the cosmos to be *finite* and ground the conditions for the possibility of knowledge and the intelligibility of the world on that presupposition. Aristotle begins with this assumption. Only if the cosmos does not infinitely expand is it possible for something to exist *as one*, and only if something can be said to be one is knowledge of it possible. However, what if this first principle of dependable knowledge (a finite cosmos) is false?

What if this assumption that we hold in that most sovereign part of the soul is a lie [*pseudōs*] and the cosmos is infinite or indefinite? In this case, everything changes. The measure of something as one can no longer serve as the model of intelligibility for all of the reasons Aristotle offers to the contrary. Consequent to the shift to the infinite, the principle of finitude becomes a lie in the most sovereign part of the soul. In the quoted passage above, Socrates claims that neither human nor god would tolerate its presence there. From these words in book II, one assumes that, as the first principle of "finitude" becomes unacceptable, the human being would find it *compelling* and *necessary* to intellectually accommodate "the infinite" or some other principle into one's understanding of the organization of the world.

Because of what may be an incommensurable relation between the *logos* and *what is*, there exists the possibility—even, necessity—that one may involuntarily hold a lie in the soul regarding the way being is organized. Because of this more profound unstable relation between discourse and being, *voluntary* lies are possible for the human being to tell. Even Socrates' *voluntary* irony finds its origin there. However, even though Socrates suggests that no one would voluntarily tolerate the presence of the *involuntary* lie in the soul in book II, in book VII this act is precisely one of the marks of the bastard. Instead of being "angry" by the disclosure of the lie, the soul of the bastard "is not irritated but tolerates [its lack of learning], like a wild animal, defiling itself in lack of learning [*amathia*]" (535 d). In this case, the bastard refuses to turn as a consequence of suffering the *aporia*. To appeal to our previous example of the principle of the finite, the bastard fails to be shaken to his foundations by the loss of the finite cosmos in a way that occasions novelty, but instead brooks no innovation in the founding principles.

Here, in the articulation of the bastard of book VII, we have the curious expression of a voluntary acceptance of an involuntary lie. One is left with the impression that such a comportment is common in human life. So much of human life requires a voluntary acceptance of an involuntary lie. To extend our examples beyond cosmological organization, one may invoke the ideological political commitments animating human societies. For instance, the enlightenment thought enshrined in the first line of the *Universal Declaration of Human Rights* that governs social organization in modern democratic societies: that each human being is born with an inherent dignity and a set of inalienable rights (United Nations General Assembly 1947, 1). A similar ideological sentiment is expressed in the Declaration of Independence of the United States. "We hold these truths to be self-evident, that all men are created equal, that they are endowed by their Creator with certain unalienable rights, that among these are Life, Liberty and the pursuit of Happiness" (Jefferson, et al. 1776). Of course, from the point of view of any biological entity on earth, these enlightenment assertions grounded on a metaphysical account born in a particular historical period are lies. That is to say, there is no such thing as inherent dignity or inalienable rights; and further, human beings are not created equal. These are ideological images that float by on the cave walls that become, nevertheless, necessary for the stable organization of the cave.

The ambiguity involved in determining how to read Socrates' assertions here is not limited to the fact that there is something bastard-like in every human being, insofar as every human belongs to a cave whose walls are meaningful because they are painted with lies. Always, or for the most part, human beings easily "accommodate" themselves to such important and world-organizing ideological lies. That is to say, the human being is in some measure always already a bastard. In addition to this difficulty for the argument in favor of bestowing the new study of dialectic on only "genuine" natures, there is the one inherent in the organization of the text itself. Namely, it appears that *Kallipolis* produces *nothing but* bastards. These latter characteristics of the bastard describe each and every citizen of *Kallipolis* insofar as the law givers employ what, in book III, they explicitly name a lie, a "noble lie" (414 b).

After Socrates asserts that they must contrive the noble lie, Glaucon asks what he means. Tempering Glaucon's expected incredulity, he responds by suggesting that what he proposes is "nothing new." Perhaps it has happened everywhere at the founding of a human society. In fact, such a "Phoenician thing," he says, "has already happened in many places before" (414 c). By "Phoenician thing," Socrates refers to the myth that relates Cadmus' founding of the city of Thebes. Like the noble lie for which Socrates advocates, the myth of Cadmus includes a narrative about the order of reproduction of a people; for, the inhabitants of Thebes are to have originated autochthonously. The story goes that, after the hero Cadmus had slayed a dragon, he planted the teeth of the dragon in the ground at the behest of Athena. The human beings that sprouted from these plantings became the fathers of the noblest families of Thebes (Chisholm 1911, 931). Presumably, the people of Thebes understand themselves through this myth of their autochthonous origins.

Socrates exhorts Glaucon and Adeimantus to tell the citizens of their city a similar origin myth.

> "First, I will set to work persuading the rulers themselves and the soldiers, then the rest of the city . . . that they were in truth under the earth being formed and reared . . . When the work was brought to completion, the earth, their mother, delivered them. And now, just as if the land [xōra] were a mother and nurse, for her sake they deliberate about and defend it . . . and think of the other citizens as brothers and born of the earth" (414 d—e).

This lie serves as the ground for the self-understanding that each citizen has in relation to its city and its citizenry. Each citizen of *Kallipolis* owes a great part of his/her identity to the organizing power of the lie. It is the ideological source for the feeling of belonging to this community and communicates a measure by which each citizen may distinguish between sameness and otherness, inside the city and outside the city, us and them. It may be argued that, without this or a similar lie, there are no such distinctions. The only people excluded from the lie in *Kallipolis* are the law-givers (who, like Solon, may be exiled from the city they found). Like the prisoners in the cave, these citizens are told that they have been formed below the earth. However, this is a clear metaphor for the kind of formation unique to human nature. Human natures are formed by discursive environments, like those presented in the underground cave allegory. Our law-givers, Glaucon, Adeimantus, and Socrates, are of course subject to their own world-forming myths. That is to say, insofar as they are "like" the prisoners (515 a), they too are bastards, accommodating themselves to lies that govern the organization of Athens. However, as so-called founders of a mythologically-grounded society themselves, they stand outside of the lies told to the citizenry of *Kallipolis*. Thus, even as founders of the city, they themselves are not of the city—they originate the lie, but do not accommodate themselves to it in the same way as the citizenry.

Moreover, the noble lie serves to organize the breeding regime of the city. The forces of necessity that show themselves as erotics in human life are only secondarily controlled by law. The laws themselves are grounded upon the lie. The city's rational control of the sexual practices, gender roles, and class organization (all of which have meaning in relation to the power of *erōs* and, thus, necessity) is codified by the laws, but its *false* necessity is felt as a consequence of the originating lie. Every citizen accommodates him/herself to the lie, measures him/herself to other citizens through the lie, and conducts his erotic and gendered life in accordance with the moral necessity provided by this arbitrary contrivance, the noble lie. Of course, in the unfolding of the drama in the *Republic*, the rational lie fails to control erotics and/or necessity and the city collapses into tyranny. But at its origin, every citizen in *Kallipolis* seems to be a bastard, insofar as each "accommodates" itself to the noble lie.

Socrates again returns to the theme of the children distanced from their fathers toward the end of book VII; however, this time his images are cast in relation to the problem of misology. Even though the comportment achieved in the activity of dialectic represents the culmination of human nature, it nevertheless remains dangerous. This comportment is a (if not the) source of the tragic in human life. Dialectic reveals itself as *deinos*; that is to say, it is both wonderful and terrible at the same time. When the human being undergoes the practice of dialectical questioning, she is opened to the possibility of misology. Socrates says,

> "Have you considered," I said, "how great is the harm now being brought into being by dialectic [*dialegesthai*]?"
>
> "What kind?" he said.[9]
>
> "Certainly, they are filled with lawlessness [*paranomia*]," I said.
>
> "Very much," he said (537 e).

As we have elaborated in the previous chapter, Socrates referred to dialectic as the "song" [*nomos*] itself just a few pages earlier. Now, dialectic is said to be the source of "lawlessness" [*para-nomia*]. Dialectic is a comportment in which one sings the song, but it is equally subject to the possibility of modifying the key or corrupting the melody. Following this assertion about practitioners of modern dialectic, Socrates asks Glaucon if he is surprised these people suffer from it and if he feels sympathy [*suggignoskō*] with them. The term *suggignoskō* is ambivalent here; for, according to Liddell, Scott, Jones (1940), it may mean what Bloom has translated: namely, "to sympathize" as in "to feel fellow feeling with," so as "to make an exception for," or "to excuse." This appears to be the way that Socrates repeats the term at 539 a. But, in addition, among other things, it may mean "to own" or "confess one's error." In the latter case, Socrates would be asking Glaucon if he sees himself in the image of these lawbreakers. The latter interpretation would be supported by the fact that Glaucon's projections of the image of Gyges' ring may be interpreted as an example of the use of dialectic in the service of lawlessness.

However the reader is to interpret *suggignoskō*, Glaucon finds Socrates' use of the term ambiguous too. He asks, "why should I?" (537 e). In order to answer the question, Socrates employs another image, the image of a sort of orphan, an adopted child.

> "It is like the adopted child [*hupobolimaios*]," I said, "reared in wealth, in a large and great family, among many flatterers. Having become a man, he perceives [*aisthanomai*] that he does not belong to those stated to be his parents and cannot find those who gave birth to him. Can you divine [*manteuomai*] how he would be disposed toward the flatterers and toward those who made the adoption, in the time when he did not know about it, and in the time when he did know? . . . I divine [*manteuomai*] that he would be more likely to honor his mother and his father and . . . his other kin. . . . in the time when he did not know the truth. And perceiving [*aisthanomai*] which *is*, I divine [*manteuomai*]

that he would loosen the honor [for his kin] and increase it for the flatterers" (537 e - 538 b).

Why this image should clarify Glaucon's confusion about the reasons he ought to sympathize with the philosophical lawbreakers is not immediately apparent. However, the image does offer another orphan for comparison with the practice of dialectic. It is an image that puts on display the potential dialectic holds for engendering a misological comportment in its practitioner.

The adopted child raised by parents that he has *been told* are his own functions in society in the expected way. He adheres to the social customs of heeding what his parents say and doing what he can to help cultivate the welfare of his kin. In this case, the child ignorant of his adoption resembles Polemarchus' interpretation of Simonides' just person: he does good to his friends and nothing bad (332 a). Perhaps there is nothing to distinguish the character of the changeling child from the "genuine" one in its youth. Moreover, both children reflect the social commitments of the *polis* like individual bees reflect the hives. The change comes when each child reaches adulthood. Once the adopted child comes of age, qua human, he learns the *truth*. He comes to recognize that he is held to his parents and kin only through something like social convention. There is no paternal connection, no *necessary* bind to his kin.

In a certain way, this truth sets him free. Without the pressures of necessary obligation, he becomes loosened from the binds of the cave. He has seen "that which *is*" (538 b). The vision of the truth frees him from the obligations he felt toward his parents and opens him to redirecting his productive energies. One can say that he abandons the cave. Consequently, for the "adoptive kin ... he would not care" (538 c). Instead, he *turns* his attention increasingly toward the influence of the flatterers, adopting their way of life and having "open [*aparakaluptos*] relations with them" (538 c).[10]

With this image, Socrates gives another analogy for the practice of dialectic. In the picture that Socrates presents, the child is raised by parents who instill within the child the cultural expectations of *oi polloi*. They plant the discursive seeds of what counts as just, wise, courageous, moderate and beautiful. However, there comes a time in maturity in which the young person "perceives that which *is*" (538 b). It is clear that the person in the example has practiced dialectic, since coming to know *that which is* remains the stated goal of the practice. In the example given, through the practice of dialectic, the parents are exposed as false origins.

In my reading, this discovery that one has false parents must be what happens analogously in the course of the activity of dialectic.[11] That is to say, when the human being comes into maturity, he undergoes the tragic awareness that there is no necessary ground for the validity of the meaning of the most important concepts that govern human life. Coming to maturity and developing the primary work of the human being means suffering the comportment in which these concepts become brought into question. That is to say, coming to human maturity means that one runs the risk of losing one's father. This reading is further confirmed by the passage that follows. Glaucon announces that he does not understand how the image is a metaphor for the practice of "arguments," or dialectic. Thus, Socrates says,

> It is certain that we have from childhood opinions about the just and the beautiful by which we have been raised as by parents, obeying them as rulers and honoring them (538 c).

The *logoi* of *oi polloi* have communicated to us the most important concepts. We are their children, insofar as they have raised us and instilled within us our convictions about what is just and fair through which we evaluate the world, others, and ourselves. Like bees in the hive, we obey these organizational concepts as our rulers and we honor them—perhaps even unconsciously. In addition to these practices of obeying and honoring, there are others too. Namely, there exist those practices "opposed" to the latter. Which is to say, there are practices that "possess pleasures that flatter our soul and pull it to them. They do not persuade those who are moderate [*metrios*]. Each of these [latter] honor the inherited opinions [*patrios*] and obey them as rulers" (538 d, translation altered). What are the practices that possess pleasures that flatter the soul? Perhaps we would want to argue that they are akin to those that bring relishes (but also poetry, architecture, sculpture and rhetoric) into cities and that eventually engender within cities the necessity for war—that is to say, both sets of practices belong to all human societies. However, it is important to state that *philosophy is neither of these practices*, at least if Socrates' activities are the model for the practice of philosophy. Mindlessly obeying the norms set by the king or queen bee and honoring them is not what Socrates does. Instead, he shatters his interlocutors' self-understanding of the most important concepts through incessant questioning. Nor does he abandon these concepts as if they were irrelevant in the reality of human life (in favor of, say, the accumulation of money and power). Rather, the activity that we observe in our protagonist most of all is the one that comes next in the text. Socrates asks questions.

It is precisely the activity of the question that destabilizes the honor offered to the ancestral things, to the discursive parents that have raised one. Moreover, the image of Socrates' activity appears in the description of the effect of the question.

"When, to such a one as this, a question is posed: 'What is the beautiful?' and, after answering what he heard from the lawgiver, the argument refutes him, and refuting him many times and in divers manners, throws him into the [confusing] opinion that what the law says is no more beautiful than ugly, and in like manner too about the just and good and that which he most held in honor. After this what do you think he'll do . . . ?"

"Necessarily [*anagkē*]," he said, "he will not honor or obey them as before" (538 d—e).

The practice of Socrates runs the risk of turning his interlocutors into orphans, insofar as his questions invariably force them to admit that they do not know what they thought they knew. The parents turn out to be adoptive. Prior to the encounter with Socrates, the philosopher, they conduct their lives in accordance with the ancestral things without question, obeying and honoring them. One might argue that in this condition citizens lead lives in accordance with natural necessity, since it belongs to human nature to "have from childhood opinions about the just and the beautiful by which we have been raised as by parents, obeying them as rulers and honoring them" (538 c). It is only when they encounter a Socrates, a Parmenides or a Zeno—whether in youth (Polemarchus) or old age (Cephalus)—that "argument's" questions loosen them from the self-evidence that one's parents really are one's parents. And when the human being becomes orphaned from his discursive parents and loses their necessary self-evidence, misology—this distrust of discourse and its connection to reality—becomes likely.

Socrates argues that every precaution against this misology must be taken. In youth, in particular, dialectic must be discouraged. For, youth employ arguments without the necessary ground: "they misuse [discursive refutations] as if they were a game, always using them to contradict. And imitating the ones who have refuted them, they refute others" (539 b). Certainly, in the halls of every modern philosophy department dwell at least a few of these "youth," whatever their age. Socrates may be referencing the students who pay to learn arguments from sophists like Thrasymachus. However, in addition to these, one can imagine the often youthful interlocutors of Socrates suffering this same experience and then imitating him to refute others. To be sure, one might argue that a possible consequence of Socrates' questioning of Polemarchus in book I is precisely a loss of the ancestral conviction subtending his commitment to justice. Polemarchus may become alienated from his father. He is already an adopted son of Athens, living outside of its interior limits in the Piraeus as an alien.

Whether Socrates' dialectical questioning corrupts the youth he encounters or not, the only real precaution he offers against it here is waiting for a time.

Humans, he suggests, should wait until they are older before engaging in arguments. "Someone older . . . would not be willing to participate in such madness. He will imitate the one willing to converse [*dialegesthai*] and search for the truth rather than imitate the one who plays and contradicts for the sake of a game" (539 c). According to Socrates, if youth are subject to dialectical refutation, they treat it as play and become orphaned from dialectic's source of seriousness. To conduct one's arguments in the service of play, then, is to remain alienated from *what is*. Indeed, the question each poses (the youth and the older man) may be identical. The "older man" may ask the same question as the "youth." However, there is a difference not betrayed by the words, grammar, or form of the question. There is no difference of content or form between the two questions. Yet they are not the same. Socrates observes the difference to lie in the *comportment* of the interlocutor. One plays and the other is serious. One is an "orphan" and the other is "genuine." Yet, there is no way to perceive this difference in the words used.

Of course, as usual, what appears to be Plato's commitment to the expression of human finitude does not seem to allow him to permit his discourse to arrive at a final conclusion regarding these matters: only three Stephanus pages earlier Socrates excused himself for speaking outside the limits of *play* and behaving too seriously, "I forgot . . . that we were *playing* and spoke too eagerly" (536 c, emphasis added). Thus, either the entire *Republic* is merely a game not to be taken seriously insofar as its limits are determined by the soul-conditions of its youthful interlocutors, or play plays a more profound role in the human being's necessary conditions than the legal framework Socrates constitutes will allow. Despite the rigorous restrictions established by the rule of law, play continues to bubble up through its surface.

Dialectic might be one of the necessary components of human nature—like erotics and play—that, despite reason's attempts to codify it, circumscribe it within limits, and control it with law, continues to move along in accordance with its own necessary path. The attempt to restrict it quickly becomes a whack-a-mole game. Insofar as dialectic is *deinos*, it already belongs to the human being both as "genuine" (insofar as it emerges as a response to *aporia* and gives rise to the novel and the original) and as "bastard" and "orphan" (insofar as it is a source of the alienating effect of "misology"). Because of human finitude, knowing in advance which of these consequences might emerge from dialectic may not be possible. Dialectic might be, to take a phrase from Heidegger, "the saving power" (Heidegger 1977, 34) But one does not know from where it comes or to where it is going. As such, it belongs to necessity, and the vision of the good as a mechanism by which the human may transcend her finitude is an illusion built into human nature already. This illusion would then be already an effect of necessity.

NOTES

1. Steadiness and ease of learning are found in book VI. "Natures that easily learn, remember, that are shrewd and quick and the rest, you know that these natures full of youth and magnificence do not willingly grow together with dispositions that that choose orderly lives which are quiet and stable [*bebaios*]" (503 c).

2. Jonathan Fine offers a similar interpretation of this passage (Fine 2011, 242).

3. Fine interprets *ō makarie* as an important example of Socratic irony. He argues that Plato has Socrates employ this phrase as a pedagogical act of speech, exhorting his interlocutor to critically assess something he has said. "Not only is *ō makarie* consistently ironic," he argues, "but it tends to occur in a narrow set of circumstances in which Socrates' interlocutor is deficient in criticism and Socrates exhorts him to think more critically" (Fine 2011, 239). While I agree that the use of the vocative phrase is often ironic (though not always) and that it frequently has the function of calling attention to something the interlocutor says in a critical way, I'm not sure its use is always *pedagogical*. In the cases I cite, it is not always clear that Glaucon perceived the irony or consciously received the exhortation and/or criticism—which would seem to be a necessary consequence if Glaucon is to learn something. Moreover, by the end of the dialogue, I do not see evidence that Glaucon has been educated. In fact, as I have already indicated, he appears to be assenting to Socrates' questions without reflection, appearing to desire to simply arrive at the end of the discussion.

4. The clear line of demarcation that I am drawing between the application of a human concept to a "nature" as a "bastard" and that of a natural concept to a "nature" as, say, "bodily strength" is problematic. At this time (and others), there exists an ideological concept (probably derived in some way from conventional selective practices in husbandry) of a "purebred" Athenian offspring that comes to be as a consequence of the breeding of two "purebred" Athenian citizens. And this ideological concept circulates in the ancient Athenian period of Socrates (Kamen 2013). Thus, the qualification calls to mind the breeding regime of the *Kallipolis*, the city that, in just a few pages, will begin its decline as a consequence of a failure to calculate the nuptial number and, thereby, produce what we might call bastard offspring within the regime. Further, in certain respects, the philosopher can be said to possess many of the defining characteristics of a bastard or an orphan. The philosopher is disconnected from the father insofar as the critical questions that the philosopher poses are precisely those derived from his city (or father). Philosophy takes place in Piraeus, which is precisely the space of the bastard/orphan: the space connected to Athens proper, but distanced from it, just like the foreigners who inhabit it.

5. *Kallipolis* has been compared to a "community of animals" husbanded like they live on a farm (Saxonhouse 1978, 892).

6. By switching the term "bastard" for the term "orphan" here, there exists a conspicuous similarity between these orphans and the legal children of book V, who also have lost the legitimate biological connection to their fathers and mothers. The law rendered the children legally parented, but not biologically parented.

7. James Adam notes that *megaloprepēs* is meant by Plato to be the opposite of *aneleutherōs* and *smikrologos* (1902, 487 a). Stanley Rosen points to the connection

to Aristotle's *Ethics*, highlighting the differences on this issue between Aristotle and Socrates' account in Plato. "'Liberality' has nothing to do with spending money (as it does for Aristotle) but refers to something that reminds us of Aristotle's 'greatness of soul' (*megalopsuchia*). What I shall call Socratic greatness of soul has to do with speech, not deed, and with the erotic inclination toward comprehensiveness and depth of knowledge. . . . Socrates again applies what will later be a technical term in Aristotle's ethics: 'magnificence' (*megaloprepeia*). In Aristotle, the term refers to the proper expenditure of large sums of money on splendid public buildings and the like, whereas liberality concerns spending small sums in the proper way. For Socrates, on the other hand, the attributes in question are the mark not of a gentleman but of a philosopher, and so of someone who, in the just city, neither possesses nor spends money" (2005, 231).

8. This is the same verb [*exapataō*] that Socrates employs when he warns his interlocutors that he may deceive them with his images in book VI (507 a).

9. Again, here we may have another instance of Glaucon's poor memory. This subject played a crucial part in the turning of the dialogue in book VI. Adeimantus' accusation against philosophy ought to be fresh on the mind.

10. As we observed in the previous chapters, Socrates argues that the uncorrupted practice of philosophy would be rare, if not impossible, because the environment in which great natures are born is always or for the most part filled with flatterers that wish to exploit these natures and take advantage of the benefits that being associated with a great nature will bring them. Such associations are again alluded to here.

11. As for the children of *Kallipolis*, it should be noted that, in a way, all of them have false parents. There is no necessary connection between parent and child, since that relationship has been reconstituted by the law-givers precisely through social law. Further, at the end of book VII, Socrates advises that the children avoid corruption by being taken away from their parents, by being orphaned: "everyone in the city who happen to be older than ten they will send out to the fields, taking the children far away from the habits of their parents" (540 e - 541 a).

Chapter 9

Necessity and Democracy

After Socrates comes to the end of his questioning regarding the natures that would be most suited to receiving an education in dialectic, the long detour necessitated by Polemarchus' and Adeimantus' interruption would seem to be complete. They had forcibly turned the conversation toward Socrates' too brief explanation of *Kallipolis'* attempts to control erotics, gender dynamics, and the order of the family through its rationalist legal framework. Now, at the beginning of book VIII, Socrates asks if anyone can recall where they had taken the detour. Glaucon claims to remember, although he appears incredulous regarding Socrates' intentions. After suggesting that, then as well as now, Socrates presents his arguments as if they are complete even though they are unfinished, Glaucon says that he recalls that the conversation was forcibly turned away from the formulation of the four constitutions "that miss the mark *if this one is right*" (544 a, emphasis added; c.f., 449 a).

Whether by luck or necessity, the point at which the dialogue turned toward erotics at the end of book IV was an important foreshadowing. For, it is precisely the problem of erotic necessity slipping through the controlling fingers of calculative reason that generates the decline of the city into the other four regimes. The explanation of the legal organization of erotics in the city compels Adeimantus and Polemarchus to seize hold of Socrates' argument and turn it in a new direction, a detour lasting three books. The failure of the legal organization of erotics compels the city to turn, change shape, and decline. Yet, it seems as though Socrates is incapable of offering an account of the erotic movement without help. In order to give expression to the manner in which the phenomenon of movement will envelop *Kallipolis*, Socrates will invoke the Muses.

> Do you want us to pray, like Homer, to the Muses to proclaim "how" faction [*stasis*] 'first broke out.'"[1] and should we say that they speak to us in the manner of tragedy [*tragikōs*], as if we were children? (545 d—e).

As we discover in the *Timaeus* (2001, 19 b—c), *Kallipolis* is presented as a static entity. That is to say, according to Socrates himself, it does not belong to the order of nature—in it lies no principle of metabolism or change.[2] It is, rather, a hypostatization. Perhaps one could even liken it to a painting (to reference book X), or a mere abstract concept. Indeed, from Parmenides' thinking to Newton's *Principia*, movement has long been a difficult phenomenon to grasp for reason, for arguments, for propositions. It may be that Socrates invokes the Muses for this reason. To give expression to natural movement governed by necessity, one requires possession by the Muses. What follows the question above is spoken by the Muses. In a certain way, the Muses relieve Socrates of his personal responsibility for the words given. His mouth and voice are like a vessel, filled with the words of others flowing through them.

Prior to the Muses speaking, Socrates' words surrounding the four regimes suggest moral failure. Free decisions and choices are made by the rulers of the regime that lead to faction within its classes: "every polity changes in the part that has the rule, when faction/division [*stasis*] is born in it. But if it is of one mind, however small it is, it is not possible to move" (545 c—d). At the beginning of book V, just before the turn toward the question of the laws governing *erōs* and child rearing, the language used to describe the cities in decline may equally be interpreted morally: "I call such a city and such a man [*anēr*] good; the others I call bad and missing the mark" (449 a).

However, from the perspective offered by the muses, the decline of the city is a matter of necessity.[3] Quite apart from any free decisions made by the ruling faculties, decay belongs as a mark of finitude[4] in all the things that come into being, even well-educated philosophical natures (even the model of the philosopher that the law-givers' *Kallipolis* produces).

"It is difficult to move a city so organized. But since for *everything that has come into being there is ceasing to be*, such a bringing together will not remain for all time; it will be dissolved [*luō*].[5] And this will be its dissolution [*lusis*]: fruitfulness [*phoras*] and barrenness [*aphoria*] of soul and bodies come not only to plants in the earth but to animals on the earth when life-cycles for each join together a revolution [*periphora*] of circles . . . Even though they are wise, those you have raised as rulers of the city will nonetheless not happen upon [*tugxanō*] the [right] prosperous birth and barrenness [*aphoria*] for your kind with calculation and sensation" (546 a—b, emphasis added).

According to the muses, all things that come into being suffer decay in accordance with necessity. Even if the *Kallipolis* produces philosopher kings to look over itself, it will be moved. In accordance with Socrates' previous words, philosopher rulers have good memories and learn quickly, yet their quickness is tempered by stability and tenacity. These philosophers are in possession of wisdom, courage, moderation and justice. Moreover, they have undertaken the highest studies in the manner of the "genuine" (rather than the "bastard"); and, consequently, they have come to see *what is*, coupled with it and produced offspring. Further, they have seen *the good* by somehow singing the song itself: dialectic. Presumably, if they exist, the moral character of a philosopher ruler is unimpeachable. Their free decisions and choices cannot be better grounded.

Yet, despite being in possession of all these necessary traits and having conducted themselves in perfect order, the muses say that the philosophers and their city are still subject to an untranscendable force of corruption, a force that operates underneath the philosophers and folds them into itself. The city will "dissolve" in accordance with its class of animality for which "life-cycles for each join together a revolution of circles" (546 a). In book X, we find that it is the Spindle of Necessity that spins "all the revolutions" (616 c). The "revolutions" that organize the life-spans of different species are a matter of necessity. Therefore, regardless of the precautions and moral stability of the philosopher kings, the *Kallipolis* will cycle through the revolutions belonging to its animality and dissolve in accordance with *anagkē*.

Whatever it is that the philosopher rulers think they are doing in bestowing a rational order in accordance with thought onto the city, there exists a different order that folds the philosophers, their reasoning, their actions, their words and propositions, their laws, and all the other citizens into itself and lights it up in a new way. It is a tragic image of human nature, insofar as the self-determination of human beings comes to be seen as an illusion of reason. This other order (necessity) renders all of those distinctions irrelevant by bestowing the same organic revolution upon them all indifferently. The city has its life-span, the "revolving of [its natural] circles," regardless of the high quality of the technologically constructed law. What even the titles of these "philosophers," "auxiliaries," and "merchants" mean in the context of *Kallipolis* circulates in the limits of the political framework—but all of this is cast in a revolving trajectory indifferent to *Kallipolis'* goals, a "revolution" that changes the offices' meaning as *Kallipolis* changes shape. The city has its finite revolution and the entities that make up the city come to have meaning in accordance with the point upon the circle in which this revolution finds itself and them. It is a *hermeneutical* revolution, a hermeneutical turning of circles in which the classes of human beings and the private human beings that inhabit the revolving city shift meaning along the trajectory of transformation. Book VIII traces these transformations of meaning within the regimes and within the private humans.

In this chapter we consider book VIII's presentation of the democratic regime through the lens of necessity. While one finds the concept of necessity distributed throughout the morphological movements of the city in book VIII, I will focus primarily on the shape of democracy. For, the language of necessity appears in conjunction with what might be conceived in opposition to it: the language of freedom. Indeed, even though "freedom" is conceived as "the good" for this regime, the word *anagkē* appears in the presentation of democracy more often than freedom [*eleutheria*]. Moreover, in my view, democracy holds a unique position among the mortal manifestations along the transient trajectory of *Kallipolis*. Traditionally, Socrates' presentation of democracy in book VIII has been used to paint a picture of "an elitist Plato, opposed to democracy and hostile to the masses" (Saxonhouse 1998, 273). This is the standard view, even as numerous voices have challenged this interpretation for many years.[6] In this chapter, my reading will lean toward the more favorable views of democracy in book VIII. The structural organization of Socrates' democracy occasions philosophy and the "aristocratic" organization of the soul; however, at the same time, it makes possible the horrors of the tyrannical soul. That is to say, I will argue that Plato has Socrates present democracy as a tragic regime—both wonderful and terrible at the same time.

To begin the analysis, I will offer a reading of the *love* that animates each of the regimes. The idea of "the good" serves as the primary feature of all of the regimes. Love for this good defines the changing hermeneutical soil out of which grow different types of regimens and different types of private citizens. In each regime, the good appears to the citizens in a different way. While the good is the central idea around which each regime revolves, it shows itself in very different ways in each regime. This makes all the difference; for, all the classes of the citizenry organize their lives around this idea and the laws are interpreted in its light.

The reader will recall from the previous chapters that the discussion surrounding the good was unable to produce an explicit interpretation. Socrates said that he did not know what the good is and remained incapable of giving an account of it. At the behest of Glaucon to state his *opinions* about it, he said he was willing to give an account of "the child of the good" as it appeared to him. However, everything contained in that account, he warned, held the potential to deceive. Therefore, we are unable to articulate precisely what the principle around which the aristocracy operates. The for-the-sake-of-which everyone does what they do in the aristocracy remains hidden from us, except as the rather empty, contentless concept of "the good." One might wish to appeal to the concept of knowledge of *what is* as the good supported by the love of the citizens of *Kallipolis*; however, as we elaborated extensively in our analysis, the good was said to be "beyond being" and knowledge is said to be knowledge of *what is*. Thus, in a very profound sense, the true principle of order of our law-givers' city ("if this one is right" [544 a]) remains necessarily absent to us. With the absence of an account of the good, Plato presents perhaps *the* serious hermeneutical problem of the dialogue as a whole. The space containing the principal idea of the good that bestows meaning upon all of the concepts and actions of *Kallipolis'* citizenry remains empty of content.

However, as the city moves along its mortal trajectory, the meaning of the good in each subsequent regime begins to carry more content. For instance, as the city moves into a timocracy, we find that the idea of the good is disclosed as victory and honor: "the most evident thing in it is one alone under the power of spiritedness: love of victories [*philonikiai*] and of honors [*philotimiai*]" (548 c). The love that animates the lives of the citizens in a timocracy, the good around which the world comes to have meaning, is the idea of honor. Honor mediates the interpretation of the laws, drives decisions about how youth become educated (549 a), the relations between classes of citizens, and even the way one understands parental roles (549 c).

From the love of honor, Socrates describes the way that the population moves towards the love of money or wealth, a dramatic shift in the city's constitutional vision of its good. "Against men who love victory and honor, they finally become lovers of money-making and money. And they applaud and marvel at [*thaumzō*] the wealthy man and bring him to the ruling offices, while they hold the poor in no honor" (551 a). According to Socrates, the more that the citizens honor money-making and wealth, the more their love of virtue and honor shrinks. What was formerly a dishonorable action no longer means the same thing if it is performed in exchange for money. The laws are reshaped in accordance with the accumulation of wealth. And the individuals who have achieved success at money-making are brought into the ruling offices as examples of virtue and leadership. All the citizens, rich or poor, desire the accumulation of wealth as their good.

The decline of the oligarchy appears to occur in the moment in which the poor seem struck by a form of self-consciousness. Prior to the turn, all citizens are possessed by a love of wealth and, insofar as wealth is the good, those that possess the most wealth are honored above all else. However, during events in which the wealthy and the poor encounter each other, the rich are seen by the poor in a new light. In warfare, for example, the poor and the rich are together side by side in the battlefield. When you have a "lean, sun-tanned, poor man placed in battle with a rich man reared in the shaded indoors, having a lot of excess flesh" (556 d), the fit and energetic poor man recognizes that the slothful rich man is easily winded and weak (556 d). In these moments, the poor begin to question whether the wealthy ought to be honored at all. Instead the poor begin to think that the wealthy "are nothing" (556 d) and do not deserve to rule anyone. The recognition creates the conditions for a transformation of regime. Interior faction ensues between rich and poor. If the poor win, suggests Socrates, democracy results.

What is the great love of the citizenry of democracy? What is the good that animates the thoughts, speeches and actions of the democratic polis? Freedom.

> "What is the way these men organize their life?. . . . Certainly, first of all, they are free [*eleutherōs*]? And the city becomes full of freedom [*eleutheria*], free speech [*parrēsia*], and license [*exousia*] in it to do as each wishes?"
>
> "To be sure, this is what is said" he said (557 a—b).

According to Socrates, the unifying love of the citizens in a democratic regime shows itself as "freedom." Precisely why the love of money gives rise to the love of freedom in the city's necessary mobile trajectory remains unclear. However, freedom is the love that animates the citizenry. We have additional confirmation that the love that compels [*anagkazo*] the citizens of the regimes is in fact the good of these regimes a couple of pages later. After Socrates has already said what is quoted above about the love pervading democracy, Adeimantus asks "How do you say that it [democracy] defines [the good]?" Socrates replies, "Freedom . . . for surely you would hear that this is the most beautiful thing in a democratic city" (562 b—c). *Eleutheria* shines out as the good and it illuminates the citizens' desires and loves.

Earlier, in our analysis of "the child of the good," we observed that Socrates argues that light remains the "third thing" that lies in between the faculty of sight and the thing seen. The sun, we saw, emits the light that allows things to appear to us in a certain way, in a particular light, shaping the very meaning of the things. Perhaps initially, we imagine that light is neutral. It illuminates entities in the world *as they are* without influencing the way the entities appear. However, light is not neutral; it bestows a meaning that remains uninterrogated by vision.

In chapter 5, we suggested that, even though Socrates does not offer an explicit interpretation of the good, his analogy betrayed a kind of structural relation that may be applicable to the good and to the things in the world that appear good to humans. We needed to conceive of a third thing between the power of sight and the beings in the world that light up the things *as* "good." At the time, we challenged Socrates' radical separation of necessity from the good by offering an interpretation of the third thing as *erōs* and desire. The third thing that lights up the beings in the world *as* "good" is love. While light as a third thing mediates our ocular/sensuous relation to the beings in the world, desire as a third thing mediates our relation to beings in the world as good or not. As such, *erōs* and desire are disclosive and revealing. However, like light, *erōs* is not neutral; the meaning of *the good* changes as the city moves through its mortal trajectory. With metamorphosis, desire also changes. In the shape-shifting that *Kallipolis* undergoes as it passes through these forms of its mortality, we see that it is precisely the idea of the good in each regime that lights up the beings in the city, the meaning of the citizens of the city, the meaning of the actions of the city, the meaning of its laws all appear desirable in accordance with the idea of the good.

However, on my reading, democracy's good remains unique among them. In the context of the aristocracy, the idea that animates the *polis* permeates the city and its classes. The good unifies at both the individual and the political level. The *oi polloi* and the private, individual citizen organize life around the idea of the good (though, again, neither Socrates, nor the interlocutors, nor the reader knows what this means). Further, in the timocracy, the political and the private are both animated by the idea of honor. The individual lives her life in accordance with this first principle. Even if the private individual remains incapable of accomplishing much in the way of honor, the world is lit up for her by this desire. Thus, both at the level of the political discourse of *oi polloi* and its structure of education, and also at the private level, the good that animates desire is "honor." In addition, both the political and the private desire that animates the oligarchy is the desire for the good of wealth. Yet, democracy's good does not function in the same way. It occasions a split between the private and the public.

In democracy "freedom" is the good. At the political level, the desire for freedom mediates the relation between the power of vision and the beings in the world and coats these beings (laws, speeches and actions, artifacts and animals) with meaning. However, at the level of the private, Socrates says that this good "frees" the individual citizen to live a private life in accordance with *varying* ideas of the good. "And where there is license, it is clear that each would set up [*kataskeuazō*] the estate [*kataskeuē*] of life privately [*idios*] as it pleases each" (557 b). That is to say, insofar as freedom is the good in a democratic regime, one may organize one's private life, one's soul, in accordance with different regimes, different ideas of the good.[7] For this reason, Socrates says that democracy is likely the most beautiful [*kalos*] regime.

> It happens that this is the most beautiful polity: just like a many-colored [*poikilos*] garment embellished [*poikillō*] in all bright colors, embellished [*poikillō*] with all characters [*ēthos*], it would also appear [*phainō*] most beautiful. And many perhaps . . . like boys and women beholding sparkling [*poikilos*] objects, would judge this to be the most beautiful polity (557 c).

How one is to interpret this last line remains controversial. On the one hand, one may read Socrates' remarks here to indicate that he presents the claim that democracy is the most beautiful shape of the declining city with some irony. In this interpretation, what "boys and women" think is most beautiful should elicit some skepticism on the serious person's part. However, David

Roochnik challenges this reading by suggesting that Glaucon's youthfulness is presented as a benefit and that women throughout the *Republic* are viewed in a respectful light (1998, 81–84).

When our interpretation attends to the split that is occasioned by the idea of *the good* between the public and the private in the democracy, I think that, for Plato in the *Republic*, democracy stands in a unique and privileged position in the organization of regimes. The democratic constitution may be multi-colored and beautiful without being a perfect, immobile statue; indeed, it may be beautiful like a tragedy is beautiful, insofar as it is tragically *deinos*, both wonderful and terrible at the same time. The word *poikilos*[8] is found throughout the *Republic* in complex [*poikilos*] ways. After reviewing its use throughout the text (please see the note in the previous sentence), I do not think that we can say that the passage affirms either a positive compliment or a negative ironic judgment without qualification. Indeed, on the one hand, *poikilos* is sometimes used to convey a meaning that is something like Odysseus' wiliness, insofar as Odysseus is capable of presenting one face on his surface and another, even opposite interior motivation, hidden under his mask (c.f., for example, 365 c; 561 e). In this way, we may suggest that Socrates' irony is *poikilos*—he says one thing on the surface, but actually means another. Thus, whatever work Socrates' irony performs in the dialogues, in a way, it can be said to appear *poikilos* like democracy. We might even apply the term to Plato, insofar as he presents *arguments* that convey one interpretation, while the *dramatic* events and movements of the dialogue either subvert it or occasion a different interpretation. From this perspective, Plato is indeed wily and his dialogue appears *poikilos*. However, Odysseus' wiliness is precisely his heroic quality bestowed upon him by natural necessity. It is what enables him to stand out and succeed, even as it alienates him and prevents him from being able to return home. Is democracy in the *Republic poikilos* in this sense? That is to say, both beautifully heroic and tragic at the same time?

Another way that *poikilos* is seen in the text applies to the current passage in book VIII as well. In a few instances, *poikilos* is contrasted with singularity, as if to describe a plurality—a complex, shape-shifting multiplicity. In these instances, the being described as *poikilos* opposes a unity that stays the same all the time. In book VII, we see this meaning at play when Socrates criticizes contemporary astronomy as only interested in looking at visible ornaments [*poikilma*] on the ceiling, as opposed to looking (intellectually) for something that stays the same and is not subject to becoming (529 b—c). In addition, the tyrant's soul is *poikilos*, qua *never the same*—a churning civil war of an infinity of competing desires (568 d). In this case, contrasting the tyrannical soul with the aristocratic regime is instructive. The tyrannical soul is ruled by an infinite chaos of shape-shifting, seething, foaming desires, while the aristocratic regime is ruled by an unchanging unity. Of course, as we know from the oracular presentation of the muses, this is a false impression; for, the tyrannical soul remains part of the mortal trajectory of the very same aristocratic regime. As such, the interpretation that claims that there exists a radical distinction between the two is itself *poikilos* in the Odyssean sense articulated above. On the surface, according to reason and *o logos*, they are stated to be separate; but, according to the necessity hidden underneath this surface argument, we observe that they are the same mortal being.

Democracy is *poikilos* insofar as, at the private level, it is bejeweled with each polity and with the idea of the good that animates each regime.

"And, blessed one," I said, "it is a fitting place to search for a constitution."

"Why?"

"Because, through its license, it holds all species of polities, and it seems likely [*kinduneuō*] necessary [*anagkaios*] to one wishing to arrange a city as we were doing just now, to go to a democratic city. He would choose [*eklegō*] the form [*tropos*] that pleases him, like a man going into a bazaar of constitutions. And, having chosen [*eklegō*], he would thus set up his polity" (557 d).

From the point of view of logical necessity—that is to say, from the point of view of the framework of human technological reason in which a constitution is drafted in accordance with the craftsman's method in such a way that it contains no self movements (Plato 2001, 19 b—c) but exists only as an unchanging abstraction—the movement away from aristocracy into democracy may be interpreted as a decline without qualification. It moves from static being to a complex becoming, dividing itself in many ways. The aristocratic constitution remains a static hypostatization, an artifact that should not be subject to innovation, erotic desire, or metabolic change. However, from the point of view of natural necessity, democracy may represent a form that contains a certain potential for rebirth, but in a specifically human way at the level of the private. Whatever freedom is, it functions as a sort of necessary organic signal for the human in which a form of cell division begins to take place. The city becomes for the first time a complex, quasi-multicellular organism. While the political organism retains its unity (through freedom), under its dermatological surface its organic tissues begin to differentiate. Each cell in the city has the same political genetic code, but despite this, the tissues develop their own identities—there are brains, hearts, sexual organs, digestive systems, and perhaps also microbiota (the foreign residents and divinities in Piraeus) making their influences felt and living in accordance with the good that organizes their tissues. Each human lives its life in accordance with a desire to perform a different function. Freedom at the political level enables the differentiation of tissues at the private level. To use a metaphor from the realm of mycology, democracy is the moment in the "turning of [natural life] cycles" [546 a) when the human fungus begins to sporulate. That is to say, each individual spore is set free to organize a new regime within itself.

The manner in which this selection of regimes for the soul occurs is through ocular experience and a desire for pleasure. And this origin of selection is the same for each soul, *even for the souls that choose to organize themselves aristocratically*. Socrates says that the citizens of this democracy are witness to every sort of political organization, insofar as each kind of regime and each kind of good are *lived* out before one. There exist aristocratic souls in the democracy who have organized their private lives in accordance with the relevant good (if it exists). They walk down the catwalk modeling this life for their fellow citizens. There are lovers of money and honor whose shining example will no doubt inspire many citizens to imitate them. In addition there are democratic men, barely holding onto their identities while chasing after the satisfaction of ever-changing goods and desires. A youth may observe the tyrannical soul conducting his life in accordance with tyrannical desires. The youth may "not consider everything sufficiently" (619 c) and decide to model himself after the tyrant's image. This choice [*airēsis*] occurs in the Myth of Er to the human being raised in what appears to be an aristocracy as we have accounted for it in the previous chapters. For, after death, "he was among those that came from heaven, *having lived in a well-arranged [tassō] polity* in his former life, participating in virtue by *habit*, without philosophy" (619 c—d, emphasis added).[9] Consequently, we see that, as a citizen in this democracy, one *chooses* to organize one's soul in accordance with the impression made by the lives being led around one.

In the quotation from book VIII above, "to choose" is Bloom's translation (Bloom 1991) here of *eklegō*.[10] Often, in other translations, one finds the term rendered as "to select" (compare for instance: Reeve 2004, 374 e). The latter term appears a handful of times in the *Republic*. Despite the similarities between the choices made in the Myth of Er and the choices of the democratic citizens in book VIII, Plato does not use the same term for each "choice." In both book VIII and book X, souls look at lives and select among them. In book X, one finds the expected term *aireō* instead of book VIII's *eklegō*; but the similarity of the two passages warrants consideration. As in the afterlife articulated in the Myth of Er, the democracy occasions the question about the best life to lead. In the best of circumstances (in both locations), the plurality of choice occasions an opportunity for reflective observation. However, there nevertheless remains a sort of "wandering cause" here. In both cases, there exists a certain arbitrariness to the choice, a choice driven by desire (a watermark of necessity) that appears not to be totally transparent to the chooser. It seems, indeed, unthinkable that a soul from an aristocracy would choose the life of the tyrant, despite having heard what sorts of torments he will suffer. Then again, he has lived a life organized by the concept of a good that has not been determined by philosophy, but by rote habit.[11]

For this reason, from a practical point of view, it appears to me that philosophy as practiced by Socrates can only occur in a democracy. Socrates hints that there may be other regimes besides these five, insofar as these are only "the ones having names" (544 c). Further, he raises additional doubts by adding a conditional: "*if* there are five arrangements of cities" (544 e). That is to say, nature may have necessitated other organizations that are not apparent to us or to other humans and, thus, not articulated in names "no less among the barbarians than the Greeks" (544 d). Consequently, there may be other regimes that give rise to the philosophical comportment. This qualification granted, I would like to suggest that, in the case of the five shapes isolated in the description of the mortal trajectory of the aristocracy, the comportment in which dialectical questioning arises is only possible in a democracy. At the very least, the bee-hive of *Kallipolis* would never tolerate the "dream" leading to itself. As has been said by others, the aristocracy brooks no innovation; therefore, one must live in a democracy in order to give birth to *Kallipolis'* constitution in speech (Roochnik 2003; Saxonhouse 1996).

Because the individual citizen "chooses" the image by which each will organize his or her soul, the democracy is unique among the regimes. A soul born into an oligarchy is appropriated by the surrounding *oi polloi* and their idea of the good—wealth. She does not have the opportunity to select or even to evaluate the quality of the life for which wealth is the love she seeks to satisfy. She loves wealth by rote. In the timocracy, the youth seeks out the satisfaction of honor and victory without reflection. As such, the movements of the humans in such regimes (if any actually exist) resemble the movements of bees—provided that bees are not accorded a share in the life of the intellectual comportment of the *question*. The soul is organized by rote and, at least theoretically, there is no division between *oi polloi* and the *idiotes*. As we know from books VI and VII, the mark of philosophy lies precisely in this division between the public and the private. But what about the aristocracy? Is not the aristocracy the place in which philosophy determines the lives of the rulers, at the very least? First, as I have suggested throughout our analysis of the philosophical nature, the model of the philosopher in *Kallipolis* remains questionable. If Socrates is a philosopher, the manner in which he conducts his life in practice is very different from the conceptual example of the philosophical nature articulated in books IV and VI. Secondly, prior to books VI and VII, the education system of *Kallipolis* appropriates the minds and bodies of the youth and molds them after its idea of the good (whatever it may be). Unlike the democracy, there are no occasions for the citizens of

Kallipolis to suffer *aporia* such that they may "turn," question the good, affirm it and take possession of it at the level of the private. It would seem that philosophy cannot occur without the movement of "turning" engendered by a certain loss or loosening [*aporia*] of one's attachment to the conceptual economy engendered and maintained by *oi polloi*. As we know from book VI, the many cannot be philosophical. This is true not because "most people" are not philosophical (which is a separate issue) but because, from an ontological point of view, philosophy requires the shock of *aporia* and this can only occur at the level of the private.

Further, in the aristocracy, only a tiny minority (if *anyone* actually meets the special criteria of possessing the natural characteristics) will undergo the aporetic training of the new studies which culminate in dialectic. That is to say, only a tiny minority, if any, will be animated by the idea of the good philosophically and not by rote, by mere habit.[12] But even for this philosophical minority, their questions are not productive; for, innovation in the aristocracy is not tolerated. *The philosophy of Kallipolis creates no concepts.* The split between the public and the private that the idea of freedom engenders in the democracy makes possible the experience of the question at the level of the private soul. The idea of the good first becomes a *question* in the democracy. The questions in the democracy first necessitate a *choice* as to how one should live, like the question that leads Socrates in the Pireaus of the democracy to say to Thrasymachus: "the *logos* is not about just any random thing [*epi tugxanō*], but about the way one needs [*xrē*] to live" (352 d). If nothing else, such an experience occasions an authentic philosophical comportment: *aporia*. Subsequent to this experience, one has become alienated from *oi polloi* for the first time. From the point of view of the private, the contrast in the Myth of Er between Odysseus—who chooses a private life—and the up-and-coming tyrant is striking; for, the latter had come from something like a *Kallipolis* "having lived in a well-arranged [*tassō*] polity in his former life, participating in virtue by *habit*, without philosophy" (619 d).[13]

Thus, on the one hand, along the *necessary* trajectory of the mortal life-cycle of *Kallipolis*, democracy's good—freedom—occasions the split between the public and private. The split enables the emergence of philosophical aporetic questioning. Consequently, the love for freedom in the democracy makes possible the creation of concepts, constitutions, and the rebirth of the aristocracy in the novel mode of "choice" at the level of the private. And yet, with apparent equal necessity, the emergence of the good of "freedom" marks the moment of a turn toward tyranny. The idea of the good as freedom necessitates. On the one hand, it necessitates in the sense of occasioning something "unavoidable" *sine qua non* within the life-cycle of *Kallipolis*. On the other hand, it necessitates in the sense of the "wandering cause," which introduces, like so many of the images offered in the *Republic*, a contradiction of reason, an irrationality. The love for freedom gives rise to rebirth and philosophical novelty. Yet, it also gives rise to the tyranny of the unnecessary desires that tear both cities and souls apart. That is to say, freedom is beautifully tragic.

NOTES

1. Adam thinks that Socrates refers here to Homer's *Iliad* XVI, 112; but Shorey points instead to *Iliad* I, 6.
2. See Winslow, 2021. "Difference in Plato's *Timaeus*" in *Graduate Faculty Philosophy Journal*.
3. Jacob Howland acknowledges this when he writes of "the seemingly inevitable transformation of the truly aristocratic regime (*Kallipolis*)" (Howland 2004, 150).
4. The mortal character of the human city plays an important part in Claudia Baracchi's reading of book VIII and the decline of the city (Baracchi 2002, 76).
5. Saxonhouse (1998, 274) argues that interpreters have been mistaken in assigning the word "decline" to describe what occurs in book VIII to *Kallipolis*. She points out that the words used are "change" and "movement," not decline. While I agree that Plato interpretation has perhaps overemphasized the idea of descent, still, we do have a reference to a "decline" in the mouths of the muses, insofar as the city must die and be dissolved [*luō*]. It is a mortal being, after all, and does not merely "change," but dies—even if it may be, like Er, eventually reborn.
6. For example, in *Beautiful City*, David Roochnik argues "the *Republic* actually offers a qualified and cautious defense, rather than a resounding condemnation of democracy. This defense is specifically dialectical. In other words, it is not stated as an isolated political thesis expounded explicitly and then substantiated at a particular juncture of the work. Instead, it emerges from the dialogue as a whole, from the very fabric of the work understood as a dialectical activity which, as Socrates says, is probably only possible in a democracy" (Roochnik 1996, 2; see also 77, 78–82). See also Saxonhouse 1998 and Monsoon 2000.
7. Given the presence of these regimes in the democracy, I disagree with Saxonhouse's interpretation (1998) that the democracy in the *Republic* contains no *eidē*. At the level of the private, it contains, in fact, every *eidē*. There exist souls in the democratic regime that are organized in the manner of aristocratic, timarchic, democratic, oligarchic and tyrannical regimes (if not more). As will become clear, this is both a strength and a weakness—it is the democracy's tragic-heroic feature.
8. The first instance of *poikilos* in the *Republic* occurs in book II. Adeimantus presents the arguments derived from education provided by the poets to assert that it is better to *appear* just, while doing unjust things. He quotes what has been attributed to Simonides: "I must trace around me a shadow painting of virtue in order to deceive those who come near, but keep behind it the wise Archilochus' crafty and changing [*poikilos*] fox" (365 c, translation altered). In my view the meaning of *poikilos* in this

passage carries the connotation of manifold shape-shifting. Odysseus, for instance, might be said to be *poikilos*, insofar as can shift in speech and appear to be of one mind, even though, underneath his mask of appearance, he is of another.

The next occurrence of *poikilos* appears in the purgation of the city of corrosive forms of education in book III. Socrates says that, in the study of music, it is necessary that the rhythms allowed in the city not be too "complex [*poikilos*] or multifarious" (399 e). For instance, the law-givers should not allow polyrhythms in the music played in the city—rhythms should not change too much or strive after complexity, but remain simple.

In book IV, we find another instance of *poikilos*. Socrates casts an image of people who are unhealthy because of their poor habits. They seek out treatments from medicine, but only so that they can continue to live in their unhealthy fashion. "Their medicine makes no progress, but only makes their illnesses more complex [*poikilos*] and worse (426 a). The appearance of illness grows more *manifold*, increasingly more deeply embedded in a manifold complexity. One thinks of a biofilm. Originally, one might have thought that biofilms are composed of a colony of a single species, but then one discovers that it is actually a very complex web of hundreds of species.

After these early instances, we jump to book VII and find the term employed as a noun in the context of the new studies. Specifically, Plato uses it in the study of astronomy as Socrates understands it. As we observed earlier, the new study of astronomy does not consist of an empirical analysis of the visible heavens. "If someone were looking at something by leaning his head back and studying ornaments [*poikilma*] on a ceiling, it seems as though you would say that he is looking at them with his understanding, not with his eyes" (Reeve 2004, 529 b). "These ornaments [*poikilma*] in the heavens, since they are ornaments [or 'have been embroidered': *poikillō*] in something visible, may certainly be regarded as having the most beautiful and most exact motions that such things can have. But these fall far short of the true ones" (Reeve 2004, 529 c). Here, it appears as though *poikilma* (qua emergent and manifold appearance) is contrasted with something with sameness and universality.

For the passage from book VIII currently under consideration in this chapter, Plato uses the term four times: "It happens that this is the most beautiful polity: just like a many-colored [*poikilos*] garment embellished [*poikillō*] in all bright colors, embellished [*poikillō*] with all characters [*ēthos*], it would also appear [*phainō*] most beautiful. And many perhaps . . . like boys and women beholding sparkling [*poikilos*] objects, would judge this to be the most beautiful polity" (557 c- d).

Further in book VIII, we find the term used to convey a meaning similar to the earlier instance: "democracy . . . would have these and other things sister to them. It would be . . . a sweet polity, without rulers and complex [*poikilos*], distributing a certain equality to equals and unequals similarly" (558 c). The democratic state is not singular, but manifold, containing a complexity of private regimes each animated by a different good.

Once the democratic city has been described, Socrates moves to the articulation of the emergence of the democratic man. "We should say how the democratic person comes to be from the oligarchic one. . . . When a young person . . . raised without education, stingily, tastes the honey of the drones, and keeps company with . . . clever beasts who have the powers to provide manifold and subtle [*poikilos*] pleasures" (559 d). While the democratic city has every regime (in private) living in its borders, the democratic man has every regime living within his soul. As such, a *complex manifold* [*poikilos*] of pleasures compete for prominence with him.

The language used to describe the democratic city is also used to describe the democratic soul. "I think . . . the man is a manifold [*pantodapos*] and full of a great number of habituated dispositions [*ēthos*], the fair and manifold [*poikilos*] man, like the city. Many men and women would envy his life because it contains the most patterns of constitutions and ways of life [*tropos*]" (561 e). He is "beautiful" and admired by both men and women (not just boys and women). However, the use of *poikilos* appears again to convey that this person has a plethora of types of souls competing inside of him. He may be envied because he can, like Odysseus, present himself in many different ways, but there may be nothing underneath this surface presentation, or inside he may be subject to civil war.

At the end of book VIII, *poikilos* is used to describe the tyrant and his regime. "Let us speak again of the tyrant's court, that beautiful, diversified, and manifold/complex [*poikilos*] thing that is never the same: from where will it be fed" (568 d). What appears to be distinctive here is the kaleidoscopic character of the tyrant. Similar to the elemental, it is never the same. As soon as one thinks one can point to the element water, it is already turning into some other element. It always churns and never remains the same. In this way, it is the perfect contrast to the aristocracy. The aristocracy is singular, always the same. The tyranny is most many-colored [*poikilos*], never the same.

Book IX offers a remarkable chimerical image of the human being, a soul whose three parts are unified into one. The desiring part of the soul is described as *poikilos*. "Mold, then, one idea for a manifold/complex [*poikilos*], many-headed beast that has a ring of heads of tame and savage beasts and has the power to change them and grow them all from itself" (588 c). In this case, we must think of the faculty of desire as complex and manifold.

The next instance of poikilos occurs in book X in the account of imitation. Socrates says, "the disposition apt to be vexed involves much and manifold/complex [*poikilos*] imitation, while the prudent and quiet character, which is always nearly equal to itself, is neither easily imitated nor to be understood when imitated" (604 e). Like several of the previous instances, *poikilos* is contrasted with self-sameness and self-possession.

Finally, one finds the term in the final image of the *Republic*: the myth of Er. Socrates describes the largest whorl of the spindle of necessity as *poikilos*: "the largest whorl is manifold/complex [*poikilos*] (616 e).

9. David Roochnik proposes the disturbing possibility that the choice of tyranny may be the fate of almost every human being: "The startling feature of the myth is that because of the 'exchange of evils and goods for most souls,' this fate [choosing the tyrant] seems to await almost everyone [as souls cycle through the various 1000 year journeys]. . . . This millennium of pleasure, however, will presumably stupefy the soul so that, as Er's story has it, it will next be disposed to choose the life of a tyrant, which, in turn, will lead to eternal damnation" (Roochnik 2003, 124).

10. Even though *eklegō* occurs several times in the *Republic* in rather important places, neither Shorey nor Adam offer commentary. For the sake of usefulness, I will review the occurrences here. We find it in book II, when Socrates says that the law-givers must select [*eklegō*] which natures will be best to guard the city (374 e). In book IV, it occurs again in a metaphor that we have already analyzed above. Socrates uses the image of dyeing wool to describe what it is like to ensure the virtues are color-fast in the souls of the guardians. The people in this profession carefully select [*eklegō*] wools that will most hold the dye (429 d & e). The next instance of *eklegō*, we find in book V. Socrates argues that women must be included among the guardian class if they meet the criteria that we employed to select [*eklegō*] the males. At 536 c, Socrates uses the term again to describe the selection criteria of the nature who receives the new studies. They must not be older men. Then, finally, we find the term twice in the current passage of book VIII.

11. The constitution for which our law-givers have given articulation is also not informed by a concept of the good with any content.

12. Jacob Howland holds a similar reading insofar as he writes "whereas the philosopher is said to have a vivid paradigm of the Ideas within his soul, the nonphilosophical citizens of the *Kallipolis*, who remain within the cave, have images of the Ideas 'painted' onto their souls by the philosophic rulers" (Howland 2004, 151). By "vivid paradigm," I assume he means that the philosopher is in possession of a living conception achieved as a consequence of being compelled by *aporia* into thought. In contrast, the vision of the nonphilosophical citizens of the aristocracy is achieved by mere rote imitation.

13. Jacob Howland too observes the likeness shared between Kallipolis and this "'orderly regime'—that in crucial respects resembles the Kallipolis (Howland 2004, 151).

Chapter 10

The Spindle of Necessity

What happens to *Kallipolis* after it dies? Once *Kallipolis* has reached the end of its mortal life, after it has been "carried around [its natural] circles [of life]" (546 a), it may be that its decaying body begins to sporulate and some of its individual, private cells begin to disperse, abandoning *Kallipolis* and leaving their identification with it behind. The individual, private cells that survive the collapse are blown by the winds of necessity. With some luck perhaps they happen [*tugkanō*] to land in fruitful hermeneutical environments in which each may either found cities of his/her own or find like-minded communities in which to integrate in accordance with the prevailing love for the good after which each has molded him/herself. But what of the soul of *Kallipolis*, the supposed soul writ large, writ as the constitution of the city-in-speech brought into discursive being by the law-givers? Is it reborn?

In book X at the end of the text, Socrates tries to convince Glaucon that one must be cautious about the kinds of speeches one allows into the garden of the soul; for, if the wrong sort of speech finds a place to germinate and grow there, the regime in the soul is at risk (608 b). He describes this sort of diligence of the soul regarding speeches as a contest [*agōn*]. "For the contest [*agōn*] is great . . . greater than it seems—this contest that concerns becoming good or bad" (608 b). Glaucon joins Socrates in this claim, and adds that "anyone else would [agree] too" (608 b). However, given the scarcity of souls organized by the idea of the good in the aristocratic sense, Glaucon's remark cannot be taken seriously. Perhaps aware of the contradiction between Glaucon's stated *opinion* and the *reality* of human affairs, Socrates tries to produce what *appears* to be a dialectical argument for the existence of the immortal soul. Presumably, the end of persuasion motivates Socrates' argument. If he can persuade Glaucon that his soul is immortal, the opinion would help to ensure Glaucon's diligence in attempting to accomplish a well-ordered life. Plato accentuates the assertion of immortality by intensifying the dramatic response of Glaucon when Socrates asks him if he "had not perceived [*aisthanomai*][1] . . . that our soul is immortal and never dies" (608 d). The reader feels compelled to hesitate at this claim; for, Plato inserts a delay of surprise in Glaucon's response, adding the line: "he looked me in the eyes in wonder [*thaumazō*] and said, 'by Zeus, not I. You can say this?'" (608 d). Glaucon's shock remains curious; for, Socrates has already more than hinted at the idea of an immortal soul in book VI. There, speaking to Adeimantus, he says "we will not leave off our attempts before we either persuade [Thrasymachus] and the others, or make something serviceable for that life when, born again, they happen upon [*entugxanō*] such *logoi*" (498 d). Moreover, given that the idea of immortality is something already circulating in the Athenian conceptual economy, the idea would not be new to Glaucon. As Adam points out, "the doctrine itself had of course long been an article of the Orphic and Pythagorean creeds . . . , and we must not suppose... that it is the novelty of the idea which occasions Glauco's wonder" (1902, 498 d). Therefore, it is not the first time that the character Glaucon would have heard of an "immortal soul," either in the context of his education in Athens, or in the context of the conversation on this evening with Socrates. Why, then, does Plato have Glaucon respond in this dramatic way?

Perhaps Glaucon is shocked because Socrates uses the language of *aisthēsis*. It is one thing to say that the poets claim in *mythoi-logoi* that the soul is immortal; but it is something else to say that one has sensed, perceived, or observed it oneself. No one has in fact perceived [*aisthanomai*] the workings of necessity as it ushers souls into being and back out of it again. Even though they subtend all human endeavor—whether metabolic, reproductive, enthusiastic, rationalistic, or noetic—these workings of necessity remain hidden [*lanthanomai*] from human perception and from propositional argument. On my reading, as will become clear in this chapter, the Myth of Er gives expression to this finitudinal relation to necessity.

In any case, Socrates solicits more disbelief when he claims that perceiving that the soul is immortal is "nothing hard" (608 d). One can sense the incredulity in Glaucon's response: "I would with pleasure hear from you this thing that is not difficult" (608 d). What follows this curious exchange is a proof of the immortal soul. It is presented in a form resembling dialectic, if in fact dialectic takes the shape of *elenchus*. However, as we noted above, Socrates had already suggested that Glaucon is neither capable nor ready to pursue that sort of work. Thus, the series of questions and answers that follow must be an imitation of dialectic in shape only.

Earlier, we have already suggested that the content and form of propositions and definitions are not self-sufficient *logoi* or entities of meaning; but rather they rely upon a semantic ecosystem. Consequently, the interpreter must seek this meaning outside of the mere content or logical form of the proposition. Here, in the "proof" of the immortal soul, we observe that the elenchic question and answer of a socratic conversation also requires attention to sources of meaning outside of the bare form of the question and its answer. While the conversation that follows betrays the form of elenchus, it would appear that it lacks fertility—it produces nothing capable of life—it is, in the words of the *Theaetetus*, a wind egg (Plato 2004, 151 e). To be sure, the supposed proof of the immortal soul has convinced few. According to Julia Annas: "this is one of the few really embarrassingly bad arguments in Plato, and though Glaucon is quickly satisfied with it, we have good reason not to be" (Annas 1981, 345). If we presume, as I think we should, that Plato knows that he is having Socrates produce a "bad argument," then we ought to be compelled to ask why he inserts it into the drama.[2]

As indicated earlier, Glaucon appears to me to be disengaged in the conversation. Like Thrasymachus in book I, Glaucon seems to be mostly "gratifying" Socrates with answers simply to move the conversation along. The question arises, therefore, whether the soil in which the conversation is planted lacks a necessary nutrient. For instance, in his exchange with Callicles in the *Gorgias*, Socrates says that there are three things that subtend a meaningful conversation, a conversation that really "tests" one's judgment: knowledge [*epistēmē*], good will [*eunoia*] and frank speech [*parrēsia*] (1998, 487 a). Thus, in order for a meaningful conversation to occur, Socrates often points to the necessary ingredient of that signal feature of the democratic political constitution: *parrēsia*, "free speech" or "frank speech." While, as we suggested in the previous chapter, "free speech" takes on some negative connotations in Socrates' description of the democratic regime, it remains a *necessary* feature of the philosophically productive conversation throughout the dialogues. In the words of our previous chapter, *parrēsia* is *deinos*—it possesses a tragic potential, being both wonderful and terrible. Insofar as it shows itself in philosophy, it is required for a fruitful testing of one's opinions. One must be willing to answer a question about a phenomenon with an answer that reflects how it really appears to one. As with propositions and definitions, there are sources of meaning that shape both the form and the content of questions and answers—*parrēsia is one of them*. A question can be posed with frank speech or without it; an answer can be offered with freedom or without it. However, the evidence for the presence of frankness does not appear in either the content or the form of the question or answer, but shines out (if at all) in another way.

Meno's opening question in the dialogue with the same name asks Socrates if he thinks that virtue is something teachable, or acquired through practice, or, if neither of these, something that comes to humans through nature or in some other way (1903, 70 a). One could argue that this question lacks *parrēsia*; for, if, as seems likely, Meno poses the question only to acquire from Socrates additional weaponry for future argumentative contests, then he does not pose the question from a deep desire to get to the bottom of virtue.

Like many young people, he pursues philosophy as if it were a language game. That is to say, to him, philosophy is a contest in logical necessity. The "winner" of this contest successfully proves the logical inconsistency of his interlocutor. But the need and desire, the *erōs*, to flesh-out the subject matter is not animating such a "philosopher"—what motivates is rather the honor and reputation of the victory, the win.

In addition to questions, answers too are not abstract assertions solely concerned with logical consistency and divorced from a discursive meaning horizon. One ingredient in the food web of answers, suggests the dialogues, is *parrēsia*: the freedom to say how it really appears to one without concern for reputation or vanquishing one's opponent. Among other dialogues, the urgency to speak frankly and to state how things genuinely *appear* to one is highlighted in the *Theaetetus*. Socrates often exhorts Theaetetus to "offer" himself to him (for example, 2004, 151 b) and to *eagerly* [*prothumos*] respond to Socrates' questions with answers that genuinely appear to Theaetetus to be the case (for example, 2004, 151 e). In fact, Theaetetus stumbles upon the problem of speaking frankly about what is in his "heart" after he is forced to confront his interpretation of the being of knowledge inspired by the hearsay accounts of Protagoras. Theaetetus grasps that, if he is to remain consistent with his previous answers, he must respond to Socrates' question in opposition to the way the subject now appears to him. His "tongue" must contradict his "heart." In answer to Theaetetus' dilemma, Socrates swears by Hera and appeals to Euripides' *Hippolytus*. In this play, Hippolytus claims to have sworn to keep his oath by his lips, but not by his mind/heart [*phren*] (Euripides 1991, ln 613). Socrates says, "if you answer [in accordance with your previous answer] . . . there will turn out to be something Euripidean about it, for your tongue will be unrefuted by us, but your heart will not be unrefuted" (Plato 2004, 154 d). There exists the possibility, therefore, for the human being to speak (or write, or gesture) only by the tongue. On the one hand, this may take the form of a lie. One says the opposite of what one thinks. On the other hand, in accordance with logical necessity, it may take the form of a statement without genuine commitment—as when one answers a question about Parmenides in an undergraduate philosophy exam with: "Parmenides claims all things are one." Technically, this claim is coherent. However, one says it by rote, lacking the erotic enthusiasm or "*prothumia*" (Plato 2004, 148 d) to speak for Parmenides and, as such, to speak frankly as to how it appears to him. However, if one is to speak frankly, to speak freely, the words must be imbued by the heart—that is to say, they are informed by a "good will" and a "frank" comportment. In contrast to Theaetetus, Theodorus persistently resists frank speech. Socrates attempts to goad him into answering for Protagoras several times. But out of concern for his reputation, he declines. Instead he asks Socrates to interrogate Theaetetus.

Even when Socrates appeals to Theodorus' debt to Protagoras as one of his intellectual "orphans," Theodorus denies his inheritance by saying that he turned away from "bare words" towards geometry years ago (2004, 165 a). Eventually, Theodorus is dragged into the elenchus. However, it remains a question if he speaks freely in the service of the conversation, or if he holds something in latency. That is to say, it is a question whether he speaks by the tongue or by the heart; for, it is impossible to perceive [*aisthanomai*] the soul of a *logos*, to perceive how the soul accompanies speech as it flows out into the world. Every instance of so-called Socratic irony attests to this.

Thus, is Glaucon speaking from the tongue during the discussion of the immortal soul, or from the heart? Does Glaucon speak frankly, with *parrēsia*, and state how things really appear to him? Or, like Thrasymachus in book I, are his responses merely gratifying Socrates? It is not possible to perceive the soul of the *logos* from the mere words on the page, whether propositions, definitions, questions or answers. The *logoi* are rather embedded in this rarely perceptible meaning horizon. But there are hints in the dramatic movement that signal that the conversation is producing a "wind egg" (Plato 2004, 151 e). For instance, it is telling that Adeimantus does not interject and demand an explanation of the instances of "question begging" (Roochnik 2003, 121; Rosen 2005, 379) that occur in the elenchic conversation developing the concept of the immortal soul. Why? Perhaps the two young men are exhausted after conversing all night—a feature of human necessity and finitude as they impose themselves upon speech; perhaps Adeimantus no longer possesses the mental fortitude to come forward now and "stand by his brother," to step into the conversation as he has many times earlier and "come to [Glaucon's] defense" "if he leaves anything out" (362 d).

In any case, the unproductive elenchic argument proving the existence of the immortal soul passes over into a myth about this soul's journey into the afterlife. Glaucon, with a "quite so" (613 c), soberly capitulates to the claim that Socrates has reversed his opinions about the just and the unjust human beings that he articulated in book II through the myth of Gyges Ring. Ostensibly, the story [*apologos*] that comes next fills the need to give expression to all of the "prizes, wages, and gifts" (613 e) that come to just and unjust men in death. And, indeed, this is Socrates' stated intention when he says "[these prizes] are nothing in multitude or magnitude compared to those that wait for each person when finished [dead]" (614 a). It may be that one would want to argue that the historical accounts of the practices of humans toward the unjust and just are subject to the influence of myth and even fiction. However, when the discourse turns toward the kinds of things that the soul undergoes in death, myth becomes necessary for obvious reasons—no one has perceived [*aisthanomai*] that the soul is immortal. While it is true that the myth depicts the human soul undergoing punishments and joys in death in proportion to its actions while alive, the myth of Er reveals much more than this.

On the one hand, it marks the mortal end of the dialogue and the constitution it has brought into being. The dialogue and *Kallipolis* reflect entities "carried round [their] circles of life" (546 a) *in speech* as the drama unfolds. Out of the erotic urges of the participants, the city-in-speech came into being. Socrates was again its midwife. It emerged in its *infancy* as the city of need. "Our need [*chreia*]" made it (369 c). In its infancy, it is the city of "utmost necessity" [*anagkē*] (369 d), brought into being because no one is "self-sufficient but in need of much" (369 b). With time, the city perceives its lack in a more sophisticated sense and desires relishes (372 c)—it begins to distinguish between the general satisfaction of hunger and the pleasures of dinner and dessert. That is to say, the city in speech grows into toddlerhood. As it matures, the city and its citizens require primary education. Music and gymnastics are established in its soul (books III and IV). Eventually, it grows into adulthood. The middle books of the *Republic* (books VI and VII) mark the passage into maturity. For the first time, through *aporia* and the philosophical endeavor, the soul of *Kallipolis* is able to take responsibility for itself and its *logoi*, and to give birth to novel ideas. However, this grasp of itself in good order is short lived (as it is for all of human life [608 c]). *Kallipolis* begins to decline (books VIII and IX). In its final *logoi* (the arguments supporting the immortal soul), the dialogue about *Kallipolis* is lacking in erotic desire and urgency. These arguments give the impression of being used up and tired, until, finally, the *logos* of *Kallipolis* passes beyond in the form of a myth in which it promises resurrection.

Therefore, the necessary cycles of the living, the "revolving of [the natural] circles" (546 a) of mortal beings like *Kallipolis*, the "revolving of [the natural] circles" that becomes expressed in the *Republic*, include the resurrection of souls and their *logoi*. In fact, Socrates actively resurrects the soul and *logos* of Er in an *apologos*. The myth of Er is a resurrection of the soul of Er, of his speeches (this pam-phylian, this representative of "all" "races"). If Socrates' speech in imitating Er's speech can be said to be an imitation of the speech of "every human" (as the name of Er's tribe implies), then the myth of Er may be said to depict the movements of human *logos*, the movement of human discourse and perhaps even human reason. Socrates conducts a resurrection of Er precisely through an *imitation* of his speech.

In the *apologos*[3] of Er, as with other images presented in the *Republic*, Socrates practices one of the forms of the style of imitation restricted in *Kallipolis*, the Homeric. That is to say, for the most part he presents himself as if he were Er speaking, but on occasion Socrates reminds the listener that his own body is the vessel of the speech by saying things like "and he [Er] said . . . " Like Homer, Socrates' style of imitation is mixed

(393 a—c): sometimes his speech is an imitation of Er's, and sometimes he speaks for himself (a style of imitation *supposedly* without imitation). Of course, the source of the discourse becomes more complicated by the human limits of time and memory: Socrates is relating the entirety of the *Republic* in the form of Homeric imitation insofar as the conversation occurred "yesterday" (327 a). Thus, in fact, Socrates imitates Socrates imitating Er. We may wonder if the imitation is still Homeric without the security provided by immediacy. Moreover, when we zoom out to the author of the dialogue, we observe that Plato tells the *apologos* of Er in the most dangerous form of imitation, the form thoroughly banned from *Kallipolis*—he hides [*lanthanomai*] behind Socrates' imitation of Er and never speaks for himself as himself (394 b). Indeed, as Rosen points out "the characters about whom Plato writes are already dead at the time of the composition of the dialogue" (2005, 381); Plato's imitation of them is simultaneously a resurrection of their postmortal, if not immortal, souls. He stands behind them, unseen, pulling their strings by way of a form of imitation heavily censored in *Kallipolis*.

It is not only this inconsistency that reveals a problem with the educational paradigm of the city. To be sure, the fact that Plato and the character Socrates practice styles of speech restricted from use in *Kallipolis* ought to raise questions about how seriously we are to take the city's censorship of poetry and discourse. However, the problem of the freedom of speech also shows itself in these stylistic choices. If the practice of philosophy and *elenchus* relies upon the willingness of the participants to offer frank speech, then the style of imitation supposedly without any imitation is the only one that can be used (394 b). For this reason, I doubt Stanley Rosen's observation when he writes that the myth of Er is a speech that "could be admitted into the beautiful city" (Rosen 2005, 381). Perhaps from the point of view of content, the myth would be allowed; however, from the point of view of style [*lexis*], the form of imitation that serves as the speech's body precludes it from the city. Still, frank speech [*parrēsia*], a condition for dialectical fruitfulness, can be said in many ways. As I have tried to show in other settings,[4] any human's ability to speak for him/herself, as him/herself, without imitation (393 d) is called into question by the conditions of human discourse. There are no *logoi* that spontaneously arise in one without imitation.[5] Every meaningful word that any human being can utter is always already an imitation. And most "ideas" to which humans give expression and elaboration (like justice, wisdom, courage, moderation and the good) are imitated by us most often in the most dangerous way—pure imitation. For, each time we resurrect these concepts, we remain unaware of the source/sources of our conception of justice, for example. Even though we resurrect them by imitating them unawares, the authors stay hidden in the background, pulling our strings. The allegory of the cave presents an image of this phenomenon. Thus, if frank speech is the style of imitation in which one does not imitate, it does not exist. However, if the meaning of *parrēsia* does not imply speaking without imitation, without repetition—if speaking frankly does not mean to speak with an originality without qualification, then *perhaps it does exist* in the way we have cited in the character of Theaetetus. Saying how things genuinely appear to one is not the same as pretending to originate a discourse—that's what Thrasymachus does. Instead, Theaetetus acknowledges that his way of seeing holds a debt to Protagoras; and he allows it to undergo interrogation *vis à vis* a certain "resurrection" or "wakeful imitation" of Protagoras.

Thus, in addition to the stated purpose of the image (showing the prizes and punishments of souls after death) the *apologos* of Er makes visible the final image of the mortal trajectory of the city in speech and of all souls in speech. The souls will be resurrected insofar as they are imitated (e.g., when the souls select a paradigm of life [617 e–618 a]). Even if immortal souls are merely fictive images, it belongs to human life to resurrect both the dead and the living by imitating their discourses and by viewing the world through the lens that the *logoi* provide.

In addition to the explicit image about prizes and punishments, and the implicit image of the resurrection of human speech, the Myth of Er makes explicit an interpretation of the workings of necessity insofar as it subtends individual human lives, before, during and after life. There exists an entire system to which all humans belong but to which they remain oblivious during their life—Er is compelled [*anagkazo*] to die, to witness, and to be resurrected with a *logos* about his experience that he is to relate to the living. The *apologos* of Er gives an account of this system of necessity.

The image depicts the movement of souls in accordance with necessity. In advance of perception and awareness in death, the deads' movements are determined insofar as they have been integrated into greater, architectonic cycles of a regulated motion. Once their souls have departed life, they find themselves in the middle of a journey already underway: "he said that when he stepped out, his soul was made to go with many others and they arrived at a certain mysterious [*daimonios*] place" (614 b—c). In death, Er wakes to find himself already on the way somewhere. Who or what has sent him? What is the origin and cause of the sending? To what end does he journey? About all of this, he remains in the dark. Similarly to those born into life, he, in death, is *born* already on the way.[6] The movements carry him to an end and a purpose that remains hidden from him.

The moving souls arrive at a mysterious place, a place described as *daimonios*, as demonic. The location holds meaningful weight insofar as it is a place of decision, a crossroads of sorts into which all the souls are coming and going as from a kind of origin. Perhaps the space is "mysterious" because of this decisive feature: everyone must come and go from here. The space is marked by holes in the ground going into the earth aligned with two holes in the sky going into the heavens (614 c). All of the souls arriving and departing are moving into or out of these holes. Adam presents the space in the following way.

What transpires in this space of decision is not decided by the moving souls—they do not decide but are placed on the conveyor belt governed by the *necessary* rules already at work in advance. Indeed, judges sit in wait for them in the daimonic place (line AB), attaching signs to them before sending them on their way into the holes. Those souls judged unjust receive signs on their backs detailing their deeds and made to go [*poreuesthai*] down to the left (AC'), while those judged just receive signs on their fronts and made to go [*poreuesthai*] up to the right (BC) (614 c). Consequently, the souls' motions into and out of the daimonic place are governed by a system of necessity that transcends their awareness and their control. Insofar as they are made to go [*poreuesthai*], the movements of their journey are the opposite of the one that characterizes the origin of philosophical movement: impass (*aporia*). The souls are compelled [*anagkazō*] to pass through, without the rupture in movement that characterizes the philosophical endeavor. Neither the ones that were

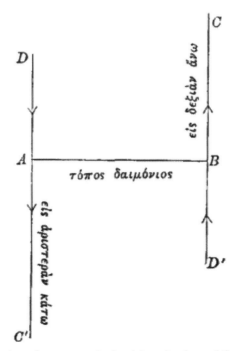

Figure 10.1. Depiction of movement in the daimonic place of the judges
Adam 1902, 614c., 435

just and passed through heaven, nor the ones that were unjust and passed through the earth experience the philosophical rupture in necessity. The philosophical movement here belongs to Er. He is not permitted (or made) to pass through [*poreuesthai*], rather he is made to stop [*a-poreuesthai*], stare, and listen to those that arrive. As a messenger, like Hermes and Iris,[7] Er represents this finite break (*aporia*) in the flow of necessity. He is the philosopher here. However, that is not to say that his movements are totally free, or that his reason lifts him out of being made to move in accordance with necessity. Rather, through his journey he *is made to* see how necessity envelops him and all humans within itself in ways that remain for the most part hidden to us.

Again, Socrates' stated intention in offering the *apologos* of Er was to give expression to the prizes and penalties received in death for just and unjust actions performed in life. However, after the limited account of judgment in the daimonic place, very little is stated in the myth about what most souls experience in the journey under the earth or through the heavens. Once the souls complete their thousand-year journeys through the passages of the holes, they return to the daimonic place, gather together in a meadow, and discuss with one another what they have experienced. All the details are left out except for a quick mathematical description explaining the intensity of prizes and penalties in proportion to the acts of justice and injustice done. Socrates offers the excuse one sees from him frequently in the dialogue, "to describe it all would require all time, Glaucon" (615 a). Whatever the reasoning, the myth devotes little time to the purpose for which it was offered. One exception to this is the account of the suffering of Ardiaeus the Great, a brutal tyrant in the region of Pamphylia.[8] In the Meadow, one of Er's companions who had risen out of the journey through the earth said that, as Ardiaeus approached the mouth leading to the demonic place after his thousand year journey through the earth, the mouth rejected him: he, other tyrants, and even some private persons were instead seized by savage [*agrios*] men, flayed, dragged skinless upon the ground and thrown into Tartarus. The mouths in the earth (curiously, *not* the judges) deemed their deeds to be too unjust to be curable by punishment (615 c—d).

On my reading, the next lines are important; for, all of the souls that are traveling through the earth display terror upon approaching this mouth that empties them upon the daimonic place. After their experience of a thousand years of punishment, they still do not know whether their crimes in life have been sufficiently penalized. Like so much of what happens in accordance with the *necessary* movement of souls, they remain in the dark about the system of judgment to which they belong. Knowledge does not rule here. Presumably, every soul has performed some *unjust* acts in the course of its life. Further, it seems likely that every soul has performed some *just* acts in the course of its life. By what measure are the souls judged by which they will be sent on a journey through the heavens or through the earth? We are not told. Is it a simple mathematical calculation? For instance, if you committed one more unjust act than the sum of just acts, is that the measure by which you are sent on a journey through the earth? The calculus remains a mystery. Therefore, the souls who approach the mouth after their thousand year journey through the earth are unsure if they will be admitted and allowed to continue to the meadow or will be skinned 'alive' and thrown into Tartarus as incurable. They approach the mouth and suffer the greatest fear (616 a). That is to say, they do not know the standards by which they will be judged in advance. They remain in the dark in many ways regarding the measures by which the system of necessity governs their movements. As was shown by the failure to properly calculate the nuptial number, the *logos* of human calculation brushes up against its limit here in death. The phenomenon of *erotic necessity* and the phenomenon of *mortal necessity* (related as birth is to death) belong to regions of necessity, not reason. Indeed, reason may be said to hover on their surfaces, like a boat upon a murky ocean—the pilot can observe the waves the ocean produces, he may sense the currents that carry the boat in a certain direction, but he cannot see what is occurring in the depths. The human, insofar as she may grasp the world through rational appropriation, remains in a non-transcendable limitation regarding it. The nature and work of the human, *logos*, enable the human to cast dependable static images and models, among which the human finds herself at home. But what belongs to the *wandering cause*—the motions of the erotic, of birth, of death—these motions cannot be totalized into the rational systems that the human necessarily employs to understand itself and its world.

The absence of an account detailing the pleasure and pains of justice and injustice signals to the reader that the myth Socrates relates is not really about these consequences pertaining to justice—at least, it is not primarily about these. The movements of necessity, which somehow folds justice into itself, shines out as the primary subject matter of the *apologos* of Er. In my view, the myth raises a question about the relation of the vast reach and complexity of natural necessity to the comparatively miniscule and insignificant work of a private human choice. Moreover, I would argue that the myth raises this question as though the *apologos* were the *Republic* writ small. That is to say, the entire drama of the *Republic* betrays the human struggle to raise itself above the waves of necessity by means of its heroic powers of *logoi*. It may appear to do so periodically; but its achievements inevitably become swallowed up by and incorporated into the waters of oblivion. Such is the tragic element of the heroic human trait bestowed upon humans by *nature*—which is already to say *necessity*.

Er states by means of his triple resurrection (that is, his resurrection through Socrates, who states through Socrates, who states through Plato) that, after spending seven days on the plane, the group he accompanied was again set into motion. They were made to stand up again and made to pass [*poreuesthai*] further along their journey together (614 b) without knowing why or to what end. Four days into this journey, they observe a straight light (*phōs euthu*) in the distance. From this point of view, the light seen is stretched through heaven and earth. Socrates says that it looked like a rainbow, although brighter (614 b). Adam believes that the straight light may be interpreted as the Milky Way. In a way not immediately intuitable from the passage, Adam argues that the column of light both travels around the entire cosmos and serves as its central axis (he provides images for his commentary [Adam 1902, 443–444]). Further, Adam points out that these passages—which articulate a kind of cosmological order—have generated a great deal of controversy over the centuries (Adam 1902, 441). He argues that the picture created by the description of "the pillar of light" and the one produced immediately after by "the spindle of necessity" are inconsistent and impossible to reconcile with one another (1902, 441). Consequently, he calls into question whether the images are meant to be a "serious astronomical theory" (1902, 441). But what if Plato has no intention of introducing novel scientific theories through the *apologos*?[9] One might instead ask whether Plato has Socrates employ images that circulate in the conceptual economy of Athens (images, mixed from theoretical and poetical sources)[10] to put on display the way the human imagination organizes the world for itself. As such, all the debate about the coherency or incoherency of "Plato's theory of astronomy" as presented *in a myth* simply reinforces the text's portrayal of the hermeneutical rootedness of the human imagination and perhaps even its reasoning.

In any case, it is this light, whatever its source, that holds together the cosmos (616 c). This is no unimportant function, given that so many of its parts will be shown to be under persistent, differing and contrasting motions—as Er observes next. To be sure, the light beam proves to be their destination and, after another day's journey, the group arrives at the light column and penetrates to the center of it. From here, they not only observe the manner in which the light binds to the heavenly cosmos, but they also perceive the "spindle of necessity [*anagkēs atrakton*]" (616 c), stretching down from the highest positions from a hook.

The spindle of necessity is said to be that by which "all the orbits/spheres [*periphora*] are turned" (616 c). Which orbits? On the one hand, it may be that the spindle turns the celestial bodies. Adam reads the text in this way (1902, 440–452). He provides a careful analysis of the structure in accordance with the cosmos as well as an assessment of the historical debates surrounding it. Socrates nowhere refers to the celestial bodies, however. He says that the spindle resembles those we have here. It has a long, central stem made of adamant. As already mentioned, the top of the stem is attached to the heavens by hooks. Lower on the stem, one finds a whorl by which Necessity turns the entire spindle and, thus, all orbits. The whorl of the spindle is said to be a composite structure. It consists of eight concentric hemispheres nested into one another as if it were a Jawbreaker candy split in half with the stem of the spindle passing through its center as a diameter. As said above, these nested hemispheres may depict an image of the spheres of the celestial bodies; for, each of the spheres move independently: "The spindle as a whole is moved in a circle with the same revolving movement [*phora*], but within the revolving [*periphero*] whole the seven inner circles revolve [*periphero*] gently in the opposite direction to the whole" (617 a). In this reading, the outermost sphere turns in opposition to the others. According to Adam, it is the sphere of the fixed stars. The other spheres that fit inside of the outermost are the *wandering* ones, the spheres on which the planets are carried. Adam argues that the width of the rims of each sphere ought to be read as the distance between the heavenly bodies. In accordance with the description Socrates gives (at 616 e - 617 a), Roochnik repeats Adam's scheme like so:

"The whorl of the Fixed Stars (no. 1)[11]
" " " the Sun (no.7)
" " " the Moon (no. 8)
" " " Venus (no. 6)
" " " Mars (no. 4)
" " " Jupiter (no. 3)
" " " Saturn (no. 2)
" " " Mercury (no. 5)" (Roochnik 2004, 125).

It seems certain that Plato wishes to have Socrates present an image of the whorl of the spindle of necessity in a way that betrays an analogy to the cosmos and its motions. Most importantly for my reading, it is necessity's rules and organization that are shown to be at the origin of these movements that resemble those of the cosmos.

Whether the image explicitly employs the language of the celestial bodies or not would appear to be irrelevant. For, necessity underlies the turning of *all* "orbits [*periphora*]" (616 c).[12] If anything, the lack of an appeal to precise language allows us to include not only the celestial rotations under the rule of necessity, but to broaden its influence beyond heavenly movement to other sorts of "rotations." For, *all* cycles of movement are governed by her. In our analysis of the muses' statements at the beginning of book VIII, we observed that the muses use the same term there to describe the cycles of life of living things as is used in the *apologos* to describe the circuits of the whorl.

> Not only to plants in the earth but also to animals upon the earth comes to be a bearing and barrenness of soul and bodies *when life-cycles for each complete an orbit [periphora] of circles* (546 a, emphasis added).

Thus, if necessity underlies the turning of all orbits [*periphora*], this includes the movements of both the "soul and bodies" of earthly living things too, not only those of celestial entities. The turning of the whorl mythologically governs the motions of the planets, to be sure; however, the threads spun out at the top of the spindle weave together the lives and movements of the living *and the dead*. Mythologically, then, necessity employs the movements of planets and the celestial spheres to weave together the mortal trajectory of living things.

Moreover, from this description, nothing stops us from concluding that necessity subtends the rotations of the human mind as well. The turns of *logos*, too, are subject to "bearing and barrenness of soul." On the one hand, the animation of *logos* by necessity may be observed in the very activity of soul—speaking, thinking, conversing are forms of rotating and turning. Moreover, sometimes they are productive and sometimes, as we have seen above, they are barren, producing wind eggs. *Logos* too has a mortal, finite constitution. However, necessity governs the formal forms of *logos* too, insofar as the movements (or orbits) of the syllogism compel [*anakazo*] the *logos* forward from premise, through premises, and toward conclusion. This is not only a *temporal* necessity. The structure of the syllogism betrays an *a priori* order and force before anything is asserted, before the first premise. The first premise becomes inserted into a *space* already rule-governed by a motive force and already prepared to compel the *logoi* forward in a specific arrangement—this *chōra* is *necessity*.[13] It is necessity that drives the *logoi* of the *syllogism and the other apodeixeis* through their cycles. However, the space of necessity into which the *logoi* become inserted (and, thereby become meaningful), *remains outside the content or even form of the discourse*—that is to say, necessity remains unspoken and, in an important sense, unheard by the speaker. Therefore, the myth may offer an image of necessity as the origin of "all orbits." That means: not only of celestial rotation, and not only of biological rotation, but also of discursive and intellectual *turnings* as well. However, these are not enlightenment-era necessities; nor is this concept of necessity exhausted by the three forms articulated by Aristotle in *Metaphysics delta*. As we have argued throughout this book, erotic necessity and mortal necessity belong to Plato's images of necessity in the dialogues. If all of these cycles and rotations belong in an unavoidable sense to necessity, it means that not only bodies are subject to the "wandering cause" and to what "happens to be" [*tugxanō*]. It may be that soul cycles—discursive and intellectual systems as well as the syllogisms and propositions that constitute them—too are subject *to wandering* when viewed from the point of view of Platonic necessity. Such wandering in the intellectual systems betrays a tragic finitude inherent to the ontological organization of the human (and her *logos*) in the world.

After giving an account of the whorl and its differentiated spheres, Er states that the spindle was seen to be turning in the lap of Necessity. Claudia Baracchi has noted the distance between the figure of necessity and the actual rotation of the spindle; moreover, there exists a distance in vocalization as well (Baracchi 2000, 191). For, while the figure of necessity remains motionless and silent, her spindle emits much music and sound as it turns. On each of the spheres of the whorl sits a siren. As they move in a circle with their associated sphere, each siren vocalizes a different pitch, "sounding together [*sumphoneo*]" to produce "a single harmony" (617 b). Further, the "daughters of Necessity" (617 c), the ancient Moira, both take turns spinning the spindle and sing in accord with the sirens' harmony: Lachesis sings a *logos*, weaving together a tale of what has been, Clotho weaves a *logos* of "what is," and Atropos sings of "what will be" (617 c). Through the mediation of the fates, Necessity organizes all movement in accordance with an articulation of a temporality of *being*—indeed, even for "what is" (which was stated to be radically distinct from movement in book VI). I would like to relate this existence of distance between necessity and her effects in both sound and movement to another present in the organization of the text: the distance in both the movement and vocalization of the con-versation (which is, of course, a form of *turning*) between the reader of the *Republic* and the fictional origin of the conversation. Necessity operates behind the scenes, in silence and by means of an indirect causality. In a similar way, Plato too operates behind the scenes, in silence and by means of an indirect causality. Like the distance between the reader and the mythological origin of the conversation, necessity remains several levels removed from appearance (and hearing).

In book IV, after building the city in speech, Socrates says that, all along, justice has "rolled at our feet from the beginning" (432 d). Justice was so near to us that we failed to notice that it was already there, as if justice were the keys we were searching for that lie already in our hands. Justice subtended the conversation around justice (the political things that make this conversation realizable) and made possible the search for it. Similarly, necessity too was already there from the beginning, already rolling around under feet prior to the conversation. The structures of necessity, like erotic necessity, already subtend the human search for meaning and the forms that these searches take. However, they appropriate us to their movements without being seen as we move through our intellectual endeavors. They rule from the beginning, prior to forms and prior to the actions of demiurges (Plato 2001, 52 d). Like justice and necessity, Plato too operates behind the appearances in our experience.

As readers, we undergo the drama that unfolds between the characters of the play, as well as the contents and forms that the characters choose to elaborate. However, we remain in the dark about the fact that our experience of these characters is set into motion in advance, from the beginning, by Plato who composes our experience at a level deeper than the surface arguments of the dialogue or any conclusions articulated by the characters. In a certain sense, therefore, Plato is to the drama (the fictional life in the text) as necessity is to a human life and its intellectual endeavors.

Socrates does not say that Er mentioned a soul who offered an account of the organization of the Spindle of Necessity. From Socrates' speech, it appears that Er and the other sojourners may have understood all of the workings of the Spindle from simple observation. For the next step of their journey, however, a spokesperson appears. While the group stood before Lachesis (she who sings of what has been), they were organized at a distance from each other in preparation for an activity as individuals. It is *necessary* for each sojourner to choose their next mortal resurrection. In order for this choice to occur, they require instruction from a spokesperson, a spokesperson who serves as a vessel for the *logos* of this goddess Lachesis. The spokesperson addressed them from a podium and said:

> Here is the *logos* of Lachesis, the virgin daughter of Necessity. "Ephemeral souls: this is the beginning [*archē*] of another death-bringing cycle of the mortal race. A daimon will not randomly draw your lot [*lagxanō*], but you will choose [*aireō*] a daimon. The first to choose [*aireō*] a life by which he will be joined by necessity [*anagkē*] is the first to randomly draw the lot [*lagxanō*]. Virtue is without a master, each will have more or less of her as each honors or dishonors her. The blame [*aitia*] is for the one having chosen; the god is blameless." (617 d—e).

In the myth so far, all the movements performed by the travelers in death have been governed by necessity. Here, for the first time, the system into which the souls are enfolded *necessitates* a choice. The souls are differentiated from each other and, at least ostensibly, from the system of necessary movement. They are at the origin [*archē*] of their next mortal journey. Even though they are at the *archē*, they are also in the middle and at the end; for, the *archē* of the next journey signals the completion of the last and the entire sojourn through death lies in the middle, between the previous life and the next. According to Lachesis, the spirit [*daimōn*] of their next life begins now. It is as though an individual soul is not merely *alive* when it is born into its mortal trajectory in life; rather, a daimon already possesses the soul. That is to say, a soul is born already organized in some way, already on the way somewhere, already differentiated somehow. And each individual soul at the *archē* chooses the "*daimōn*" that it will become. Lachesis suggests that this organization is not a matter of chance, as if necessity threw the dice and the daimon entered the equivalent soul. Rather, in opposition to her name (the name *lachesis* is derived from *lagxanō*), it is *the soul* that chooses the organization that will rule over it once it is born. Lachesis says that, once the soul chooses, the daimon is woven into it by necessity. The only apparent arbitrary character of the choice is the order in which the choice occurs among the present souls. The lots in accordance with which the order of choice originates appear to be sent by the wandering cause (necessity) through Lachesis (the apportioner of lots [Hesiod 1914, ll. 218]). Therefore, says the goddess who sings of what *has been*, all blame rests with the one who chooses, not with the divine.

At first glance, the soul's free choice of a daimon appears to introduce a rupture into the system of necessity. At the very least, it raises a question about the reach of necessity in human life. However, because necessity already includes the "wandering cause" for the Platonic text, the emergence of "choice" on the scene does not necessarily imply the arrival of radical chance or the coming to be of something from nothing. That is to say, "choice" is not a disruption of the webs of necessity. In this instance, free choice cannot mean the kind of freedom understood as radical spontaneity—the kind of free action that violates necessity. Perhaps one could even argue that freedom is not opposed to necessity here. What sort of choice, then, is it? In what follows, rather than a free choice originating outside of the structure of necessity, I will argue that the choice is in fact fully circumscribed by necessity.

Among the first things one notices in what follows is that Socrates' description of the opportunity for the sojourners to choose a daimon for their coming mortal journey resembles the freedom that the democracy of book VIII occasions for its citizens to select a regime among the available ones for their own souls. In book VIII's treatment of the democracy, Socrates had said that, thanks to its freedom [*exousia*], the regime was full of different forms of political constitution. Every paradigm [*paradeigma*] (557 e) of regime exists in a democracy. Each citizen is free to choose a regime and then fashion his soul in imitation of it. The paradigms are lived out before one in the form of tyrannical, aristocratic, timarchic, oligarchic and democratic (if not more) individual souls. Many things can influence one's desire to choose among them and to live out one's life in accordance with a particular regime. In the *apologos* of Er, too, the spokesperson lays out "the paradigms [*paradeigma*] of lives on the earth" (618 a) for the souls to choose among. However, the diversity of possible lives is greater than in the democracy. Instead of limiting the choice to political regimes (although those are present too: for instance, many forms of tyranny [618 a]), the lives available that Er relates included those of beauty, of noble birth, and even other living things. As in the democracy, choosing a paradigmatic daimon means choosing a certain organization of soul (618 b).

In our analysis of the democracy, we observed that the manner in which this choice of regimes for the soul occurs is through ocular experience and a concept of the good mediated by desire and love. This is true even for the souls that choose to organize themselves aristocratically. Socrates says that the citizens of this democracy are witness to every sort of political organization, insofar as each kind of regime and each kind of good are *lived* out before one. There exist aristocratic souls in the democracy who have organized their private lives in accordance with the relevant good (if it exists). They walk down the catwalk modeling this life for their fellow citizens. There are lovers of money and honor whose shining example will no doubt inspire many citizens to imitate them. Further, a youth may be compelled by the presence of a tyrannical soul conducting his life in accordance with tyrannical desires. Thus, as in the democracy, in *the other place* described in the *apologos* of Er, one *chooses* to organize one's soul in accordance with the mediation of experience (and the loves and desires generated by it) as one looks at the paradigms set before one. That is to say, historical experience of the soul conditions its loves and desires which in turn shape the choice of life.

However, in Er's space in *between* the life already lived and the life to come, experience plays an even more important role in the description of what influences one's "free" choice. In the democracy, the choice is mediated by an experience almost arbitrary in comparison. It depends upon the kinds of lives lived around one and the consequent constitution of one's desires. However, in the context of the choice in death, it depends upon the kind of life the soul has already lived and the sorts of punishments and prizes one receives in death as a consequence of one's actions during that life. Er relates that "most choose in accordance with the habituated customs of their former life" (620 a). He observes Orpheus choose the life of a swan because his life (and death) had driven him toward a hatred of women. Out of his continued rage against human beings, Ajax was *compelled* to choose the life of a lion. From out of pitiable [tragic], comic [comic], or wondrous [philosophic?] experiences in their lives, he observed women driven to choose the life of men and men compelled to choose the life of women. Moreover, he observed animals that had lived more musical lives *compelled* in consequence to choose the life of humans. That is to say, in all of the examples that Er witnesses, *necessity* plays a crucial role in the selection of future lives. It is from out of "what has been," the song of the daughter of necessity, Lachesis, that all of the souls Er observes choose the kind of song that Atropos will sing when she sings of what *will be* by necessity.

Even the soul that appears to hold the most potential and whose choice the text seems to affirm the most, the soul of Odysseus, chooses in accordance with the flow of historical necessity. After his life filled with glory and public heroism, after his thousand year journey in the afterlife in which he labors and recovers from love of honor, Odysseus searches with effort for and chooses the life of a private man (620 c). Given that the choice appears cast in a positive light, one feels some compulsion to see in Odysseus the example of philosophy. It appears that the episode is often read this way.[14] However, none of the features that the *Republic* has presented of the philosophical nature and education are present here. Not only was Odysseus not raised in the educational curriculum of *Kallipolis*, but also there is no indication that he has undergone the education of the higher studies.[15] Certainly, there exists no evidence that he has spent his time in the mathematical disciplines of book VII in preparation for dialectic. There seems to be no reason given in the text to connect Odysseus' choice to the practice of philosophy. If the philosopher king is the model for philosophy, then there may be no philosophers choosing lives in the *apologos* of Er—unless, that is, the practice of philosophy actually reflects the work that Socrates performs more than the philosopher kings of the *Republic*. Like Socrates, Odysseus is wily and wears discursive masks. Moreover, it may be that his "labors" have driven him into an *aporia* regarding the meaning of honor from which he has recovered. In any case, regardless of his philosophical status, Odysseus, like the others, is compelled to choose his paradigm "in accordance with the habituated customs of [his] former life" (620 a).

The other conspicuous choice that occurs in this scene is made by the human who drew the first lot. Like Odysseus, who seems to have known from the beginning which life he wanted, the first to choose selected immediately with determination. However, instead of a private life, this soul went directly for the greatest tyranny (619 b). "Not having examined everything" (619 b), he chose a life that would condemn him to eat his own children, commit other evils and probably suffer the fate of those cast into Tartarus. At first sight, this choice appears to have the opposite origin as the others. Rather than being *compelled* by the "habituated customs" of his former life, his choice seems to originate arbitrarily. For, this human being had been habituated in what appears to be an aristocracy. After death, "he was among those that came from heaven, *having lived in a well-arranged [tassō] polity* in his former life, participating in virtue by *habit*, without philosophy" (619 d, emphasis added). Why would a person for whom every precaution of *Kallipolis* was taken, a person who has lived a virtuous, orderly life and spent one thousand years roaming through the bliss of heaven instantaneously choose the life of the most horrific tyranny? However, there is no indication in the text that the soul who chose tyranny chose it arbitrarily; Er does not suggest that the tyrannical choice is an exception to the rule of the "habituated customs." Therefore, if the person is compelled from the habituated customs of his previous life and after-life, then it is in his "virtuous" and "orderly" life (without philosophy), followed by the journey through the heavens wherein lies the danger of tyranny. Indeed, given the fact that almost every citizen in *Kallipolis* lives in this way, save the guardians, one must ask if all of its citizens would choose the same form of resurrection? According to Socrates, philosophical natures are rare. Even *Kallipolis* has few. Moreover, there are doubts that philosophy is even possible in *Kallipolis*. Consequently, one may wonder if even the guardians are saved from this choice made *necessary* by their "habituated customs." *At the very least*, everyone in the city, with the (merely) *possible* exception of a guardian or three, appears likely to suffer this fate. There is apparently nothing in their "habituated customs" to cause hesitation before making the choice to organize themselves tyrannically after all.

David Roochnik proposes the disturbing possibility that the myth makes the choice of tyranny the eventual fate of almost every human being: "The startling feature of the myth is that because of the 'exchange of evils and goods for most souls,' this fate [choosing the tyrant] seems to await almost everyone [as souls cycle through the various 1000 year journeys]. . . . This millennium of pleasure, however, will presumably stupefy the soul so that, as Er's story has it, it will next be disposed to choose the life of a tyrant, which, in turn, will lead to eternal damnation" (Roochnik 2003, 124). On Roochnik's suggestion, the *apologos* of Er may communicate a system of punishments and prizes that eventually (after many lives and afterlives) leads all souls to a "virtuous" and "orderly" life (without philosophy) and, then, a thousand year journey through the heavens. As such, every soul would eventually find itself in the horrifying position of the man who chose tyranny.

Therefore, in every case, the souls choose in accordance with historical experience and habituated customs derived from that experience. Choices are not made from out of some free rational will that breaks free of the system of necessity; it is not a rational choice that tames the wandering cause. Rather, what appears now to the chooser as good, desirable, love-worthy and choice-worthy is thoroughly compelled and enveloped by the song of the daughter of necessity, Lachesis, who sings of what has been. If *what is* must be conceived, as it is in book VI, as something in opposition to *what becomes* and what moves, then none of the choices made here are informed by a knowledge of *what is*. In the *apologos* of Er, rather, *what is* makes itself manifest in the song of Clotho, who takes her position in spinning the spindle of necessity following *what has been*. Indeed, Clotho's song, another song of a daughter of necessity, is the song of the choices of the souls before being bound to a future necessity in the song of Atropos.

Perhaps this is the reason that Er describes the spectacle of choice in human life in the same terms as those dramatic discourses of self-reflection: tragedy, comedy[16] and philosophy. Er speaks as if he had seen these forms of performance in *the other place*, saying that the choices were "pitiable [*eleeinos*], laughable [*geloios*], and wonderful [*thaumasios*] to see" [620 a]. By framing it this way, Er situates the human choice of the kind of life to live precisely upon the stage of the mirroring spectacles of tragedy, comedy and philosophy. These forms of discourse sing the song of human life back to the human being. The figures who work behind the scenes to organize the necessary movements that subtend human life brought Er down as he reached his limit to witness the tragedy, comedy and philosophy occasioned by human choice. These forms of discourse each serve to put on display "the entire danger for a human being" (618 b) in being offered the capacity to choose by necessity. As suggested earlier, the spectacle of choice in the myth of Er is mirrored in the *Republic* as a whole—that is to say, the *apologos* of Er is the *Republic* writ small. The entire drama of the *Republic* betrays the human struggle to raise itself above the waves of necessity by means of its heroic powers of *logoi*. It may appear to do so periodically; but its achievements inevitably become swallowed up by and incorporated into the waters of oblivion. Such is the "pitiable [*eleeinos*], laughable [*geloios*], and wondrous [*thaumasios*]" [620 a] feature of the heroic human—choice. It is the heroic, yet tragic, gift bestowed upon humans by *nature*—that is to say, *necessity*.

NOTES

1. Glaucon uses *aisthanomai* in his account of Gyges' ring. He argues that those who "perceive" that someone has the power of the ring without using it would privately criticize him, while publicly extolling him (360 d).

2. This difficult hermeneutical question cannot occur to anyone who does not make the distinction between Plato, the writer, and Socrates, the character. Annas shows that she does not when she writes: "Plato himself goes on to say that we don't perceive the true nature of the immortal soul." And further: "Plato does not see, or is unmoved by, the question-begging nature of the argument" (Annas 1981, 346). Not only does Plato not "say" the argument, but there is likely, as everywhere in Plato, some extra-argumentative condition of necessity to which the characters often remain oblivious that is shaping the conversation and what the characters say in it.

3. At the beginning of the "myth of Er," Socrates says "I will not, however, tell you an *apologos* of Alcinous . . . but rather of a strong man, Er" (614 b). According to Adam, the books 9–12 of the *Odyssey* were known as the *alkinou apologoi*. However, he also refers to an additional "proverbial application" of the term *apologos* for a long and tedious story (1902, 614 b).

4. I analyze Socrates' presentation of the styles of imitation in my "On Mimetic Style in Plato's Republic" (2012).

5. "Do the poets *and the men who say anything* fall into one of these patterns of style or the other, or make some mixture of them both? (397 c, emphasis added).

Chapter 10

6. I appropriate a Heideggerian philosophical theme here. Insofar as the human finds herself "thrown" into a world already articulated, already animated in certain directions and with certain ends, the human is born in the middle of a movement, and is carried along to ends about which she remains in the dark. In death, Er too *is born* already on the way (Heidegger 1993).

7. Claudia Baracchi helpfully brings together commentary in the dialogues linking the figures of Iris and Hermes, both messenger gods, to the philosopher. She brings our attention to the link between the work of the philosopher and the messenger god Iris in the Theaetetus (155 d), and the task of interpretation mirrored in both Iris and Hermes in the Cratylus (407 e - 408 b). Baracchi does so in order to offer an interpretation of Er as a philosopher. "Just like Er, then, the philosopher must be a messenger, hovering between worlds and weaving them together in their irreducibility. He must always come back and speak, recount, relate what he has observed, that is, undergone. In this respect it might be opportune to point out the ubiquity, in the Platonic dialogues, of the characterization of the philosopher as a messenger" (Baracchi 2002, 180).

8. Ardiaeus appears to be a purely fictional invention (Adam 1902, 438).

9. Adam further distances his own interpretation from those that would attempt to resolve the impossibilities in order to locate a scientifically coherent theory in the myth. He writes "it should be remembered that Plato's object in this passage is not to furnish a scientific account of the celestial mechanism: see 616 D, E, 617 A. We are dealing with a work of literature and not of science, and the machinery of a myth ought not to be rigorously scrutinized from the scientific point of view" (Adam 1902, 447).

10. For instance, that of Parmenides: see Morrison's *Parmenides and Er* (1955).

11. As we noted in chapters 6 and 9, the term Plato has Socrates say that Er used to describe the sphere of the fixed stars is *poikilos* (616 e). Like the democracy, then, the sphere so often associated with everlastingness by Aristotle (1998 *Physics*) is here said to be "diversified" or "manifold."

12. On my reading, all movements here (celestial and biological, erotic and mortal) are governed by necessity. The movements from life to death, the movements from death to the judges, the movements through the judgments and rewards, the movements to life from death. The only exception *may* be the choice of life in which the god is held blameless. But this assertion is mythological and *not* dialectically achieved. While I agree with Rosen's supposition that "one may wish to claim that the punishment of injustice and the rewarding of justice is an intrinsic necessity of the mythical cosmos," I am not sure that "it cannot have been established by chains and spindles" (Rosen 2005, 383–384). That is to say, while one might need to distinguish between human technological *logical* necessity and what we have called *natural* necessity, I'm not sure natural necessity's movements may be divided up in the way Rosen seems to suggest.

13. See *Timaeus* (2001, 52d - 53c). The concept of necessity (which is another name for *chōra* in the *Timaeus*) I am describing here resembles that explanation of the infinitesimal by Leibniz (see his *Letter to Varignon* [1969]). For the latter, the infinitesimal serves as an order without extension or magnitude. In my view, the necessity

The Spindle of Necessity 235

of the *chōra* conveys a similar meaning and function. However, it seems doubtful that, for Leibniz, the ratio which constitutes the meaningful order of the infinitesimal prior to extension or magnitude is given to *wander* as it is here.

14. Rosen appears to read it in this way. "As it turns out, the happiest life for the wise man is philosophy together with the quiet of the private life in which one minds one's own business" (Rosen 2005, 386).

15. While it seems unlikely that Odysseus has undergone the necessary education, he does share aspects of the private nature stopped from corruption in book VI: "After having seen sufficiently the madness of the many, and that no one doing the things of the *polis* does anything healthy . . . Taking all of these things into calculation, he keeps quiet and attends to his own things [rather than politics] . . . Seeing others filled with lawlessness, he is pleased [*agapaō*] if somehow he himself can live his life here free [*katharos*]of injustice and unholy deeds, and depart [this life] with beautiful hope, graciously and cheerfully" (496 c–e).

16. For a rich analysis of laughter in the Platonic dialogues, see Sonja Tanner's *Plato's Laughter: Socrates as Satyr and Comic Hero.*

Bibliography

Adam, J. 1902. *The Republic of Plato*. Ed. James Adam. New York: Cambridge University Press.
Annas, J. 1981. *An Introduction to Plato's Republic*. Oxford: Oxford University Press.
———. 1994. "Plato the Skeptic" in *The Socratic Movement.* Ed. Paul Vander Waerdt. Cornell: Cornell University Press.
———. 1997. "Understanding and the Good: Sun, Line, and Cave" in *Plato's Republic: Critical Essays*. Ed. Richard Kraut. Lanham, MD: Rowman & Littlefield.
Aristotle. 1959. *Ars Rhetorica*. Ed. W. D. Ross. Oxford: Clarendon Press.
———. 1924. *Metaphysics: Volumes I and II.* Ed. W.D. Ross. New York: Oxford University Press.
———. 1984. *Nicomachean Ethics*. Trans. Hippocrates Apostle. Grinnell, IA: The Peripatetic Press.
———. 2000. *On Coming to Be and Passing Away*. Trans. E. Forster. Cambridge MA, Harvard University Press.
———. 1995. *Aristotle's Physics: A Guided Study*. Trans. Joe Sachs. New Brunswick: Rutgers University Press.
———. 1998. *Physics*. Ed. Sir David Ross. Oxford: Oxford University Press.
———. 1986. *Politics*. Trans. Hippocrates Apostle. Grinnell, IA: The Peripatetic Press.
———. 1960. *Posterior Analytics. Topica.* Translated by Hugh Tredennick, E. S. Forster. Loeb Classical Library 391. Cambridge, MA: Harvard University Press.
Aristophanes. 1938. "Birds" in *The Complete Greek Dramas. Vol. 2*. Trans. Eugene O'Neill, Jr. New York: Random House.
———. 1853. "Clouds" in *The Comedies of Aristophanes*. Trans. William James Hickie. London: Henry G. Bohn.
Baracchi, C. 2002. *Of Myth and War in Plato's Republic*. Bloomington: Indiana University Press.
Barney, R. 2008. "Eros and Necessity in the Ascent from the Cave." *Ancient Philosophy*. V28, 1–16.
Benardete, S. 1989. *Socrates' Second Sailing: on Plato's Republic*. Chicago: Chicago University Press.

Bergson, H. 1911. *Creative Evolution*. Trans. Arthur Mitchell. New York: Henry Holt and Company.
Brann, E. 1966. 2004. *The Music of the Republic*. Philadelphia: Paul Dry Books.
Bromberg, J. 2012. "Academic Disciplines in Aristophanes' *Clouds*." The Classical Quarterly. V62:1, 81–91.
Burnyeat, M. 2000. "Plato on Why Mathematics Is Good for the Soul." *Mathematics and Necessity: Essays in the History of Philosophy.* Ed. T. Smiley. 1–81.
Canguilhem, G. 2008. *Knowledge of Life.* Trans. Stefanos Geroulanos and Daniela Ginsberg. New York, Fordham University Press.
Chaucer, G. 1970. *Chaucer's Canterbury Tales.* Ed. Vincent Hopper. Barron's Educational Series, Inc.
Chisholm, H., Ed. 1911. "Cadmus" in *Encyclopædia Britannica*. Vol. 4. Cambridge University Press.
Cornford, F. M. 1937. *Plato's Cosmology: The Timaeus of Plato*. Indianapolis: Hackett Publishing Company.
Deleuze, G. 1994. *Difference and Repetition*. Trans. Patton.
Diels, H. 1906. *Die Fragmente der Vorsokratiker*. Ed. Hermann Diels. Berlin: Weidmannsche Buchhandlung.
Euclid. 1956. *The Thirteen Books of the Elements*. Trans. Sir Thomas Heath. New York: Dover Publication, Inc.
Euripides. 1995. Trans. David Kovaks. Cambridge, MA: Harvard University Press.
Ewegen, S.M. 2020. *The Way of the Platonic Socrates*. Bloomington: Indiana University Press.
Ferrari, G. 2000. *Plato: The Republic*. Cambridge: Cambridge University Press.
Fine, J. 2011. "Laughing to Learn: Irony in the Republic as Pedagogy" in *Polis: The Journal for Ancient Greek and Roman Political Thought*. V28:2, 235–249.
Frede, M. 1992. "Plato's Arguments and the Dialogue Form" in *Oxford Studies in Ancient Philosophy, Supplementary Volume*. Eds. James Klagge and Nicholas Smith. New York: Oxford University Press.
Gadamer, H.G. 1980. *Dialogue and Dialectic: Eight Hermeneutical Studies on Plato*. Trans. P. Christopher Smith. New Haven: Yale University Press.
———. 2010. *Wahrheit und Methode: Grundzüge einer philosophischen Hermeneutik*. Tübingen: Mohr Siebeck.
Gonzalez, F. J. 1995. *The Third Way: New Directions in Platonic Studies*. Lanham, MD: Rowman and Littlefield Publishers, Inc.
———. 1998. *Dialectic and Dialogue: Plato's Practice of Philosophical Inquiry*. Evanston: Northwestern University Press.
Gordon, Jill. 1999. *Turning Toward Philosophy: Literary Device and Dramatic Structure in Plato's Dialogues*. University Park, PA: Pennsylvania State University Press.
Griswold, C. 1988. *Platonic Writings, Platonic Readings*. New York: Routledge Press.
Heidegger, M. 1977. "The Question Concerning Technology" in *The Question Concerning Technology and Other Essays*. Trans. William Lovitt. New York: Harper Torchbooks.

———. 1993. *Sein und Zeit*. Tübingen: Max Niemeyer Verlag.
Heraclitus. 1906 *Die Fragmente der Vorsokratiker*. Ed. Hermann Diels. Berlin: Weidmannsche Buchhandlung.
Hesiod. 1914. *Theogony*. Trans. Hugh G. Evelyn-White. Cambridge, MA: Harvard University Press.
Howland, J. 2004. *The Republic: The Odyssey of Philosophy*. Philadelphia: Paul Dry Books.
Hyland, D. 2011. "Aporia, the Longer Road, and the Good" in *Graduate Faculty Philosophy Journal*. V31:2, 145–175.
———. 1995. *Finitude and Transcendence in the Platonic Dialogues*. Albany, NY: State University of New York Press.
Iamblichus. 1818. *Life of Pythagoras, or Pythagoric Life*. Trans. Thomas Taylor. London: J. M. Watkins.
Irwin, T. 1977. *Plato's Moral Theory: The Early and Middle Dialogues*. Oxford: Clarendon Press.
Kahn, C. H. 1987. "Plato's Theory of Desire." *The Review of Metaphysics*. V41:1, 77–103.
———. 1996. *Plato and the Socratic Dialogue*. Cambridge: Cambridge University Press.
Kamen, D. 2013. *Status in Classical Athens*. Princeton: Princeton University Press.
Klein, J. 1977. *Plato's Trilogy*. Chicago: University of Chicago Press.
Kneale, M., and W. Kneale. 1984. *The Development of Logic*. Oxford: Oxford University Press.
Kraut, R. 1997. *Plato's Republic: Critical Essays*. Ed. Richard Kraut. Lanham, MD: Rowman & Littlefield.
Krohn, A. 1876. *Der Platonische Staat*. Halle: R. Mühlmann.
Leask, I. 2016. "Performing Cosmic Music: Notes on Plato's Timaeus" in "Sacred Music: Perspectives on Performance," ed. Róisín Blunnie and Orla Flanagan, special issue of *REA: A Journal of Religion, Education, and the Arts*.
Liddell, H., Scott, R., Jones, H. 1940. *A Greek-English Lexicon*. Oxford: Clarendon Press.
Liebert, R.S. 2010. "Apian Imagery and the Critique of Poetic Sweetness in Plato's *Republic*." *Transactions of the American Philological Association (1974–2014)*. V140:1, 97–115.
Long, C.P. 2007. "Socrates and the Politics of Music: The Preludes of the *Republic*." *Polis*. V24:1, 70–90.
Lyons, J. 1967. *Structural Semantics: An Analysis of Part of the Vocabulary of Plato*. Oxford: Oxford University Press.
Mason, 2006. "Plato on Necessity and Chaos" in *Philosophical Studies*. V127, 283–298.
McCoy, M. 2020. *Image and Argument in Plato's Republic*. Albany: State University of New York Press.
———. 2008. *Plato on the Rhetoric of Philosophers and Sophists* Cambridge: Cambridge University Press.

Miller, M. 2007. "Beginning the *Longer Way*" in *The Cambridge Companion to Plato's Republic*. Ed. G.R.F Ferrari. Cambridge: Cambridge University Press.

Monsoon, S. 2000. *Plato's Democratic Entanglements: Athenian Politics and the Practice of Philosophy*. Princeton: Princeton University Press.

Morrison, J. 1955. "Parmenides and Er." *The Journal of Hellenic Studies*. V75, 59–68.

Nails, D. 2000. "Mouthpiece Schmouthpiece" in *Who Speaks for Plato?* Ed. Gerald Press. Lanham, MD.: Roman and Littlefield.

Newton, I. 1999. *The Principia*. Trans. Bernard Cohen and Anne Whitman. Berkeley, CA: University of California Press.

Nussbaum, M. 1986. *The Fragility of Goodness*. Cambridge: Cambridge University Press.

Palumdo, L. 2022. "Bee Imagery in Plato's Dialogues" in *Arete in Plato and Aristotle*. Eds. Ryan Brown and Jay Elliott. Sioux City, Iowa: Parnassos Press.

Plato. 2011. "The Cratylus" in *Socrates and The Sophists*. Trans. Joe Sachs. Indianapolis, IA: Focus Publishing.

———. 1996. *Parmenides*. Trans. Albert Keith Whitaker. Newburyport, MA: Focus Publishing.

———. 1903. "Phaedo" in *Platonis Opera*. Ed. John Burnet. Oxford: Oxford University Press.

———. 1990. *Plato in Twelve Volumes, Vol. 2*. Trans. W.R.M. Lamb. Cambridge, MA: Harvard University Press.

———. 1998. *Plato: Gorgias*. Trans. James H. Nichols Jr. Ithaca, NY: Cornell University Press.

———. 1996. *Plato: Sophist*. Trans. Eva Brann, Peter Kalkavage, Eric Salem. Indianapolis: Hackett Publishing Company, Inc.

———. 2004. *Plato's Theaetetus*. Trans. Joe Sachs. Newburyport, MA: Focus Publishing.

———. 2001. *Plato's Timaeus*. Trans. Peter Kalkavage. Newburyport, MA: Focus Publishing.

———. 1902. *The Republic of Plato*. Ed. James Adam. New York: Cambridge University Press.

———. 1991. *The Republic of Plato*. Trans. Allan Bloom. New York: Basic Books.

———. 1969. *The Republic* in *Plato in Twelve Volumes. Vol. 5&6*. Trans. Paul Shorey. Cambridge, MA: Harvard University Press.

———. 2000. *The Republic*. Trans. Tom Griffith. Cambridge: Cambridge University Press.

———. 2004. *Republic*. Trans. C.D.C. Reeve. Indianapolis: Hackett Publishing Company, Inc.

———. 2007. *Republic*. Trans. Joe Sachs. Indianapolis: Focus Publishing.

Plutarch. 1936. *Moralia. V.* Trans. Frank Cole Babbitt. Cambridge, MA: Harvard University Press.

———. 1976. *Moralia. XIII. Part 1. Platonic Essays*. Trans. Harold Cherniss. Cambridge, MA: Harvard University Press.

Press, G. 2000. *Who Speaks for Plato? Studies in Platonic Anonymity*. Lanham, MD: Roman & Littlefield.

Proclus. 2006. *Commentary on Plato's Timaeus*. Trans. and Ed. Harold Tarrant. Cambridge: Cambridge University Press.

Robinson, R. 1941. *Plato's Earlier Dialectic*. Ithaca, NY: Cornell University Press.

———. 1971. "Plato's Separation of Reason from Desire." *Phronesis* 16, 38–48.

Roochnik, D. 1990. *The Tragedy of Reason: Toward a Platonic Conception of Logos*. New York: Routledge.

———. 2003. *Beautiful City: The Dialectical Character of Plato's Republic*. Ithaca, NY: Cornell University Press.

Rosen, S. 1993. *The Quarrel between Philosophy and Poetry*. New York: Routledge, Taylor and Francis Group.

———. 2005. *Plato's Republic: A Study*. New Haven: Yale University Press.

Ryle, G. 1966. *Plato's Progress*. Cambridge: Cambridge University Press.

Saxonhouse, A. 1978. "Animal Imagery in the Republic" in *The American Political Science Review* V78, 888–901.

———. 1998. "Democracy, Equality, *Eide*: A Radical View from Book VIII of Plato's *Republic*" in *The American Political Science Review* V92:2, 273–283.

Sallis, J. 1996. *Being and Logos: Reading the Platonic Dialogues*. Bloomington: Indiana University Press.

———. 1999. *Chorology: On Beginning in Plato's Timaeus*. Bloomington: Indian University Press.

Simondon, G. 2020. *Individuation in Light of Notions of Form and Information*. Trans. Taylor Adkins. Minneapolis: University of Minnesota Press.

Smith, N. 1997. "How the Prisoners in Plato's Cave Are 'Like Us'" in *Proceedings of the Boston area Colloquium in Ancient Philosophy* XIII. 188–204.

Stenzel, J. 1964. *Plato's Method of Dialectic*. New York: Russell & Russell.

Strauss, L. 1964. *The City and Man*. Chicago: University of Chicago Press.

Swammerdam, J. 1758. *The Book of Nature, or, The History of Insects*. Trans. Thomas Flloyd. London: C. G. Seyffert.

Tanner, S. 2017. *Plato's Laughter: Socrates as Satyr and Comic Hero*. Albany, NY: State University of New York Press.

Taylor, A.E. 1928. *A Commentary On Plato's Timaeus*. Oxford: Oxford University Press.

Tigerstedt, E.N. 1977. *Interpreting Plato*. Upsala: Almqvist & Wiksell.

United Nations General Assembly. 1948. *The Universal Declaration of Human Rights*. New York: United Nations General Assembly.

Vlastos, G. 1941. "Slavery in Plato's Thought" in *Philosophical Review*. V. 50:3, 289–304.

———. 1971. "The Paradox of Socrates" in *The Philosophy of Socrates: A Collection of Critical Essays*. New York: Anchor Books.

———. 1991. *Socrates, Ironist and Moral Philosopher*. Ithaca: Cornell University Press.

Waerdt, P.V. 1994. *The Socratic Movement*. Ed. Paul Vander Waerdt. Cornell: Cornell University Press.

Wantzel, L. 1837. "Recherches sur les moyen de reconnaître si un Problème de Géométrie peut se résoudre avec la règle et le compas." *Journal de Mathématiques Pures et Appliquées.* V2, 366–372.

Winslow, R. 2007. *Aristotle and Rational Discovery: Speaking of Nature.* New York: Continuum International Publishing Group.

———. 2009. "The Life of Thinking in Aristotle's de Anima" in *Epoche.* V13:2, 299–316.

———. 2012. "On Mimetic Style in Plato's Republic" in *Philosophy and Rhetoric.* V45:1, 46–64.

———. 2013. "Aristotelian Definition and the Discovery of *archai*" in *Bloomsbury Companion to Aristotle.* Ed. Claudia Baracchi. London: Bloomsbury Publishing.

———. 2021. "Difference in Plato's *Timaeus.*" *Graduate Faculty Philosophy Journal.* V42:1, 3–24.

Zhmud, L. 2006. *The Origin of the History of Science in Classical Antiquity.* Trans. Alexander Chernoglazov. Berlin: Walter de Gruyter.

———. 1998. "Plato as 'Architect of Science.'" *Phronesis* V43, 1–44.

Index

Adeimantus' role, 31
Adeimantus' slander, 9–13, 179
akribes [precise], 40, 49, 130–31
allegory of the cave, 50, 51, 58, 60, 61, 64, 79–106, 123, 157, 163, 219
Apology, 21
aporia [impasse], 19, 20, 38, 41, 64, 79, 83, 86, 88–89, 91–92, 107–10, 112–16, 119–20, 121–23, 130, 134–35, 136–38, 139–40, 154, 164, 175, 183–84, 194, 208, 218, 221–22
Aristotle, necessity, xiii–xiv, xvii; *Ethics,* 30, 38, 92–93, 100, 196; *History of Animals,* 102; *Metaphysics,* xiii, 65, 119, 155, 186–87, 226; *On the Soul,* 56, 59, 65; *Politics,* 64; *Posterior Analytics,* 78; *Physics,* xiii, xvii, xix, 132–35, 143, 234; *Rhetoric,* 160
arithmetic, 41, 111–20
astronomy, 41, 107, 118, 123, 124, 126, 128–36, 137, 142, 204, 210, 224

bastard, 175–96, 199
bees, 18, 89–90, 99–103, 125, 149, 183, 191, 207
Bendis, xvii, 26, 86, 160, 171, 173

Cephalus, 4, 6, 19, 26, 46, 63–64, 66, 86, 193
child of the good, 51–64, 84, 94, 95, 200, 202
city of pigs, 102, 111
comedy, xvi, xvii, 135, 184, 230, 232, 233

deinos [terrible/wonderful], xvii, 8, 24, 175, 184, 189, 194, 204, 215
Delian problem, 126
democracy, 11, 16, 142, 177, 200, 202–8, 209, 229–30, 234
dialectic, xii, 8–10, 25, 26–27, 30, 35, 36, 38–39, 41, 49–50, 60, 75–76, 125, 147–70, 175, 177, 180–83
divided line, 3, 50, 51, 58, 60, 69–78, 80–83, 96–97, 104, 114, 122, 123, 132, 143, 150, 155, 158, 162, 165, 166, 172, 183–84, 189–92, 194, 207, 208, 213, 214, 219, 231
dog, philosopher, 2–3, 33, 40
dialogue form and necessity, xvii, xviii, 1, 25, 30, 35, 43, 69, 78, 110, 30, 148, 151–53

Empedocles, 87, 105, 169
Euclid, 72, 74, 122, 123, 127, 130, 132, 153

Euthyphro, 21

finitude, xvi, 64, 75–76, 83, 93–94, 105, 110, 111, 134, 148, 165, 184, 187, 194, 198, 217, 227

Gyges, 7, 9, 31, 37, 190, 217, 233

harmonics, 107, 118, 136–40
Heraclitus, 46, 87, 105
hive, bee, 18, 89–90, 99–103, 125, 149, 183, 191, 207

Meno, 47, 103, 107–8, 110–11, 122, 127, 140–41, 215
misology, 30, 99, 189, 190, 193, 194
myth of Er, 33, 82, 142, 206, 208, 211, 214, 218–20, 233

necessity as chance [*tugxanō*], xv, xviii, xix, 1, 14–15, 20–21, 22, 27, 29, 33, 40, 69, 96, 175, 180, 229
necessity as erotic, xv–xvi, 1, 3, 5, 12, 14, 26–29, 39, 52, 54, 61, 64, 66, 69, 82, 105, 136, 160, 167, 175, 179–80, 181, 189, 197, 202, 218, 223, 226, 234
necessity as growth, orderly movement, xv, 1, 14–15, 16, 26, 168, 180
necessity as wandering cause, xiii–xv, xix, 14–15, 20, 22, 107, 118, 120, 122, 127–28, 169, 206, 223, 226, 229, 232
necessity, geometrical, xvi
necessity, logical, xiii, xv–xvi, 4, 18, 81, 83, 110, 122–23, 165, 167, 205, 216, 234
necessity, natural law, 69
necessity, spindle of, xii, 82, 136, 142, 199, 211, 213–33
necessity vs. good, ix, 18, 45, 122
Newton, necessity, xiv, xix, 122, 131
nuptial number, 82, 195, 223

Odysseus, xvii, 33, 204, 208, 210, 211, 230–31
oligarchy, 201, 203, 207

Parmenides, 30, 81, 110
parrēsia [frank/free speech], 202, 215–17, 219–20
Phaedo, 6, 7, 78, 93, 162
Phaedrus, xix
plane geometry, 41, 107, 118, 120–23
poikilos [complex, multicolored], 177, 203, 204–5, 209–11
Polemarchus, 6, 19, 64, 70, 86, 109, 191, 193
private wage earners, xi, 17, 20, 37–38

ship parable, 10–11
Simonides, 6, 30, 191, 209
skepticism, xx, 1
slander against philosophy, 9–13, 179
solid geometry, 41, 107, 118, 123–28, 140
Sophist, 78, 86–87, 89, 105, 151, 154
spindle of necessity, xii, 82, 136, 142, 199, 211, 213–33
Symposium, xix, 105, 153

Theaetetus, xiv, 141, 215–16, 220, 234
thaumatopoioi [puppeteers], 17, 74, 84–86, 90, 93, 94, 105
Timaeus, xiii–xv, xix, 5, 35, 44–45, 55–56, 81, 137, 144, 167–70, 198
timocracy, 31, 201, 203, 207
Thrasymachus, 9, 37–38, 49, 70, 77–78, 86, 131, 156, 162, 177, 208, 215, 217
tragedy, xvi–xvii, xviii, xix, xx, 1, 13, 32, 60, 64, 104, 135, 149, 168, 175, 184, 189, 191, 199–200, 204, 209, 215, 223, 227, 230, 232–33
tugxanō [chance happening], xv, xviii, xix, 1, 14–15, 20–21, 22, 27, 29, 33, 40, 69, 96, 175, 180, 229
tyranny, xv, 31, 189, 208, 209, 211, 229, 231, 232